Military Small Arms of the Twentieth Century

By Ian Hogg
and John Weeks

DIGEST BOOKS, INC.,
NORTHFIELD, ILL.

Published in the United
States by Digest Books, Inc.,
540 Frontage Rd., Northfield,
Illinois 60093.

Manufactured in the United
States of America.

While every care has been taken to
ensure that the material appearing in
this book is factually accurate, it is
probable that in some cases slight
alterations might ultimately be found
necessary—particularly with the
appearance on the market of new types
of weapons. The authors and the editor
would therefore be pleased to hear of
any such amendments which have
escaped their notice or which have been
announced after Military Small Arms had
gone to press. Please write care of
the publishers (Arms and Armour Press,
2-6 Hampstead High Street, London
NW3 1PR, England); all aid will be
gratefully acknowledged.

ISBN-0-695-80406-5
Library of Congress Catalog
Card Number: 73-83466

Produced by Arms and Armour Press and Duotech Graphics

Military Small Arms of the Twentieth Century

Military smallarms of the twentieth century is a comprehensive illustrated history of the small-calibre hand-held firearms issued to the world's armies in the troubled years of the present century, whose seven decades have seen more radical changes in weapon design than the preceding six hundred years. In these pages are the weapons of the most violent and costly wars—in both human and monetary terms—seen by history.

The Russo-Japanese War, 1904-05, foreshadowed in its use of the machine-gun the trenchscape of Flanders, Paschendaele and the Somme which was to follow within ten short years. The imaginative handling by the Japanese of their Hotchkiss machine-guns, purchased at the century's turn from France, left a profound impression on those alert to the weapons' possibilities. It was a lesson learned well by the emissaries of Imperial Germany.

World War 1, 1914-18, was the most bloody of conflicts in which thousands of lives were lost to obtain, retain or regain mere feet of the shell-torn 'front': here the machine-gun reigned supreme, the supreme arbiter of trench warfare and the dealer of death to luckless combatants on all sides. To the Germans' Maxim and the British Vickers—themselves near cousins—was accorded the doubtful accolade of having killed more often than any other class of weapon. These and the infantry's rifles (Germany's Mauser, Britain's Lee-Enfield, France's Lebel and Berthier, Russia's Mosin, Austria's Mannlicher, America's Springfield) are featured alongside the first hesitant attempts to provide truly workable self-loading rifles, at first regarded with universal suspicion by the military authorities.

World War 2, 1939-45, brought still further developments, for, although the rise in the interwar years of airborne warfare had led to an apparent diminution of the smallarms' role, most battles and campaigns remained land-fought. The American army began the war in the process of issuing its troops with a self-loading

rifle: this, the renowned M1 Garand, foretold of things to come. Further research led to such things as the German MG42 and FG42 and the appearance of the short-cased Pist Patr 43 'intermediate' round, all of which were the leaders in their respective fields and all of which influenced smallarms design for many years.

The 'Cold War' following upon World War 2, and the lessons of the Korean War (1950-3) accelerated armies' demands for automatic or self-loading rifles—Fabrique Nationale's SAFN and FAL, Russia's AK and SKS, the United States' M1 and M14—until even the British Army, for long the conservative champion of the bolt-action rifle, adopted the FAL in 1957.

Indo-China, Vietnam, and the internecine struggles in Southeast Asia showed the need for a lighter rifle suited to the stature of the smaller native troops; this led in 1964 to the adoption by the US Army of the Stoner-designed M16, whose 5.56mm (0.223in) bullet's lethality belies its unimpressive size. The M16's appearance has spurred Europe's leading designers to search for the rifles from which the next generation will be chosen.

Contents

The contents of **Military smallarms of the twentieth century** are divided by weapon class and are paginated as such within sections. Each section has a chapter number and each page is numbered within that chapter—instead of in relation to the book as a whole. Hence page 3.24 is the twenty-fourth page of the third section, and 6.02 is the second page of the sixth; the index relies upon this method.

Acknowledgements

In the course of preparing this book, the authors have sought the help of many individuals, manufacturers, museums, and official agencies. Most responded with alacrity, sending sales literature, photographs, and information concerning themselves and their weapons. It is with gratitude, therefore, that we extend our thanks to the following individuals:

Mr A J R Cormack

Mr Don Crean

Mr Les Field

Lieutenant-Colonel D Hermansson, of the Royal Swedish Army

Major F W A Hobart, of the Applied Thermodynamic Branch, Royal Military College of Science, Shrivenham

Mr J E Hunter, Curator of the US Army Infantry Museum, Fort Benning, Georgia, USA

Major F Myatt, MC, Curator of the School of Infantry Museum, Warminster, Wiltshire

Mr Tom Nelson

Mr Bob Owens

Mr Peter Simpkins, Keeper of the Exhibits, Imperial War Museum, London

Mr H J Woodend, Keeper of the Pattern Room, RSAF, Enfield Lock

Among those who supplied information concerning their products were the following companies:

(Armalite)	Armalite Incorporated, Costa Mesa, California, USA
	Artillerie-Inrichtingen, Hembrug-Zaandam, Netherlands
(Beretta)	Pietro Beretta SpA, Gardone-val-Trompia, Brescia, Italy
	Breda Meccanica Bresciana SpA, Brescia, Italy
	BSA Guns Limited, Birmingham, England
	Cadillac Gage Company, Detroit, Michigan, USA
(CETME)	Centro de Estudios Técnicos de Materiales Especiales, Madrid, Spain
(Colt)	Colt Industrial Incorporated, Hartford, Connecticut, USA
	Cooper-Macdonald Incorporated, Baltimore, Maryland, USA
	Dansk Industri·Syndikat AS 'Madsen', København, Denmark
	Direction Téchnique des Armements Térrestres, Saint-Cloud, France
	Eidgenössisches Waffenfabrik, Bern, Switzerland
(FN)	Fabrique Nationale d'Armes de Guerre SA, Herstal-lèz-Liège, Belgium
	Harrington & Richardson Incorporated, Worcester, Massachusetts. USA
(Heckler & Koch)	Heckler & Koch GmbH, Oberndorf/Neckar, West Germany
	Howa Machinery Corporation, Nagoya, Japan
	Interarmco Limited, Alexandria, Virginia, USA
	Mauser-Werke AG, Oberndorf/Neckar, West Germany
(NWM)	Nederlansch Waapenen et Munitiesfabrik NV 'de Kruithoorn', s'Hertogenbosch, Netherlands
(Remington)	Remington Arms Company Incorporated, Bridgeport, Connecticut, USA
(SIG)	Schweizerische Industrie-Gesellschaft, Neuhausen-am-Rheinfalls, Switzerland
(Walther)	Carl Walther Sportwaffenfabrik, Ulm/Donau, West Germany
	M P Weibel AS, København, Denmark
	Winchester-Western Division of the Olin-Matheson Chemical Corporation, New Haven, Connecticut, USA

ACKNOWLEDGEMENTS

The following museums and official bodies proved most helpful:

Firearms Department, Birmingham City Police, England
Home Office Forensic Laboratory, Nottingham, England
Imperial War Museum, London, England
Musée d'Armes, Liège, Belgium
Musée de l'Armée, Paris, France
Museu Militar, Lisbon, Portugal
Museum of Science and Technology, Birmingham, England
(RSAF) Pattern Room Collection, Royal Small Arms Factory, Enfield Lock, Middlesex
Royal Artillery Institution, London, England.
(RMCS) Royal Military College of Science, Shrivenham, Wiltshire, England
(SIM) School of Infantry Museum, Warminster, Wiltshire, England
(USIM) US Infantry Museum, Fort Benning, Georgia, USA
(USMC) US Marine Corps Museum, Quantico, Virginia, USA

The majority of the photographs credited to the collections held at RSAF Enfield Lock, the School of Infantry Museum, and the Royal Military College of Science were photographed by the authors. The authors and publishers much appreciate the permission granted by the various governing bodies to photograph weapons in their care, and especial thanks are due to Mr H. J. Woodend of the Royal Small Arms Factory at Enfield Lock for his assistance.

Special thanks are due to Mr John Walter, of the Arms and Armour Press, for his diligence in supervising the manuscript's course and for making available much of his own research on bolt-action rifles. Similar thanks are also due to Mr Joseph Schroeder Jr, of Digest Books Inc, for his helpful criticisms of certain parts of the script and for making available much pistol information from his own files.

Ian Hogg/John Weeks
Summer 1973

Introduction
Weapons and their operation

Before beginning any study of smallarms mechanisms, it is as well to examine a few definitions and terms so that the explanations and discussions in later chapters can be more easily understood. For the most part, this introductory chapter is concerned with presenting an outline of the more common expressions used in the descriptions of smallarms and in explaining—in broad terms—how the various methods of operation function. This is not intended to be a scholarly treatise, and those who wish to take the subject further are advised to study the advanced books which are specifically written for this purpose.

Definitions

1.1; smallarms system. A smallarms weapon system is taken to consist of the gun and the round of ammunition which is fired from it.

1.2; the barrel. The chamber leads forward into the bore, which in the vast majority of modern weapons is rifled. The number and depth of the grooves is a question almost of preference between makers but the rapidity of twist dictates the rate at which the bullet will spin when it emerges from the muzzle. This stabilises the bullet along its longitudinal axis by imparting to it gyroscopic stability which resists efforts to change its direction, and eliminates drift tendencies caused by mass variations in the actual projectile; if spin was absent, the unbalanced projectile would fly in anything but a true direction. The ideal shape, weight and diameter of the bullet are fixed by the laws of external ballistics. The function of the barrel is therefore threefold: it guides the bullet in the required direction, it gives the bullet velocity by containing the expanding gases which force the bullet forward, and it imparts a rotatory stabilising effect by spinning the bullet.

1.3; the chamber and the bolt. The chamber has to withstand a considerable pressure and an equally considerable amount of heat. For instance, in Fabrique Nationale's Fusil Automatique Léger (FAL) the chamber pressure is about 22 tons per square inch, and the gas temperature is in excess of 2500°C. It is therefore necessary to seal the rear of the chamber, which is done by using some form of bolt or breechblock. The breech unit is bored to permit passage of a firing pin or striker, the function of which is to give a sharp blow to the priming cap in the base of the cartridge case and so ignites the propellant.

1.4; the operating cycle. The bolt closes the breech opening and is generally locked in place until the pressure is reduced to a safe level, after which the breech can be opened either by hand or by some automatic means. If an extractor is attached to the bolt-head the empty case can be withdrawn and subsequently ejected from the weapon, and as the bolt goes backward it can be made to compress a spring—thus storing energy which can be subsequently used to drive the bolt forward again; The bolt can also be made to cock a firing mechanism. On its way forward the bolt can strip a round from a magazine, push it into the chamber, and support the base of the round (usually by locking the bolt to the barrel or the receiver). The energy stored in the spring during the cocking action can then be used to drive a pin into the primer.

This series of operations takes place every time a weapon is fired and the sequence may be performed either by hand or by an automatic mechanism. It is generally referred to as the 'operating cycle' and is summarised thus:

1 Chambering
2 Locking (supporting the base of the cartridge case)
3 Firing
4 Unlocking (removing the support to the base of the cartridge case)
5 Extraction
6 Ejection
7 Cocking
8 Feeding

These portions of the cycle need not necessarily take place in this order, cocking, for example, could occur before unlocking or before extraction, but all smallarms have to go through the cycle regardless of its precise order (provided they are intended to use conventional metallic cartridges.

Gas operation

2.1; gas operation. In all machine-guns the fundamental source of operating energy is the high-pressure gas created by the rapid combustion of the propellant charge. This is true in a general sense of guns operated by the blowback systems, recoil systems, or any other system of true automatic operation—but in spite of the fact that the ultimate source of operating energy in all machine-guns is the pressure of the propellant gases, the term "gas operation" is reserved for a particular type of operating system in which the pressure of the gases is employed in a specific way.

In a typical gun which uses the system of gas operation, an opening or 'port' is provided in the wall of the barrel. When the projectile has passed this opening, some of the following high-pressure gases are tapped off through the orifice to act upon a piston or some similar device for converting the pressure of the gases to thrust. This thrust is then utilised through a suitable mechanism to provide the energy necessary for performing the automatic functions required in sustained fire.

The gas-powered operating mechanism can take many forms, but the most commonly used device consists of a simple gas cylinder and a piston which is driven rearward to transfer its energy to the bolt by direct impact. In some cases the piston may be driven forward instead of rearward but this does not involve any significant change in the principle of operation. Even the nature of the member which is acted upon by the gas pressure is subject to great variation. Instead of being a conventional piston, this member can be in the form of a sleeve, a slide, or any other device arranged to receive an impulse from the gas pressure.

The methods used for transferring energy from the piston to the gun mechanism are also extremely diverse both in form and function. Instead of transmitting energy directly to the bolt, the piston itself sometimes moves through a very short stroke and transfers its energy by impinging on an intermediate rod or lever. Large numbers of devices have been designed to minimise the shock involved in the energy transfer through the use of levers, links or cams. In certain instances the shock of transfer is reduced by causing the piston to load intermediate springs which subsequently transfer their stored energy to the mechanism with greater smoothness.

The principles involved in gas operation can be outlined by considering the general character of the pressures and forces which result from the firing of the cartridge in an elementary gun provided with a gas port and a piston. The diagram shows the condition which exists immediately after the cartridge is fired, as the bolt is rigidly locked to the barrel in order to support the base of the cartridge case against the thrust produced by the ignition of the propellant charge. This thrust acting on the base of the projectile drives it forward and as the projectile moves through the bore of the gun, the gases expanding behind the projectile also move—so that the centre of mass of the gaseous propellant travels forward at almost 50% of the projectile's velocity. The same force which moves the projectile and powder gases forward produces an equal and opposite

a gas piston
b operating rod
c receiver
d bolt
e locking shoulders

1 bullet travelling towards gas port
2 bullet past gas port

reaction which attempts to drive the entire gun to the rear. This reaction, known as the recoil force, is explained in more detail in a later section.

As soon as the projectile has passed the gas port the high-pressure gases behind the projectile start to flow into the gas cylinder and to build up a pressure against the piston. For any given barrel and cartridge the rate at which this pressure builds up depends on a number of factors: these are complex and will not be discussed here, but it should be noted that the amount of gas which ordinarily flows into the cylinder is extremely small and has no significant effect on the muzzle velocity of the projectile.

After the projectile has passed the gas port, and as it moves through the bore and leaves the gun, the pressure within the barrel decreases. The manner in which the pressure decays for a given propellant charge will be influenced by the length of the barrel, but the pressure inside the gas cylinder eventually approximates to that in the bore. The gas piston is therefore subjected to a driving force for only a very short time, as the pressure starts to act on the piston when the projectile passes the gas port and ceases to act when the residual pressure reaches that of the atmosphere. The entire process takes approximately 5 milliseconds (0.005 sec).

Owing to the short time in which the pressure acts and the necessity to have the breechblock locked while there is pressure in the bore, the force exerted on the piston cannot be used directly to drive the bolt back but can only be employed to accelerate the piston mass; the kinetic energy so acquired is later used to carry out the automatic cycle.

The amount of energy stored in the piston as the result of the applied impulse is determined by the mass of the piston: the lighter the piston, the greater becomes the energy produced by a given impulse. Thus the conditions of pressure, the location of the gas port, the size and shape of the orifice, the piston area and the piston mass all have an influence on the amount of energy which can be obtained from the action of the piston. By proper selection and control of these factors the piston energy can be regulated, so that low values or very high values of energy can be achieved at will. It is comparatively easy under practical conditions to achieve extremely high values of piston energy in gas-opened guns, but unless the gas operation is carefully controlled the action of the piston may be so violent that it can literally smash the breech mechanism.

2.1.1; types of gas operation. Over the years the design of gas-operated guns has crystallised into three distinct categories: long-stroke piston types, short-stroke piston types, and direct gas action types. Other systems, however, have been mooted in the past, some of which have seen experimental use.

2.1.1(1); long-stroke piston. In this the piston is attached directly to the breechblock and controls the block throughout the automatic cycle. The piston is of necessity massive and therefore comparatively slow-moving, moving the entire length of the bolt stroke. This means that the energy available, although adequate, is not excessive. Since the piston is either permanently fixed to the bolt—as in the L7A2 GPMG—or holds the bolt as in the L4A4 Bren, there are small impact shocks and energy losses when the piston is accelerated.

2.1.1(2); short-stroke pistons. In a short-stroke piston design, the piston itself generally has a short movement: possibly no more than 0.5in (12.7mm). The piston weighs less than 1oz (28.4gm) and so receives an impulsive blow which rapidly accelerates it. It is in contact with an actuating lever of light weight which is connected to the bolt, and the actuating lever absorbs the energy of the piston thereafter passing it to the bolt. This system is very suitable for rifles and is usually found in this application.

2.1.1(3) direct gas action. In this method of operation the gas tapped from the barrel is led back along a tube which enters an expansion chamber formed in the bolt carrier. The carrier is driven to the rear and unlocks the bolt from the barrel, or in some designs from the body of the weapon, and carries it rearward. This system is used in the French Fusil MAS Mle 49 and also in the Armalite Ar15/M16 series of rifles. The system usually leads to a light weapon, but there are greater chances of fouling than with other systems owing to the deposition of the products of combustion in the gas tube.

2.1.2; drawbacks of gas operation. The main drawbacks to a gas-operated system are these:

2.1.2(1); fouling. The gas cylinder often becomes clogged with fouling, and so slows down the rate of fire. Gas ports can also become restricted, which leads to slower piston action.

2.1.2(2); fumes. Gas from the cylinder has to escape to the open air. In a vehicle this usually means that it vents into the crew compartment.

2.1.2(3); barrel changing. There are engineering difficulties in arranging a satisfactory way of changing the barrel.

Blowback operation

2.2.1; simple blowback operation. The blowback operation of a smallarm can be defined as "a method of operation in which the energy required to carry out the cycle of operations is supplied to the bolt by the backward movement of the cartridge case caused by the gas pressure".

There are several variations in the way a blowback system can be made to operate, and the first factor affecting the operation is that of the conditions inside the chamber and their effect on the behaviour of the cartridge case.

When a round is fired the propellant burns and produces some 14,000 times its volume of gas. This gas is burnt and the flame temperature is in the order of 2,700°C; the pressure caused by the rapid burning of the propellant builds up very quickly and in the first half millisecond (0.0005sec) it has reached its peak value. This in a current 7.62mm NATO round is about 22.3ton/in^2.

If the case is resisted by a locked bolt, the forward movement of the front part of the cartridge case expands the caseneck to fill the gap between the case and the chamber; the rearward movement of the case's base takes up any excess cartridge head space. Beyond this process of putting the walls of the case in tension there is no case movement, but if the bolt is free to move it is driven backwards by a force equal in magnitude to the pressure multiplied by the cross-sectional area of the bore.

The actual operation of the simple blowback system is uncomplicated. The gas pressure exerted on the base of the case drives the unlocked bolt to the rear, while the empty case pushes itself out of the chamber and is ejected from the gun. The return spring, which has absorbed energy, then drives the bolt forwards to feed a round from the magazine. The round is chambered and when the trigger is operated the weapon is fired. The system does not lend itself to full automatic fire. The limitations of scope and calibre of the simple blowback system makes is suitable only for hand-operated low-power pistols; for the military applications one must look to a more sophisticated arrangement.

2.2.2; blowback with advanced primer ignition (API). Instead of firing from a stationary bolt, the bolt in this case is moving forward when the primer is struck. This means that the forward momentum of the bolt must be destroyed by the firing impulse before the bolt can be stopped and driven back. As a result, the force needed to accelerate the bolt backwards is reduced and the time during which it is accelerated rearwards is also reduced. This means that a lighter block can be incorporated. Two good examples of this principle are the M3A1 and the Sten; in the Sten submachine-gun the cap is struck by the fixed firing pin while the bolt still has 0.0030in to travel to the breech face. The propellant immediately burns and the pressure in the case increases. Peak pressure is reached when the case is still 0.0018in from the breech, and the block continues forward to touch the breech face with minimum velocity before starting back. It can be seen from this simple explanation that the design of these parts is a delicate matter and the success of the whole operation of the weapon depends to a great extent upon two features, the first of which is the mass of the bolt and its spring force and the second the characteristics of the ammunition. We shall return to this latter point.

One small disadvantage to API is the fact that the gun must always fire from an open bolt, which means that on pulling the trigger there is a delay while the bolt travels forward to the breech, and this delay—together with the attendant bolt movement—is not conducive to an accurate delivery of the first shot. Some training is also required before the firer becomes accustomed to the pause after pulling the trigger and to the shift of centre of gravity as the bolt runs forward. Another feature which slightly affects the first few rounds of a burst is the fact that the bolt moves from the trigger sear for the first shot, but from the buffer for subsequent shots (which gives rather more forward velocity). The first is therefore chambered at a slower speed than the optimum, and so the bolt comes back rather faster than normal. In other words it recoils harder and this can affect the placing of the next shots, although it is a phenomenon of fairly small dimensions and it dissipates after two or three rounds.

For submachine-guns it is rare to supply more than one type of ammunition, and where this has been done in the past it has not been mixed. If ammunition of different characteristics is mixed and fed into a gun working on an advanced primer ignition system it can lead to difficulties, for the bolt has to be balanced to one particular type of round and another type may easily have quite different chamber pressures and bullet weights. If the two are fed alternately the motion of the bolt is likely to become upset; the gun may stop firing in time, or the action of the bolt may become progressively more violent until something breaks. Both these actions have happened with trial guns.

2.2.3; blowback with delay, hesitation blowback, or retarded blowback.
Although advanced primer ignition represents a saving of weight in the breech-block compared to a pure blowback system, it can only be used in small-calibre submachine-guns and very heavy 20mm cannon carried on heavy mountings. It is not suitable for a rifle-calibre weapon because not only is the breech mechanism heavy but, by the nature of its construction, it must be an open-breech firing system which leads to inaccuracy for two reasons—the change in the position of the centre of gravity as the bolt reciprocates, and the long lock-time which is found in any open-breech system.

To be able to use a rifle-calibre weapon and to have one of an acceptable weight, a system known as 'delayed blowback' has been developed over the years. The essence of the system is that the breechblock is delayed in its backward travel while the projectile is in the bore and thereafter the residual pressure is utilised to carry out the cycle of operations. It must be remembered that pressure in the region of 6ton/in² exists at the muzzle of a rifle firing a 7.62mm NATO round and this takes about 0.005 sec (5 milliseconds) to decay. This pressure is quite adequate to produce the required bolt velocity, but arrangements must be made to delay the speed of breech opening so that (while the bullet is in the bore) the case cannot drive the bolt backward to expose enough unsupported brass to produce a casehead separation.

There are many current examples of this system, most of which use some simple arrangement incorporating a mechanical disadvantage system although a few utilise surplus gas forces.

The essential part of the delayed blowback design is that it must not be uniform in its action, as it must impose the maximum restraint on the movement of the bolt immediately after firing—yet as soon as the pressure drops off the mechanism must allow the bolt to move with progressively increasing freedom as it accelerates backwards.

Modern weapons use a light and simple system which reduces the movement of long arms, with their associated moments of inertia, by means of either a simple roller system or a bell-crank lever. In each case a two-part block is used.

When the firing takes place the gas pressure forces the front face of the block to the rear. The front part of the block carries two rollers which engage in recesses in the body of the weapon, and before the breech can move these rollers must be forced inwards to clear their supporting surfaces; this is done by the reaction of the body to the firing force. The inward movement of the rollers is resisted by the inertia of the rear part of the breechblock as it is driven back by the action of the rollers over the inclined plane at the front end. By the time the rollers are finally free from the body, the bullet is leaving the muzzle and the residual forces then carry out the cycle of operations. To eliminate any danger of casehead separations, the G3 (together with some other similar designs) makes use of a fluted chamber; this prevents the cartridges adhering to the chamber walls by floating them on a layer of gas which is able to flow around the case by way of the flutes.

2.2.4; locked-breech blowback or locked-breech, blowback-assisted. This system has been used in varying ways in the past. The breechblock is locked to the body at the time of firing and so the block itself can be of a minimum weight and size. After the point of maximum pressure has passed, the breech is unlocked and the cycle of operations is carried out by simple blowback. The method of breech unlocking may be achieved either by gas, by recoil or even by primer projection—but it must be emphasized that of the eight parts of the cycle of operation seven are carried out by energy obtained from simple blowback. Only the unlocking process depends on some other system.

The use of gas action to unlock has so far been almost entirely confined to weapons whose size puts them outside the scope of this book, for the most part 20mm cannon.

Another unlocking method which has been favoured in the rifle calibres is recoil. The Breda modello 30, the Fiat-Revelli and the Johnson are three notable examples from among many who have achieved locked-breech blowback with greater or lesser complexity. The Breda uses a rather involved way of locking its bolt, by using a threaded sleeve over the breech into which the bolt head fits. The sleeve, or 'fermeture nut' as it is more properly called, then rotates and holds the bolt head to the breech when its threads engage with lugs on the bolt—literally screwing it up tight. The rotational movement is quite naturally small and the thread pitches very coarse.

On recoil, the barrel moves rearwards in bearings, and the 'nut' is unlocked by an inclined plane striking a stud on the nut. The bolt is then blown to the rear by residual gas pressure. A speciality of the Breda is the fact that the recoil could be slowed by dust and sand in the barrel bearings, and so—when the bolt was unlocked—the chamber pressure was too low to operate the blowback part of the cycle. This was overcome by adjusting the recoil to allow the breech to open more quickly; such an adjustment is comparatively rare in this system of operation.

2.2.5; summary of blowback action. The modern blowback-operated small-arms are extremely efficient and highly versatile. It has taken many years for them to be accepted by the traditionally conservative military but they are now in general use in many parts of the world, particularly on the continent of Europe. The cautious military were, however, quite sensible in their apparent reluctance to accept blowback since it does have some distinct drawbacks. For a given round the performance will not be as good as from a locked breech of comparable dimension, since some energy is taken up in opening the breech while the bullet is still in the bore. The system also tends to produce more fumes at the breech, which makes it less acceptable for weapons which have to be fired in such confined spaces as armoured vehicles.

These two limitations have been largely overcome in the most modern designs, but one which is common to all is the virtual impossibility of providing a variable-power adjustment in the system when it is operating in adverse conditions or becoming fouled from prolonged firing. In most designs an attempt is made to cater for this by making the system a little too powerful when it is clean and properly lubricated, and so the action is noticeably harsh on first firing.

Recoil operation

In the recoil system provision is made for locking the bolt to the barrel and these parts are mounted in the gun body so that they can slide to the rear. The gun is fired with the bolt locked to the barrel, and these parts remain locked together as they are thrust back by the pressure resulting from the explosion of the powder gases. In some guns the energy derived from this motion is used to perform the entire cycle of operations; in others the energy derived from recoil may only perform certain functions in the cycle or may merely supplement the energy derived from another system of automatic operation.

The distinguishing characteristic of the recoil system is that the energy used for operation is obtained from the recoil movement of the barrel and bolt while these parts are locked together. Any gun in which the bolt is locked to the barrel while there is pressure in the chamber will be subject to some recoil action, but (unless the recoil is put to use in operating the mechanism) the gun need not necessarily employ the recoil system.

In a gun operated purely by recoil the bolt remains locked to the barrel until the chamber pressure has become zero and therefore there are no problems (such as are encountered in blowback) resulting from movement of the cartridge case under pressure and lubrication of the ammunition is unnecessary. The number of different machine-guns employing recoil operation is very large and an examination of these weapons will reveal an extreme diversity of mechanical detail and functional arrangement, but in spite of these dissimilarities all recoil-operated weapons can be placed in one of two basic subclasses: long recoil or short recoil.

2.3.1; long recoil operation.   Long recoil is defined as a system of operation in which energy for operating the gun mechanism is obtained from a recoil movement which is greater than the overall length of the complete cartridge.

The cycle starts with a cartridge in the chamber and the bolt locked to the barrel. When the cartridge is fired, the barrel and bolt recoil together and during this phase the retardation offered by the springs is relatively small: the only significant factor in limiting the recoil acceleration is the mass of the recoiling parts. The resistance of the springs gradually slows the recoiling mass until it stops at the extreme position and starts forward again. At this point the bolt is still locked to the barrel. The moment the barrel starts to move it unlocks the bolt (which now stays at the fully recoiled position) and the barrel goes forward extracting the case, which stays held by the extractor against the face of the bolt until forced away by the ejector. When the barrel is almost at its forward run-out position, it operates a catch which releases the bolt. The bolt now moves forward faster than the barrel and catches it, at the same time feeding a fresh round into the breech. The breech locks at run-out and the bolt then trips the sear to release the striker and start the cycle afresh. The barrel gains a good deal of kinetic energy while 'running-out' (moving forward), and this is absorbed by large buffers at the forward end of the body. Some of the bolt energy is dissipated through these buffers also, but not necessarily all since it is sometimes possible to arrange that the next round is fired before all the bolt energy is dissipated.

In general the long recoil system is better suited to the larger calibres of cannon and certain types of shotgun, which are not touched upon in this book. The greatest drawback to the system for the smallarms designer is that the sequence of operations is wasteful of time. Throughout the recoil movement nothing happens beyond recoil, and this can be considered to be essentially wasted. All the automatic actions have to happen on the forward stroke, and even then slowly, for the first part of the barrel movement is only used to extract the case. Ejection and feeding cannot begin until the barrel is well forward, and firing is delayed until the barrel is at rest after having runout. For these reasons the long recoil system only lends itself to low rates of fire. Where these are no handicap it does offer some advantages; the recoil energy is comparatively low, since most of it is employed in accelerating the mass of the barrel and bolt, and since this energy can be absorbed during the time of rearward movement of the mass it can be kept within reasonable limits. The trunnion pull can therefore be kept low, and the stresses on the parts of the gun's mechanism can be reduced. These considerations have led to its introduction in at least one type of gun for small armoured vehicles, and in some automatic sporting shotguns.

2.3.2; short recoil operation. In a short recoil weapon, the bolt remains locked to the barrel for only a portion of the recoil stroke. After unlocking occurs, the barrel can move only a short distance with the bolt until it is stopped.

before firing

end of recoil

barrel return

bolt return

a barrel spring
b bolt lock
c bolt
d unlocking device
e bolt spring
f bolt latch
g lock open
h spent case being extracted
i bolt latched
j latch lugs engaged
k bolt unlatched

a barrel spring
b counter recoil buffer
c recoil buffer
d bolt lock
e accelerator
f unlocking cam
g backplate buffer
h bolt spring

1 start
2 bolt unlocked, acceleration begins
3 acceleration complete
4 barrel latched, bolt returning
5 barrel unlatched, bolt loading

The bolt continues to move to the rear, completing this movement by virtue of the momentum it possessed at the time of unlocking (although it may receive additional momentum through the action of a mechanical device, known as an accelerator; which transfers some of the energy of the barrel to the bolt). In either case the rearward motion of the bolt continues until the opening is sufficient for feeding and the bolt is then moved forward to close and lock the breech. In some guns the bolt pushes the barrel back to the firing position, but in others the return motion of the barrel is accomplished independently before the bolt closes.

The outstanding feature of the short recoil system of operation is that, by proper design, high cyclic rates can be attained. The bolt is unlocked without unnecessary delay shortly after the projectile has left the muzzle and then the bolt, which is already moving with considerable rearward velocity, is propelled to the rear at even greater velocity by the combined effects of the accelerator and residual breech pressure. With this the recoil movement of the bolt, and its return to battery, are accomplished in a very short time.

The possibility of achieving high rates of fire with little difficulty make the short recoil system most attractive to the designer of smallarms and it has been frequently used for several applications. Aircraft guns are ones which generally need high rates of fire, and in the past the well-known Browning (whose cyclic rate was high for its day) utilised this system—so, too, did the German MG 15 and its derivatives. The design of such guns demands considerable care since the very high rates of fire which they achieve leads to formidable accelerative forces acting upon the moving parts, and it is vital that everything moves smoothly and positively without excessive shock or friction. This is particularly true of the accelerator, which has to complete its action within one or two thousandths of a second and will therefore be imparting quite a violent motion to the bolt. The mechanism for a fast-firing short-recoil gun requires to be both simple and strong. Everything must be compact, rugged, and should not need delicate adjustment for effective functioning. Where this has been achieved the designs have worked remarkably well, though it has to be admitted that some have shown themselves to be sensitive to adverse operating conditions.

The amount of energy available to operate a recoil system is relatively small, and guns using the short recoil principle are sometimes near to the limits of working when in mud or dust. One means of increasing the useful power is by means of muzzle boosters, or recoil intensifiers. These work by trapping some of the muzzle blast and using it to apply a heavy thrust to the front face of the barrel. This additional thrust causes the recoiling parts to have a higher velocity and hence a higher rate of fire. It alternatively overcomes the retarding effect of the dust and dirt. It is important not to have too powerful a muzzle booster, since this can lead to violent recoil, and so to excessive pounding of the moving parts.

A further difficulty with the system is that it does not lend itself easily to adjustments for varying rates of fire, or for varying power in the ammunition. The Maxim series could be adjusted in their rates of fire by varying the tension in the return spring, but this is a relatively clumsy method, albeit a convenient one. In this respect of adjustment the recoil system of operation is at a disadvantage when compared to the popular gas systems; the system does not entirely compensate for this drawback by its more compact dimensions and light working parts.

Breech locking

Breech locking is the function of the mechanism which supports the cartridge case on firing. The object is to ensure that the cartridge case is positively supported by a locked mechanism until the gas pressure has fallen to a safe level (in automatic weapons) or until it is desired to remove the case in a manually-operated mechanism.

There are too many different kinds of locking mechanism in use to be covered in a brief survey such as this, and so some of the most common types have been singled out for description. Almost all systems will be found to be closely related to one of the following:

3.1; rotating bolts
3.2; tilting breechblocks
3.3; lug systems
3.4; toggle systems
3.5; non-ramming breechblocks
3.6; revolver systems

The first four mechanisms employ breechblocks which move along the prolonged axis of the barrel and are therefore able to ram the round and extract the case in addition to their more obvious functions, but by doing so they demand a certain length or space behind the breech in which to operate. The cramped confinement of a turret has led the designers of the 30mm Rarden cannon and the M73 machine-gun to revive a rare type of locking system, the non-ramming breechblock.

3.1; rotating bolts.   The bolt is pushed forward to ram the round and then the knob is turned into a recess in the receiver body to lock; lugs are generally added to the bolt for greater locking strength. No rearward travel is wasted in unlocking, because the bolt is turned and there is no significant axial movement.

Light machine-gun bolts are usually hollow with a cam-slot cut in them. The piston post engages in this and rotates the bolt by pressure on one face or the other. Locking is achieved by lugs as on the bolt-action rifle.

The lugs should ideally be symmetrically placed, but there have been many weapons in which they were not and this only upsets their performances in theory. There are two basic methods of mounting the lugs: at the front or at the rear of the bolt. Rear lugs allow a separate bolt head to be used, and this can be changed independently of the bolt to adjust cartridge head space, and it also permits a simpler and more easily cleaned chamber. Forward lugs, for example the Mauser action, allow the receiver to be lighter and shorten the stress paths in the metal of the bolt/breechblock and the receiver.

3.2; tilting breechblocks.   The tilting-block system is strong and simple, and well suited to single-shot or automatic weapons. The best known and most common examples are found in the Czech ZB series and in the British Bren light machine-gun. In these weapons the piston extension tends to raise the breechblock during forward travel, and when the block stops at the face of the breech the ramp forces the locking shoulder into a recess in the body and locks the action. At the same time the face of the breechblock is 'squared-off' to the breech. Unlocking is achieved by the underside of the piston post bearing on a crossbar of the breechblock, and withdrawing the locking shoulder by camming action.

The direction in which the bolt tilts is immaterial, but it always pivots on its forward edges.

3.3; lug systems.   Lugs comprise the largest and most varied group; with these the breechblock does not turn, but a lug or lugs move with respect to it. The block is usually roughly rectangular in shape and the lugs are hinged to it—generally at the forward end. The following descriptions will probably be sufficient to show the remarkable variety and ingenuity of design in this group. It will be seen that in general the masses (and thus inertiae) of the moving parts are low, so permitting high accelerations and high rates of fire.

3.3.1; German Kar 43. This is a gas-operated semi-automatic rifle introduced in 1943. The locking action is shown in the drawing and is self-explanatory; the unlocking cycle may be less obvious, but as the striker is driven to the rear by the piston it withdraws support from the lugs, and a small push on the bearing surfaces X–X is sufficient to cause them to move out of engagement. There is no actual pivot, but the design allows the lugs to swing in their housings. It is a compact and efficient unit.

Gewehr 43; Germany, 1943
1 locked
2 unlocked

Degtyarev; Russia, c.1926
1 striker carrier
2 locking recesses
3 lugs
4 bolt

3.3.2; Russian Degtyarev system. This is another simple design, based on Friberg's design of c.1872, improved in 1907 by Kjellmann. The two struts are hinged in recesses in the bolt at their forward end and are forced outwards by the striker to lock into the body. The struts are withdrawn by cams on the piston extension (not shown in the diagram), which act on studs machined on each strut. After withdrawing the lugs, the piston extension then carries the bolt to the rear.

3.4; toggle systems. Toggle-locking systems are obsolete, but at least two weapons survive in service in various parts of the world using this type of lock. Toggles have only ever been used with recoil-operated weapons but the action is rather slow and complicated; the principle is similar to a 'knee joint', which when bent is easily bent further—but when straight is rigid.

A source of weakness with toggle systems is the number of joints, all of which can wear, and the long stress path in the body. The system was utilised by the Parabellum pistol, the Maxim machine-gun and the Vickers machine-gun (both often gas assisted), the Parabellum light machine-gun, the Fürrer (Swiss) guns, and the American T2E1 Pedersen self-loading rifle.

3.5; non-ramming breechblocks. Until the 30mm Rarden cannon and the US M73 tank machine-gun were produced the use of non-ramming breech-blocks had almost completely died out among smallarms, apart from one important exception—the Martini-action competition rifle and the Madsen-system machine-guns. The non-ramming block can be extremely compact, but it requires an external mechanism to feed the rounds and sometimes to eject them. With the Rarden and M73 the requirement for short inboard length in a vehicle is so pressing that the extra mechanical complication is considered worthwhile, but in a weapon which has to be used in any other environment this would not be so. This system theoretically allows a higher rate of fire because the moving parts are light and the movement small.

3.5.1; Martini hinged block. This is the simplest method of all for breech closure, but it becomes hopelessly complicated when it is desired to load successive rounds. It is, in fact, purely a single-shot system to which a number of parts have to be added at a considerable cost in complexity to produce an automatic weapon.

3.5.2; Rarden and M73 sliding block. This is no more than a miniature version of an artillery-type sliding breechblock, rotated through 90° and opened and closed by a system of cams and studs actuated by the long recoil of the barrel. The M73 is of 7.62mm calibre and so the masses of the working parts are comparatively low. The breechblock moves horizontally in the barrel extension. In both designs the ramming mechanism is quite complicated and ingenious.

3.6; revolver systems. Revolver systems are an interesting example of the revival of an apparently obsolete design. Some of the earliest repeating arms used a revolving cylinder but for high-powered rounds it was soon abandoned as the gas leak between barrel and cylinder was excessive. However, the system in a modified form is now used in some high-speed guns carried in aircraft, notably in the American 'Vulcan' rotary multibarrel guns based on the old Gatling principle. (It must, however, be noted that in the Vulcan and the Gatling the cartridges are chambered directly into the barrel.) Whatever the use the design is roughly the same, and the following general description of a hand-held revolver is sufficient to bring out the principles.

The rounds are fed into a cylinder which contains a number of chambers. The cylinder rotates on an axis in line with the barrel and indexes each round into line, until on lining up with the barrel the base of the cartridge is supported by a fixed or 'standing' breech, through which the firing pin moves: the advantage of the design lies in its simplicity. The mechanism need only rotate the cylinder and cock the action, and there have been many different ways of achieving this. For years the revolver system has been held by many to be the only completely reliable one; it is, however, sensitive to wear, and slight play between cylinder and barrel can lead not only to escapes of gas, but misalignment of the chamber and bore.

Handguns

There has always been a certain element of doubt about the pistol's precise function in military service; ostensibly issued as a weapon for personal protection, it has often appeared to be a social symbol. To be of combat value, however, the handgun must be robust and capable of discharging a bullet which will effectively disable the recipient, and it is now generally accepted that nothing smaller than 9mm or 0.38in can do this. (In the past pistols of 7.65mm, and even 6.35mm, have been pressed into emergency military service; these cannot be taken as representative of the trend of military thought.) The provisions of various conventions on soft-nosed bullets kept soft and expanding-point bulleted ammunition from military service to improve the anti-personnel performance of such weapons as the Mauser C96, but it is notable that the original 7.65mm Parabellum bullets were flat-nosed for this reason.

Amongst cartridges of 9mm calibre there are a number utilising bullets of similar diameters and similar weights, but the 9mm Parabellum has displaced its competition, particularly since 1945. The much weaker 9mm Short, once commonly seen in Italy and Central Europe, has now diminished in military importance but the Soviet Bloc has recently produced its own 9mm round—an intermediate step between the 9mm Parabellum and the 9mm Short.

In the military field the only competitor to which the 9mm calibre is now submitted is the .45 Auto Colt, a cartridge of awesome stopping power.

The twentieth century has seen the automatic pistol supersede the revolver as a standard military weapon, although a number of nations still arm para-military or second line troops with revolvers. For a long time the argument was that six reliable shots were better than eight or nine doubtful ones, and in the early days of the automatic pistol (or, more particularly, automatic pistol ammunition) development there was in this some truth. Another criterion was the stopping power of the bullet, and a heavy revolver firing a large bullet at relatively low velocity certainly delivered a more telling blow than an automatic pistol firing a smaller bullet at a higher velocity. Many designers attempted to get round this by producing pistols firing at exceptionally high velocities, but a small fast bullet (if it is stable) does not have the shocking effect of a larger and slower one.

World War 1 was the testing ground for all the various theories; every pistol of repute—and some disreputable ones—found their way to the Western Front. When the war was over and the analysts sat down to discuss future handgun design, the general tendency was away from the heavy and powerful weapons for one simple reason: the difficulty of training hasty wartime draftees to shoot them. It must be noted, however, that the recoil-absorbing properties of the automatic pistol enabled better shooting in .45 calibre by the average soldier, and the combat effectiveness of the bullet was beyond doubt. The 9mm Parabellum calibre, exemplified by the German Parabellum pistol, had also appeared satisfactory, and although many Western agencies felt that the Luger was insufficiently robust for active service the German army made no change in either their pistol or choice of calibre.

During the inter-war years few new designs of military pistol were introduced, although there was a tendency towards designing automatic pistols fitted with sear devices to obtain fully automatic fire; these novelties had little practical value. Germany discarded the Parabellum in favour of the P-38 (a

▼Typical revolvers of the last decades of the nineteenth century, many of which lasted in the hands of the troops well into the twentieth. **1 France**, Revolver Réglementaire Modèle 1874, calibre 11mm. **2 Italy**, Pistola à Rotazione Bodeo Modello 1889; this specimen is marked as the product of N & V Castelli of Brescia and was made in 1922, calibre 10.35mm. **3 Switzerland**, Ordonnanz-Revolver Modell 1882 System Schmidt, calibre 7.5mm. **4 Belgium**, Revolver Nagant Modèle 1878, calibre 9mm. **5 Austria-Hungary**, Revolver Modell 1898 System Rast & Gasser, calibre 8mm (all RSAF).

Walther design), selecting this as a better mass-production proposition. This weapon also introduced the double-action feature to military pistols; it had previously been necessary to carry an automatic pistol with a round in the chamber and the hammer cocked, with a round in the chamber and the hammer carefully lowered into the firing pin, or empty and requiring the slide to be operated when the gun was needed for action. The Walther design provided a pistol which could be carried with the chamber loaded and the hammer down against a locked striker, and which could be fired simply by pulling the trigger.

With the exception of the P38 and the Soviet Tokarev of 1930/33 (modified Colt patterns) World War 2 was largely fought with the pistols which had seen action in 1914–18. The British and Canadian Armies ultimately brought an automatic pistol into limited use, the Browning GP35, but this did not become general issue in the British Army for another ten years. The postwar years have seen little innovation other than the general acceptance of the double-action feature pioneered by Walther, though few of these designs have found their way into general military stocks. The future does not appear to hold anything in the way of a notable breakthrough in the pistol field, for there seems little possibility of improvement on the conventional patterns and improvement can only be in the field of lightness—by the greater incorporation of lightweight high-strength alloys and simplified manufacture and maintenance.

PISTOLA AUTOMATICA BALLESTER MOLINA
Argentina
Hispano Argentino Fabrica de Automoviles SA, Buenos Aires
0.45in ACP

The Argentine Government, after having used the Mannlicher pistol for some years, adopted the Colt M1911 pistol under the title 'Pistola Automatica Modelo 1916'. This was later augmented by supplies of the M1911A1 under the title 'Modelo 1927'. Production of the M1927, with technical assistance from the Colt factory, was eventually begun in Argentina and continued there for many years.

It was ultimately decided to develop a local variation of the Colt pattern and this subsequently appeared as the Ballester Molina (known also as the 'Hafdasa' from the contraction of the maker's name—as both titles appeared on the slide). It is a virtual copy of the Colt M1911 and, seen from a distance, the two are practically indistinguishable. The Ballester Molina differs in the form of the hammer and in the absence of a grip safety; the trigger is pivoted at the top rather than sliding, and there is a different notching of the slide's finger grips. The construction is that of the Colt, utilising a locked-breech system of Browning's pattern in which ribs on the barrel top surface engage with slots formed in the slide, together with a swinging link mounted beneath the breech and tied to the frame. There are subtle variations in the formation of butt and grips, and the pistol seems to suit a small hand better than the Colt; it is of inferior finish compared to the Colt, although apparently similarly reliable. A number of these pistols were taken into service by the British Army during World War 2, notably for issue to clandestine units.

Length: 9.00in (228mm)
Weight unloaded: 2lb 8oz (1.14kg)
Barrel: 5.00in (127mm), 6 grooves, right-hand twist
Magazine: 7-round detachable box
Muzzle velocity: c.860fps (262mps)

MANNLICHER SELBSTLADEPISTOLE MODELL 1901 and MODELL 1905
Austria-Hungary
Osterreichische Waffenfabrik-Gesellschaft, Steyr
7.63mm Mannlicher-patrone

Like all Mannlicher designs manufactured at Steyr, these pistols are pieces of excellent workmanship: well-balanced and exquisitely made, they were worthy of better success than they attained. Their failure was firstly due to the fact that the guns were competing against the weapons of Peter-Paul Mauser and Georg Luger and that, secondly, they were designed around a cartridge peculiar to the Mannlicher—and hence not commonly available.

The operation is unique; the Modell

01 is a blowback pistol with a delay device to ensure that the breech pressure drops to a suitable level before case extraction begins. A heavy spring keeps a cam in engagement with a notch on the recoiling breech and the initial recoil force is taken up in overcoming this spring's resistance, so delaying the opening of the breech for a brief period. The magazine—like those of most other Steyr products—is an integral part of the weapon within the butt and must be loaded from a charger. The magazine is provided with a release catch to empty the gun without recourse to operating the slide.

There were two major variations of the pistol, the patterns of 1901 and 1905; the former is readily distinguished by the chequered grips and the barrel-mounted rearsight, and the latter (which is actually marked 'Md.1905') has grooved grips and a rearsight mounted on the breechblock. Approximately 9,500 of both types were manufactured, of which little more than 1,000 were of the 1901 design. The Modell 1905 was adopted by the Argentinian army; Argentina's state crest is found on these guns.

Length: 9.68in (246mm)
Weight unloaded: 2lb 0oz (0.91kg)
Barrel: 6.18in (155mm), 4 grooves, right-hand twist
Magazine: 8-round internal box (1901),
Muzzle velocity: c.1025fps (313mps)

MANNLICHER SELBSTLADEPISTOLE MODELL 03
Austria-Hungary
Osterreichische Waffenfabrik-Gesellschaft, Steyr (?)
7.65mm Mannlicher-patrone

Originally designed in 1896, this weapon—in common with the earlier Mannlicher pistols—is a delight to the eye and perfectly finished of the finest materials, although it is a good deal more scarce than the earlier guns. Like the 1901 design it was in competition with the Mauser as a military weapon and, although it was tried by several nations, no one adopted it as a service weapon. The design used a locked breech of the prop-up type with a concealed internal hammer, and the cartridge was almost identical to the more common and more powerful 7.63mm Mauser round. The pistol was generally turned down on the grounds of its comparative unreliability, which was due to insufficiently strong manufacture for such a powerful cartridge, the lock and firing mechanism in particular being too highly stressed. It was also unusual in having a double-pressure trigger rather like that of a military rifle—and this, with the stock attachment found on a few examples, made the M03 an above average stock-fitted pistol for long-range shooting. A few of these weapons were made with longer barrels and long-range tangent

◁Mannlicher's selbstladepistole Modell 1901; this is a prototype weapon, made c.1900 by F von Dreyse of Sömmerda (RSAF).

◁Mannlicher's selbstladepistole Modell 1903; note this gun's vague external resemblance to the Mauser C96, although internally the two are quite different (RSAF).

▶An example of the 8mm Repetierpistole Modell 1907—the 'Roth-Steyr'—shown together with its cartridge. Note the cocking piece protruding from the rear of the receiver, unusual in a pistol of this class (RSAF).

▶The Pieper-designed Modell 1908 pistol manufactured in Austria by Osterreichische Waffenfabrik-Gesellschaft of Steyr (RSAF).

sights, and some were permanently fitted with stocks, perhaps for evaluation as cavalry carbines, but the few which were made all seem to have been used as hunting weapons and none ever saw even unofficial military service.

Length: 11.00in (279mm)
Weight unloaded: 2lb 4oz (1.02kg)
Barrel: 4.50in (114mm), 6 grooves, right-hand twist
Magazine: 6-round internal box
Muzzle velocity: c.1100fps (335mps)

8MM REPETIERPISTOLE M07 ('ROTH-STEYR')
Austria-Hungary
Osterreichische Waffenfabrik-Gesellschaft, Steyr, and Fémáru Fegyver és Gépgyár, Budapest
8mm Repetierpistole-patrone M07

The Roth-Steyr holds the distinction of being the first self-loading pistol to be adopted for general service by the army of a major power, having been officially taken into the service of the Austro-Hungarian cavalry in 1908. Later issued to the Flying Corps it became known unofficially as the 'Flieger-Pistole' and, although long obsolete, it is still to be found in the more obscure corners of the Balkans. This is remarkable in view of the fact that in common with many contemporaries it was produced in a single calibre—one which was never used by another weapon—so that ammunition

resupply must be very difficult.

Like most Steyr-manufactured designs, the magazine is integral with the butt and must be loaded by a charger. The striker mechanism is also unusual in that the self-loading action of the weapon only partially cocks the striker; full cocking is done by the initial pressure on the trigger, which draws back the striker and then releases it. Should the cartridge fail to fire, it is necessary to pull back the bolt to arrive once more at the partially-cocked condition; the mechanism is not double-action. This system is said to have been demanded by the authorities so that there would be less likelihood of the inadvertent discharge of a fully-cocked pistol by a cavalryman on a skittish horse.

Length: 9.18in (233mm)
Weight unloaded: 2lb 4oz (1.02kg)
Barrel: 5.18in (131mm), 4 grooves, right-hand twist
Magazine: 10-round internal box
Muzzle velocity: c.1090fps (332mps)

STEYR-SELBSTLADEPISTOLE MODELL 1908
Austria-Hungary
Osterreichische Waffenfabrik-Gesellschaft, Steyr
7.65mm automatic pistol (0.32in ACP)

This peculiar weapon was designed by the Pieper company of Liège, who also manufactured a small number under

their own name, but the principal manufacture was done at Steyr and the gun was issued in some numbers to the Austrian police. Some later saw emergency service in World War 1.

It appears to be a highly ingenious design until careful thought robs the unusual features of some of their attraction. In the first place the gun has a thumb-catch on the left side which (when pressed) allows the barrel to hinge forward so that a cartridge can be loaded directly into the chamber. This movement also disconnects the above-barrel recoil spring from the breechblock so that the block can be drawn back and pushed forward to cock the internal hammer—but this should only be done when the magazine is either empty or withdrawn, since the action otherwise feeds the top round out of the magazine and on to the ground. There is no extractor fitted as the design relies on residual gas pressure to blow out the spent case as it drives the breechblock back, until the ejector deflects the case through the side port. This means that ammunition malfunctions—especially misfires or stuck cases—cannot be cleared by operating the slide since this will only try to load a fresh round and compound the mischief. Pieper had a habit of coming up with odd designs, but it is a little surprising to find that Steyr should bother producing one of them.

Length: 6.38in (162mm)
Weight unloaded: 1lb 6oz (0.63kg)
Barrel: 3.63in (92mm), 6 grooves, right-
   hand twist
Magazine: 7-round detachable box
Muzzle velocity: c.900fps (274mps)

9MM REPETIERPISTOLE M12 ('STEYR-HAHN')
Austria-Hungary
Osterreichische Waffenfabrik-Gesell-schaft, Steyr
9mm Repetierpistole-patrone M12, 9mm Parabellum
The M12 is a first-class design and deserved wider acceptance than it received. Accepted by the Austro-Hungarian army in 1912, it is a locked-breech design using a rotating barrel to lock the slide and the barrel together on firing. Like all Steyr designs the magazine is integral with the butt and must be loaded from a charger, and—also a common feature with Steyr weapons—the M12 takes a unique cartridge which is uncommon elsewhere, being larger and more powerful than 9mm Parabellum and almost the same size as (but not interchangeable with) the Bergmann-Bayard round.

Approximately one quarter of a million of these weapons were rebarrelled to take the 9mm Parabellum round when the Austrian army was absorbed into the German army in 1938, and these are recognisable by the figures '08' stamped on the left side of the slide. In an attempt to distinguish between this and the earlier Roth-Steyr, the M12 is often referred to as the 'Steyr-Hahn' (or 'Steyr-with-hammer') as the Roth model had a bolt and striker mechanism. The M12 is also known by the commercial designation M11 and under the German service term of Pistole 12(ö). It was also adopted by the armies of Chile and Romania.

Length: 8.50in (216mm)
Weight unloaded: 2lb 3oz (1.02kg)
Barrel: 5.10in (128mm), 4 grooves, right-
   hand twist
Magazine: 8-round fixed
Muzzle velocity: c.1100fps (335mps)

PISTOLE AUTOMATIQUE BROWNING, MODELE 1900
Belgium
Fabrique Nationale d'Armes de Guerre, Herstal-lèz-Liège
7.65mm automatic pistol (0.32in ACP)
The Modèle 1900 was the first Browning design to be manufactured by Fabrique Nationale of Herstal, the result of experimental models of 1898 and 1899—and the beginning of a long association. The mechanism is unusual in having the recoil spring in a tube above the barrel, connected to the reciprocating breech-block by a lever in such a fashion as to double as the firing spring and the recoil spring: an elegant engineering solution and also keeping the parts to a minimum. The barrel is fixed to the frame; the slide and breechblock are driven back on firing, pulling on the recoil spring. As the

◁The 9mm Repetierpistole Modell 1912 ('Steyr-Hahn'). The gun has a magazine contained within the angular butt, which must be loaded through the top of the action from a charger. Guns bearing a stamp '08' on the lower left side of the slide in front of the trigger-guard have been converted to fire 9mm Parabellum ammunition.

◁The Pistole automatique Browning of 1900, the first of John Browning's successful pistols and the first to be made by Fabrique Nationale (RSAF).

◁John Browning's Modèle 1903 pistol, widely adopted as a police weapon, and service issue in several European countries (FN).

slide returns the striker is held cocked by the sear, placing the recoil spring under additional compression to give the necessary motive power to the striker.

Although produced in vast numbers, the 1900 type was little used as a military weapon, as most armies of the time were a little suspicious of the self-loading pistol and more than a little contemptuous of such a small calibre as a combat loading. Some guns are, however, known to have been used by the armies of Tsarist Russia, Belgium and—possibly—Holland. In addition to Fabrique Nationale's production, reputed to run into millions, numbers of various cheap Spanish and Chinese copies are to be found.
Length: 6.75in (170mm)
Weight unloaded: 1lb 6oz (0.64kg)
Barrel: 4.00in (101mm), 6 grooves, right-hand twist
Magazine: 7-round detachable box
Muzzle velocity: c.950fps (290mps)

PISTOLE AUTOMATIQUE BROWNING, MODELE 1903
Belgium
Fabrique Nationale d'Armes de Guerre, Herstal-lèz-Liège
9mm Browning Long
This is the Belgian-made version of the John Browning design which was also produced as the Colt 0.32in and 0.380in pistols. Blowback operation is used, which sounds dangerous in this calibre, but the weapon is chambered for the 'long' Browning cartridge which although slightly longer than the 9mm Parabellum is actually somewhat weaker. A robust and accurate pistol, the Mle 03 was widely adopted on the Continent as a military and police weapon and large numbers are still in use. It is the weapon responsible for the fact that the word 'Browning' is, in French common parlance, synonymous with the words 'automatic pistol'. The armies of Sweden, Serbia and Turkey were amongst those to whom the Mle 03 was issued; some of the Swedish guns (known as the Pistol m/1907) were manufactured by Husqvarna Vapenfabrik to a licence granted from Fabrique Nationale.
Length: 8.00in (203mm)
Weight unloaded: 2lb 0oz (0.91kg)
Barrel: 5.00in (127mm), 4 grooves, left-hand twist
Magazine: 7-round detachable box
Muzzle velocity: c.1050fps (320mps)

PISTOLE AUTOMATIQUE BROWNING, MODELE 1910
Belgium
Fabrique Nationale d'Armes de Guerre, Herstal-lèz-Liège
7.65mm automatic pistol (0.32in ACP), 9mm Short (0.380in automatic pistol)
This model is variously referred to as that of 1910 or the 1912, having been designed in 1910 and first marketed in 1912; it was a considerable improvement on the 1900 model and served as a pattern for innumerable imitations and

copies. The most important feature lies in the mounting of the recoil spring around the barrel, giving the weapon a light and handy appearance. A grip safety is fitted, acting on the sear since the pistol is striker-fired.

The Browning 1910 was extensively sold commercially and widely adopted on the Continent as a police pistol. It was also frequently purchased by military officers as a personal weapon and was used in small numbers by many armies, as a second-line weapon, to augment their normal issues. It is still manufactured in Belgium for sale in the United States.
Length: 6.00in (152mm)
Weight unloaded: 1lb 5oz (0.60kg)
Barrel: 3.50in (89mm), 6 grooves, right-hand twist
Magazine: 7-round detachable box
Muzzle velocity: c.925fps (282mps)

PISTOLE AUTOMATIQUE BROWNING, MODELE 1922 (or 10/22)
Belgium
Fabrique Nationale d'Armes de Guerre, Herstal-lèz-Liège
9mm Short (0.380in automatic pistol), 7.65mm automatic pistol (0.32in ACP)
This pistol is a Browning design, with the recoil spring around the barrel. The 1922 model is no more than the 1910 pattern with the barrel extended by 1in (25mm) to improve the accuracy, and the frame extended to increase the magazine's cartridge capacity. The existing design of slide was modified to accept an extension nosepiece attached by a bayonet joint in a praiseworthy attempt to utilise existing machine tools and components—a technique pioneered by Walther some years earlier in a similar design.

This weapon, in 9mm Short or 7.65mm automatic pistol chambering, was widely adopted for use by military and police forces all over the Continent and was also adopted in 1940 as a substitute standard weapon issued to men of the German Luftwaffe—the Pistole 626(b). The gun is striker-fired and a grip safety is fitted. The armies of Holland, Yugoslavia, France, Greece and Turkey numbered amongst those equipped with the Mle 22 pistols.
Length: 7.00in (178mm)
Weight unloaded: 1lb 9oz (0.73kg)
Barrel: 4.50in (114mm), 4 grooves, left-hand twist
Magazine: 9-round detachable box
Muzzle velocity: c.875fps (266mps) (9mm Short)

PISTOLE AUTOMATIQUE BROWNING, MODELE A GRANDE PUISSANCE (FN GP35)
Belgium
Fabrique Nationale d'Armes de Guerre, Herstal-lèz-Liège (see notes)
9mm Parabellum
This pistol was introduced in 1935 by Fabrique Nationale to John Browning's design and represents the logical improve-

ment of earlier types, notably the Colt 0.45in M1911. The major difference lies in the disposal of the Colt's hinged link which effects barrel/slide unlocking on recoil and the substitution of a shaped cam on the underside of the barrel, which operates against a fixed stud in the frame to do the same job. Stripping is also rather easier than with the Colt; a slot in the butt of all earlier Belgian (and some Canadian) specimens permits a holster stock to be fitted, and in many cases adjustable tangent sights of varying degrees of optimism are fitted. The GP35 design's greatest asset as a military weapon is its unusual magazine capacity—13 rounds in a double row. In spite of the consequently bulky butt grip, the GP35 is easily held and is a most handy weapon in action. It has been adopted by many countries, including Britain, Canada, Belgium, Denmark and Holland (see also UNITED KINGDOM, CANADA), and during World War 2 it was also used by Nationalist China, Lithuania (who adopted the pistol in 1936), Romania and by the German army, who took over the FN factory output as the Pistole 640(b) after capturing Belgium in 1940. During the course of World War 2 many pistols were made in Canada by John Inglis & Company of Toronto; many of these were despatched to China.

Length: 7.75in (197mm)
Weight unloaded: 2lb 3oz (1.00kg)
Barrel: 4.65in (120mm), 4 grooves, right-hand twist
Magazine: 13-round detachable box
Muzzle velocity: c.1100fps (335mps)

AUTOMATICKY PISTOLE VZ/22, AUTOMATICKY PISTOLE VZ/24
Czechoslovakia
Ceskoslovenská stán Zbrojovká, Brno (vz/22); Ceskoslovenská Zbrojovká, Praze (vz/24)
9mm Short

These pistols were the earliest of a number of designs manufactured and marketed in Czechoslovakia to the designs of Josef Nickl, who had been employed prior to World War 1 by Waffenfabrik Mauser—and for whom in 1916 he had designed the vz/22 as the 'Nickl-Pistole'. Although using a low-powered cartridge, the vz/22 uses a locked breech dependent upon the rotation of the barrel for locking and unlocking. There is, of course, no necessity for locking in 9mm Short calibre and the later vz/27 (0.32in ACP) reverted to blowback principles. In general terms the vz/22 had no particular virtues, although a sound weapon of first-class quality, and many are still in use.

The 1924 design, also in 9mm Short and also a locked-breech weapon, is no more than a logical development of the vz/22. Assembly is slightly more easy, a magazine safety has been added and, on the later models, the wooden butt grip based on the original Mauser type was replaced by one of hard rubber and bearing the CZ monogram.

▲The Browning-designed Modèle 1910 pocket pistol (FN).
▲The Modèle 1922 (or Mle 10/22) pistol, clearly showing the extension to the front of the slide and the longer grip.

▲▷▷Three views of the Browning-inspired GP35 pistol; right side, left side and with the shoulder-stock/holster (FN).
▷A comparison between the vz/26, top, and the vz/27, bottom (RSAF).

Length: 6.00in (152mm)
Weight unloaded: 1lb 8oz (0.70kg)
Barrel: 3.55in (91mm), 6 grooves, right-
  hand twist
Magazine: 8-round detachable box
Muzzle velocity: c.970fps (295mps)

AUTOMATICKY PISTOLE VZ/26, AUTOMATICKY PISTOLE VZ/27
Czechoslovakia
Ceskoslovenská, Zbrojovká, Praze
7.65mm automatic pistol (vz/27), 9mm Short (vz/26 and vz/27)

The vz/27 is the successor to the vz/22 and vz/24, and it is generally encountered as a 7.65mm blowback pistol with the barrel attached to the slide by ribs in the Colt fashion. An earlier experimental design, the vz/26, was also made (generally found in 9mm Short calibre) in which the barrel and the breech are locked together on firing by the same rotating system used on the vz/24. Certainly there is no requirement for breech locking in either calibre. The external difference between the two vz/27 variations lies in the cutting of the finger-grip grooves in the slide: the blowback model has vertical grooves while the locked-breech model has the grooves obliquely inclined to the top front of the slide. The locked-breech models also have a magazine safety which prevents the trigger being moved unless the magazine is in place. Early models have butt grips of wood and are marked on the top rib CESKA ZBROJOVKA ASV PRAZE, while later models made after the German occupation are inscribed BOHMISCHE WAFFEN-FABRIK PRAG and in many cases have plastic butt grips. The German weapons, known as the Pistole 27(t), are often found in a slightly simplified form. Production of the vz/27 was resumed after 1948, such output being distinguishable by the marking NARODNYI PODNIK.

Length: 6.25in (158mm)
Weight unloaded: 1lb 9oz (0.70kg)
Barrel: 3.90in (100mm), 6 grooves, right-
  hand twist
Magazine: 8-round detachable box
Muzzle velocity: c.920fps (280mps)
  (7.65mm ACP)

AUTOMATICKY PISTOLE VZ/38
Czechoslovakia
Ceskoslovenská Zbrojovká, Praze
9mm Short

This is a terrible weapon and there seems to be no good reason for its existence: it is clumsy to hold and point and the lockwork is double-action only, so that accurate shooting is out of the question. It scores in only one respect as it is perhaps one of the easiest pistols to strip and clean, since the simple release of a catch allows the barrel and slide to hinge up at the muzzle so that the slide can be pulled from the barrel. The pistol is of good manufacture, well finished of good material.

While some authorities have claimed that this pistol is chambered for a special version of the 9mm Short cartridge developed by the Czech Government for military use only, we have neither seen the cartridge in question nor even any official record of its existence—and all the specimens of this pistol so far examined seem to function quite satisfactorily with the standard 9mm Short round. A few examples with a conventional sear and a hammer grooved for manual cocking have also been noted.

Length: 8.11in (206mm)
Weight unloaded: 2lb 1oz (0.94kg)
Barrel: 4.65in (118mm), 6 grooves, right-hand twist
Magazine: 8-round detachable box
Muzzle velocity: c.980fps (299mps)

AUTOMATICKY PISTOLE VZ/50
Czechoslovakia
Ceskoslovenská Zbrojovká, Strakoniče
7.65mm automatic pistol (0.32in ACP)
This is no more than a slightly modified Walther Modell PP, and the modification seems to have been done for the sake of it since it adds nothing to the functioning. There is a slight difference in the shape of the frame and the trigger-guard, the grip is changed slightly and the contour of the hammer is also different from the original Walther pattern. The biggest change is in the repositioning of the safety catch on the left side of the frame instead of the slide. In this position it works directly on the lockwork instead of demanding some rather complex machining and fitting of operating pins in the slide, which simplifies manufacture if nothing else. The double-action lockwork of the Walther is retained.

Length 6.60in (167mm)
Weight unloaded: 1lb 7.5oz (0.70kg)
Barrel: 3.75in (97mm), 6 grooves, right-hand twist
Magazine: 8-round detachable box
Muzzle velocity: c.920fps (280mps)

AUTOMATICKY PISTOLE VZ/52
Czechoslovakia
Ceskoslovenská Zbrojovká, Strakonice
7.62mm náboj vz/30 (Soviet M30)
The vz/52 is a considerable improvement over its immediate predecessors, although it is notable that there still seems to be evidence of Mauser design techniques just as there were on prewar pistols. It is a recoil-operated pistol with an unusual locking system. Chambered for the 7.62mm Soviet pistol cartridge (which is virtually the 7.63mm Mauser round), a locking system is very necessary and the design is loosely based on a Mauser patent of 1910, modified along lines first developed in Poland and later incorporated into the MG42. Two rollers lock the barrel and slide together during a short recoil stroke and are then cammed out of engagement with the slide, permitting the slide to recoil fully, extract, return and chamber a fresh round. As the new round is chambered, the slide and barrel move forward and the locking rollers are once more forced into engagement.

Neat, strong and elegant as the system

▼The Czechoslovak automaticky pistole vz/38 (RSAF).
▼The vz/52 pistol, which incorporates an unusual roller-locking system (RSAF).
▼The Bergmann-Bayard pistol, shown here in a civil version but supplied in a similar type to Denmark (RSAF).

is, it seems unnecessarily complex when compared with Browning designs, although the vz/52 is probably the smoothest-shooting pistol using a cartridge of the 'Tokarev/Mauser' type.
Length: 8.25in (209mm)
Weight unloaded: 1lb 15oz (0.90kg)
Barrel: 4.71in (120mm), 4 grooves, right-hand twist
Magazine: 8-round detachable box
*Muzzle velocity: c.1300fps (396mps) **

PISTOL MODEL 1910, MODEL 1910/21
Denmark
Ancien Etabblissements Pieper, Herstal-lèz-Liège, Belgium; Haerens Tojhus, København
9mm patron m/10 (Bergmann-Bayard)
This weapon is one of the many designs produced by Theodor Bergmann in the early years of the century, although he himself only manufactured a very small number—perhaps no more than 1,000—and in 1907 the manufacturing rights and existing parts were acquired by Pieper. Originally known as the Bergmann 'Mars', Pieper renamed it the Bayard Modèle 1910, but such was the influence of its inventor's name that it is invariably known as the Bergmann-Bayard. Bergmann had initially begun supplying the Spanish Government in 1905 and this contract was thereafter fulfilled by Pieper, although details of the pistol were changed. The barrel became slightly longer, forged integrally with the barrel extension, and the rifling was changed from the original 4-groove right-hand twist to 6 grooves left-hand twist. The pistol was also said to have been adopted at this time by the Greek Army.

The layout of the pistol, although vaguely reminiscent of the Mauser C96, is a logical development of earlier Berg-

* The muzzle velocity given is using the standard Soviet M30 cartridge, but some reports aver that the Czechs use a heavier loading in their service round, giving a velocity of approximately 1650fps (504mps). This is difficult to credit since a velocity of this speed in a pistol of this weight would be virtually uncontrollable.

mann designs and owes nothing to Mauser. The great difference between this weapon and its forerunners is the utilisation of a much more powerful cartridge and a positive breech locking system. The bolt is locked by a plate beneath, which engages in slots in the bolt and is supported by a ramp on the frame. On firing, the barrel and bolt recoil slightly until this lockplate rides down the ramp and unlocks the bolt—which is then free to move back while the barrel is held. Another refinement absent on earlier Bergmann pistols is a firing-pin withdrawal spring which keeps the point of the pin inside the bolt during loading.

After having been tested by various governments in a variety of calibres, the pistol was adopted in 1911 by the Danish Army as the Pistol m/10, made under contract by Pieper. Supply was terminated by World War 1 and in 1922 the Danes decided to make their own; the indigenous produce differed from the original Pieper issues by the use of large wooden or plastic grips and by having the lock cover-plate retained by a screw instead of by a spring catch. They were marked 'm 1910/21' with Danish inscriptions, although some of the original Pieper models were reworked to 1921 standard by the addition of the new plastic grips and these were also marked 'm 1910/21' (but still bear the original Belgian markings).
Length: 10.00in (254mm)
Weight unloaded: 2lb 4oz (1.02kg)
Barrel: 4.00in (101mm), 4 or 6 grooves, left or right-hand twist (see above)
Magazine: 6 or 10-round detachable box
Muzzle velocity: c.1300fps (395mps)

PISZTOLY 'TOKAGYPT 58'
Egypt (United Arab Republic)
Fémaru és Szerszámgépgyár NV, Budapest
9mm Parabellum
This is no more than a slightly improved copy of the Soviet TT33 (Tokarev) pistol manufactured by FES of Budapest (in 9mm Parabellum) for use in the Egyptian military forces. The improvements on the original design are no more than skin

deep—a better-shaped grip is provided, owing to a plastic one-piece butt grip, and a better quality of finish and manufacture than that usually found on the native Soviet products is also apparent. A safety catch has been added and the calibre changed to 9mm Parabellum.
Length: 7.65in (192mm)
Weight unloaded: 1lb 15oz (0.91kg)
Barrel: 4.50in (114mm), 6 grooves, right-hand twist
Magazine: 7-round detachable box
Muzzle velocity: c.1150fps (350mps)

PISTOOLI MALLI 35 (Pistol M35, 'Lahti')
Finland
Valtion Kiväärithedas (VKT), Jyväskylä
9mm Parabellum
The Lahti pistol, often simply known as the L35, takes its name from the designer of the weapon, Aimo Lahti. The weapon was adopted as the official pistol of the Finnish Army in 1935, replacing the Pistoli m/23 (a Parabellum), and was later adopted by Sweden as the Pistol m/40. The L35 is exceptionally well made and finished, and is particularly well sealed against the ingress of dirt; as a result it is remarkably reliable in sub-zero conditions, although a little heavy by modern standards. An unusual design feature of the Lahti lies in the provision of an accelerator, a device more usually associated with a machine-gun in which it is utilised to increase the fire-rate. In the pistol, however, the accelerator is specifically intended to ensure the operation of the action at sub-zero temperatures. It is impossible to strip the gun completely for cleaning or for repairs without the services of a trained armourer and access to a workshop, but it should be said that the likelihood of components breaking or wearing out is so remote that the armies in which the pistols serve are obviously prepared to discount the chances.
Length: 9.68in (245mm)
Weight unloaded: 2lb 11oz (1.22kg)
Barrel: 4.18in (105mm), 6 grooves, right-hand twist
Magazine 8-round detachable box
Muzzle velocity: c.1150fps (350mps)

►The Finnish m/35 pistol, designed by Aimo Lahti and bearing external affinity to the Parabellum. The VKT monogram on the grips (for Valtion Kiväärithedas—State Rifle Factory) distinguishes the Finnish gun from the Swedish version made by Husqvarna (RSAF).

▲The French Modèle 1892 revolver, often known as the 'Lebel' after the president of the commission responsible for its adoption (RSAF).

▲The Le Français of 1928, one of the more unusual self-loading pistols.

Marketed by SFAC of Saint-Etienne, sales were few (RSAF).

▲The French Modèle 1935A self-loading pistol, manufactured by Société Alsacienne de Construction Méchanique (SACM) (RSAF).

PISTOLE REVOLVEUR MODELE 1892 ('Modèle d'Ordonnance' or 'Lebel')
France
Various State-owned factories
8mm Cartouche Mle 92

The Modèle 1892 is sometimes known as the 'Lebel', although it is a matter of some doubt whether or not Nicolas Lebel had anything to do with the design and development of this weapon. The Mle 92 was introduced to the French Army in 1893 and remained in use until 1945, as the French had meanwhile failed to design and issue a suitable self-loading pistol other than the Modèle 1935. The revolver is a relatively simple double-action six-chamber revolver, using a lock mechanism similar to that employed by the Italian 1889 design (see ITALY): it was built on a solid frame with a cylinder which swung out to the right for loading, a feature of arguable usefulness as most shooters are right-handed. One of the better features of the Mle 92 was that the left sideplate could be unlocked and swung forward to expose the lock and trigger mechanism for repair or cleaning, and one of the defects (shared by most other revolvers of that period) lay in the small and underpowered cartridge.

Length: 9.36in (238mm)
Weight unloaded: 1lb 14oz (0.84kg)
Barrel: 4.60in (117mm), 6 grooves, right-hand twist
Magazine: 6-round cylinder
Muzzle velocity: c.750fps (228mps)

PISTOLE AUTOMATIQUE MILITAIRE LE FRANCAIS, MODELE 1928
France
Société Française d'Armes et Cycles, Saint-Etienne
9mm Browning Long

The 1928 'Militaire' Le Français is the senior model of a series of pistols of similar design made by SFAC of Saint-Etienne and it embodies a number of novel and distinctive design features. The gun operates on the blowback system but has the recoil spring augmented by a leverage device which also functions as a recoil buffer. The barrel pivots downwards through about 15° to permit cleaning and loading single rounds, and withdrawing the magazine automatically unlocks the barrel and allows it to tip forward. The lockwork is double-action and there is no provision to allow the slide to be manually operated.

To operate the Le Français the magazine is inserted in the normal fashion; at the bottom of the magazine an external loop or clip holds an additional round which is removed and, with the barrel tipped forward, inserted into the chamber. The barrel is then closed. Pulling the trigger will now fire that round, owing to the double-action lock, and the blowback action extracts and reloads from the magazine in the usual way. The firing mechanism is hammerless and the striker does not actually cock until the trigger is drawn back to fire the first round. The only drawback to the system is that the slide closes on an empty chamber after the last round has been fired and the firer is given no warning

Alternatively, after loading the magazine into the gun, it can be withdrawn about 0.25in (6.40mm) and locked there, clear of the slide. The pistol can now be loaded with single rounds, the first into the tipped barrel and subsequent rounds by releasing the barrel (by using the barrel catch) to reload. This allows a slow fire to be kept up, with a full magazine in hand for emergencies. Much the same system had been used earlier on the Webley and Scott automatic pistol and, of course, it was a common feature in bolt-action rifles

Introduced early in 1929, the Le Français failed to catch on, although it is an interesting example of what might have been; perhaps it was a little too unusual in its concept and, by that time, the 9mm Browning long cartridge was considered too weak to be practical.
Length: 8.00in (203mm)
Weight unloaded: 2lb 6oz (1.09kg)
Barrel: 5.25in (134mm), 6 grooves, right-hand twist
Magazine: 8-round detachable box
Muzzle velocity: c.1000fps (305mps)

PISTOLE AUTOMATIQUE MODELE 1935A, PISTOLE AUTOMATIQUE MODELE 1935S
France
Manufacture d'Armes de Chatellerault (MAC), Manufacture d'Armes de Saint-Etienne (MAS), Manufacture d'Armes de Tulle (MAT), Société Alsacienne de Construction Méchanique (SACM) and Société d'Applications Générales, Eléctriques et Méchaniques (SAGEM)
7.65mm Long
Taking the Colt 0.45in M1911A1 as a starting point, Charles Petter of SACM made a number of improvements and embodied them in this French service pistol. The principal differences lie in the system of housing the recoil spring, the use of a single wide locking rib on top of the barrel, the provision of a magazine safety and a safety catch on the slide, and the positioning of the hammer and lockwork in a separate sub-assembly.

A variant known as the 1935S reverses the barrel locking system by forming the lug on the undersurface of the slide-top and the recess in the material of the barrel. This model is recognisable by a straight butt and a slightly protruding barrel muzzle, whereas the principal model — the M1935A — has the butt curved to better suit the hand and has the muzzle flush with the front edge of the slide.

These weapons, which are generally known as the MAS1935A and 1935S, are little known and rarely seen. They are, moreover, of only academic interest outside France as they are chambered for the 7.65mm Long automatic pistol cartridge peculiar to the French army.
Length: 7.45in (189mm)
Weight unloaded: 1lb 10oz (0.76kg)
Barrel: 4.30in (109mm), 4 grooves, right-hand twist
Magazine: 8-round detachable box
Muzzle velocity: c.1000fps (305mps)

PISTOLE AUTOMATIQUE MODELE 1950
France
Materiels d'Armes de Saint-Etienne
9mm Parabellum
The French never seem to have excelled in weapon design until after World War 2. The only prewar pistol of any merit was more or less copied from earlier Browning designs and chambered for an odd and ineffective round, but after the war work began on a pistol which was ultimately adopted as the Modèle 1950. The weapon is once again basically the Colt M1911A1/Mle 1935S in 9mm Parabellum calibre but with some small changes, the most important of which is in the matter of safety.

A cross-bolt safety catch, as used in the 1935 Petter-designed pistol, is retained in the Mle 50 and replaces the frame-mounted catch of the Colt. This is a sensible move in a way, since the users would have become used to the earlier system and, since the use of safety catches is largely instinct, leaving it in a familiar place would obviate retraining. A magazine safety is also fitted to prevent firing the round in the chamber when the magazine is removed; this is one of those features which look good on a specification sheet or sales brochure but which are of dubious utility in a combat pistol.
Length: 7.60in (192mm)
Weight unloaded: 1lb 8oz (0.68kg)
Barrel: 4.40in (112mm), 4(?) grooves, right-hand twist
Magazine: 9-round detachable box
Muzzle velocity: c.1100fps (335mps)

REICHS-COMMISSIONS-REVOLVERE, MODELL 1879 and MODELL 1883
Germany
Various manufacturers, amongst them V C Schilling & Cie, J P Sauer & Sohn, C G Haenel & Cie (all of Suhl), Gebrüder Mauser & Cie, Oberndorf-am-Neckar, and Königlich Gewehrfabrik Erfurt
10.6mm Revolver-patrone
These revolvers are the designs approved by the various commissions which were charged in the late 1870s with providing new weapons for the German army. In view of the number of advanced revolver designs appearing at that time the Reichs-revolver was remarkably conservative. reflecting the viewpoint of most contemporary military authorities.

The two models differed only in barrel length, the M79 (also known as the 'Trooper' or 'Cavalry' model) having a 7in (178mm) barrel and the M83 (also known as the 'Officer' or 'Infantry' model)

▶The officers' version of the Reichs-Commissions-Revolver, Modell 1883, manufactured in Suhl by Schilling (VCS) and Haenel (CGH), whose initials appear in an oval on the left side of the frame (RSAF).

▼The Mauser C96 mit Sicherung neuer Art (new pattern safety device), of c.1912. This is a wartime gun in 9mm Parabellum, note the figure '9' impressed in the grip, which explains the relatively inferior finish of the gun compared to Mauser's peacetime products (RSAF).

▼The 9mm Parabellum C96 showing the differences between a charger of 7.63mm ammunition (left) and one of 9mm (right) (RMCS).

▼A sample of the Westinger-system schnellfeuerpistole of 1936, with the selector set at 'N' (normal). This gun was supplied to China in the late 1930s; the ideographs read 'Made in Germany'.

having a 5in (127mm) barrel. Apart from that, they were normally found as solid-frame single-action non-ejecting six-shot revolvers of robust construction. Loading was done through a gate on the right side, as the hammer could be pulled to half-cock to release the cylinder. Unloading—or ejecting spent cases—was done by withdrawing the cylinder axis-pin and removing the cylinder, then using the axis-pin or a suitable rod to punch out the cases.

Although superseded in 1908 by the Parabellum, numbers of these weapons remained in second-line service throughout World War 1 and sufficient remained in private hands to make it worth one manufacturer's while to market commercial 10.6mm ammunition until 1939.

(data: Modell 1879)
Length: 12.20in (310mm)
Weight unloaded: 2lb 5oz (1.04kg)
Barrel: 7.20in (183mm), 6 grooves, right-hand twist
Magazine: 6-round cylinder
Muzzle velocity: c.670fps (205mps)
(data: Modell 1883)
Length: 10.25in (260mm)
Weight unloaded: 2lb 1oz (0.94kg)
Barrel: 4.96in (126mm), 6 grooves, right-hand twist
Magazine: 6-round cylinder
Muzzle velocity: c.640fps (195mps)

MAUSER-SELBSTLADEPISTOLE CONSTRUCTION 96 ('C96')
Germany
Waffenfabrik Mauser AG, Oberndorf-am-Neckar
7.63mm Mauser-patrone and others

The Mauser-Selbstladepistole C96 was apparently invented by the three Feederle brothers, probably in 1894, and patented in 1895 in the name of Peter-Paul Mauser. The prototype, chambered for the 7.65mm Borchardt round with a 10-round magazine and a spur hammer, was completed in the first months of 1895 and first fired on 15th March. The rest of 1895 was spent testing the prototype guns in conditions of the utmost secrecy until in January 1896 Mauser pronounced that his company was ready to begin the manufacture of 'preproduction' pistols, about 110 of which were manufactured in nine months—including guns chambered for the 7.65mm Borchardt cartridge with magazines of 6, 10 and 20 rounds, and a very small number of 6mm specimens with 10-round magazines. The magazines, all of which were integral with the frame, were loaded through the top of the action from chargers.

True production began in October of 1896, when the design was finalised around the 7.63mm Mauser round which was in reality no more than a 7.65mm Borchardt in which the bullet was more securely anchored, for it had been found that the C96 was extremely hard on the ammunition held in the magazine. Assorted magazines—6, 10 and 20 rounds —were provided for the guns, although the 20-round unit was discontinued.

At the beginning of 1897 a mechanical change was made when a supplementary locking lug was added to the underside of the bolt and several minor modifications were made to the mechanism, particularly in the method of supporting and guiding the mainspring housing.

The C96 failed to attract the favourable attention of the German military authorities, and with the emergence of the Parabellum Mauser's chances receded. C96 pistols were, however, supplied to the Regia Marina d'Italia and to Turkey and Russia. Almost all C96 pistols were capable of being fitted to a hollowed wooden shoulder-stock/holster. with which they were often supplied.
Length: 12.25in (312mm)
Weight unloaded: 2lb 12oz (1.25kg)
Barrel: 5.50in (139mm), 6 grooves, right-hand twist (4 grooves in early weapons numbered below c.100000)
Magazine: 10-round integral box
Muzzle velocity: c.1425fps (434mps)

Selbstladepistole C96 mit Sicherung C02. In 1902, Mauser attempted to improve the C96 by patenting a revised form of safety device—the so-called 'gelenksicherung' or 'hammer safety'—which consisted of a lever on the left side of the hammer. The safety lever could be used for single-hand cocking, which was a virtual impossibility with the standard pistol hammer (designed for cocking against a horseman's saddle), and although the hammer could still be dropped in the 'safe' position the lever blocked the hammer nose from the striker.

Selbstladepistole C96 mit kurzer Auszieher, c.1905. In 1905 Mauser modified the C96 by the addition of a shorter extractor, a small hammer which no longer obscured the rearsight when resting on the striker, and a two-lug firing pin retainer. It must be noted that transitional models exist with similar features, but still possessing the old long extractor.

Selbstladepistole C96 mit Sicherung neuer Art, c.1912. The 'new safety'—'Sicherung neuer Art'—could only be applied when the hammer was manually retracted from contact with the sear; those pistols with the older pattern of safety device could have it applied regardless of the position of the hammer. Pistols fitted with this safety had the entwined letters NS on their rear surface.

Mauser Selbstladepistole C96, 9mm Parabellum, 1915. During World War 1, the German authorities soon realised that they were in desperate need of smallarms of every description, and that it would be most useful if a supply of Selbstladepistolen C96 could be made available in 9mm Parabellum. As a result of investigations made in mid-1915 by the Gewehr-Prüfungs-Commission, Mauser began the production of 150,000 C96 pistols in the desired calibre; the weapons were marked on the grips with large red-stained figures '9', although there are those in existence with black staining. Some guns first chambered for Mauser's semi-experimental 9mm 'Export' cartridge—which had a longer case than the 9mm Parabellum—are thought to have been rebarrelled for the latter calibre.

'Bolo-Modelle'. The so-called 'Bolo' pistols were made in c.1920 and supplied in large numbers to Soviet Russia ('Bolshevik'—hence 'Bolo'). The principal difference was the fitting of a 3.88in (99mm) barrel in order to evade provisions of the Versailles Treaty. The term is, however, often misapplied—given loosely to any short-barrelled Mauser of any age.

Selbstladepistole M711. A version of the basic C96 manufactured c.1930, the 7.63mm M711 was provided with detachable magazines of 10, 20 and 40 rounds. A semi-automatic contemporary of the Schnell/feuerpistolen, it saw no military application.

Selbstladepistole M30 mit Universel-Sicherung. This was a 7.63mm 10-round magazine version of the C96 strengthened and fitted with a new pattern of safety similar in basic principle to the Sicherung C02, although it did not permit one-hand cocking. The safety could be applied with one hand, and effectively blocked the striker, which meant that the hammer could be dropped in safety on a loaded chamber. Pistols of this type were supplied to Norway and China.

Schnellfeuer-selbstladepistole M30 Zwanziglader, 1931. Sometimes called the M712, the original 'rapid-fire pistol' was manufactured to the patents of Josef Nickl. One hundred pistols of this type were delivered to Yugoslavia in 1933–4 (as the 'Modell-S') and 1000 went to China in 1931, where the market was being flooded by inferior—but cheaper—copies emanating from Spain and from China itself. Few of this class of weapon can be considered as anything other than aberrations: without suitable shoulder-stocks they climb much too rapidly as full-automatics and are extremely wasteful of ammunition.

Schnellfeuer - selbstladepistole system Westinger, 1936. The 1936 pattern, made to the designs of a Mauser engineer named Karl Westinger, was introduced as a belated attempt to win back some of the market which had been flooded by Mauser's cheap competitors, notably those of Spain. Notwithstanding sales of some Westinger pistols (which were offered in both 7.63mm Mauser and 9mm Parabellum calibres) to China, the war intervened before the pistol had time to become a commercial success: it is at any rate unlikely that it had the potential to become so.

SCHWARZLOSE-SELBSTLADE-PISTOLE, 1895 PATENT, MODELL 1896, or MODELL 1898
Germany (Austria)
Made for A W Schwarzlose GmbH, Berlin, by an unknown manufacturer
7.63mm Mauser-patrone
Andreas Schwarzlose was an ingenious and versatile designer who patented a wide variety of weapons in the period 1892 to 1912. This pistol was the first of his many designs to be produced in any quantity, but it unfortunately arrived on the market shortly after the Mauser C96 and less than 1,000 were actually made. It suffered by comparison with extant weapons and was consequently not commercially successful. The remaining stocks were apparently sold by an enterprising Berlin salesman to the Russian revolutionary movement of 1905, but the shipment was intercepted by the Russian authorities; the pistols were then distributed to the frontier police and similar official bodies and hence specimens of this pistol are more common in Russia than elsewhere.

The locking system is a turning bolt opened by a stud in a fixed guide ring riding in a helical groove in the bolt. This rotates and unlocks the bolt during recoil, after which the bolt reciprocates in the normal way, ejecting on the rearward stroke and reloading on its return. The Schwarzlose also ranks amongst the first designs to incorporate a hold-open device.

The pistol is well-balanced and fits the hand excellently, but the mechanism was complicated and turned out to be unreliable unless maintained in a perfect condition. In addition, the powerful cartridge gave a violent action which led to rapid wear on many surfaces.
Length: 10.75in (273mm)
Weight unloaded: 2lb 1oz (0.94kg)
Barrel: 6.43in (163mm), 4 grooves, right-hand twist
Magazine: 7-round detachable box
Muzzle velocity: c.1400fps (426mps)

PARABELLUM-PISTOLEN, 1898-1945
Germany
Deutsche Waffen- und Munitions-fabriken, Berlin (originally)
7.65mm Parabellum-patrone, 9mm Pist Patr 08 (9mm Parabellum-patrone)
The history and development of the Parabellum pistol is an involved affair—itself the subject of several specialised studies—and much of it is only of marginal interest to these pages. As a result only essential detail is included here

The Parabellum was a direct descendant of the Borchardt-Selbstladepistole, designed in 1893 by Hugo Borchardt and placed on the commercial market in the following year by Ludwig Loewe & Cie of Berlin. For its time the strange-looking gun was a revelation, but within three years improved pistols began to appear (notably the Mauser Selbstladepistole C96) and sales of the Borchardt rapidly declined until, in c.1898–9, production was discontinued.

There were, however, sufficient good features of the M93 to warrant continued development, although Hugo Borchardt had by now become disenchanted with the gun (or perhaps he believed it to be incapable of further improvement) and the succeeding designs were the work of Georg Luger, of the newly-formed Deutsche Waffen- und Munitionsfabriken. Luger's first patents were granted in 1898 and covered a transitional pistol representing a halfway stage between the Borchardt and the perfected Parabellum, which appeared in 1900 when it was adopted by the Swiss as the *Parabellum-Pistole, system Borchardt-Luger, Modell 1900*.

The variations which followed upon the success of the 1900 pattern pistol—and there were many—made use of the same operating principle with but minor alterations. Luger was a champion of recoil operation, and his pistol made use of the rearward-moving barrel to break open a toggle-lock by moving the centre of the pivot above the line of the bore. This permitted the lock to continue to break upwards as the breechblock moved directly towards the rear of the receiver, compressing the return spring (in a housing at the rear of the handgrip) as it did so. The compressed spring then returned the breechblock to its position behind the barrel and as the block re-turned so the entire barrel/receiver assembly—which was capable of about 6mm free movement before being brought to rest—returned to the firing position, locking the toggle by ensuring that the centre of the pivot lay below the centreline of the bore. The mechanism was well made of the finest materials then available, with the result that in the Parabellum DWM had one of the finest automatic pistols of its day; there were faults in the design, it is true—especially in the pattern of trigger mechanism (although it was adequate enough for military purposes) and the fact that the gun's feed was a little delicate in opera-tion. This stemmed from the recoil action which, although it was capable of smoothly handling powerful cartridges, returned the mechanism to battery by weak spring pressure; with cartridges loaded to a slightly lower pressure than normal, it was quite possible for the breechblock to recoil insufficiently far to clear the top cartridge in the magazine, from which position it either returned to an empty chamber or jammed against the base of the cartridge case. The Para-bellum, however, served the German Army (amongst others) well through two world wars, and although theoretically replaced after 1941 by the Pistole 38 (a Walther design) the earlier weapon was never entirely displaced in German service.

7.65mm Parabellum-Pistole Modell 1900, after 1906 occasionally known as 'alterer Modell'. The M00 was the original pistol, adopted by the Swiss and extensively tested by various other countries (see APPENDIX), chambered for Luger's 7.65mm bottleneck cartridge. The pistol was fitted with a grip safety, which was depressed by the hand before the gun could fire, at the rear of the handgrip and a manual safety lever was placed on the left rear side of the receiver where it could easily be operated by the thumb of the firing hand (provided

◁The Borchardt-selbstladepistole of 1893, prototype of the Parabellum and used to a very limited extent in World War 1 (RSAF).
◁The Borchardt with its shoulder stock/holster (RSAF).
◁The 9mm Parabellum-Marinen-Pistole Modell 1904; note the grip safety (RSAF).
◁The 9mm Parabellum-Pistole Modell 1908 (RMCS).
▶The 9mm Parabellum-Pistole Modell 1908, right side (RMCS).

of course, that the firer was right-handed). The toggle unit was partially cut away at the rear and a toggle-lock was fitted into the right 'toggle finger-grip'. A flat leaf spring was placed in the rear of the handgrip where it bore on the breech mechanism through an intermediate crank; when the later coil-spring guns were introduced, the leaf spring guns were christened 'alterer Art' (old pattern) or 'alterer Modell' (old model) as a means of distinguishing the two types.
Length: 8.31in (211mm)
Weight unloaded: 1lb 14oz (0.84kg)
Barrel: 4.80in (122mm), 4 grooves, right-hand twist
Magazine: 8-round detachable box
Muzzle velocity: c.1150fps (350mps)
9mm Parabellum-Pistole, 1902. The 1902 pattern was the first of Luger's pistols to use his 9mm Parabellum cartridge, which had been developed in 1901 from the 7.65mm type: in a moment of genius, Georg Luger had simply removed the bottleneck from his earlier cartridge to provide a straight-cased 9mm round, whose heavier bullet went some way to allay the objections of the authorities who would otherwise have taken the 7.65mm Parabellum if a heavier bullet, with greater stopping power, had been available. Luger's solution also had the important advantage of using the same case base size as the 7.65mm round, which ultimately meant that most of the existing machine facilities and spare parts could be used in the modified guns. Although few 9mm guns—which are usually known as the 'M02'—were produced, the pattern provided adequate development for the later P08. The gun was mechanically similar to the 1900 design (from which it could be readily recognised by the heavier barrel which destroyed much of the aesthetic appeal of the previous 7.65mm guns) and possessed a cut-away toggle, a toggle-lock and a leaf recoil spring.
9mm Parabellum-Marinen-Pistole Modell 1904 ('Marine Modell 1904'). The M04

was the first Parabellum to be adopted by a branch of the German armed forces, in this instance by the Kaiserliche Marine (Imperial Navy). The original pistol was in 9mm calibre with a longer barrel than the standard army P08 of later years, and it could be quickly recognised by the two-position rearsight protected by lateral 'wings'. It was also fitted with a lug at the bottom of the backstrap to which a shoulder-stock could be attached to increase accuracy at longer ranges. Mechanically, the M04 was an interesting transitional variety which represented a midstage between the 'alterer Modell' and the 'neuer Modell' as it married the leaf recoil spring and the toggle-lock with a new type of toggle finger grip which, flat sided, was only partially knurled about its circumference; the opportunity was also seized to add a combined extractor/loaded chamber indicator to the breechblock in accordance with Georg Luger's 1904 German patent. This, which later appeared as a feature of the 'new' models, showed the word GELADEN when a round had been chambered. Very few M04 pistols seem to have survived.
Length: 10.50in (267mm)
Weight unloaded: 2lb 2oz (1.00kg)
Barrel: 6.00in (152mm), 4 grooves, right-hand twist
Magazine: 8-round detachable box
Muzzle velocity: c.1200fps (366mps)
9mm Parabellum-Marinen-Pistole Modell 1904, system of 1906. Although still known to the Kaiserliche Marine as the M04, a modified version of the navy pistol was introduced in 1906; in accordance with the new patterns of the same year, the leaf recoil spring was eliminated in favour of a coil-spring and the toggle-lock was discarded.
9mm Parabellum-Marinen-Pistole Modell 1904, system of 1908. The 1908 variation of the M04 was the navy's equivalent of the army P08, from which it differed only in the length of the barrel and in the sighting arrangements.
7.65mm and 9mm Parabellum-Pistolen,

'neuer Art', 1906. The patterns of 1906 replaced the leaf recoil spring with one of coil type and eliminated the toggle-lock device which on previous models had appeared on the right toggle finger-grip. All guns produced to the modified system were fitted with the patented extractor/loaded chamber indicator which had first appeared on the naval pistol of 1904, and all made use of the grip safety. Two basic types were offered in the new range: the 7.65mm pistol was really the pattern of 1900, modified by the addition of the new spring and toggle unit, and the 9mm version was a revision of the gun of 1902.
9mm Parabellum-Pistole Modell 1908. The model of 1908, usually known simply as the P08 (from the German Army's contraction of 'Pistole 08'), is undoubtedly the most famous of all the Luger-designed pistols. The gun was based on the 9mm Pistole 'neuer Art' of two years previously, with the elimination of the grip safety mechanism and the revision of the manual thumb safety which as a result moved downwards (instead of upwards) to a 'safe' position, at which point an extension on the lever rose to block the sear. The original produce came from the workshops of Deutsche Waffen- und Munitionsfabriken, but in 1914 guns began to appear from the Königlich Gewehrfabrik Erfurt—the government arsenal at Erfurt in Thuringia. At about the same time the opportunity was taken of adding a shoulder-stock lug and a hold-open device to the magazine follower, although it seems that some pre-war guns were also so fitted.

The P08 had a long production life, surviving as it did the provisions of the Treaty of Versailles; apart from various postwar commercial produce emanating from such firms as Simson & Cie of Suhl, production arrangements passed c.1930 to Mauser-Werke AG of Oberndorf, although weapons continued to be produced under the DWM trademark until 1933–4—possibly for reasons of security. P08 pistols were also manufactured in

Suhl by Heinrich Krieghoff Waffenwerk, and it is said that the majority of these were procured by the Luftwaffe. Over 9,000 Parabellum pistols were manufactured in the period c.1922–4 by the British firm Vickers-Armstrongs & Co Ltd, of Crayford: these were supplied to Holland. The Swiss arsenal at Bern also made many for the Swiss army, and some were also produced for commercial sale.

By 1936, it was realised that the days of the P08 were almost over and in the following year possible replacements appeared in the form of the Mauser HSv (of which all too little is known), and the Walther Armee Pistole and Heeres Pistole. It was eventually decided that the Walther Heeres Pistole should be adopted by the Oberkommando der Wehrmacht as the Pistole 38, and instructions were accordingly passed to Carl Walther Waffenfabrik for the instigation of a suitable production line.

In July of 1941 Mauser-Werke were also in a position to begin production of the P38, and in June of the following year they manufactured the last P08—the last batch of which were accepted by the Wehrmacht in November. The P08 nevertheless remained in widespread service until the war's end, as insufficient quantities of the P38 were forthcoming to permit the replacement of all the Luger-pattern pistols.

Length: 8.75in (223mm)
Weight unloaded: 1lb 15oz (0.85kg)
Barrel: 4.00in (102mm), 6 grooves, right-hand twist
Magazine: 8-round detachable box
Muzzle velocity: c.1150fps (350mps)

9mm Parabellum - Artillerie - Pistole Modell 1908 (often known as the 'Modell 1914', 'Modell 1917' or 'die länge Pistole 08'). The Artillerie-Pistole's precise date of introduction is a little elusive for although specimens have been noted dated 1914–1915 over the chamber it is quite possible that the Germans rebarrelled standard P08 guns—which as the Parabellum barrel merely screws into the barrel is quite possible—to save time. There are also grounds for supporting an introduction date of 1917, as it seems unlikely that there would have been a tactical requirement for weapons of this pattern some three years before.

The Artillerie-Pistole was fitted with a 7.50in (192mm) barrel and a special tangent-leaf rearsight graduated to 800 metres, although the gun was otherwise identical to the standard P08. It was issued with a flat 'board' type stock for use as a carbine. Towards the end of World War 1 the Germans issued the pistol with 32-round spring-operated helical 'snail' magazines manufactured to the designs of the Austro-Hungarians Tatarek and von Benkö, who had patented the device in 1911. In service the magazines proved troublesome and unwieldy, but they continued in use until the Armistice and were also used on the embryonic Bergmann submachine-guns of 1918. It was found that the original

flat-nosed cartridges were ill-suited to the helical magazine, and so a round-nosed bullet was developed to counter the troubles: this bullet has since become standard.
Length: 12.24in (313mm)
Weight unloaded: 2lb 5oz (1.06kg)
Barrel: 7.50in (192mm), 6 grooves, right-hand twist
Magazine: 8-round detachable box or 32-round helical 'snail' magazine
Muzzle velocity: c.1250fps (381mps)

WALTHER SELBSTLADEPISTOLE MODELL 6
Germany
Carl Walther Waffenfabrik AG, Zella-Mehlis (then Zella St. Blasii)
9mm Pist Patr 08 (9mm Parabellum)
The firm of Carl Walther had been manufacturing automatic pistols since 1908 and, in response to a 1915 request from the German Army, they produced an enlarged version of the commercial Modell 4 as a military weapon. The resulting Modell 6 is a blowback weapon, and since the calibre is 9mm Parabellum it leads to the use of a heavy slide and a very strong recoil spring to withstand the heavier forces. Very few of these pistols were made and manufacture was discontinued in 1917.
Length: 8.25in (210mm)
Weight unloaded: 2lb 2oz (0.96kg)
Barrel: 4.75in (121mm), 4 grooves, right-hand twist
Magazine: 8-round detachable box
Muzzle velocity: c.1100fps (335mps)

MAUSER SELBSTLADEPISTOLE MODELLE 1910, 1914 and 1934
Germany
Mauser-Werke AG, Oberndorf-am-Neckar
6.35mm automatic pistol (M10 and M34), 7.65mm automatic pistol (M14 and M34)
The Modell 34, known sometimes as the 'Mauser-Pistole alterer Art' to distinguish it from the HSc, was a cleaned-up version of the design which first appeared in 1910. Although looking rather more of a nineteenth-century product than most of its contemporaries it was a sound pistol, immaculately finished, and it shoots well. Of the blowback variety, the assembly is such that the barrel can be removed for cleaning without disturbing the rest of the weapon. A typical example of Mauser craftsmanship is the butt grip, a one-piece wrap-around unit usually carved from wood (they were sometimes of hard rubber) and fitted with the utmost precision.

This pistol was originally produced as a commercial weapon, with the additional possibility of adoption by various European police forces. In this application it was successful but, with the outbreak of war in 1939, it was taken into military service as a substitute standard pistol and largely issued to the Kriegsmarine (German navy) and Luftwaffe (airforce); many of the examples found today bear

▷An example of the Mauser-selbstlade-pistole of 1914 in 6.35mm calibre. Note the Mauser monogram 'WM' (Waffenfabrik Mauser) on the grip (RSAF).

▷The Beholla self-loading pistol, manufactured in Suhl by Becker & Hollander, although other markings are known on pistols of this type. A typical small-calibre pistol pressed into German service in World War 1 (RMCS)

▷RM & M's 'Dreyse' army pistol, a blowback type firing the powerful 9mm Parabellum cartridge. These unusual guns can be dangerous if fired in a well-worn condition (RSAF).

the markings of one or other of these services.

(data: Modell 1934)
Length: 6.25in (159mm)
Weight unloaded: 1lb 5oz (0.60kg)
Barrel: 3.40in (87mm), 6 grooves, right-hand twist
Magazine: 8-round detachable box
Muzzle velocity: c.975fps (297mps)

BEHOLLA-SELBSTLADEPISTOLE
Germany
Becker & Hollander, Suhl (originally)
7.65mm automatic pistol (0.32in ACP)
This simple and sturdy blowback pistol was designed just prior to World War 1 by Stenda, with the intention of marketing it commercially. Before these plans got under way the war began and the German army began demanding supplies of pistols, and, since the standard P08 could not be produced fast enough, the Beholla was selected as a substitute standard weapon for staff officers and others whose pistol had no need to be of the same heavy calibre as the combat pattern. Manufacture was contracted to a number of companies and the design will be found bearing such names as 'Beholla', 'Menta', 'Stenda', 'Leonhardt' or others, depending upon the manufacturer.

The design is quite simple, leading to rapid manufacture and a trouble-free life, but it is remarkable in that the gun cannot be dismantled without using a vice and a tool kit. A hole in the slide gives access to a locking pin which has to be driven out with a drift before dismantling can begin. With this removed, the slide is locked back and the barrel driven from its mounting with a hammer, after which the rest of the weapon can be stripped.

Manufacture ceased in 1918, but so many thousands were made that they are still relatively common.

Length: 5.50in (140mm)
Weight unloaded: 1lb 6.5oz (0.64kg)
Barrel: 2.88in (73mm), 6 grooves, right-hand twist
Magazine: 7-round detachable box
Muzzle velocity: c.900fps (274mps)

DREYSE 'HEERES-SELBSTLADE-PISTOLE'
Germany
Rheinische Metallwaaren- und Maschinenfabrik AG, Sömmerda
9mm Pist Patr 08 (9mm Parabellum)
The Dreyse was one of the first commercial pistols to be produced in 9mm Parabellum, and (since this was the standard army round) small numbers were used by officers and soldiers alike during World War 1, although it was never accepted as an official weapon and no more than a few thousand were actually produced. The gun was also employed by police and other para-military organisations in Germany.

It resembles the earlier 7.65mm Dreyse design in appearance, but has an unusual feature in that the recoil spring can be disconnected for cocking. This is necessary since the pistol is of the blowback type; to handle the powerful 9mm cartridge the recoil spring has to be extremely powerful, making cocking in the normal way—pulling the slide back against the spring—very difficult. To cock the Dreyse the knurled grips which form the rearsight are gripped and pulled up to unlock the top rib, which disconnects the slide from the recoil spring and allows the slide to be pulled back and pushed forward, chambering a cartridge and cocking the striker. With the breech closed, the rib is replaced, re-engaging the recoil spring, and the gun is ready to be fired.

Another unusual feature of design is that the striker spring is not fully compressed when the gun is cocked, additional pressure being applied when the trigger is pulled.

Many 9mm Dreyse pistols found today have the locking lugs of the top rib somewhat worn and firing the pistol is a trifle hazardous, since the rib can jump open and the slide can then recoil violently with unfortunate results to the pistol and, in extreme cases, to the firer.

Length: 8.12in (206mm)
Weight unloaded: 2lb 5oz (1.05kg)
Barrel: 5.00in (126mm), 6 grooves, right-
    hand twist
Magazine: 8-round detachable box
Muzzle velocity: c.1200fps (366mps)

LANGENHAN 'HEERES-PISTOLE'
   (also known as the 'Heeres-Modell' or
   as the 'FL-Selbstladepistole')
Germany
Fritz Langenhan & Cie, Suhl
7.65mm automatic pistol (0.32in ACP)
Originally designed as a commercial weapon, this pistol was adopted by the German army during World War 1 as a substitute standard weapon and the entire production went into military service.

It is a blowback weapon, accurate and handy to use but of peculiar construction. The breechblock is a separate unit held in the slide by a stirrup-lock which forms the rearsight, and which is itself retained by a large screw at the rear of the block. The frame is cut away on the right side so that the breechblock is only supported on the left. Provided all the mating surfaces are unworn, and the lock screw is secure, the pistol works well—but once wear takes place the lock screw and stirrup tend to loosen during firing and there is a considerable danger that, after twenty or thirty rounds, the breechblock might be blown into the firer's face.

Length: 6.60in (168mm)
Weight unloaded: 1lb 7oz (0.67kg)
Barrel: 4.15in (105mm), 4 grooves, right-
    hand twist
Magazine: 8-round detachable box
Muzzle velocity: c.925fps (281mps)

▶Langenhan 'Army' model; Sauer's Modell 1913 (top) and 'Behörden Modell' (bottom) compared; Walther PP (All RSAF).

SAUER-SELBSTLADEPISTOLE 'BEHORDEN MODELL'

Germany
J P Sauer & Sohn, Suhl
7.65mm automatic pistol (0.32in ACP)
This blowback pistol, used by military and civil police in Germany in the 1930s and 1940s, is sometimes referred to as the 'Behörden' ('Authorities') model. It is generally the same as the 1913 pattern (the so-called 'Old Model') with a more rounded butt and a redesigned trigger mechanism. The breechblock is a separate unit held in the rear of the slide and retained by a large knurled cap. A signal pin is fitted in the breech which protrudes through the rear of the cap when a cartridge is chambered, and some models were equipped with a tiny 'grip safety' fitted into the front surface of the trigger.
Length: 5.75in (146mm)
Weight unloaded: 1lb 6oz (0.62kg)
Barrel: 3.03in (77mm), 6 grooves, right-hand twist
Magazine: 7-round detachable box
Muzzle velocity: c.900fps (274mps)

WALTHER SELBSTLADEPISTOLE MODELL PP

Germany
Carl Walther Waffenfabrik AG, Zella-Mehlis
Various calibres—see text
This pistol, introduced in 1929, was a radical improvement on anything which had passed before. It was the first totally successful self-loading pistol which incorporated a double-action mechanism, and it exhibited a clean and streamlined shape. It was originally produced as a police pistol—hence the initials PP (for Polizei Pistole)—for holster use by uniformed officers, and it was later employed by the German services in large numbers. Originally developed in 7.65mm automatic pistol calibre, models were also made in 0.22in Long Rifle, 6.35mm automatic pistol (rare) and 9mm Short chambering, all of which are almost identical in external appearance. An uncomplicated blowback weapon, an interesting innovation found in the centrefire models was the provision of a signal pin which floated in the slide and pressed on the rim of the chambered round so that the end of the pin protruded just above the hammer and gave a visual and tactile indication that the weapon was loaded.

Since the end of World War 2 this pistol has been copied with or without permission in a number of countries. It is once again being manufactured by its original inventors.

In c.1931–3 Walther produced an enlarged blowback PP in 9mm Parabellum for possible military adoption, which they called the MP (Militärisches Pistole): it was not successful.
Length: 6.38in (162mm)
Weight unloaded: 1lb 9oz (0.71kg)
Barrel: 3.35in (85mm), 6 grooves, right-hand twist
Magazine: 8-round detachable box
Muzzle velocity: c.950fps (289mps)

WALTHER SELBSTLADEPISTOLE MODELL PPK

Germany
Carl Walther Waffenfabrik AG, Zella-Mehlis
Various calibres—see text
The Walther PPK is a smaller edition of the PP, intended to be issued to plain-clothes police and hence easily concealed. In mechanism and construction it is almost identical with the PP, the only differences lying in the dimensions and construction of the butt. On the PP the butt is forged to shape, with two separate side-pieces of plastic. On the PPK the frame forging is a simple rectangle and the plastic grip is a one-piece wrap-around component which produces the final shape. Like the Modell PP, the PPK can be found in 0.22in, 6.35mm, 7.65mm and 9mm Short calibres, although the 7.65mm is by far the most common and no more than a few 6.35mm pistols ever seem to have been made.
Length: 5.83in (148mm)
Weight unloaded: 1lb 5oz (0.58kg)
Barrel: 3.15in (80mm), 6 grooves, right-hand twist
Magazine: 7-round detachable box
Muzzle velocity: c.950fps (289mps)

SAUER-SELBSTLADEPISTOLE MODELL 38H

Germany
J P Sauer & Sohn, Suhl
7.65mm automatic pistol (0.32in ACP)
This is a vastly different weapon from anything which had previously come from Sauer, and it is undoubtedly among the best of its kind. But for World War 2 it might well have been a considerable commercial success, although almost the entire production was taken over by the army and Luftwaffe; manufacture ended with the close of the war.

The Modell 38H is a blowback pistol of conventional pattern, but of superior design and heavier than most of its contemporaries, giving it good shooting qualities. It has a double-action trigger mechanism and, in addition, an unusual thumb-operated catch just behind the trigger which will release the internal hammer under control and allow it to be safely lowered on a full chamber. The lever can also be used to enable the hammer to be cocked by thumb pressure for deliberate single-action fire. When the hammer is down, a straight pull on the trigger will cock and fire if speed is more important than accuracy. A manual safety (omitted on specimens produced in 1944–5) was also provided.

▲Sauer's Modell 38H of 1938 (RSAF).
▼Walther's Modell PPK of 1931 (RSAF).

Length: 6.75in (171mm)
Weight unloaded: 1lb 9oz (0.72kg)
Barrel: 3.27in (83mm), 4 grooves, right-hand twist
Magazine: 8-round detachable box
Muzzle velocity: c.900fps (274mps)

MAUSER SELBSTLADEPISTOLE MODELL HSc
Germany
Mauser-Werke AG, Oberndorf-am-Neckar
7.65mm automatic pistol (0.32in ACP)

The Mauser HSc was introduced in c.1938–9 as a commercial venture (having been preceded by three experimental designs—HS, HSa and HSb—of 1935–7) and represented a considerable advance in design. It is a double-action pistol using blowback operation, and it is of very streamlined and clean appearance. The hammer is concealed within the slide, leaving only a small lip protruding sufficiently to allow it to be thumb-cocked, and the safety catch on the slide is unusual in that it lifts the entire firing pin into a recess and takes it out of alignment with the hammer: a most positive form of safety.

Though produced as a commercial venture, the HSc was taken into service for use by the German navy and airforce in considerable numbers during World War 2. A slightly improved version is once more in commercial production.
Length: 6.00in (152mm)
Weight unloaded: 1lb 5oz (0.60kg)
Barrel: 3.38in (86mm), 6 grooves, right-hand twist
Magazine: 8-round detachable box
Muzzle velocity: c.960fps (291mps)

PISTOLE 38 (P38), now known as PISTOLE 1 (P1)
Germany
Carl Walther Waffenfabrik, then of Zella-Mehlis, now of Ulm; and others
9mm Pist Patr 08 (9mm Parabellum)

In 1936–7 the Walther concern developed their double-action Modell AP or 'Armeepistole' as a potential military weapon. This made use of a locked breech and a concealed hammer, but when submitted to the Oberkommando des Heeres (OKH, the army command) the pistol was returned with a request that a visible external hammer should be substituted for the internal one. This was done, and the pistol was formally adopted in 1939 as the Pistole 38, the desire for which was brought about by the army's request for a more modern service pistol easier to manufacture than the old Parabellum-system Pistole 08.

In its early days (1937–8) a number of what later became the P38 were sold under the tradename 'Heerespistole' or 'HP', some of which were marketed in 7.65mm Parabellum in addition to those in 9mm Parabellum, although experimental guns were produced in 0.45in ACP and 0.38in Super: military demands soon absorbed the majority of Walther's entire production capabilities and so the com-

mercial guns are now rarely encountered. Breech locking is performed by a wedge-shaped locking block beneath the breech; when the pistol is fired, the barrel and the slide recoil together for a short distance until the locking block is driven down to disengage the slide and halt the barrel. The P38 is fitted with a double-action trigger mechanism—in common with Walther's earlier PP (1929) and PPK

(1931)—and a signal pin protrudes from the slide to indicate that the gun is loaded.

The demands of wartime production ultimately proved to be more than Walther could handle, and so various other concerns were impressed into the manufacture of the P38. Amongst those participants were Waffenfabrik Mauser AG of Oberndorf, who assembled complete pistols and whose first deliveries were made in 1941, and Spreewerke GmbH of Berlin. Use was also made by the Germans of the various captured arms plants, including Fabrique Nationale d'Armes de Guerre and Waffenwerke Brünn (Brno, Czechoslovakia), to manufacture certain vital components.

Walther resumed production of the P38 after the close of World War 2, and it was again adopted as the Bundeswehr's official sidearm under the new designation of Pistole 1. It is also used in Austria and elsewhere, and a number of prewar commercial specimens were supplied in 1939 to the Swedish Army (where the gun was known as the Pistol m/39).
Length: 8.38in (213mm)
Weight unloaded: 2lb 2oz (1.00kg)
Barrel: 5.00in (127mm), 6 grooves, right-hand twist
Magazine: 8-round detachable box
Muzzle velocity: c.1150fps (350mps)

'VOLKSPISTOLE'
Germany
Mauser-Werke AG, Oberndorf (?)
9mm Pist Patr 08 (9mm Parabellum)
This weapon, which exists only in prototype form, appears to be a late 1944 design intended for cheap production and issue to the Volkssturm towards the end of World War 2.

The specimen bears no markings and it cannot be attributed to any particular maker with certainty, but examination points to it having been a development of Gustloffwerk (Suhl) since it operates on a delayed blowback system similar to that developed by Barnetske for the Volksgewehr 1–5 self-loading rifle. Gas is tapped from the chamber and directed forward into the slide to delay the breech opening.

◁ Mauser-Werke's HSc (Hahn-Selbstspanne—hammer, self-cocking) which, together with the Walther PP and PPK and Sauer's Modell 38H, represented the zenith of German pocket pistol design (RSAF).
◁ The Pistole Modell 38, the Walther design selected to replace the Parabellum on the inventory of the German forces (RSAF).
◁ The Volkspistole, produced in 1944 as a last-ditch prototype and thought to have been made at one of Mauser's plants (RSAF).

▶ The Hungarian Pisztoly 37M. This specimen was produced in 1941 under German control, hence the slide marking (RSAF).

Firing the 9mm Parabellum cartridge, the general construction with a fixed barrel and a lift-off slide is reminiscent of Walther design and the magazine is a standard P–38 component. A smoothbore extension is fitted to the end of the barrel, probably in order to extend the pressure/space curve and ensure that the delayed blowback operation gives sufficient delay.
Length: 11.25in (286mm)
Weight unloaded: 2lb 2oz (0.96kg)
Barrel: 5.13in (130mm), 6 grooves, right-hand twist
Magazine: 8-round detachable box
Muzzle velocity: c.1250fps (381mps) (Estimated)

PISZTOLY 12M, PISZTOLY 19M ('Frommer Stop'), PISZTOLY 39M
Hungary
Fémáru-Fegyver és Gépgyár, Budapest
7.65mm automatic pistol (0.32in ACP), 9mm Short
These three pistols represent a successful class of long-recoil operated weapons, a system of operation which demands that the barrel and breech recoil, locked together, for a distance greater than that of the entire length of the cartridge. The breech is then unlocked, and the barrel is permitted to return to its original position, allowing the spent case to be ejected. The breech is then released to follow the barrel and takes a fresh round from the magazine on the way. The system had a mesmeric attraction for the designers Rudolf Frommer, Georg Roth and the Krnka family, who were responsible for a considerable range of weapons embodying the principle and who had produced experimental long-recoil pistol models in 1900 and 1901.

It is open to question exactly why they

went to such lengths to secure a locked breech on these weapons, as the power of the 7.65mm automatic pistol or 9mm Short cartridges hardly demand it.

The Pisztoly 12M was adopted by the Honved—the Hungarian branch of the Austro-Hungarian reserve formations—in 1912, and was chambered for the 7.65mm cartridge. Some weapons were made in 9 mm Short during World War 1, but a revision was made to 7.65mm when the Frommer was adopted in 1919 as the official weapon of the new Hungarian Army. The last model, the 39M in 9mm Short, does not seem to have been adopted by the services.

The Frommer weapons are reasonably well made of sound material, but they are ugly and awkward and have little to commend them.
(data: Pisztoly 19M)
Length: 6.50in (165mm)
Weight unloaded: 1lb 6oz (0.61kg)
Barrel: 3.80in (95mm), 4 grooves, right-hand twist
Magazine: 7-round detachable box
Muzzle velocity: c.920fps (280mps)

PISZTOLY 29M, PISZTOLY 37M
Hungary
Fémáru-Fegyver és Gépgyár, Budapest
9mm Short (29M), 7.65mm automatic pistol (0.32in ACP) and 9mm Short (37M)
There is little of remark in the 37M pistol adopted by the Hungarian Army in 1937, when it replaced the 9mm Short 29M of similar appearance and slightly different construction. The 1937 design is a sound and workmanlike blowback weapon, rather more robust and heavy than is usual in 7.65mm calibre, which makes it rather more comfortable and accurate to

shoot than some of the commercial lightweights. It was also made in limited numbers in 9mm Short chambering, a popular paramilitary cartridge in Eastern Europe in the middle 1930s.

A number of these pistols were made for the German Army as Pistolen 37(ü), and these are distinguished by the slide marking P MOD 37 KAL 7.65, whereas the Hungarian service models are marked FEMARU-FEGYVER ES GEPGYAR PT37M. The German occupation model also had a thumb-operated safety catch on the rear of the frame in addition to the grip safety of the original pattern.

(data: Pisztoly 37M)
Length: 7.17in (182mm)
Weight unloaded: 1lb 11oz (0.77kg)
Barrel: 4.33in (110mm), 6 grooves, right-hand twist
Magazine: 7-round detachable box
Muzzle velocity: c.920fps (280mps) (7.65mm ACP)

PISTOLA AUTOMATICA GLISENTI MODELLO 10, PISTOLA AUTOMATICA BRIXIA MODELLO 12
Italy
Metallurgica Bresciana Temprini, Brescia; Societa Siderugica Glisenti, Torino
9mm cartucchia pallottola modello 10 ('9mm Glisenti')

The precise relationship between the Brixia pistol, so named after its manufacturers, and the Glisenti pistol accepted into the Italian service in 1910 is at best uncertain.

The first patents for the design were filled in the United Kingdom in September of 1906 by Societa Siderugica Glisenti, who claimed a date of 30th June 1905, under the terms of the 1901 Patents Act. The original drawings accompanying the patent indicate that the gun—which is said to have been designed by the Swiss Hänsler and Roch—was originally conceived for a bottlenecked cartridge which is sometimes referred to as the 7.65mm Glisenti.

It has been stated that the Brixia was issued in 1905 to the officers of the Italian Carabinieri as the 'Pistola automatica, sistema Hänsler-Roch, modello 05', and although it has been indicated that this was also known as the 'Brixia' it seems more likely that this was an early 'Glisenti' gun, and that the manufacturers were Societa Siderugica Glisenti. In 1907, however, representatives of Glisenti offered the pistol to the British Army, although it had by then been redesigned for a 9mm cartridge dimensionally almost identical to the 9mm Parabellum. In this form, however, the Glisenti was adopted by the Italian Army in 1910 and it seems almost certain that the 'Brixia' pistol appeared on the scene two years later; it is unfortunate that the precise link between the Glisenti company and MBT is so elusive, but it may be that MBT were Glisenti's successors.

Both pistols are outwardly similar (although the Brixia lacks the Glisenti's grip safety) and internally identical, relying as they do on a swinging wedge-lock of marginal efficiency. Both bear some external resemblance to the Parabellum, although the internal arrangements are in a way reminiscent of the Mauser C96. While they are locked-breech types, the power of the lock is minimal and a more powerful cartridge would tax the design strength to its limits; another weakness is that the whole left side of the frame is a detachable plate which robs the frame of much-needed torsional strength. Since the chambers of the Glisenti and the Brixia will accept the 9mm Parabellum cartridge, which is identical in size to the cartucchia pallottola M10 (but a far more powerful loading), these two hazards are very real. When used with the right ammunition, the two Italian guns are reliable enough, but it is noteworthy that the Beretta designs were a good deal more popular with those to whom they were issued.
Length: 8.22in (207mm)
Weight unloaded: 1lb 13oz (0.85kg)
Barrel: 3.91in (100mm), 6 grooves, right-hand twist
Magazine: 7-round detachable box
Muzzle velocity: c.1050fps (320mps)

PISTOLA AUTOMATICA BERETTA MODELLO 1915
Italy
Pietro Beretta SpA, Brescia
7.65mm automatic pistol, 9mm Glisenti (experimental), 9mm Short

This pistol was produced by the well-known Beretta company for military use in World War 1. It is a simple blowback pistol and it was normally provided either in 7.65mm Auto Pistol or 9mm Short. A small number were, however, provided with stronger recoil spring and an added buffer spring, and chambered for the Italian service 9mm M10 (Glisenti) cartridge—with which cartridge they are as safe as with the other loadings; since the Glisenti round is dimensionally similar to 9mm Parabellum but weaker in loading, it follows that using Parabellum cartridges in the pistol could lead to dangerous pressures and the possibility of a serious accident.

The firing mechanism is a concealed hammer and, after the last round is fired, the slide is held open by the breech face striking the magazine follower. On the 7.65mm pattern it is unusual that there is no positive method of ejection (although the 9mm guns used conventional ejectors) and the extracted case is ejected by the firing pin protruding from the breechblock at a position of full recoil. Manufactured to a long-obsolete design the Modello 1915 was at best a wartime expedient and was far outclassed by subsequent models from the same company.
Length: 5.85in (149mm)
Weight unloaded: 1lb 4oz (0.57kg)
Barrel: 3.32in (84mm), 6 grooves, right-hand twist
Magazine: 8-round detachable box
Muzzle velocity: c.875fps (266mps) (9mm Short)

PISTOLA AUTOMATICA BERETTA MODELLO 1922, BREVETTO 1915/19
Italy
Pietro Beretta SpA, Brescia
7.65mm automatic pistol, 9mm Short

At the end of World War 1 the Modello 1915 was redesigned and produced as an improved commercial venture in the 9mm Short calibre which was then becoming very popular. The general appearance was slightly changed, principally in the design of the slide which is built to surround the muzzle and carry the foresight. The finish of these pistols, at the time of their manufacture, was impeccable.

The principal change in the pistol's action was a complete redesign of the lockwork, giving a much improved trigger

◁The Glisenti pistol, modello 1910 (RSAF).

▶The 9mm (short) Beretta pistol of 1915 (Beretta).

▶Beretta's 7.65mm pistol design of 1915. It does not possess a conventional ejector, instead making use of the firing pin (Beretta).

▶The 7.65mm Beretta pistol, model of 1922 although marked as the patents of 1915 and 1919 (Beretta).

▶The 9mm (short) pistol modello 1923 (Beretta).

pull. The system of holding the slide open on the magazine follower was retained, and thus demanded a hard pull to remove the empty magazine and the operation of the slide to reload when a full magazine was inserted—which was unfortunate.

This pistol, made to the 1915/19 system, was officially known as the 'modello 1922'—serving as a form of prototype for the succeeding 9mm gun of 1923. The slide is marked PISTOLA AUT. BERETTA 7.65 BREV. 1915–1919.

Length: 5.75in (146mm)
Weight unloaded: 1lb 7oz (0.67kg)
Barrel: 3.50in (87mm), 4 grooves, right-hand twist
Magazine: 7-round detachable box
Muzzle velocity: c.975fps (297mps)

PISTOLA AUTOMATICA BERETTA MODELLO 1923, BREVETTO 1915/19 (ie: 1915/15 system)
Italy
P Beretta, Brescia
9mm cartucchia pallottola modello 10 ('9mm Glisenti')
The Beretta modello 1915 and modello 1915/19 in 7.65mm were made and issued in vast numbers, but since the official Italian automatic pistol round of the time was the 9mm Glisenti it was decided to produce an enlarged version to accept that cartridge.

The modello 1923 was otherwise similar in design to the later 1931 pattern, and similar to the preceding 1915 and 1922 designs, but with an external ring hammer. It was still a blowback, as the Glisenti's cartridge was of relatively low power, but since the 9mm Parabellum round of much greater power will also chamber in the pistol, there is an amount of hazard if the wrong ammunition is used.

It may be that this was the reason for the pistol being discontinued fairly quickly, few being made after c.1925. Total production was small, and the gun is today uncommon. The slide is marked PISTOLA–BERETTA–9M BREV. 1915–1919–MO 1923.

Length: 7.00in (177mm)
Weight unloaded: 1lb 12oz (0.80kg)
Barrel: 3.50in (87mm), 4 grooves, right-hand twist
Magazine: 7-round detachable box
Muzzle velocity: c.1000fps (305mps)

PISTOLA AUTOMATICA BERETTA MODELLO 1931, BREVETTO 1915/19
Italy
Pietro Beretta SpA, Gardone-val-Trompia
7.65mm auto pistol (0.32in ACP)
The Modello 1931 was a direct derivation

of the preceding patterns of 1922 and 1923, but in 7.65mm calibre only. Although used in small numbers by the Italian army, the modello 31 is usually recognisable by the appearance on the wooden grips of a medallion bearing an R/anchor/M device—signifying service with the Regia Marina d'Italia (Italian navy). The slide is marked PISTOLA BERETTA 7.65 BREV. 1915–1919–MO 1931, and the characteristics are essentially similar to those of the later Modello 1934, for which the 1931 design served as a basis.

PISTOLA AUTOMATICA BERETTA MODELLO 1934, BREVETTO 1915/19
Italy
Pietro Beretta SpA, Gardone-val-Trompia
7.65mm automatic pistol, 9mm Short
The 1934 Beretta is mechanically an improved model of the 1915, with the addition of an external hammer similar to that of the 1923 and 1931 patterns and a generally cleaner exterior. Well-made and finished of first rate material, they are excellent pistols although somewhat underpowered for military use. In common with previous models the magazine follower acts as a slide-stop when the last shot has been fired, which is inconveni-

ent in practical use; an independent slide stop would have been an improvement. It should be noted that models in 7.65mm calibre are somewhat uncommon.

(data: 9mm Short model)
Length: 6.00in (152mm)
Weight unloaded: 1lb 7.5oz (0.69kg)
Barrel: 3.75in (94mm), 4 grooves, right-hand twist
Magazine: 7-round detachable box
Muzzle velocity: c.825fps (251mps)

PISTOLA AUTOMATICA BERETTA MODELO 1935
Italy
Pietro Beretta SpA, Gardone-val-Trompia
7.65mm automatic pistol
The Modelo 1935 pistol, issued to officers and aircrew of the Italian air-force, was a lightened-slide version of the standard Modelo 1934.

PISTOLA AUTOMATICA BERETTA MODELLO 1951
Italy
Pietro Beretta SpA, Gardone-val-Trompia
7.65mm Parabellum, 9mm Parabellum
After World War 2 the Beretta company decided to align themselves with the rest of the world and produce a military pistol in 9mm Parabellum calibre. The design of the Modello 1951 (or M951) appears to have been begun c.1950, but

◁The 7.65mm pistol design of 1931, precursor of the more famous 1934 type (Beretta).
◁A civil version of the Beretta pistol modello 1934, differing from the military type primarily in the design of the grips and the quality of the finish (Beretta).
▶The Beretta Modello 1951, a locked-breech pistol bearing several affinities with the action of the Walther P38. The gun shown here is of the production series: some of the prototypes were fitted with alloy slides (Beretta).

the weapon was not placed on the market until c.1957. One of the reasons for this delay may have been the original intention to make the pistol with a light alloy frame, keeping the weight down to about 24oz (0.70kg); this appears, however, to have produced a weapon which was neither accurate nor pleasant to shoot and production models were entirely of steel. The results were heavier and better-shooting weapons.

This is a locked-breech pistol utilising a locking wedge swinging in the vertical plane. Locking of barrel and breech is achieved by a pair of lugs engaging with recesses in the breech slide; unlocking is done by a floating plunger carried on the rear barrel lug which releases the locking wedge to disengage the lugs from the slide on meeting a shoulder in the frame. Relocking is done automatically on the return stroke of the slide and the breech and slide are positively locked together at the moment of firing.

An improvement on previous models of Beretta's manufacture is the adoption of a slide stop which, under pressure from the magazine follower, holds the slide open after the last round in the magazine has been fired and keeps it open until a fresh magazine is inserted. Releasing the slide stop then permits the slide to go forward and chamber the first round.

The M1951 has also been adopted by Egypt and Israel.

Length: 8.00in (203mm)
Weight unloaded: 1lb 15oz (0.89kg) (All-steel model)
Barrel: 4.50in (114mm), 6 grooves, right-hand twist
Magazine: 8-round detachable box
Muzzle velocity: c.1300fps (396mps)

MEIJI 26 NEN KENJU
Japan
State factories
9mm Meiji 26 Japanese revolver
Adopted in 1893, this is known as the Meiji 26 Nen Ken Jū (Pistol pattern of the 26th year of the Meiji era). It is of native Japanese design and manufacture insofar as it is an amalgam of features of various Western revolvers; one can but suppose that, as in the case of their self-loading pistols, patriotism held a greater attraction than efficiency. The mechanical details of the barrel latch and cylinder mechanism are copied from Smith & Wesson designs, the lock and trigger mechanism from various Continental weapons, and the general construction leans heavily on Nagant principles. The result is unfortunate.

It can charitably be described as serviceable, but little more. It is double-action only, uses a side-swinging cylinder and has a hinged cover-plate which can be opened to expose the lockwork for cleaning in much the same way as the French Modèle 1892 revolver. The

▶The Japanese Meiji 26th year (1893) revolver, a good example of a combination of features culled from various western weapons (RSAF).

▲The 'baby' Nambu version of the Taisho 4th year (1915) 8mm gun. Chambered for a tiny 7mm cartridge, the small Nambu pistols were issued to officers, although some also seem to have been used as presentation weapons (RSAF).
▲The Taisho 14th year (1925) pistol, really no more than a modified version of the earlier 1915 design manufactured with an eye to simplicity (RSAF).
▲The Type 94 (1934) pistol, adopted by the Japanese army c.1937 to supplement the old Taisho 14th year guns (which were nevertheless produced until 1945). The exposed sear is visible along the left side of the gun above the trigger and grip. It will also be noted that the recoil spring is exposed.

ammunition is unique to the weapon and although Western ammunition of some makes of 0.380in revolver might be persuaded to fit, such a practice cannot be recommended.
Length: 8.50in (216mm)
Weight unloaded: 1lb 15oz (0.88kg)
Barrel: 4.70in (120mm), 6 grooves, left-hand twist
Magazine: 6-round cylinder
Muzzle velocity: c.750fps (229mps)

PISTOLU NAMBU TAISHO 4 NEN (Nambu pistol, 4th year of Taisho era: ie, 1915)
Japan
Various manufacturers
8mm Japanese auto pistol

This pistol, designed by Kijiro Nambu, was never apparently accepted as an issue weapon although many were undoubtedly purchased by officers of the Imperial army and navy, which must have led to quasi-official recognition. The exact date of these weapons' appearance has long been a subject for debate and is normally said to have been 1904 (likely a wrong assessment of the Japanese system of chronology); the pistol seems to have been first exhibited in 1909 at the Toyama Military Academy, which points to a design date of c.1908. It is therefore concluded that the pistol's '04' designation refers to the fourth year of the Taisho reign— 1915. It is also possible that the Italian Glisenti pistol (designed in Switzerland, 1905) provided Nambu's inspiration.

The Nambu breech-lock, achieved by a floating locking block working on the 'prop-up' system, is rather better than the similar type of the Glisenti but other details are less good. This is especially true of the striker spring, which is poorly made to the extent of ultimately giving weak strikes

The Taisho 4 pistol exists in several types. The first version has a tiny cramped trigger guard and a magazine bottom of wood; the government of Siam (Thailand) acquired a small number—perhaps 500—pistols c.1916–17. All pistols of the first type have the butt grooved for a telescoping wood/metal shoulder stock. The second version of the basic gun has an aluminium-bottom magazine and a larger trigger-guard, and small version of the basic pistol, firing a tiny 7mm cartridge, was issued as a staff officers' gun.

(data: 8mm Taisho 4)
Length: 9.00in (228mm)
Weight unloaded: 1lb 15oz (0.90kg)
Barrel: 4.70in (120mm), 6 grooves, right-hand twist
Magazine: 8-round detachable box
Muzzle velocity: c.1100fps (335mps)
(data: 7mm Taisho 4 'Baby Nambu')
Length: 6.75in (171mm)
Weight unloaded: 1lb 7oz (0.65kg)
Barrel: 3.25in (83mm), 6 grooves, right-hand twist
Magazine: 7-round detachable box
Muzzle velocity: c.1000fps (305mps)

TAISHO 14 KENJU
Japan
Kokura and Nagoya Army Arsenals
8mm Taisho 14

The Taisho 14 is virtually an 'improved' Nambu 'Taisho 04' and was introduced in 1925–6, improved insofar as simplifying the design to facilitate production is concerned. There are minor changes in the internal arrangements to this end, but the functioning is basically the same; the improvements, however, did nothing to the striker spring which remained a potential source of misfires. The Japanese authorities added a safety catch, which could be operated only by the firer's free hand, and the complication of a hold-open function operated by the magazine platform was also continued on the gun. The double recoil springs, plus a magazine retaining spring (on later models), ensured that the chance of removing a magazine was good only when the weapon was well-maintained and the user's hands dry. In any other combination of circumstances, removal varies from somewhat difficult to downright impossible—a prominent factor in the untimely demise of numerous Japanese soldiers, the victims of poor design.

A modified version of the Taisho 14 was introduced c.1937–8 after experiences in Manchuria, differing from the earlier model in the provision of a large 'winter triggerguard' and the addition of a magazine retaining spring on the lower front grip-strap. This modification is sometimes called the 'Kiska Model' as it was first captured on Kiska Island in the Aleutian Group.

Length: 8.93in (227mm)
Weight unloaded: 2lb 0oz (0.91kg)
Barrel: 4.75in (121mm), 6 grooves, right-hand twist
Magazine: 8-round detachable box
Muzzle velocity: c.1050fps (320mps)

94 SHIKI KENJU
Japan
State Factories
8mm Taisho 14

The Type 94 pistol, introduced to the Japanese army c.1937 (although it had been previously offered for commercial sale), was a peculiar design which did not achieve much distribution outside the country in which it was made. The Type 94 must rate among the worst automatic pistols ever produced for service issue; although the prewar guns were well made and finished, and of good material, wartime production standards gradually declined until those made in 1944 and 1945 were almost incredibly crude. The pistol also has the sear bar exposed along the left side of the receiver, where it can be released by a sharp blow—without recourse to the trigger. The Type 94 was also capable of firing when the breech was neither closed nor locked.

The action is that of a locked-breech relying on a vertically-sliding lockplate being cammed out of engagement during recoil. It is an adequate system, but does not appear to have attracted the attention of any other manufacturer.

Length: 7.13in (180mm)
Weight unloaded: 1lb 12oz (0.82kg)
Barrel: 3.13in (79mm), 6 grooves, right-hand twist
Magazine: 6-round detachable box
Muzzle velocity: c.1000fps (305mps)

PISTOLA AUTOMATICA SISTEMA OBREGON
Mexico
Fabrica de Armas, Mexico City
.45 M1911 (0.45in ACP)

Outwardly this weapon resembles a Colt 0.45in M1911A1, with slight contour changes in the slide and a peculiar safety-catch/slide lock. Inwardly it is based on the Austro-Hungarian 'Steyr-Hahn'

system, using a helical cam on the barrel engaging with a locking lug on the frame to rotate the barrel out of engagement with the slide on recoil. It is unusual in that the pistol has followed the Colt design closely enough to have the barrel rifled with a left-hand twist, making it the only pistol in the world ever to operate on a right-hand barrel unlocking system, since the motion of unlocking is resisted by the torque generated by the bullet in its travel up the rifling.

Chambered for the Colt's 0.45in round, this is a well-designed weapon which, owing to the axial movement of the barrel on unlocking, is potentially more accurate than the Colt or Browning designs of swinging barrel; there appears to be no record of comparative tests by which this contention could be proved or disproved.

Length: 8.25in (210mm)
Weight unloaded: 2lb 5oz (1.02kg)
Barrel: 4.88in (124mm), 6 grooves, left-hand twist
Magazine: 7-round detachable box
Muzzle velocity: c.850fps (260mps)

PISTOL VIS, WZ/35
Poland
Fabryka Broni w Radomiu, Radom
9mm Parabellum

The Polish model 35 is variously known as the Radom, from the arsenal at which it was made, or as the VIS (from the initials of the designers, Wilniewczyc and Skrzypinski) and is basically a Browning with Polish overtones. The locking of breech and slide is controlled by a cam on the barrel, as in the FN-Browning GP35. On the side of the slide is a catch which drops the hammer under control on to a loaded chamber after first blocking the hammer's path to the firing pin, allowing subsequent thumb-cocking. On the frame the device which appears to be a safety catch is in fact no more than a slide lock to facilitate stripping; the only true safety device is a grip safety, although the hammer drop lever could also be considered as an additional type.

During the course of the German occupation of Poland these weapons were made for the German Army (as Pistolen 35[p]) and may be found very roughly finished and without the hammer release catch or the slide lock; the original Polish pistols are easily identified by the prominent Polish Eagle engraved on the slide and their outstanding finish and fit.

Heavier and larger than the general run of pistols chambered for 9mm Parabellum, the wz/35 is among the best —and is certainly among the more comfortable—to shoot.

Length: 8.31in (211mm)
Weight unloaded: 2lb 5oz (1.05kg)
Barrel: 4.53in (115mm), 6 grooves, right-hand twist
Magazine: 8-round detachable box
Muzzle velocity: c.1150fps (350mps)

◀The Polish pistol wz/35, usually known as the 'VIS' or the 'Radom' after the designers or manufacturers (RSAF).

PISTOLA SAVAGE DO EXERCITE PORTUGUES M/908, PISTOLA SAVAGE DO EXERCITE PORTUGUES M/915
Portugal
Savage Arms Corporation, Chicopee Falls, Massachusetts
7.65mm Cartoucho M/908 (7.65mm automatic pistol)

Portugal was the only country (apart from France) ever to adopt the Savage pistols as service issue, although the design was unofficially used elsewhere. The M/908 was the same weapon as Savage's 1907 model with a rounded cocking piece, made to the 1904 patents of E H Searle and the result of an experimental 0.45in pistol submitted to the US Army pistol trials of 1907 (when it was narrowly beaten by the Colt entry). It is more than possible, however, that the Portuguese Savage M/908 pistols were not acquired until 1914 when they were purchased to augment the Parabellum weapons, no longer available from DWM, on the Portuguese inventory. A small quantity of the later M/915 design, which differed principally in the provision of a large spur-type cocking piece, were also procured.

The operation of the Savage pistols lies in that twilight class known as delayed or retarded blowback: the barrel and slide are unlocked by the rotational movement of the barrel, resisted by the torque of the bullet taking the rifling. Since the unlocking movement is but 5°—compared, for example, with the 90° of the Austro-Hungarian M07 ('Roth-Steyr')—the effectiveness of the breech-lock is a subject of much debate. Spark photographs, taken in Germany in the 1920s, appear to have shown that the breech of the Savage opens slightly more quickly than that of the 0.25in Colt pocket pistol, which is a pure blowback design.

Length: 6.60in (167mm)
Weight unloaded: 1lb 5oz (0.57kg)
Barrel: 3.50in (87mm), 4 grooves, right-hand twist
Magazine: 10-round detachable box
Muzzle velocity: c.950fps (289mps)

PISTOLA AUTOMATICA DEL EJERCITO ESPANOL CAMPO-GIRO MODELO 1913, PISTOLA AUTOMATICA DEL EJERCITO ESPANOL CAMPO-GIRO MODELO 1913–16
Spain
Unceta y Compania, Guernica
9mm cartoucho Largo

The Campo-Giro pistol designed by Don Venancio Lopez de Ceballos y Aguirre, Count of Camp-Giro, was Unceta y Cia's first successful self-loading design, the origins of which stretched back to 1904; the first model of the Campo-Giro to be adopted by the Spanish Government was that of 1913, rapidly replaced by the slightly modified pattern of 1916 which paved the way for the highly successful line of Astra pistols.

Like their successors, the Campo-Giro

▼The Astra Modelo 400 automatic pistol, used by the Spanish army as the Modelo 1921, and the first of a long line of similar weapons (RSAF).
▼The 9mm Llama pistol, the product of Gabilondo y Cia of Elgoibar (RSAF).
▼The Star Modelo A self-loading pistol, produced by Echeverria y Cia of Eibar. This gun is in 9mm, although various other chamberings could be supplied on request. The gun bears a considerable resemblance to the Colt M1911 (RSAF).

guns are blowback weapons designed around the 9mm Bergmann - Bayard cartridge, the standard Spanish service cartridge since their adoption in 1905 of the Bergmann-'Mars' pistol. It must be noted, however, that the original model of the Campo-Giro—the modelo 1904—was designed around a special 9mm cartridge.

Although of a somewhat unprepossessing appearance, the Campo-Giro weapons are all of sound construction: they were never universal issue in the Spanish Army.

The 9mm Bergmann-Bayard cartridges, larger and more powerful than the 9mm Parabellum, are known throughout the Iberian Peninsula as the 9mm Largo
(data: modelo 13–16)
Length: 8.03in (204mm)
Weight unloaded: 2lb 2oz (1.99kg)
Barrel: 6.49in (165mm), 6 grooves, right-hand twist
Magazine: 8-round detachable box
Muzzle velocity: c.1165fps (355mps)

PISTOLA DEL EJERCITO ESPANOL ASTRA MODELO 1921, PISTOLA AUTOMATICA ASTRA MODELO 400
Spain
Unceta y Compania, Guernica
9mm cartoucho Largo
The Astra 400 is an unusual weapon in two particular respects: firstly, it is a blowback pistol using heavy and powerful cartridges and, secondly, the chamber dimensions are such that it will work—with varying degrees of success—with a number of different carridges. Although primarily chambered for the 9mm Bergmann-Bayard cartridge, most will also accept 9mm Steyr, 9mm Parabellum, 9mm Browning Long, 9mm Glisenti and 0.38 Auto Colt cartridges. The pistol was designed and manufactured by Unceta of Guernica, first appearing in commercial guise in 1921 as the Astra 400 and later adopted by the Spanish Army in 1922 as the modelo 1921. The reliability of the blowback action is obtained by using a powerful recoil spring and relatively heavy recoiling parts, and pulling back the slide of an Astra in order to load requires a vice-like grip in the fingers. The catholicity of ammunition is achieved not only by suitable selection of mesurements and tolerances in the breech and extractor but also by making the striker rather longer than usual in order that it can reach out to strike the cap of the shorter cartridges with sufficient force of blow. It has to be said, though, that the Astra is not at its best with some of the rounds—especially the 9mm Parabellum—since it does not always feed cleanly with the shorter cartridge.
Length: 9.25in (235mm)
Weight unloaded: 2lb 6.5oz (1.15kg)
Barrel: 5.50in (115mm), 6 grooves, right-hand twist
Magazine: 8-round detachable box

Muzzle velocity: c.1125fps (343mps) (with 9mm Bergmann-Bayard cartridge)

PISTOLA AUTOMATICA ASTRA MODELO 900
Spain
Unceta y Compania, Guernica
7.63mm Mauser
This is outwardly a copy of Mauser's Selbstladepistole C196, but internally it is somewhat changed from the original design. The left side of the body is formed into a sliding plate which can be removed to give access to the lockwork, which is built into the frame and not—as in the Mauser—mounted in a separate detachable unit. The barrel is screwed and shrunk into the barrel extension and not, as in the Mauser, an integral forging. The general design of the frame is much different and the weapon is heavier and more solid, but all this modification (particularly that of the lockwork) has led to an unfortunately heavy trigger pull since the mechanism has been designed more with an eye to cost than to efficiency. While the weapon is an avowed copy of Mauser's design and basic system, the recoil of the bolt and barrel while locked together is almost twice the distance covered by the Mauser—a fact which defies rational explanation.

The modelo 900 began production in 1928, aimed largely at the Chinese and South American markets where the Mauser was a prestige weapon but where the genuine article was too expensive; like the Mauser, it too was supplied with wooden stock-holster. Production ceased in 1934 in favour of the selective-fire modelo 902.
Length: 12.50in (317mm)
Weight unloaded: 2lb 14oz (1.39kg)
Barrel: 5.50in (140mm), 6 grooves, right-hand twist
Magazine: 10-round integral box
Muzzle velocity: c.1450fps (476mps)

PISTOLA AMETRALLADORA ASTRA MODELO 902
Spain
Unceta y Compania, Guernica
7.63mm Mauser
The Astra modelo 902 is an improved version of the modelo 900, made by fitting a longer barrel, adding a section to the magazine to raise its capacity to 20 rounds and arranging a switch whereby full automatic fire could be made available. This, with the shoulder stock fitted, turned the pistol into a rudimentary form of submachine-gun.

The automatic fire selector is a short lever on the right side of the frame behind the trigger-guard: set vertically to the figure '1', it gives single shot self-loading action but, turned through about 45° to the rear to the figure '20', it gives automatic fire—on pressing the trigger the gun continues to fire until pressure is released or the magazine is empty, whichever happens first. A cam on the lever

engages the trigger-bar and causes it to move an additional distance when the trigger is pressed; this causes the bar to engage a second notch on the firing sear to prevent it from re-engaging with the hammer so long as the trigger is pressed. In this situation a secondary sear, operated automatically by a recess machined in the barrel extension, delays the hammer fall until the breech is closed and thus ensures a fair blow on the striker. With the selector lever in its vertical position, the additional movement of the trigger bar is not applied and the automatic sear is overridden.

The material used in the firing mechanism is generally not of the best and, after firing a few hundred rounds under conditions of continuous operation, the amount of wear reaches the point where automatic action completely fails to take place. The weapon was only manufactured for two years—from 1934 to 1936—and specimens are rarely met today.
Length: 14.25in (362mm)
Weight unloaded: 2lb 15oz (1.36kg)
Barrel: 7.25in (183mm), 6 grooves, right-hand twist
Magazine: 20-round integral box
Muzzle velocity: c.1500fps (456mps)

PISTOLA AUTOMATICA LLAMA 9MM MARQUE IX
Spain
Gabilondo y Compania, Elgoibar
9mm—various chamberings
The Llama series of pistols, produced in a variety of calibres to suit all comers, are simply copies of the Colt 0.45in M1911A1 pistol differing only in dimensions. The model chambered for the 9mm Bergmann-Bayard cartridge was used in limited numbers by the Spanish Army for some years and also by the Spanish police units; specimens in 9mm Parabellum and 9mm Short were purchased by various combatant nations during the general pistol shortage in World War 2. A few pistols were also chambered for 0.45in ACP cartridges.
Length: 6.25in (158mm)
Weight unloaded: 1lb 5oz (0.60kg)
Barrel: 3.50in (87mm), 6 grooves, right-hand twist
Magazine: 7-round detachable box
Muzzle velocity: c.850fps (260mps)

PISTOLA AUTOMATICA STAR MODEL A, PISTOLA AMETRAL-LADORA STAR MODELO M
Spain
Bonifacio Echeverria SA, Eibar, Guipuzcoa
9mm cartoucho Largo
The Star series of pistols are well distributed throughout the world in a wide variety of calibres and styles. The military models are generally based on the outline of the 0.45in Colt M1911, though the smaller calibres are plain blowback types and the larger ones, while adhering to the Browning system of breech locking, show one or two simplifications—such as the absence of a

grip safety—intended to make their manufacture easier and cheaper.

In addition to the Spanish service calibre, the Modelo A could be supplied in 9mm Short and 7.63mm Mauser chambering, the latter especially common.

A minor aberration of the 1930s was the attempt to turn a reasonable pistol into a submachine-gun, generally one of questionable efficiency. Star made their attempt at this by modifying the 9mm Model A to achieve fully automatic fire. Some were provided with the usual type of detachable stock/holster and optimistic rearsight and with lengthened magazines holding 16 or 32 rounds, although many were without these additions. Like all other single-hand fully automatic weapons, these 'machine pistols' were useless, particularly with such a powerful chambering. Apart from problems of ammunition wastage, the guns climbed excessively in automatic fire.

The automatic versions were manufactured just prior to the Spanish Civil War (1936–9) and were known as Modelo M. A quantity were supplied to the Nicaraguan Government, but beyond that their military employment was rare.
Length: 7.95in (202mm)
Weight unloaded: 2lb 2oz (1.00kg)
Barrel: 5.00in (127mm), 4 grooves, right-hand twist
Magazine: 8-round detachable box (16 or 32-round units were available for Modelo M)
Cyclic rate: 800rpm (Modelo M)
Muzzle velocity: c.1200fps (365mps) (9mm Bergmann-Bayard)

PISTOLA AUTOMATICA STAR SUPERBA ('Star Super')
Spain
Bonifacio Echeverria SA, Eibar
9mm cartoucho Largo
The Super Star is little different from the Star Modelo A, its predecessor. There are slight changes in the butt contours, a two-piece slide stop appears instead of a one-piece type, and it is generally of a better finish. The Spanish issue models are, of course, chambered for the 9mm Bergmann-Bayard cartridge, but the pistol is commercially available in 9mm Parabellum, 0.45in Colt Auto and 0.38in 'Super Auto' calibres as well.
Length: 8.03in (204mm)
Weight unloaded: 2lb 4oz (1.02kg)
Barrel: 5.25in (134mm), 4 grooves, right-hand twist
Magazine: 9-round detachable box
Muzzle velocity: c.1200fps (365mps)

PISTOL MODEL 40
Sweden
Husqvarna Vapenfabrik AB, Huskvarna
9mm patron m/39 (9mm Parabellum)
The Pistol m/40—the Swedish-made version of the Finnish Lahti pistol (qv)— has a considerable outward resemblance to the Parabellum, but the affinity is no more than skin deep.

It is hard to avoid the conclusion that Aimo Lahti took the pistole 08 as his starting point and then began to eradicate the less desirable features. First to go was the toggle-joint—a system which is wide open to dust and dirt, delicate in adjustment, demanding in its ammunition, and (in the Parabellum at least) productive of a poor trigger pull. In the m/40, the barrel extension is a closed box inside which operates a Mauser-like bolt, thus keeping the internal components sheltered from the elements and allowing a decent trigger-sear-striker mechanism to be fitted. Breech locking is achieved by a vertical block which is cammed up and down on recoil to lock the bolt to the barrel extension. Finally, an accelerator—similar to that used on Browning machine-guns—is used to accelerate bolt movement on recoil: all this adds up to a well-built pistol which is remarkably reliable in sub-zero temperatures.
Length: 10.70in (272mm)
Weight unloaded: 2lb 7oz (1.12kg)
Barrel: 5.50in (140mm), 4 grooves, right-hand twist
Magazine: 8-round detachable box
Muzzle velocity: c.1275fps (387mps)

SELBSTLADEPISTOLE MODELL 49 (SIG P210 or SP47/8)
Switzerland
Schweizerische Industrie-Gesellschaft, Neuhausen-am-Rheinfalls
7.65mm Parabellum, 9mm Parabellum
In 1937, the SIG company obtained a number of French patents held by Charles Petter and began to develop a modern automatic pistol. After a number of prototypes and trial models, the P210 appeared. It is basically of the standard Browning locked-breech pattern and, like the FN-Browning GP35, it uses a fixed cam beneath the barrel engaging in this case with the slide lock pin to withdraw and unlock the barrel from the slide.

A notable feature of the SIG design is that the slide is carried inside the frame of the weapon rather than moving on the more common external milled surfaces. Furthermore, the workmanship and finish of SIG pistols, as is to be expected of the Swiss, is outstanding. In view of their accuracy and high quality they are rarely to be found in military inventories—being far too expensive to be issued in great numbers—although they have been adopted in Switzerland and in Denmark (as the 9mm pistol m/49).

An interesting feature is that the pistol can be readily adapted to fire either 7.65mm or 9mm Parabellum cartridges by simply interchanging the barrel and recoil springs. Conversion units to permit use of the 0.22in LR cartridge are also available.
Length: 8.50in (215mm)
Weight unloaded: 2lb 3oz (0.96kg)
Barrel: 4.75in (120mm), 6 grooves, right-hand twist
Magazine: 8-round detachable box
Muzzle velocity: c.1150fps (350mps)

▶The Swedish version of the Finnish Lahti pistol of 1935. The Swedish gun, known as the m/40, was manufactured by Husqvarna Vapenfabrik (RSAF).
▶The 7.65mm prototype for the Swiss Parabellum Modell 1900, manufactured c.1899, this pistol is an interesting stage in the history of the Parabellum (RSAF).

▲Schweizerische Industrie-Gesellschaft's P210-1 pistol, manufactured in 7.65mm and 9mm Parabellum calibres. This weapon has wooden grips and a polished finish, distinguishing it from the otherwise similar P210-2 (SIG).

▲The P210-2, essentially the same as the P210-1, but with plastic grips and a sandblasted finish (SIG).

▲The P210-6 target pistol, based on the military weapon and similar to the P210-5 (which has an extended barrel protruding in front of the slide). The gun is offered in 7.65mm and 9mm Parabellum (SIG).

AUTOMATIC PISTOL, 9MM KIRIKKALE
Turkey
Kirikkale Tûfek Fb, Istanbul
7.65mm Auto Pistol, 9mm Short

The Kirikkale is yet another copy of the Walther Modell PP. The only changes from the original design are relatively small modifications in machining, to simplify production, and a finger-rest on the magazine platform (although this was sometimes seen on original Walther weapons). Stripping, functioning and operating are exactly as for the Walther (see GERMANY).

Length: 6.65in (168mm)
Weight unloaded: 1lb 8oz (0.70kg)
Barrel: 3.83in (97mm), 6 grooves, right-hand twist
Magazine: 7-round detachable box
Muzzle velocity: c.950fps (289mps) (9mm Short)

REVOLVER NAGANT OBRAZETS 1895G ('Nagant revolver Model of the year 1895')
Russia, Tsarist and Soviet
Manufacture d'Armes Nagant Frères, Liège; and Tulskiï Oruzhenyi Za'vod, Tula
7.62mm Revolver-patron o95g (Nagant 'gas seal')

The Nagant revolver, adopted by the Tsarist Army in 1895, is of representative general appearance for the revolvers of the period but incorporates an unusual feature into the mechanism. In an endeavour to extract the maximum performance from the weapon, an attempt has been made to overcome one of the theoretical drawbacks of a revolver—the leak of propelling gas between the front face of the cylinder and the rear face of the barrel which, in theory at least, reduces the efficiency of the weapon, although in the best revolver designs emanating from highly regarded manufacturers the tolerances are such that this objection becomes negligible, until the weapon becomes worn.

The Russian M95, produced to the 1894 patent of Léon Nagant although largely based on an earlier Pieper design, incorporates a cam mechanism which—on cocking—causes the cylinder to be moved forward so that the rear of the barrel is enclosed within the mouth of the aligned chamber. The cartridge is also unusual in that the bullet is totally contained within the case and that the mouth is slightly reduced in diameter; thus, when the cylinder is pressed forward, the case mouth actually enters the barrel. On firing, the expansion of the case mouth and the enclosure by the chamber effectively combine to provide a sealed union and to prevent the leakage of gas. As the action is operated for the next shot to be fired so the cylinder is withdrawn, rotated, and returned once more to seal.

The Nagant design, produced both in Belgium and in Russia, in single-action (trooper's) form and in double-action (officer's) guise, was the only 'gas-seal' mechanism to achieve total success: various other manufacturers, particularly in Belgium, produced weapons of this form but none became widespread. The value of such a seal is in any case questionable, particularly as it is achieved at the expense of needless mechanical complication; since the gun barrel is short the bullet is within the barrel for less than one millisecond (0.001 second) and in this time there is little chance for much gas to escape. An exact comparison is difficult, owing to the problem of finding a similarly-chambered conventional revolver, but it has been shown that the French M92 service revolver (which has a barrel/cylinder gap of about 0.009in (0.25mm) and a barrel length of 3.94in (100mm) loses about 80fps (24mps) without the benefit of a gas-seal. Despite the fact that the energy stored in the projectile is dependent on the square of the velocity, this velocity loss counts for little.

Length: 9.06in (229mm)
Weight unloaded: 1lb 12oz (0.82kg)
Barrel: 4.35in (110mm), 4 grooves, right-hand twist
Magazine: 7-round cylinder
Muzzle velocity: c.1000fps (305mps)

SAMOZARIADNYIA PISTOLET TULA-TOKAREVA OBRAZETS 1930G, SAMOZARIADNIYA PISTOLET TULA-TOKAREVA OBRAZETS 1933G and variations
Union of Soviet Socialist Republics
Tulskii Oruzhenyi Za'vod, Tula (also made in Hungary and China)
7.62mm patron o30g

The TT pistols, formerly the standard weapons of the Soviet Army, are based upon the Colt-Browning design and use a swinging link beneath the barrel to unlock the barrel from the slide on recoil. Some minor modifications have been made with the intention of simplifying manufacture and maintenance: a notable feature is that the lockwork can be removed en bloc for cleaning purposes. A further and very useful modification is the machining of the magazine guide lips into the pistol itself, which means that damage to the mouth of the magazine is less likely to result in a malfunction than in most other designs of pistol.

There are several varieties of these Tokarev-designed pistols but it is difficult to ascertain exactly how many, largely owing to the confused designations ascribed to the weapons in some publications. Two varieties of the full-bore pistol have been made, normally called the TT30 and the TT33 (TT represents Tula-Tokarev) although sometimes referred to as the SPT (from samozariadnyia pistolet Tokareva—Tokarev self-loading pistol). On the TT30 the locking lugs are machined on to the top surfaces of the barrel as in the Colt M1911A1 but on the TT33 they are machined entirely around the barrel in an endeavour to quicken manufacture; there are also other smaller

▼The Russian Nagant 'gas-seal' revolver, 1895 model (RSAF).
▼The 1933 Tokarev (RSAF).
▼An East German example of the Makarov self-loading pistol, which shows a distinct Walther influence (RSAF).

differences, notably in the design of the frame and the sub-assembly carrying the lockwork. Two types of 0.22in pistol, of blowback operation but using parts common to the TT, were also manufactured: the TTR3 (or SPTR, the R representing ruchnoi—light), externally almost indistinguishable from the TT, and the TTR4, a target weapon with an extended barrel and adjustable sights.

While the Tokarev designs are perfectly serviceable, the standard of manufacture is lower than that normally found in the West. Chambered for the 7.62mm M30 Soviet automatic pistol cartridge, the TT will in most cases fire the 7.63mm Mauser (depending on the tolerance allowed by the ammunition manufacturers): because of these high-powered rounds, however, the muzzle velocity is rather higher than that generally expected in a pistol and, owing to the violent recoil, the pistols are difficult to fire with accuracy.

Length: 7.68in (193mm)
Weight unloaded: 1lb 13oz (0.84kg)
Barrel: 4.57in (116mm), 4 grooves, right-hand twist
Magazine: 8-round detachable box
Muzzle velocity: c.1375fps (418mps)

AVTOMATICHESKIA PISTOLET STETCHKINA (APS)
Union of Soviet Socialist Republics
State factories
9mm Soviet automatic pistol
As we have seen with the Star, many designers have been tempted to try their hand at converting a pistol into a sub-machine-gun. At the present time the game seems to be current on the far side of the Iron Curtain, and the Stetchkin is the Soviet entry.

It is a blowback pistol loosely based on the Walther PP but rather larger and without the double-action lock. The safety catch, on the slide, has three positions: down for safe, horizontal for single shot, and up for fully automatic fire. Hand-held automatic fire is, of course, simply a waste of time and ammunition and the Stetchkin is supplied with a wooden holster-stock almost identical to that used with the Mauser Military Model, with which attached it becomes more manageable. Chambered for the 9mm Soviet automatic pistol cartridge, the Stetchkin is unlikely to be seen outside the Soviet bloc, and there are indications that it has already been removed from service.

Length: 8.85in (225mm)
Weight unloaded: 1lb 10oz (0.76kg)
Barrel: 5.00in (127mm), 4 grooves, right-hand twist
Magazine: 20-round detachable box
Cyclic rate: 725rpm
Muzzle velocity: c.1115fps (340mps)

PISTOLET MAKAROVA (PM)
Union of Soviet Socialist Republics
State factories in USSR, German Democratic Republic; and Chinese People's Republic

9mm Soviet automatic pistol
The Walther PP impressed most people who came into contact with it for the first time during the war: so much so that many nations later produced copies, with or without benefit of licence. The Soviets were among the latter number, as the Makarov is simply an enlarged Modell PP chambered for the peculiar 9mm Soviet pistol round. This has a blunt bullet like a 9mm Short but the case, slightly longer than a 9mm Short, is shorter than a 9mm Parabellum and thus effectively clings to the Soviet tradition of chambering their weapons for their own ammunition and also preventing the use of their ammunition in anyone else's equipment. The 9mm Soviet round makes some sort of sense in being about the heaviest round that can safely be used in a blowback pistol (apart from such freaks as the Astra pistols chambered for the Bergmann-Bayard round), but it still seems to be an expensive and complicated way of going about things.

Length: 6.35in (160mm)
Weight unloaded: 1lb 9oz (0.72kg)
Barrel: 3.85in (98mm), 4 grooves, right-hand twist
Magazine: 8-round detachable box
Muzzle velocity: c.1070fps (325mps)

PISTOL, WEBLEY, MARKS 1–6
United Kingdom
Webley & Scott Limited, Birmingham (see also note below)
0.455in SAA Ball
The manufacturer of this pistol design, Webley, underwent three changes of name during the period in which these weapons were made: the company traded under the name Philip Webley & Son until 1897, when the name changed to the Webley & Scott Revolver and Arms Company Limited. In 1906 the concern became Webley & Scott Limited.

Pistol, Webley, Mark 1 (introduced in November 1887). This revolver was officially described as 'six chambered, top-opening with automatic extraction'. The butt was of the shape commonly called 'bird's head' and had a lanyard ring. The frame was locked by the familiar Webley stirrup lock mechanism.
Length: 10.25in (260mm)
Weight unloaded: 2lb 3oz (1.01kg)
Barrel: 4.00in (101mm), 6 grooves, right-hand twist
Magazine: 6-round cylinder
Muzzle velocity: c.600fps (183mps)
Pistol, Webley, Mark 1* (October 1894). Upon repair or refurbishing of the Mark 1 models, a hardened steel plate was added to the standing breech in order to approximate to the design of the Mark 2. The head of the butt grip was rounded off and the thumb-pieces on the stirrup-lock were made smaller.
Pistol, Webley, Mark 2 (October 1894). This model differed from the Mark 1 in the following respects: a hardened steel plate was used on the breech to lessen erosion, the hammer was strengthened, the grip was of a more rounded shape,

slight changes were made in the extractor components, the hammer catch spring was spiral instead of V-shaped, and the stirrup-lock thumb-pieces were smaller.
Pistol, Webley, Mark 3 (October 1897). The Mark 3 was basically the same as the Mark 2, but the attachment of cylinder to frame was improved and a cam was fitted to unlock the cylinder for removal. In 1905 a number of revolvers of this pattern were fitted with 6.00in (152mm) barrels 'to meet the requirements of officers and cadets desiring to purchase such pistols from store'.
Pistol, Webley, Mark 4 (July 1899). The Mark 4 differed from Mark 3 in that the steel was of different quality; the trigger stop was raised and the slots in the cylinder made wider, the ratchet teeth of the extractor were case-hardened and the hammer was made lighter. As in the case of the Mark 3, 1905 saw a quantity produced with the 6.00in (152mm) barrel for sale to officers.
Pistol, Webley, Mark 5 (December 1913). This differed from the Mark 4 in having the cylinder of larger diameter and rounded on the rear edge—and the body modified to suit. Fitted as standard with a 4.00in (102mm) barrel, the weapon weighed 2lb 3.5oz (1.01kg).
Pistol, Webley, Mark 1** (April 1915). Intended for Naval Service, this is the conversion, on repair, of the Mark 1 or 1* produced by fitting a Mark 4 barrel and a Mark 5 cylinder.
Pistol, Webley, Mark 2* (April 1915). Not an officially approved nomenclature, this designation arose by virtue of a number of Mark 2 pistols being fitted with Mark 4 hammers and having (*) stamped—erroneously—after the number on the barrel strap.
Pistol, Webley, Mark 2** (April 1915). Similar to the Mark 1**, a conversion of the Mark 2 by fitting the Mark 4 barrel and Mark 5 cylinder.
Pistol, Webley, 6 inch barrel, Mark 1** (June 1915). A fine example of how convoluted British nomenclature can get. This is another wartime naval expedient in which, when undergoing repair, Mark 1 or 1* pistols had the 6.00in (152mm) barrels approved for Marks 4 or 5 pistols fitted, together with a removable foresight and a Mark 5 cylinder.
Pistol, Webley, 6 inch barrel, Mark 2** (June 1915). A similar naval expedient to the foregoing model, in this case the repair of Mark 2 pistols by fitting the 6.00in (152mm) barrel, removable foresight and Mark 5 cylinder.
Pistol, Webley, 6 inch barrel, Mark 5 (May 1915). This model is identical to the Mark 5 but with the original 4.00in (102mm) barrel replaced by a 6.00in (152mm) barrel carrying a removable foresight attached with a fixing screw. The revolver weighs 2lb 5.5oz (1.07kg).
Pistol, Webley, 6 inch barrel, Mark 6 (May 1915). It differs from the Mark 5 in having a barrel 2.00in (51mm) longer fitted with a removable blade foresight, a different and more square-cut grip, and a

number of the components redesigned to facilitate more rapid production—thus making them special to this particular mark of pistol.

Length: 11.25in (286mm)
Weight unloaded: 2lb 6.5oz (1.09kg)
Barrel: 6.00in (152mm), 7 grooves, right-hand twist
Magazine: 6-round cylinder
Muzzle velocity: c.650fps (199mps)

It is interesting to note that while all these pistols are generally described as being of 0.455in (11.60mm) calibre, their actual calibre has always been 0.441in (11.20mm). The Webley pistol is still widely used among military and police forces throughout the world, particularly where those forces were originally trained and equipped by the British. There is no reason why this should not be: the Webley is among the strongest and most accurate handguns ever made, and the standard of workmanship and the quality of material is such that they will take a long time to wear out.

WEBLEY-FOSBERY SELF-COCKING REVOLVER
United Kingdom
Webley & Scott Revolver and Arms Company Limited, Birmingham (see note under Pistol, Webley, Marks 1–6)
0.455in SAA Ball

This weapon, the design of which was based on the 1896 patents of G V Fosbery, is in a class of its own—an 'automatic revolver' in which the force of recoil drives the barrel and cylinder unit back over the frame, cocks the hammer, and returns the unit by spring power to the firing position. During this movement a fixed stud on the frame is engaged in the grooves on the cylinder and the movement causes the cylinder to be rotated one-twelfth of a revolution during each stroke, thus completing one-sixth of a turn in the complete recoil cycle and hence indexing a fresh cartridge in front of the hammer.

The Webley-Fosbery was never officially accepted into military service but it was tolerated insofar as, prior to the approval of the 0.38in revolver, the British Army officer was permitted to purchase any pistol he liked as long as it accepted the issue 0.455in service cartridge. On active service in 1914–15 the Webley-Fosbery was tried and found wanting, the recoil action being easily clogged and deranged by mud and dirt.

A very few were made in 0.38in ACP calibre, and a similar pattern (in 0.32in S&W calibre) was made in the United States by the Union Arms Company.

Length: 11.00in (280mm)
Weight unloaded: 2lb 12oz (1.26kg)
Barrel: 6.00in (152mm), 7 grooves, right-hand twist
Magazine: 6-round cylinder
Muzzle velocity: c.600fps (183mps)

PISTOL, SELF-LOADING, WEBLEY & SCOTT, 0.455in
United Kingdom

Webley & Scott Limited, Birmingham
0.455in

This pistol was introduced into the Royal Navy in 1915 as the *Pistol, Self-loading, Webley & Scott, 0.455in Mark 1*. It is a solid and reliable weapon with an ungainly appearance owing to the square angle of the butt, which makes instinctive shooting difficult although deliberate shooting can be quite accurate. The cartridge is a semi-rimmed round of considerable power, which will—unfortunately—chamber in a service 0.455in revolver. This caused

◁Pistol Webley Mark 1* of 1894 (RSAF).
◁Pistol Webley Mark 3 of 1897; note the different shape of the grip and the revised extractor components at the lower front of the cylinder (RSAF).
◁Pistol Webley, 6 inch barrel Mark 2**, a conversion of Mark 2 guns (in 1915) for Naval service (RSAF).

◁Pistol, Webley, 6 inch barrel Mark 6 (RSAF).
▲The Webley-Fosbery.
▲▲Two views of the Webley self-loading pistol; the lower is that of the second pattern with an elaborate rearsight and a shoulder stock. Most guns produced during World War 1 had a simple sight.

the sudden destruction of a number of revolvers in World War 1 before the difference was appreciated. The diameter of the jacketed bullet is 0.456in (11.6mm), rather more than that of the lead revolver bullet as the revolvers' actual calibre was 0.441in (11.2mm) instead of the nominal 0.455in. This slight enlargement of the pistol bullet, together with its increased hardness and coupled with a fast-burning 7 grain (0.45gm) charge, was sufficient to build up excessive pressures and blow out the revolvers' cylinders.

The Webley pistol was also produced commercially in 9mm Browning Long and 0.38in Super Auto calibres.

The standard pattern of the Webley, the Mark 1, was fitted with a grip safety but in 1915/16 a modified 'de luxe' version was produced for trials by the personnel of the Royal Horse Artillery; in this pattern, apparently known as the **Mark 1 Number 2,** the grip safety was replaced by a mechanical catch on the hammer, a special rotating-drum rearsight (graduated to 200yd) replaced the fixed notch of the Navy weapon, and the butt was cut for a shoulder stock. With the adoption in the 1920s of a new system of nomenclature, the original pistol became the *Pistol, Self-loading, Webley & Scott, Number 1 Mark 1.* What designation, if any, was applied to the more elaborate pattern is a matter of doubt. References have been seen to the Webley 'Number 2' pistol, presumably derived from the marking 'Mk 1 No 2' on the Artillery pistol's slide. It seems, however, that this was added when the pistol was first made and not in retrospect; it is thought likely, in view of the fact that the Royal Horse Artillery's pistol was not accepted for service, that the so-called Number 2 pistol was not renamed.

The Webley is a locked-breech design, locked by oblique machined ribs on the square rear of the barrel which engage in recessed sections of the body. In the firing position the barrel and the slide are locked together by a lug on barrel engaging with a shoulder in the slide. As barrel and slide recoil so the oblique ribs slide down the recesses in the body and draw the barrel out of engagement with the slide, allowing the slide to recoil. The mainspring is an unusual V-spring concealed under the left grip. Another unusual feature was the facility to partly withdraw the magazine and lock it in place so that the top round was not loaded by the slide; in this position the gun could be fired as a single-shot, handloading each round, with the magazine held in reserve.

Length: 8.50in (216mm)
Weight unloaded: 2lb 8oz (1.13kg)
Barrel: 5.00in (127mm), 6 grooves, right-hand twist
Magazine: 7-round detachable box
Muzzle velocity: c.750fps (228mps)

PISTOL, REVOLVER, NUMBER 2 ('Enfield')

United Kingdom

Royal Small Arms Factory, Enfield Lock; Albion Motor Company, Glasgow; Singer Sewing Machine Company, Clydebank

0.380in SAA Ball

After World War 1 the British Army decided that the 0.455in bullet demanded too heavy a weapon and too great a degree of skill from the firer. Investigating possible replacements, they found that Webley & Scott were testing a 0.38in revolver for possible sale as a police weapon; with a 200-grain (12.97gm) bullet, this calibre gave the required stopping power for a combat weapon and was yet sufficiently docile to be passably accurate in the hands of hastily-trained wartime recruits. The design project was taken over in 1926–7 by the Royal Small Arms Factory at Enfield Lock and changes were made in the lockwork and trigger mechanism, largely in the provision of a hammer safety lock and a separate cylinder lock. With this modification the pistol, no longer a Webley pattern, was designated the 'Enfield' revolver or, in accordance with the system of nomenclature then used in British Service, the *Pistol, Revolver, Number 2 Mark 1*. Eventually there were three models.

Pistol, Revolver, Number 2 Mark 1 (June 1932), which was similar in appearance to the 0.455in Webley Mark 6 which it replaced but physically smaller. It was provided with a hammer mechanism which could be operated as single or double action.

Length: 10.25in (260mm)
Weight unloaded: 1lb 11oz (0.80kg)
Barrel: 5.00in (127mm), 7 grooves, right-hand twist
Magazine: 6-round cylinder
Muzzle velocity: c.650fps (198mps)

These pistols were declared obsolescent in June 1938 and all existing specimens were to be converted to Mark 1* when passing through Ordnance Factories for repair.

Pistol, Revolver, Number 2 Mark 1* (June 1938). This differed from Mark 1 in that the hammer-comb and bent were removed to allow double-action firing only. The mainspring was lightened to reduce the trigger pull (when new) from the 13lb to 15lb (5.85kg to 6.75kg) of the Mark 1 to 11lb to 13lb (4.95kg to 5.85kg); the grip sidepieces were reshaped to give a better grip, and a marking disc was recessed into the right butt sideplate. The date of introduction is of interest here, for it disproves the widely-held opinion that these double-action weapons were a wartime innovation for 'quick-draw' work by commandos and other special forces. These pistols were introduced because their principal destination was the Tank Corps, and the earlier model had the habit of snagging the hammer on various internal tank fittings.

Pistol, Revolver, Number 2 Mark 1**

▲The Pistol Number 2 Mark 1 (RSAF).
▲The Pistol Number 2 Mark 1*, as manufactured by Albion Motors of Glasgow.
▲The Smith & Wesson-made Pistol, Revolver, 0.38in S&W Number 2 (RSAF).
▲A commercial model of the Colt Army Special revolver of 1908. Note the chequered rubber grip and the monogram.

(July 1942). This was a wartime dispensation, introduced to hasten production: it is the same as the Mark 1* but with the hammer safety stop removed and one or two minor manufacturing concessions granted. These weapons were all recalled after the war and, by the addition of the hammer safety stop, converted back into Mark 1* models since without the stop they were notoriously unsafe if dropped.

PISTOL, REVOLVER, WEBLEY 0.38IN MARK 4
United Kingdom
Webley & Scott Limited, Birmingham
0.380in SAA Ball

In addition to the 0.455in pistols, a 0.38in model was brought into service during World War 2 to augment supplies of Enfield pistols. This Webley-designed 0.38in weapon was the final version of the design which had originated in 1923 as a potential police weapon which, when modified by the Royal Small Arms Factory at Enfield Lock, eventually became the Enfield pistol. Externally the Webley shows a difference in the design of the hammer and in cylinder details, and it has, of course, the Webley name impressed into the grips. The only internal difference lies in the lock mechanism, which is of original Webley design unmodified by Enfield.

The official title is *Pistol, Revolver, Webley 0.38in Mark 4*, and, although officially introduced into service—for record only—in September 1945 the pistols were actually in use early in 1942. They were declared obsolete in June 1963.
Length: 10.50in (266mm)
Weight unloaded: 1lb 11oz (0.81kg)
Barrel: 5.00in (127mm), 7 grooves, right-hand twist
Magazine: 6-round cylinder
Muzzle velocity: c.600fps (183mps)

PISTOL, REVOLVER, 0.38IN, SMITH & WESSON NUMBER 2 (Revolver '0.38/200')
United Kingdom
Smith & Wesson Arms Company, Springfield, Massachusetts
0.38in SAA Ball

This is virtually the regulation Smith & Wesson Police Model fitted with a six-chambered cylinder. The term '38/200' stems from the chambering, intended to fit the British Army 200grain 0.380in cartridge, as the design was first produced to meet British military contracts in 1940. Approximately 900,000 of these revolvers were eventually issued to Allied troops of many nations. A most accurate and handy weapon, the sole defect is a tendency of the mainspring to age during prolonged storage, which eventually leads to a light striker blow. This is only noticeable when using British Service ammunition since this demands a heavier cap blow that the commercial produce.

The finish on these weapons is a guide to their age. The first production—from April 1940 until April 1942—were polished and blued, and had barrels of 4in, 5in or 6in (102mm, 127mm or 152mm). Until January 1942 the grips were chequered walnut with a silver S & W monogram medallion let into the top. After January 1942 the grips were of smooth walnut without the medallion and, after May 1942, the finish was that of sandblasting and only 5in (127mm) barrels were fitted.
Length: 10.13in (258mm)
Weight unloaded: 1lb 8oz (0.57kg)
Barrel: 4in, 5in or 6in (102mm, 127mm or 152mm), 5 grooves, right-hand twist
Magazine: 6-round cylinder
Muzzle velocity: c.650fps (199mps)

US REVOLVERS, 1889–1911
United States of America
Colt's Patent Firearms Manufacturing Company, Hartford, Connecticut; Smith & Wesson Arms Company, Springfield, Massachusetts
.38 Long Colt, .38 Special, .45 Colt

This heading covers a number of revolver designs manufactured either by Colt or by Smith & Wesson for issue to the forces of the United States prior to the issue of the M1911 pistol.

US Revolver, Colt New Navy, M1889 (.38 Long Colt). This arm was the parent of the subsequent small-calibre revolvers which followed into the service of the army. It lacks a separate cylinder bolt and was replaced on Colt's production lines by the New Army revolver of 1892. It is recorded that 5,000 of the 1889 design were purchased on behalf of the navy authorities.

US Revolver, Colt New Army, M1892 (.38 Long Colt). In 1890 the United States Army decided that it must replace the revolvers then on its inventory with something a little more modern: after trials with the M1889 Navy revolver, it was decided to adopt this weapon provided a separate cylinder bolt could be incorporated into the design. This component was ultimately provided in the weapon, which was then adopted by the Army in 1892. Although basically a sound design, the New Army revolver—like its New Navy predecessor—was handicapped by the anti-clockwise rotation of the cylinder (apparently insisted upon by the navy experts) which tended to push the cylinder out of the frame and, when worn to a sufficient degree, meant that the cylinder and barrel were not properly aligned.

US Revolver, Colt New Army, M1894 (.38 Long Colt). Externally indistinguishable from the M1892, this weapon incorporated an additional safety feature in the form of Felton's trigger lock—a device which prevented operation of the trigger until the cylinder was fully closed. Most of the 1892 weapons were converted to this pattern.

US Revolver, Colt New Navy, M1895 (.38 Long Colt). The Navy's version of the Army's M1894, this weapon incorporates Felton's lock and has a five-groove barrel whereas the Army guns had six grooves.

US Revolver, Colt New Army, M1896 (.38 Long Colt). A minor variation of the M1894.

US Revolver, Smith & Wesson Hand Ejector, M1899 (0.38in Long Colt). A weapon of similar design to the various Colts, this weapon was also provided with a cylinder of anti-clockwise rotation. The M1899 is easily recognisable by the Smith & Wesson monogram on the grips and by the typically Smith & Wesson cylinder release-catch. Purchases of this design were relatively small: 1,000 in 1900 for the Navy and 1,000 for the Army in the following year.

US Revolver, Colt New Army, M1901 (.38 Long Colt). Another variation of the M1894, provided with a lanyard swivel on the butt and with sidepieces of a slimmer form.

US Revolver, Smith & Wesson Hand Ejector, M1902 (0.38in Long Colt). An improved version of the M1899, 1,000 of these weapons were purchased in 1902 by the United States Navy to the only contract let.

US Revolver, Colt New Army, M1903 (.38 Long Colt). The last of the line of official Army issue of this type, the M1903 is of the same pattern as the M1901 but with a slightly reduced bore diameter.

US Revolver, Colt Double Action Marine Corps, M1905 (0.38in Special). Identical to the M1903 Army weapon but in a different calibre and with a slightly different butt-shape, limited numbers of the design were procured on behalf of the Marine Corps.

US Revolver, Colt Army Special, M1908 (.38 Special). This was the last of the 0.38in calibre revolvers adopted by the services and had a service life of just one year; a reversion to clockwise cylinder rotation was made in this weapon, which was an improvement over some of the earlier guns. The frame of the M1908 was more robust than that of the New Army patterns, and the cylinder latch of a more rounded design. The reputation of the 0.38in revolvers had suffered greatly in the Phillipine campaigns of 1898–1900, where they had generally failed to stop the fanatics against whom they were used. One result of this was that quantities of 0.45in revolvers (modified Colt Double Action Army Revolvers of 1878 pattern) were hastily procured, and another was that the 0.38in calibre was replaced in the American services by one of 0.45in. It is interesting to note that the British turned the other way.
Length: 11.25in (285mm)
Weight unloaded: 2lb 4oz (1.02kg)
Barrel: 6.00in (152mm), 6 grooves, left-hand twist
Magazine: 6-round cylinder
Muzzle velocity: c.865fps (263mps)

US Revolver, Colt New Service, M1909 (.45 Colt). The last service revolver to be adopted by the United States with the exception of the wartime emergency

M1917 weapons, slightly over 21,000 of the New Service type were supplied to the Army, Navy and Marine Corps between February 1909 and April 1911. It was then replaced by the M1911 self-loading pistol. The revolvers incorporate Colt's positive lock safety of 1905, which they inherited from the Army Special model.

US PISTOL, AUTOMATIC, CALIBRE .45, M1911 and M1911A1
United States of America
Colt's Patent Firearms Manufacturing Company, Hartford, Connecticut; Ithaca Gun Company, Ithaca, New York; Remington Rand Incorporated, Syracuse, New York; Remington Arms-Union Metallic Cartridge Company, Bridgeport, Connecticut; Springfield Armory, Springfield, Massachusetts; Union Switch & Signal Company, Swissvale, Pennsylvania
.45 M1911
Nothing succeeds like success and the Colt M1911 pistols are without doubt amongst the most successful combat pistols ever invented. Incredibly robust, with more than enough lethality and stopping power from the 230gr (14.92gm) bullet—which delivers 380ft lb (52.5mkg) of energy at the muzzle—the Colt has, since its inception in 1911, armed the US Army and Navy and has been used by many other forces. Numbers were also made in 0.455in Webley & Scott chambering during World War 1 for the British Royal Navy and Royal Flying Corps, many of which were still serving in 1945.

The original M1911 model was developed from a series of improvements on Browning's 1900 design, and the first 0.45in model of 1905 competed in the United States Government Trial of 1907. In the early years of the century many inventors were pestering the world's war departments trying to secure contracts and, ultimately, the United States Army decided to hold a contest to discover which if any of the designs held promise. The Chief of Ordnance, having had some sharp things said to him about the lack of effect of the recently-introduced 0.38in revolver cartridge, laid down that all competing weapons must fire a 230gr 0.45in bullet—a round which had been developed in 1906 for a commercial Colt pistol. The Board of Enquiry met in January 1907, tested nine pistols, and reported back in April 1907—an example of alacrity which is virtually unbelievable by modern standards. As a result, 200 Colt and 200 Savage pistols were bought for extended troop trials and, after some user experience, the Colt was selected provided Browning attended to one or two small points. This was done and, late in 1911, the pistol was adopted. During World War 1 the hammer spur was made longer and, in the 1920s and as a result of war experience, further changes were made: the spur of the grip safety was lengthened, the shape of the grip was

altered, the trigger was shortened and chamfered and the frame at the rear of the trigger was also chamfered to give a better grip. With these changes the pistol became known in June 1926 as the M1911A1 and is still going strong.

While the gun is always known as the Colt, other manufacturers' names will be found on the pistols. The M1911 was made by Colt, the government arsenal at Springfield, and also by the Remington Arms-Union Metallic Cartridge Company of Bridgeport, Connecticut, during World War 1. Arrangements were also made for the manufacture of the design in Canada, but the war ended before production got into its stride and only a few were made. During World War 2, M1911A1 pistols were made—amongst others—by Colt, Remington, the Union Switch & Signal Company, the Singer Sewing Machine Company, and the Ithaca Gun Company. In addition to the military issue the pistols have also been continuously manufactured by Colt for the commercial market, and such models can be distinguished by the more elegant finish and C-prefix serial numbers. Manufacture under Colt licence has also taken place in Norway (m/1914) and Argentina (Modello 1927).

Locking of breech and barrel on the Colt is achieved by having the top of the barrel ribbed and engaging in grooves on the underside of the slide top; the barrel has a link pinned beneath it and the lower end of this link pivots about the slide stop pin. Thus, as the slide recoils, it takes the barrel with it but—as the link is held at its foot—it describes a semi-circular path with its upper end and so draws the breech down and free of the slide. The slide is thus allowed to recoil and, on the return stroke, it chambers a fresh round and pushes the barrel forward. The link now causes the breech to swing up and into engagement with the slide once more.
Length: 8.50in (216mm)
Weight unloaded: 2lb 7.5oz (1.13kg)
Barrel: 5.00in (127mm), 6 grooves, left-hand twist
Magazine: 7-round detachable box
Muzzle velocity: c.860fps (262mps)

US REVOLVER, CALIBER .45, SMITH & WESSON HAND EJECTOR, M1917
United States of America
Smith & Wesson Arms Company, Springfield, Massachusetts
.45 M1911
When the United States entered the war in 1917 the standard pistol was the Colt M1911 automatic of 0.45in calibre; supplies of this weapon were short and it would obviously take time to provide the quantities needed to supply the vastly increased army. In view of this, numbers of Colt and Smith & Wesson revolvers were purchased, more than 150,000 of the former and more than 153,300 of the latter. Since the standard round in supply was the rimless 0.45in Auto, it meant

that the revolver cylinders had to be shortened slightly and the rounds loaded in clips of three in order to prevent them sliding into the cylinder, and to give the extractor something to push against when unloading. As the Smith & Wesson has a stepped cylinder chamber, it is unnecessary to use the clips to ensure correct functioning, but without it the ejector will not operate.

These pistols remained in service until well after World War 2, although large numbers were released to the civilian market after World War 1. In order to simplify matters the Peters Cartridge Company developed a special thick-rimmed 0.45in cartridge known as the '.45 Auto-rim'; this had a sufficiently thick rim to take up space behind the cylinder and present the cap to the firing pin, and also to give sufficient rim diameter for the extractor to work against. At the same time the Smith & Wesson company produced replacement cylinders so that civilian owners could convert the guns to fire standard 0.45in revolver ammunition.
Length: 10.80in (274mm)
Weight unloaded: 2lb 4oz (1.02kg)
Barrel: 5.50in (140mm), 6 grooves, right-hand twist
Magazine: 6-round cylinder
Muzzle velocity: c.860fps (262mps)

US REVOLVER, CALIBER .45, COLT NEW SERVICE, M1917
United States of America
Colt's Patent Firearms Manufacturing Company, Hartford, Connecticut
.45 M1911
This pistol was commercially produced as the 'New Service' Model in 1897. It is a double-action revolver with swing-out cylinder and hand ejection, and it was made in a variety of calibres from 0.38in to 0.476in. It was first supplied to the United States Army in 1909 in 0.45in rimmed chambering, but was superseded by the M1911 automatic. When the United States entered the war in 1917 over 150,000 of these pistols were taken into service between October 1917 and December 1918 in order to supplement the M1911 pistol. In order to achieve uniformity of ammunition supply, the revolvers were made with a special cylinder to take the 0.45in M1911 Auto pistol cartridge, which had to be loaded by using two three-shot semi-circular clips ('half-moon clips') so that rimless rounds could be retained in the cylinder, properly located for the firing pin's strike, and to allow the extractors to have something to work against.

At the same time Smith & Wesson produced a number of similar weapons, but their cylinder chambers were stepped so that the front edge of the cartridge case was thereby located—allowing them to be loaded and fired without clips in an emergency—and this feature was adopted on later production of the Colt.

In addition to the service models, numbers of these revolvers chambered

for 0.455in calibre were supplied to the British Army in 1915–16.
Length: 10.75in (272mm)
Weight unloaded: 2lb 8oz (1.14kg)
Barrel: 5.50in (140mm), 6 grooves, left-hand twist
Magazine: 6-round cylinder
Muzzle velocity: c.860fps (262mps)

'OSS' or 'LIBERATOR' M1942 PISTOL
United States of America
Guide Lamp Corporation, Detroit, Michigan
.45 M1911

This peculiar weapon, the only single-shot pistol listed in these pages, was mass-produced during World War 2 for distribution by the Office of Strategic Services to clandestine forces in occupied countries. Designed to be made as cheaply as possible by the use of stamped metal parts, it was chambered for the United States Army's 0.45in pistol cartridge and about 1,000,000 were produced between June and August 1942 by the Guide Lamp Corporation, part of General Motors. A simple twist-and-pull breechblock was opened, a round placed in the chamber and the breech closed. After firing, the breech was opened and the empty case ejected by pushing some suitable implement down the barrel. Five extra cartridges were carried in a trap in the butt.

The accuracy of the short smoothbore barrel was sufficient for short-range work and the pistol is reputed to have been put to good use as an assassination weapon. The short range probably helped in this as it would be politic to get as close as possible before opening fire in order not to miss—otherwise the chance of a next shot would be somewhat problematic. It was supplied with a comic-strip set of graphic instructions so that language barriers—or even illiteracy—were no bar to understanding how the thing worked or what to do with it.
Length: 5.55in (141mm)
Weight unloaded: 1lb 0oz (0.45kg)
Barrel: 3.97in (101mm), smoothbore
Magazine: none, single-shot
Muzzle velocity: c.820fps (250mps)

▶The M1911 self-loading pistol, made at Bridgeport by Remington-UMC although originally manufactured by Colt (Remington).
▶The M1911A1 pistol; note the alteration to the shape of the grip which readily distinguishes the two types.

Submachine-guns

The submachine-gun, machine carbine or machine pistol—as the class is variously known—is a child of World War 1. The Italian Villar Perosa is generally credited as the first in the field although it was not of the generally accepted pattern, having been conceived as a light field machine-gun or aircraft flexible gun with an exceptionally high rate of fire from twin barrels. The 'submachine-gun' connotation came from the Villar Perosa's blowback operation and the fact that it fired a pistol round. Judged, however, by the standard of a weapon to be placed in the hands of foot soldiers with the intention of providing them with superior short-range firepower, the Bergmann Muskete must be considered the prototype for this class of weapon.

Designed in 1917 by Hugo Schmeisser, the weapon was the outcome of the 'Storm Troop' infiltration tactics evolved by von Hutier on the Russian Front and later transplanted by him to the Western Front. In these the serried lines of advancing troops marching over No Man's Land—everybody's mental picture of World War 1—was replaced by small parties of highly trained and motivated shock troops, amply armed, moving independently of each other, utilising ground and cover, and pouncing on weak spots, thus forcing the gate ajar to admit the more regimented units which followed.

For such a tactic to succeed, confidence and firepower were needed: confidence was a matter of training but firepower had to be provided. Von Hutier's firepower need was seen by Schmeisser, with the Bergmann Muskete as the result. Like other epochal inventions, one is inclined to wonder why others before had not thought of it for blowback pistols were no novelty by that time; it is worth a thought that the Bergmann was one of the first blowback pistols in existence, and, through Schmeisser (who was virtually a freelance designer at the time) Bergmann gave his name to the blowback submachine-gun.

The Bergmann MP18 is archetypal, consisting of a barrel, a heavy bolt with integral firing pin, a recoil spring, a magazine, and a wood stock with which to hold it. In order to economise on production facilities, the magazine was the Tatarek-Von Benkö 'snail' magazine developed for the Parabellum Artillerie-pistole. Since in their pistol application these magazines entered the butt at an acute angle, so they had to enter the Bergmann at the same angle—which gave the resulting weapon a rather odd appearance, but it worked once an adaptor was fitted to the magazine to position it correctly. The bolt was pulled back against the recoil spring and held by the sear. On pressing the trigger the bolt flew forward, collecting a round from the magazine and chambering it. The resistance as the round chambered caused the firing pin to impact on the cap, the round fired, the bullet departed, and the resulting reaction on the case pushed the bolt back. Owing to the bolt's greater mass compared to the bullet, it had hardly begun to move before bullet cleared the muzzle and the internal pressure dropped to a level where it was safe to remove the spent case. The energy already injected into the case and bolt gave sufficient thrust to cause the bolt to fly back, and thus the whole cycle began once again.

That, with minor variations, is the working cycle of most submachine-guns; the only great change lies in how the basic machinery is packaged. Some designers have tried to insert locking systems to hold the bolt closed in order to employ a lighter bolt (and thus a lighter and more easily aimed weapon) but most systems are either illusory or too complicated to be worth employing in what should be a simple weapon.

The principal drawbacks to submachine-guns as combat weapons are the rate of fire and the system of operation. If the bolt is light, and thus reciprocates easily, the rate of fire will be high—800 to 1,000rpm. Such a rate means that even a two-second pressure on the trigger will empty most magazines. The violence of such high-speed reciprocation causes the gun to climb and veer from the target and only the first one or two rounds will be effective. By making the bolt heavy and the recoil spring strong it is possible to cut the rate of fire by a half, but this has effects on the accuracy as most submachine-guns fire from an open bolt—or, in other words, when the gun is cocked the bolt is kept to the rear. Upon pressing the trigger the bolt is allowed to fly forwards several inches and then is stopped violently. This sudden shift in weight inevitably throws the aim, and accurate shooting with such a weapon becomes a matter of luck rather than judgement.

However, the manifold designs of World War 2 inspired many designers in the smallarms industry to try and produce weapons which at least diminished these and other drawbacks; in the pages which follow, we can sometimes discern what the designer had in mind.

PISTOLA AMETRALLADORA PAM1 and PAM2
Argentina
Fabrica Militar de Armas Portatiles 'Domingo Matheu', Rosario, Santa Fé
9mm Parabellum

The PAM1 and PAM2 are virtually identical to the US M3A1 from which they were derived; the only major differences lie in the fact that the Argentinian derivations are slightly shorter and lighter, and that they are only made in 9mm Parabellum calibre. The guns have been extensively used by the Argentine Army and police units, and they represented a break with the pre-World War 2 standards of machined construction which had until then prevailed in Argentina.

An additional feature of the PAM2 is the provision of an additional left-hand safety, which serves to reduce the number of inertia firing accidents prevalent amongst the M3 and other sub-machine-guns of World War 2. The Argentinians' guns are now well distributed amongst army and para-military forces of the South American continent.
Length: 28.50in (725mm)
Weight unloaded: 6lb 9oz (2.97kg)
Barrel: 7.85in (200mm), 6 grooves, right-hand twist
Magazine: 30-round detachable box
Cyclic rate: 450rpm
Muzzle velocity: c.1200fps (365mps)

PISTOLA AMETRALLADORA HALCON MODELO 1943 and MODELO 1946
Argentina
Halcon SA, Buenos Aires
9mm Parabellum, 0.45in ACP

These unusual looking guns were made in limited quantities in Argentina during and immediately after World War 2 and were issued both to the police (in 9mm) and the army (9mm and 0.45in). The curious shape and great loaded weight of the Halcon M43 are anachronisms in a gun produced so late in time, although it cannot be denied that examples are structurally strong and of good finish; they are also simple in operation and internally differ little from many other submachine-guns. The compensator at the muzzle helped to steady the gun during burst firing, but it must also be presumed that the excessive weight played an equally large part.

Although Halcon produced a modified weapon in 1946 in which certain modifications were made to reduce weight—most notably the substitution of a folding stock—they could not hope to compete satisfactorily with the PAM submachine-guns, and so production of the Halcon series was discontinued in the early 1950s.
Modelo 1943
Length: 33.40in (848mm)
Weight unloaded: 10lb 8oz (4.76kg)
Barrel: 11.50in (292mm), 6 grooves, right-hand twist
Magazine: 17 or 30-round detachable box
Cyclic rate: 700rpm
Muzzle velocity: c.910fps (277mps) (0.45in) c.1200fps (365mps) (9mm)
Modelo 1946
Length, stock extended: 31.10in (790mm)
Length, stock retracted: 24.04in (619mm)
Weight unloaded: 9lb 0oz (4.08kg)
Barrel: 11.50in (292mm), 6 grooves, right-hand twist
Magazine: 17 or 30-round detachable box
Cyclic rate: 700rpm
Muzzle velocity: c.910fps (277mps) (0.45in) c.1200fps (365mps) (9mm)

MACHINE CARBINES, 9MM AUSTEN, MARKS 1 and 2
Australia
Diecasters Limited, Melbourne, Victoria; W J Carmichael & Company, Melbourne, Victoria
9mm Parabellum

When the Pacific War started in 1941 Australia was desperately short of modern weapons; Britain was in no position to supply any—being in dire straits herself—and so the Australians set about producing their own, with only a limited amount of machinery and plant. Designs had therefore to be both straightforward and easy to manufacture. Submachine-guns were urgently needed for the jungle campaigns and a version of the Sten was put into production in mid-1941, combining many features of the Sten and the German MP 40. The receiver, barrel, trigger mechanism and bolt were of Sten design, but the MP 40 was the basis for the main spring, folding butt and sloping pistol grips. The resulting weapon had few vices except for the inherited Sten difficulty over feed; the Austen was, however, never made in large numbers and the total production probably did not exceed 20,000 by the time the war ended. A modification of the basic design (the Machine Carbine, 9mm Austen Mark 2) was produced, as a semi-prototype, in very limited numbers. This weapon is most readily recognisable by a two-piece cast aluminium frame. The Austen was superseded by the Owen, and the latter was the preferred arm.
Length, stock extended: 33.25 (845mm)
Length, stock folded: 21.75in (552mm)
Weight unloaded: 8lb 12oz (3.98kg)
Barrel: 7.75in (196mm), 6 grooves, right-hand twist
Magazine: 28-round detachable box
Cyclic rate: 500rpm
Muzzle velocity: c.1250fps (381mps)

MACHINE CARBINES, 9MM OWEN, MARKS 1 and 2
Australia
Lysaghts Newcastle Works, Newcastle, New South Wales
9mm Parabellum

Production of the Owen was begun at about the same time as that of the Austen and it was produced in larger numbers, reaching nearly 50,000 by 1945. Although quite large and bulky, the Owen was a first-class gun and very popular with those who used it, for it stood up well to the hard conditions of jungle fighting and stoppages were remarkably rare. Its two outstanding features were the top mounted magazine—a feature rarely seen on submachine-guns since the days of the Villar Perosa—and the provision of a separate bolt compartment inside the receiver so that the bolt was isolated from its retracting handle by a small bulkhead, through which passed the small diameter bolt. This ensured that dirt and mud did not jam the bolt and it was highly successful, although expensive in terms of space. There were many minor variations made to the Owen during its life, most of them concerning the materials of the pistol grips or the shape of the butt. In one version the trigger mechanism housing was largely cut away to reduce weight: early barrels had cooling rings, but these were soon discarded. Many Owens were painted in camouflage colours for jungle use, until they were taken out of service in the middle of the 1960s and passed to the Reserve. Three basic versions of the Owen were produced: the Mark 1 (which underwent several modifications during a production life of some three years), the Mark 1 Wood Butt, and the Mark 2—which was purely experimental with a total production of approximately 200.
Length: 32.00in (813mm)
Weight unloaded: 9lb 5oz (4.21kg)
Barrel: 9.75in (247mm), 7 grooves, right-hand twist
Magazine: 33-round detachable box
Cyclic rate: 700rpm
Muzzle velocity: c.1250fps (381mps)

9MM SUBMACHINE-GUN F1 (formerly known as the X3)
Australia
Small Arms Factory, Lithgow, New South Wales
9mm Parabellum

The Owen became somewhat out of date by the early 1960s and, although extremely popular with the troops, it had features which could be eliminated in a more modern design. Another gun—the X3—was therefore designed and the first models produced in 1962: the X3 could perhaps be described as an Australian version of the Sterling type, but this might be carrying the similarity too far. It has many features of the Sterling, particularly internally, though there are obvious differences in the trigger housing and the fact that the bolt handle is on the left side. The rearsight is a special design and the top mounted magazine of the Owen has been retained in response to the users' demands; the bolt handle has a separate cover to keep out mud and dirt (neither component moves as the gun fires). An interesting feature is the way in which the small of the butt fits into the rear of the receiver, which

▼The Austen, an Australian version of the Sten (RSAF).
▼The Owen Mark 1 (RSAF).
▼The 9mm Submachine-gun F1 (authors' collection).

is possible with the straight-line layout of the X3. It is a simple and effective gun which has performed well in the jungle war in Vietnam. So effective, indeed, that it has been adopted, with but minor modifications, as the 9mm submachine-gun F1.

Length: 28.15in (715mm)
Weight unloaded: 7lb 3oz (3.26kg)
Barrel: 8.00in (203mm), 6 grooves, right-hand twist
Magazine: 34-round detachable box
Cyclic rate: 600rpm
Muzzle velocity: c.1250fps (381mps)

MITRAILLETTE RAN
Belgium
Société Anonyme Belge Répousemetal, Bruxelles
9mm Parabellum

The RAN has never been taken into military service in any country, although it was offered to any interested buyer in the early and middle 1950s. It has, however, several unusual features and illustrates a line of thought which although not successful was at least ingenious. In general the RAN followed contemporary design in being constructed from sheet metal stampings with a one-piece wire folding stock and plastic furniture, but it differed in being more complicated and offering some extras which other designers had not thought worthy of consideration. The first was a grip safety and the second a somewhat involved ejection cover for the ejection port. The latter function was achieved by two separate covers, one inside the gun and one outside it; the inner one worked within the outer port, and the outer cover could be closed independently of it. This allowed the port to be closed when the bolt was to the rear—but other designers have accomplished this more simply. A barrel-cooling system was incorporated in which air was ducted around the breech through shallow grooves cut in the outer face of the breech, to what advantage is not now apparent since a proper cooling arrangement requires much more coolant volume than that offered by the RAN.

There were also a number of optional extras, including a folding bayonet, a bipod, a muzzle-brake, and a grenade launcher for anti-tank grenades. Quite obviously the idea was to produce a one-man weapons system: needless complication, the fact that the gun was no great improvement over existing designs and presumably the increased price, all combined to kill it within a short time.

Length, stock extended: 31.25in (794mm)
Length, stock folded: 23.00in (584mm)
Weight unloaded: 6lb 8oz (2.95kg)
Barrel: 11.75in (300mm), 6 grooves, right-hand twist
Magazine: 32-round detachable box
Cyclic rate: 630rpm
Muzzle velocity: c.1400fps (426mps)

MITRAILLETTE VIGNERON M2
Belgium
Société Anonyme Précision Liègeoise, Herstal-lèz-Liège
9mm Parabellum

The Vigneron was a light and practical submachine-gun designed in the early 1950s by a retired Belgian army officer and accepted for service in the Belgian Forces in 1953. It is similar to many other designs of the period and is made from the usual steel stampings and uncomplicated components. The barrel is longer than normal for a submachine-gun, but it also incorporates a compensator and partial muzzle-brake. This feature is nowadays thought to be largely superfluous since the advantages gained are not worth the effort and weight. The pistol grip has an integral grip safety which locks the bolt to the rear. The change lever also has a safety position and, when the lever is set for automatic fire, a slight squeeze on the trigger will produce a single shot; further pressure produces automatic fire. A wire stock telescopes into tubes alongside the receiver and the stock length can be adjusted to suit the individual firer. This is not such a great advantage as it seems as wire stocks are notoriously unstable for aimed firing. When the Belgian Army retired from the Congo, it is reported that a number of Vignerons were left in the hands of the Congolese troops and it is likely that these are still in use in that part of the world.

Length, stock extended: 35.00in (889mm)
Length, stock folded: 27.75in (704mm)
Weight unloaded: 7lb 4oz (3.29kg)
Barrel: 12.00in (305mm) including compensator, 6 grooves, right-hand twist
Magazine: 32-round detachable box
Cyclic rate: 625rpm
Muzzle velocity: c.1200fps (365mps)

METRALHADORA DE MAO 0.45IN, INA 953
Brazil
Industrias Nacional de Armas, São Paulo
.45 M1911 (0.45in ACP)

The INA is a modified version of the Danish Madsen made under licence in Brazil in a calibre of 0.45in, although improvements and adaptations have caused a gradual divergence between the INA and the parent 9mm gun, especially in the removal of the bolt retracting handle from the top of the receiver to the right side; the extractor, ejector and other lesser components have all seen improvement. All other details are similar to the original Madsen (see DENMARK).

The INA has enjoyed extensive use in Brazil—seeing service with the armed forces and the police—and it has also been exported to other South American countries.

Length, stock extended: 31.25in (793mm)
Length, stock retracted: 21.50in (545mm)
Weight unloaded: 7lb 8oz (3.45kg)
Barrel: 8.45in (215mm), 4 grooves, right-hand twist
Magazine: 30-round detachable box
Cyclic rate: 650rpm
Muzzle velocity: c.750fps (228mps)

9MM SUBMACHINE-GUN C1 (Sterling)
Canada
Canadian Arsenals Limited, Long Branch, Ontario
9mm Parabellum

The C1 submachine-gun is the Canadian version of the British Sterling, manufactured by Canadian Arsenals Limited of Ontario; all of the weapons are marked with CAL and the date of manufacture on the magazine housing.

A few modifications have been made to the original British design, particularly

◁The Belgian Mitrailette Vigneron M2, with its stock extended; note also the cuts in the top of the muzzle behind the rearsight, intended to act as a rudimentary form of compensator (RSAF).
▲The Brazilian INA 953, a modified pattern of the Danish Madsen made in Sao Paulo by Industrias Nacional de Armas (RSAF).

in the magazine and in the trigger mechanism. The capacity has been reduced from 34 to 30 and an alternative magazine holding 10 rounds can be supplied for special operations. The other obvious difference lies in the bayonet, which is that of the Canadian version of the FN rifle. Apart from these external changes there are some internal modifications which are concerned solely with the way of manufacture and do not alter the dimensions. These changes are said to make it cheaper to build. Apart from this the C1 is identical to the Sterling and its performance is
Length: 27.00in (686mm)
Weight unloaded: 6lb 8oz (2.99kg)
Barrel: 7.80in (200mm), 6 grooves, right-hand twist
Magazine: 10 or 30-round detachable box
Cyclic rate: 550rpm
Muzzle velocity: c.1200fps (365mps)

KULOMETNA PISTOLE ZK VZ/383, KULOMETNA PISTOLE ZK VZ/383H, KULOMETNA PISTOLE ZK VZ/383P
Czechoslovakia
Ceskoslovenská Zbrojovká Koucky, Brno
9mm Parabellum
The ZK vz/383, often simply known as the ZK383, is one of the oldest Czech

submachine-guns; it was first produced in the middle 1930s and was reported to be still in use in the Balkan areas in the early 1960s. A large and heavy weapon, typical of its time, the ZK383 is endowed with considerable reserves of strength. During World War 2 it was issued to troops of the Bulgarian Army and to some German units, but it has not been made since c.1948. It is similar to all the submachine-guns of its time except for a few features which are peculiar to it; the first is a bipod which appeared with the earlier versions and obviously helped accurate shooting, the second is a quick-change barrel, and the third is a removable weight in the bolt. This latter arrangement allowed the gun to fire either at 500 or at 700 rounds per minute, although it is now hard to see why this was thought necessary as the gun weighed over 10lb (4.54kg) loaded and could have a bipod to further steady it. One variation of the ZK383, the ZK vz/383H, had a folding magazine which stowed under the barrel by pivoting on a pin, and there have been police versions (the ZK vz/383P series) in which the bipod was discarded and a simpler rearsight installed.

Despite this variety and apparent complication the ZK383 sold in small quantities to the Bulgarian Army, and to

▼The Czechoslovakian vz/383 with its bipod folded down. This particular gun bears Bulgarian cyphers on the top rear of the receiver (RSAF).

Bolivia, Venezuela and other South American states; although the design is now long-obsolete, some are still used by some South American army and police units.

Length: 35.50in (902mm)
Weight unloaded: 9lb 6oz (4.33kg)
Barrel: 12.75in (324mm), 6 grooves, right-hand twist
Magazine: 30-round detachable box
Cyclic rate: 500 or 700 rpm
Muzzle velocity: c.1250fps (381mps)

KULOMETNA PISTOLE VZ/23, KULOMETNA PISTOLE VZ/25
Czechoslovakia
Ceskoslovenská Zbrojovká, Brno
9mm Parabellum

The vz/23 was designed in the late 1940s and was placed in production shortly afterwards. The weapon was present in substantial numbers in the Czech Army in 1951 and 1952 but manufacture stopped soon afterwards, perhaps because of the Soviet patronage which supplied arms to the Czech Army in enormous quantities. About 100,000 of these neat and handy little weapons were produced and many found their way to the Middle East and Cuba. Another model, the vz/25, was made with a folding metal strip stock. Both featured a bolt which had a deep recess in its forward face to allow the breech to slide inside; thus the main part of the bolt was in front of the breech when the bolt was forward. The bolt was about 8in (203mm) long, 6in (152mm) of which telescoped over the barrel, permitting a much shorter weapon; this is now—of course—quite common, but in 1950 it was novel in the extreme and made the vz/23 a definite trendsetter. Another innovation was the placing of the magazine inside the pistol grip, which can only be done when the bolt travels as far forward as it does in the 'wrap around' method; this also represents another sensible and satisfactory advance. The magazine was also a step forward since it was of the semi-triangular pattern now extensively marketed by the Carl Gustafs Stads Gevärsfactori in Sweden, and was probably the best type of magazine ever made for pistol ammunition. Two sizes were made, one holding 24 rounds and the other holding 40 rounds.

The vz/23 and vz/25 were the first postwar submachine-guns to show any significant advance in design; since then there has been a steady improvement in the directions so clearly shown by them, ultimately leading to the short, handy and simple weapons of the present day.

Length: 27.00in (686mm)
Weight unloaded: 6lb 12oz (3.09kg)
Barrel: 11.25in (282mm), 6 grooves, right-hand twist
Magazine: 24 or 40-round detachable box
Cyclic rate: 600rpm
Muzzle velocity: c.1250fps (381mps)

KULOMETNA PISTOLE VZ/24,

KULOMETNA PISTOLE VZ/26
Czechoslovakia
Ceskoslovenská Zbrojovká, Brno
7.62mm náboj vz/48

The vz/24 and vz/26 replaced the earlier vz/23 and vz/25 as the standard weapons of the Czech Army—but it is an indication of the Soviet influence that this change should have been made at all, since the only real alteration between the two sets of designs lies in the calibre. The later guns fire the 7.62mm Soviet pistol cartridge but, in the case of these submachine-guns, it is ammunition made in Czechoslovakia and loaded to give a higher velocity than the original Russian form. Apart from some obvious differences such as a new barrel, bolt and magazine, the weapon is virtually unchanged from the 9mm version. One small difference lies in the pistol grip/magazine housing which in the 7.62mm model has a noticeable forward lean, and there are some minor alterations to such items as the rearsight and sling swivels. Both the vz/24 and the vz/26 served the Czech Army from c. 1952 until the 1960s.

Length, stock extended: 27.00in (686mm)
Length, stock folded: 17.50in (445mm)
Weight unloaded: 7lb 4oz (3.29kg)
Barrel: 11.20in (284mm), 4 grooves, right-hand twist
Magazine: 32-round detachable box
Cyclic rate: 600rpm
Muzzle velocity: c.1800fps (548mps)

KULOMETNA PISTOLE VZ/61 'SKORPION'
Czechoslovakia
Ceská Zbrojovká, Brno
7.65mm auto pistol

This weapon belongs in the class of true machine pistols rather than submachine-guns; it fires a bullet of no more than marginal combat effectiveness and the whole weapon is small enough to be fired comfortably from one hand in single-shot fire. The vz/61 appears to have been designed to provide a holster weapon for armoured vehicle crews which is normally used as a pistol but which can, in emergency, provide automatic fire.

The Skorpion is a blowback weapon, and with its light reciprocating parts a high rate of fire might be expected; the designer has, however, ingeniously countered this by putting an inertia mechanism in the pistol grip. As the bolt recoils it drives a weight down into the grip, against the pressure of a spring, and at the same time the bolt is held by a trip-catch in the rear position. The weight rebounds from the spring and, on rising, releases the trip to allow the bolt to go forward. The duration of this action is very brief but it is sufficient to delay the bolt and thus reduce the rate of fire to manageable proportions. It might be expected that this action would make itself felt to the firer, but it is in fact masked by the general recoil and climb.

Length, stock extended: 20.55in (522mm)

Length, stock retracted: 10.65in (271mm)
Weight unloaded: 2lb 14oz (1.31kg)
Barrel: 4.50in (114mm)
Magazine: 10 or 20-round detachable box
Cyclic rate: 700rpm
Muzzle velocity: c.975fps (296mps)

MASKINPISTOL M/45 (MADSEN)
Denmark
Dansk Industri Syndikat AS 'Madsen', København
9mm Parabellum

One of the last wooden-stocked submachine-guns to be developed, this Madsen design had some unusual features. The breechblock is attached to a slide cover (instead of a cocking handle) which extends forward over the barrel and is formed at its front into a serrated grip. The recoil spring is wrapped around the barrel and contained within this slide.

In order to cock the weapon the slide is grasped and the entire slide and breech unit pulled to the rear—like the cocking of a giant automatic pistol. An advantage of the design is that the mass of the slide unit helps to resist the breech opening force and keep the rate of fire down, but the disadvantages are that the cover oscillates during firing and that the spring, wrapped around the barrel and confined in the slide, soon overheats and weakens in use.

A version of the basic weapon with a folding stock was also manufactured.

Length: 31.50in (800mm)
Weight unloaded: 7lb 2oz (3.22kg)
Barrel: 12.40in (315mm), 4 grooves, right-hand twist
Magazine: 50-round detachable box
Cyclic rate: 850rpm
Muzzle velocity: c.1312fps (400mps)

MASKINPISTOL M/46
Denmark
Dansk Industri Syndikat AS 'Madsen', København
9mm Parabellum

The name of Madsen has been associated with the manufacture of arms for many years and, as soon as World War 2 ended, the company started to produce for the postwar market. The m/46 submachine-gun was an attempt to overcome the drawbacks of the cheap and hastily-made wartime guns while using their manufacturing techniques to the full. The result was a weapon which was completely conventional in operation, apart from an unusual safety catch, but which offered remarkable accessibility and ease of manufacture. The gun fires from the normal open-bolt position and is capable only of automatic fire. A catch behind the magazine housing has to be grasped and pulled forward to allow the gun to fire and a second safety catch on the rear of the receiver locks the bolt in the open position. The main body of the gun is formed from two metal frames which comprise the two halves of the entire receiver, pistol grip, magazine housing and barrel bearing; a massive

▼The Czechoslovakian vz/23 sub-machine-gun with a wooden stock; 9mm Parabellum calibre (RSAF).

▼The Czechoslovakian vz/25 machine-gun with a folding metal stock, seen here in its extended position; 9mm Parabellum calibre (RSAF).

▼The Danish Madsen Maskinpistol m/1946; note the sleeve-covered folding stock and the knurled barrel nut which secures the two halves of the receiver (RSAF).

barrel nut then screws on and holds both halves together. The left-hand half can be removed, leaving all the working parts in place, and so internal inspection and cleaning are greatly simplified. The gun was well made and reliable, but it only sold in small numbers to a few South American countries and to Thailand. A modified pattern known as the maskinpistol m/50 differed in the provision of an improved retracting handle, which no longer had to be removed before the weapon was stripped.

Length, stock extended: 31.50in (800mm)
Length, stock folded: 21.50in (546mm)
Weight unloaded: 7lb 0oz (3.17kg)
Barrel: 7.75in (196mm), 4 grooves, right-hand twist
Magazine: 32-round detachable box
Cyclic rate: 500rpm
Muzzle velocity: c.1250fps (381mps)

MASKINPISTOL M/49 ('HOVEA')
Denmark
Haerens Vabenarsenalet, København
9mm Parabellum

Although bearing a considerable resemblance to the Swedish 'Carl Gustav' design, the m/49 owes its parentage to the Husqvarna company. It was originally manufactured in 1944 as a prototype for the Swedish Army but had been turned down in favour of the Carl Gustav. The gun was then offered to Denmark, who were in the market for a submachine-gun after World War 2, and the production models were all made under licence in Denmark.

There is little of note in the design; it is a simple blowback gun, designed with ease-of-production in mind and making use of the standard Carl Gustav magazine—an unusual example of standardisation which could well be copied in other spheres. The m/49 was originally made to take the Suomi drum magazine, which accounts for the oddly-shaped magazine aperture.

Length, stock extended: 31.75in (806mm)
Length, stock retracted: 21.65in (550mm)
Weight unloaded: 7lb 6oz (3.23kg)
Barrel: 8.50in (216mm), 4 or 6 grooves, right-hand twist
Magazine: 36-round detachable box
Cyclic rate: 600rpm
Muzzle velocity: c.1300fps (396mps)

MASKINPISTOL M/50, MASKINPISTOL M/53
Denmark
Dansk Industri Syndikat AS 'Madsen', København
9mm Parabellum

The m/53 is a development of the m/46 and the m/50, and differs from them mainly in the magazine which—on this model—is curved to improve the feeding and can also be used as a monopod when the gun is fired in the prone position. In common with the preceding models the receiver, pistol grip and magazine housing are contained in a novel two-piece frame hinging at the rear and locked at the front by the barrel locking nut. An optional barrel jacket carries a bayonet attachment, which is another noticeable

▲An example of the Madsen m/1953, showing the curved magazine and the modified pattern rearsight (RSAF).
▲A Madsen submachine-gun, in this case a specimen of the m/1953 type, with the barrel nut removed—whereupon the two halves of the gun, pivoting on a vertical bolt at the rear of the receiver, can be swung apart (RSAF).
▷▷Two views of the m/1931, designed by Lahti and known as the 'Suomi' (top RSAF; bottom, SIM).

departure from the previous versions. Some guns have wooden furniture on the pistol grip, and all have a distinctive leather sleeve on the tubular butt. Sales of this gun were fairly respectable and it was taken into service in some of the smaller countries of South America and Asia. It is unfortunate that the Madsen firm no longer makes armaments, and so there will be no successors to this design.

Length, stock extended: 31.55in (800mm)
Length, stock folded: 20.75in (530mm)
Weight unloaded: 7lb 0oz (3.20kg)
Barrel: 7.80in (197mm), 4 grooves, right-hand twist
Magazine: 32-round detachable box
Cyclic rate: 550rpm
Muzzle velocity: c.1250fps (381mps)

PISTOLA AMETRALLADORA CRISTOBAL MODELO 2, PISTOLA AMETRALLADORA MODELO 62
Dominican Republic
State manufacture by Armeria Fabrica de Armas, at San Cristobal
.30 M1 US Carbine
The Cristobal Modelo 2 is produced in Dominica in a factory which was originally organised with the assistance of a number of experts who had previously worked with Beretta and with the Hungarian plant at Budapest. Although the Cristobal is reminiscent in shape of the early Berettas it is rather different internally, using a simple lever system to delay the blowback opening of the bolt. The design is attributed to Kiraly, designer of the Hungarian 39M

and 43M submachine-guns. A pendant lever attached to the bolt engages with the gun body and as the bolt is driven back by the exploding cartridge it is forced to revolve the lever and disconnect it before being allowed to recoil freely. This instigates sufficient delay to allow the bullet to leave the barrel before the case is extracted.

The Modelo 62 is a more modern version using the same mechanism, but with a perforated handguard instead of the three-quarter length wooden stock and fore-end of the earlier model; the M62 may also be found with a folding skeleton butt. Both models use double triggers, the front trigger for single shot operation and the rear one for automatic fire.

Probably the most unusual feature of the Cristobal is the use of the 0.30in M1 Carbine cartridge; the lightweight bullet with its inherent lack of stopping power—compared to such rounds as the 9mm Parabellum and the 0.45in ACP—is somewhat negated by the increased velocity, which is much higher than is common with this class of weapon.

Length: 37.20in (945mm)
Weight unloaded: 7lb 12oz (3.51kg)
Barrel: 16.10in (409mm), 4 grooves, right-hand twist
Magazine: 25 or 30-round detachable box
Cyclic rate: 575rpm
Muzzle velocity: c.1850fps (563mps)

KONEPISTOOLI M/26 ('SUOMI'), KONEPISTOOLI M/31 ('SUOMI')

Finland
Oy Tikkakoski Ab, Sakara
7.63mm Mauser (m/26), 9mm Parabellum (m/31)
The 'Suomi' (named after the Finnish term for Finland) submachine-guns were manufactured to the designs of Aimo Lahti and produced by the State-owned Tikkakoski plant. The first model to be adopted by the Finnish Army was the m/26 which was itself preceded by a series of experimental weapons dating back to 1922; the m/26, chambered for the 7.63mm Mauser round, was distinguished by a large buffer housing extending from the rear of the receiver and by a severely-curved 36-round box magazine. Few of these weapons were produced, as the design was replaced within a few years by the improved m/31 — an outstandingly successful weapon which is probably still to be found in the more remote parts of the world and which was actually produced in Sweden, Denmark and Switzerland. Although heavy by modern standards, the m/31 is capable of surprisingly good accuracy from the design's long barrel; it is, of course, made in the 'old style' with all the components either machined from solid stock or forged from heavy gauge material. The bolt handle is at the rear of the receiver and works much in the way of a bolt-action rifle in that it is pulled to the rear to retract the bolt and then pushed forward and turned down—to remain stationary while the bolt moves within its housing. The barrel

▼▼Two views of the m/1944-46, based on the Soviets' PPS but chambered for the 9mm Parabellum round (authors' collection).
▼The French MAS 38, a promising design which deserved a better fate; being chambered for the odd 7.65mm Longue cartridge was no help (RSAF).

dismounts from the jacket reasonably easily and the bolt has a fixed firing pin, but the most significant feature of the Suomi design lies in the magazine. Box magazines of 20 rounds and 50 rounds were provided and so, too, was a large drum holding 71 rounds: the drum was copied by the Soviets for the PPSh 41 and has since become notorious as a symbol of Communist involvement. It is probable that Lahti drew on the drum magazine of the Thompson weapons for his inspiration, and he made a very good job of copying it for, despite the loaded weight of 5lb 8oz (2.49kg), the magazine unit is remarkably robust. A smaller drum containing 40 rounds was also developed and, c.1955, all the remaining m/31 guns were converted to take the Swedish 36-round box magazine used on the Swedish Army's m/45 submachine-gun.

(data: m/31)
Length: 34.50in (875mm)
Weight unloaded: 10lb 12oz (4.90kg)
Barrel: 12.50in (318mm), 6 grooves, right-hand twist
Magazine: 20, 36, 40 or 50-round detachable boxes, or 71-round drum
Cyclic rate: 900rpm
Muzzle velocity: c.1300fps (396mps)

KONEPISTOOLI M/44
Finland
Oy Tikkakoski Ab, Sakara
9mm Parabellum
The m/44 is a copy of the Soviet PPS43 design, with suitable modifications made to the magazine and feed to enable the 9mm Parabellum cartridge to be used. The weapon is a simple blowback type, capable only of automatic fire and made from as many simple stampings and pressings as possible: the modified feed unit, however, permits the use of the 71-round drum of the earlier m/31 submachine-gun as well as the other box magazines. In common with the m/31, the m/44 was modified—c.1955—to take the 36-round Swedish box magazine design. At the time of writing the m/44 is the standard submachine-gun of the Finnish Army, but it is possible that it will be replaced in front line service by the rynnäkkökivääri (assault rifle) m/62.

It is interesting to note that the manager of Oy Tikkakoski at the time when the m/44 was produced, Willi Daugs, fled at the close of World War 2 to Spain by way of Sweden and Holland. He took with him copies of the manufacturing drawings of the m/44, which later appeared in Spain as the DUX 53 (see GERMANY).
Length, stock extended: 32.50in (825mm)
Length, stock folded: 24.50in (623mm)
Weight unloaded: 6lb 3oz (2.84kg)
Barrel: 9.75in (247mm), 4 or 6 grooves, right-hand twist
Magazine: 71-round drum, or 36 or 50-round detachable box
Cyclic rate: 650rpm
Muzzle velocity: c.1250fps (381mps)

KONEPISTOOLI M/44-46 ('SUOMI')
Finland
Oy Tikkakoski Ab, Sakara
9mm Parabellum
The m/44-46 was derived from the earlier m/44, itself a copy of the Russian PPS43; production of the m/44 carried on into the postwar years, although the Finns were to a degree hampered by the terms of the peace treaty signed with the USSR. The slight postwar modification which led to the m/44-46 concerned the standardisation for the gun of the 36-round box magazine used on the m/45 ('Carl Gustav') submachine-gun of the Swedish armed forces, apart from which the Finnish m/44-46 differed from its predecessor only in the standard of finish as more care could be spared in times of peace. Unlike the m/44, the 1946 pattern would not accept the standard Suomi 71-round drum magazine.

The gun served in the Finnish forces until the late 1950s, but it has now been phased from service in favour of the assault rifle designs of 1960 and 1962; it is, however, likely that the Finns are holding the submachine-guns in reserve.
Length: 32.50in (828mm)
Weight unloaded: 6lb 3oz (2.84kg)
Barrel: 9.80in (248mm), 4 grooves, right-hand twist
Magazine: 36-round detachable box
Cyclic rate: 650rpm
Muzzle velocity: c.1320fps (402mps)

MITRAILLETTE MAS MODELE 38
France
Manufacture d'Armes de Saint-Etienne, Saint-Etienne
7.65mm Long Auto Pistol
Derived from the SE-MAS of 1935, the MAS38 submachine-gun was first made in 1938 and continued in production until 1949, a limited number being manufactured for the German occupation forces during the war years. The MAS38 was a good and workmanlike design, well-made and somewhat in advance of the contemporary thinking. It was reasonably light, and diverged from the general contemporary pattern of one-piece wooden stocks extending well up the barrel and of relatively complicated mechanisms. Although primarily made from machined steel stock, the MAS contained nothing that was strictly unnecessary and so managed to avoid the weight penalty

A slide on the right-hand side of the receiver engages with the bolt and, on being pulled to the rear, cocks the weapon and opens the ejection port at the same time; it then stays to the rear. A sprung plate covers the magazine housing when the weapon is not loaded. The bolt moves in a tube which contains a long recoil spring and which is not in line with the barrel. The bolt therefore reaches the breech at an angle and the bolt face is machined to allow for this. The stock is almost in a straight line with the barrel and this, combined with the comparatively low-powered round

which it fires, endows the gun with good accuracy and low recoil. The MAS38 was never produced in any calibre other than 7.65mm Long and was consequently of no interest to other European nations. A 9mm version might well have enjoyed commercial success.
Length: 25.00in (635mm)
Weight unloaded: 6lb 4oz (2.88kg)
Barrel: 8.75in (222mm), 4 grooves, right-hand twist
Magazine: 32-round detachable box
Cyclic rate: 600rpm
Muzzle velocity: c.1150fps (350mps)

MITRAILLETTE HOTCHKISS 'TYPE UNIVERSEL', 1949
France
Société de Fabrication des Armes à Feu Portatives Hotchkiss et Cie, Saint-Denis
9mm Parabellum
The Hotchkiss 'Universal' was introduced shortly after World War 2 and appears to have been designed with the intention of overcoming all the disadvantages shown by the wartime guns. It was originally produced as a self-loading police weapon but was soon marketed in a selective fire version, and small numbers were taken into the French Army for extended trials. The many ingenious features of the design led to over-complication, manufacturing difficulties and even more difficult maintenance problems in the field, and the 'Universal' fell from production by the early 1950s.

The most notable feature of the design was its ability to be folded into a surprisingly small unit; the butt and pistol-grip could fold underneath the body, the magazine and its housing folded forward beneath the barrel, and even the barrel could be telescoped into the receiver to produce a package no more than 17.25in (438mm) long.
Length, stock extended: 30.60in (776mm)
Length, stock retracted: 21.25in (540mm)
Weight unloaded: 7lb 8oz (3.41kg)
Barrel: 10.75in (273mm)
Magazine: 32-round detachable box
Cyclic rate: 650rpm
Muzzle velocity: c.1300fps (396mps)

MITRAILLETTE MAT MODELE 49
France
Manufacture d'Armes de Tulle, Tulle
9mm Parabellum
The MAT was adopted by the French Army in 1949 and was their standard submachine-gun throughout the Algerian and Indo-China fighting. Like its predecessor, the MAS38, it is a simple and effective design with few frills. It is mainly made from heavy gauge steel stampings and has a minimum of machined parts—and the effort to reduce manufacturing costs has given it a 'square' look. The folding wire stock looks very similar to that of the United States' M3 submachine-gun, and the pistol grip has plastic furniture and a grip safety. The magazine housing is

unusual in that it pivots forwards to lie under the barrel when it is necessary to carry the gun in the smallest possible package, and the housing also serves as the forward hand grip. The magazine is a single-feed box very similar to that of the Sten, which was not noted for its reliability or freedom from stoppages, and it is probable that the MAT inherited this failing.

In all other respects the gun is entirely conventional and its strength and robustness survived considerable active service.

Length, stock extended: 26.00in (661mm)
Length, stock folded: 16.00in (406mm)
Weight unloaded: 8lb 0oz (3.63kg)
Barrel: 9.00in (228mm), 4 grooves, left-hand twist
Magazine: 32-round detachable box
Cyclic rate: 600rpm
Muzzle velocity: c.1200fps (365mps)

MASCHINENPISTOLE 18/I (MP18/I)
Germany
Theodor Bergmann Waffenbau AG, Suhl
9mm Pist Patr 08 (9mm Parabellum)

The MP 18/I is an historic weapon and a landmark in the story of the sub-machine-gun. Development of the weapon started in 1916 and over 30,000 had been made by November 1918. It was designed by Hugo Schmeisser, whose name is so well known in the smallarms field, and it was the first true blowback submachine-gun although it has to be admitted that the Beretta of 1918 runs a very close second. The MP18/I set the fashion for the pattern of submachine-guns until c.1938, and its influence can clearly be seen on all the designs of the 1920s and early 1930s. Few were used in World War 1, but some were issued in 1920 to the police of the Weimar Republic.

The gun was originally meant to use the "snail" magazine of Tatarek and von Benkö produced for the Parabellum pistol, with which an adaptor had to be used to prevent the magazine fouling the bolt; this proved unsatisfactory and was corrected after two or three years of use by the police forces. A straight box magazine was substituted and it came in two sizes, of 20 or 32 rounds.

The MP18/I was comparatively simple, very strong, not too difficult to manufacture and—except for the initial feed troubles—very reliable. It was a success from the very beginning and later designers who abandoned its principles frequently found themselves in difficulties.

Length: 32.00in (812mm)
Weight unloaded: 9lb 4oz (4.26kg)
Barrel: 7.75in (196mm), 6 grooves, right-hand twist
Magazine: 32-round helical drum
Cyclic rate: 400rpm
Muzzle velocity: c.1250fps (381mps)

MASCHINENPISTOLE 28/II (MP28/II)
Germany
C G Haenel Waffen- und Fahrradfabrik AG, Suhl
7.63mm Mauser, 7.65mm Parabellum, 9mm Pist Patr 08 (9mm Parabellum), .45 M1911 (0.45in ACP), 9mm Mauser Export(?)

The MP28/II was a direct descendant of the MP18 and is substantially similar, apart from several modifications and improvements; the main difference is that a selector mechanism is incorporated so that single shots may be fired. A separate firing pin and an improved mainspring are the chief internal changes and, apart from a new rearsight, the external appearance is little changed. The gun was intended purely as a commercial proposition and in this it was entirely successful, for large numbers were made both in Germany and under licence in other countries, and specimens was used in Europe and South America. The customer could virtually state his preferred calibre and the gun would be modified to suit. In 0.45in ACP it is perhaps noteworthy that the magazine capacity was reduced to 25, although there was no standardisation in capacity and there were a few 20-round magazines made for 9mm Parabellum. Like its predecessor, the MP18, the MP28/II was strong and survived considerable ill treatment. Its greatest military use was in the Spanish Civil War, when it made an enormous impression and can truly be held responsible for the frantic rush —by those countries sensible enough to see its potential—to manufacture comparable weapons.

Length: 32.00in (812mm)
Weight unloaded: 8lb 12oz (3.97kg)
Barrel: 7.75in (196mm), 6 grooves, right-hand twist
Magazine: 20, 32 or 50-round detachable box
Cyclic rate: 500rpm
Muzzle velocity: c.1250fps (381mps)

MASCHINENPISTOLE 34/I ('Bergmann MP34'), MASCHINEN-PISTOLE 35/I
Germany
Manufactured for Theodor Bergmann & Companie GmbH by Carl Walther Waffenfabrik AG, Zella-Mehlis (MP 34), and by Junker & Ruh AG, Karlsruhe (MP35)
7.63mm Mauser, 9mm Pist Patr 08 (9mm Parabellum), .45 M1911 (0.45in ACP)

The Bergmann is one of several German weapons developed in neighbouring countries in order to avoid the restrictions of the Versailles Treaty, for in this case the prototypes were made in Denmark. Only small numbers of the MP34/I were made, and the military version was the slightly improved MP35/I. The MP35/I was the standard submachine-gun of the Waffen-SS, who sensibly stuck to one type, and their demands made up the entire output of the factory during World War 2; the total production was in the region of 40,000—hardly a large number.

The Bergmann was very well made and finished, and it had a few unusual features—the most obvious of which was

◁The Mitrailette MAT 49, an unusual design in which the magazine could be folded forward under the barrel (RSAF).
▲The Bergmann MP18/I, the first successful machine-gun and the prototype for a whole series of similar guns. It is shown with the Tatarek-von Benkö 'snail' magazine, one of the weapon's drawbacks (RSAF).
▲The MP28/II, a derivative of the MP18 manufactured by C G Haenel of Suhl; the old 'snail' magazine was discarded in favour of a more standard pattern of box (RSAF).
▲The MP34/1, in this case a long-barrelled version manufactured for Ethiopia (Abyssinia) in c.1935. The gun, made by Carl Walther, bears the ion of Judah on the receiver (RSAF).

the fact that the magazine fed from the right-hand side. The bolt handle was also peculiar to the make, as it projected from the rear of the receiver and had to be rotated and pulled back to retract the bolt. The advantage claimed for this dubious complexity was a stationary handle when firing and no bolt slot into which dirt could get. Another feature was a 'double-acting' trigger. The gun fired semi-automatically when the trigger was pulled half-way back. Further pulling caused it to force the secondary trigger to engage, giving automatic fire. Although the Bergmann MP34 was offered in a variety of calibres, and with optional long and short barrels, the SS version was short-barrelled and always in 9mm Parabellum.

Length: 33.00in (840mm)
Weight unloaded: 8lb 15oz (4.05kg)
Barrel: 7.75in (196mm), 6 grooves, right-hand twist
Magazine: 24 or 32-round detachable box
Cyclic rate: 650rpm
Muzzle velocity: c.1250fps (381mps)

◁A Spanish-made (Vollmer-designed) EMP submachine-gun. The fore-pistol grip is characteristic of this gun (RSAF).

◁The MP38 submachine-gun; the longitudinal grooving on the receiver is characteristic of this model, and was absent from the later MP40. The device over the muzzle is a blank-firing device which permitted the gun to operate with blank ammunition (RSAF).

◁The MP40 submachine-gun, a modified form of the MP38 intended for easier mass-production. There are several types of magazine and magazine housing, with and without ribbing (SIM).

◁An example of the MP41, a version of the MP38/40 series making use of a permanent wooden stock. It was not a success (RSAF).

MASCHINENPISTOLE ERMA, SYSTEM VOLLMER (MPE)
Germany
Erfurter Maschinenfabrik B Geipel GmbH (Erma-Werke), Erfurt
9mm Pist Patr 08 (9mm Parabellum)
The MPE was produced in relatively small numbers and in several variations from c.1930 until 1938, when the manufacturers turned to the production of the MP38. The Erma 'machine pistol' was developed from the prototype Vollmer pattern of the early 1920s, first submitted to the German Army in 1925 and produced by the Vollmer factory at Biberach until the design ultimately attracted the favourable attention of the Heereswaffenamt, when Erma-Werke quickly acquired production rights. The result was a simple gun which made use of seamless steel tubing for as many parts as possible, perhaps the beginnings of the move towards cheap and simple submachine-guns which later became more readily apparent. The MPE had a mainspring contained within a telescopic housing and the bolt handle locked into a safety slot, but the most prominent feature was the vertical wooden foregrip, which appeared on few other designs. The gun first appeared in combat in the hands of the Bolivian and Paraguayan Armies during the Chaco War of 1932-5; it later served through the Spanish Civil War (1936-9) and in the hands of the Wehrmacht until replaced c.1942 by the MP40, after which time the surviving Erma guns were passed to the reserve.

Some of the Spanish-built copies made c.1940 are chambered for the 9mm Bergmann-Bayard cartridge rather than the 9mm Parabellum more typical of the German-made guns: it is thought that some still serve the Spanish security forces and that others remain in small numbers throughout the world.
Length: 35.50in (902mm)
Weight unloaded: 9lb 2oz (4.15kg)
Barrel: 10.00in (254mm), 6 grooves, right-hand twist
Magazine: 25 or 32-round detachable box
Cyclic rate: 500rpm
Muzzle velocity: c.1250fps (381mps)

MASCHINENPISTOLE 38 (MP38), MASCHINENPISTOLE 38/40 (MP 38/40)
Germany
Erfurter Maschinenfabrik B. Geipel GmbH (Erma-Werke), Erfurt
9mm Pist Patr 08 (9mm Parabellum)
This was probably the most famous military submachine-gun of all time and it has gone down into history under a quite incorrect general name—the Schmeisser. In fact, Hugo Schmeisser had nothing to do with its design or early manufacture; it was first produced in the Erma factory and bears many innovations of that firm, although Schmeisser did take a hand in the manufacture of the MP40. The MP38 was made to specifications drawn up by the Oberkommando der Wehrmacht (OKW) and

from the first it was a leader in its field. It was the first submachine-gun to have a successful folding butt, the first to be made entirely without any wood in its stock or furniture, and the first to be specifically intended for use by a fast moving mechanised army. Like its predecessor, the MP18/I, it set a fashion which was followed by practically every other gun and even today its influence is still apparent. The MP38 suffered, however, from two drawbacks. The first —shared with the MP40—was the single-column feed system, which was inefficient and led to jams, and secondly the gun was expensive and time-consuming to make owing to the large number of machining processes and the use of high-quality steel. Not long after the war started, the German authorities found that they could not afford the time and expense involved in making the MP38.
Length, stock extended: 32.75in (832mm)
Length, stock folded: 24.75in (629mm)
Weight unloaded: 9lb 0oz (4.14kg)
Barrel: 9.75in (247mm), 6 grooves, right-hand twist
Magazine: 32-round detachable box
Cyclic rate: 500rpm
Muzzle velocity: c.1250fps (381mps)

MASCHINENPISTOLE 40, MASCHINENPISTOLE 40/II, MASCHINENPISTOLE 41 (MP40, MP40/II, MP41)
Germany
Erfurter Maschinenfabrik B Geipel GmbH, Erfurt; C G Haenel Waffen- und Fahrradfabrik AG, Suhl; Osterreichische Waffenfabrik-Gesellschaft, Steyr
9mm Pist Patr 08 (9mm Parabellum)
The MP38 proved to be too expensive to manufacture in time of war and the MP40 was introduced as a simplified version. It was substantially the same weapon, differing only in such matters as the ejector, the magazine catch and the receiver; the major and most important difference was that it had been designed for mass production methods utilising a minimum of machining operations and the opportunity was taken of utilising sub-assemblies which could be subcontracted to a host of minor firms throughout the Reich. The components were only brought together for final finishing and assembly. As far as possible the use of high grade steel was avoided and many parts were made of sheet-steel stampings; spot welding was used extensively at the joints. The result was a highly practical and effective gun, the manufacture of which was copied within several years by almost every other nation, and the basic idea of building in sub-assemblies for a limited life is still followed by every maker of submachine-guns. The MP40 went through several variants and there were minor differences between the models made in different factories, but the external changes were few. The most interesting version was produced in late 1943; this was a dual magazine gun—

the MP40/II—made in an effort to keep pace with the 71-round drum of the Soviet PPSh41. It allowed two magazines of 32 rounds to be held in the housing and slid across one after the other. It was not a success, largely owing to the increased weight of the unit. A wooden stock gun based on the MP40, usually known as the MP41 or the MP41/I, was also produced. It, too, was unsuccessful largely because the concept strayed from that pioneered by the MP38 and the MP40.

The standard version has had a long military life and can still be found in service in some small countries.

Length, stock extended: 32.75in (832mm)
Length, stock folded: 24.75in (629mm)
Weight unloaded: 8lb 12oz (3.97kg)
Barrel: 9.75in (248mm), 6 grooves, right-hand twist
Magazine: 32-round detachable box
Cyclic rate: 500rpm
Muzzle velocity: c.1250fps (381mps)

MASCHINENPISTOLE 'GERAT POTSDAM'
Germany
Mauser-Werke AG, Oberndorf-am-Neckar
9mm Pist Patr 08 (9mm Parabellum)
Although by no means an outstanding

▲▲▲Three versions of the MP3008, the Germans' emergency derivative of the British Sten Mark 2. The top gun (RSAF) is representative of the standard type. The second gun (RSAF), although of crude manufacture, is an attempt to produce a rather more serviceable weapon; it is thought to have been made in 1944 by the important Hamburg firm of Blohm & Voss. The third illustration (SIM) represents one of the last stages of the transition; poorly made of poor material, the weapon would not have lasted long in use.

weapon, the 'Gerät Potsdam' was certainly one of the most interesting and unusual submachine-guns produced during World War 2 and perhaps at any time. It was a careful and deliberate attempt to produce an identical copy of another design, in this case the British Sten Mark 2, and much effort went into ensuring that the resulting copy was indistinguishable from the original. Even the markings were reproduced. Although it is possible to find differences, at the time these guns were made few people would have known what to look for, and the copies would have been accepted. They were intended to be used by German guerilla units in Allied-occupied countries and, while some were used in France in 1944, it was not in their intended role as the German guerilla movement never started. Between 25,000 and 30,000 of these weapons were made and the making of them involved the Mauser-Werke plant in a prodigious effort under conditions of great secrecy. It was all to no purpose and remains one more example of the extraordinary way in which the German High Command would follow some impulsive scheme to the detriment of the regular war effort.

Length: 30.00in (762mm)
Weight unloaded: 6lb 9oz (3.00kg)
Barrel: 7.75in (196mm), 2 or 6 grooves, right-hand twist
Magazine: 32-round detachable box
Cyclic rate: 550rpm
Muzzle velocity: c.1250fps (381mps)

MASCHINENPISTOLE 3008 (MP3008)
Germany
Mauser-Werke AG, Oberndorf-am-Neckar; C G Haenel Waffen- und Fahrradfabrik AG, Suhl; Erfurter Maschinenfabrik B Geipel GmbH, Erfurt, and others
9mm Pist Patr 08 (9mm Parabellum)
The MP3008 is another example of a weapon deliberately copied from the Sten, but in this case the motives were different. In the last few months of 1944 the German High Command was desperate for cheap and simple weapons with which to replace the staggering losses in Russia, and to arm the raw battalions of young men who were to make the last stand against the Allies. At the same time the Volkssturm and various guerilla bands were forming, all demanding arms. The British Sten had been one of the outstandingly successful designs of the war, despite its drawbacks, and it was noted for its economy of material and uncomplicated design. Accordingly, it was copied in a cruder and simpler form, and several firms—including Mauser-Werke—manufactured as many as the circumstances allowed. The resulting guns differed widely in finish and some were among the worst finished ever made, but they worked—which was all that was required of them. The most obvious difference from the Sten was in the vertical magazine which fed upwards into the receiver. There

were other minor changes, particularly in the design of the butt and in the joining and pinning of the components. Approximately 10,000 of these weapons were made and, although few saw action, it was remarkable enough that these guns had been manufactured in the chaotic conditions then prevailing in a Germany where raw materials and machining facilities were in equally short supply.

Length: 31.50in (800mm)
Weight unloaded: 6lb 8oz (2.95kg)
Barrel: 7.75in (196mm), 6 or 8 grooves, right-hand twist
Magazine: 32-round detachable box
Cyclic rate: 500rpm
Muzzle velocity: c.1250fps (381mps)

MASCHINENPISTOLE ERMA 44 (MPE44 or EMP44)
Germany
Erfurter Maschinenfabrik B Geipel GmbH, Erfurt
9mm Pist Patr 08 (9mm Parabellum)
This extraordinary weapon does not seem to have been produced in any numbers and it may never have proceeded beyond the prototype stage. The design was made either in 1942 or in 1943 at the Erma factory and few have survived. It is a submachine-gun with the manufacturing processes reduced to the absolute minimum with the result that the finished gun is crude almost beyond belief. Barrel, body, butt and pistol grip are all made from steel tube of the same diameter and wall thickness: in fact the barrel, body and butt are one tube alone. The shoulder piece is also tubular. The magazine housing and muzzle brake are welded on to the body and other attachments are riveted. The magazine housing accepts the dual magazines in the same way as the MP40 variant and, similarly, MP40 magazines are used. The bolt and spring are of the same type as Erma-Werke patented and used in their more conventional designs and the trigger mechanism is extremely simple. The sights are set well above the barrel line in robust protectors. Behind the rearsight a strengthening web is welded to form a bridge over the weak point of the magazine housing, while at the same time forming part of the rearsight protector. The EMP44 is an object lesson in simple design and it obviously worked, although how well is not known. It was never adopted for service.

MASCHINENPISTOLE DUX MODELL 53
Germany (Spain)
Fabrica de Armas de Oviedo, Oviedo
9mm Pist Patr 08 (9mm Parabellum)
The DUX53 was a hybrid weapon designed by the Germans Daugs and Vorgrimmler, produced in Spain and used in Germany. The design was originally that of the Finnish konepistooli m/44 (see FINLAND) which was in turn based on the Soviet PPS43: the drawings of the m/44 had been taken from Finland at the end of World War 2 and ultimately

arrived in Spain, where they were used as the basis for the prototype of the DUX53 series, the DUX51. One thousand of the DUX53 were purchased by the Bundes-Grenz-Schütz, the West German border guard, and were used by them for several years. The West German Army also spent some years testing the weapon and, indeed, some were modified by J G Anschütz GmbH of Ulm-am-Donau, some by Mauser-Werke of Oberndorf-am-Neckar, and some by J P Sauer & Sohn of Köln: none was accepted by the army. Eventually, Anschütz produced a modified weapon called the DUX59, a much-streamlined version of the DUX53, which never gained acceptance by the military authorities.

The family resemblance between the DUX53, the Finnish m/44 and the Soviet PPS43 is very close indeed—none too surprising considering the design linkage—but the DUX uses a 50-round box magazine of 'Suomi' design and purchased from Switzerland where it had been made under licence. The DUX was largely made from sheet-steel stampings and was angular and unattractive in appearance; capable only of automatic fire, it was, by the standards of the day, a little heavy although otherwise reasonably efficient.

Length, stock extended: 32.50in (825mm)
Length, stock folded: 24.25in (615mm)
Weight unloaded: 7lb 11oz (3.49kg)
Barrel: 9.75in (245mm), 6 grooves, right-hand twist
Magazine: 50-round detachable box
Cyclic rate: 500rpm
Muzzle velocity: c.1200fps (365mps)

WALTHER MASCHINENPISTOLEN LANG (MP-L) and KURZ (MP-K)
Federal Republic of Germany
Carl Walther Waffenfabrik, Ulm-am-Donau
9mm Pist Patr 08 (9mm Parabellum)
The Walther MP is a blowback weapon utilising steel stampings for most of its basic structure. The bolt is overhung, the bulk of it being above the axis of the barrel and overlapping the breech in the closed position, and it is located on a guide rod which also carries the return spring. The sights are an ingenious combination of open sights for snap shooting and an aperture and barleycorn for more accurate aim when time allows.

Two models are available, long and short, the sole difference lying in the length of the barrel and its associated handguard. These weapons were developed in 1963 and, although evaluated by several military authorities, have yet to be officially adopted by any armed forces.

(data: MP-L)
Length, stock extended: 29.40in (746mm)
Length, stock retracted: 18.20in (460mm)
Weight unloaded: 6lb 10oz (3.00kg)
Barrel: 10.25in (260mm), 6 grooves, right-hand twist
Magazine: 32-round detachable box

▲The Walther MP-L, top, and MP-K (bottom); both are shown with the stocks, which hinge around the rear of the receiver, folded forward (Walther).

Cyclic rate: 550rpm
Muzzle velocity: c.1150fps (350mps)
(data: MP–K)
Length, stock extended: 25.98in (659mm)
Length, stock retracted: 15.01in (381mm)
Weight unloaded: 6lb 4oz (2.80kg)
Barrel: 6.78in (173mm), 6 grooves, right-hand twist
Magazine: 32-round detachable box
Cyclic rate: 550rpm
Muzzle velocity: c.1100fps (335mps)

MASCHINENPISTOLE 5 (MP5), MP5A2 and MP5A3
Federal Republic of Germany
Heckler & Koch GmbH, Oberndorf-am-Neckar
9mm Pist Patr 08 (9mm Parabellum)
The MP5 is derived—by way of the earlier HK54—from the successful Heckler & Koch rifle series insofar as it uses the same type of roller-locked delayed blowback operation, thus permitting it to fire from a closed bolt with a considerable improvement in accuracy.

Constructed largely of stampings, with plastic furniture, the MP5 is a well-built and reliable weapon which at present forms part of the equipment of the German Bundespolizei and Bundes-Grenz-Schütz (border police), and it is currently being evaluated by other agencies.

There are two variations of the MP5 at present available: the MP5A2, which has a permanently attached plastic stock, and the MP5A3 with a telescopic metal stock. Both are capable of automatic or single-shot fire and can be fitted with any of three different magazines.
(data: MP5A2)
Length: 26.77in (680mm)
Weight unloaded: 5lb 6oz (2.45kg)

▲The MP5A2 (Heckler & Koch).   ▼The MP5A3 (Heckler & Koch).

Barrel: 8.85in (225mm), 4 grooves, right-hand twist
Magazine: 10, 15 or 30-round detachable box
Cyclic rate: 650rpm
Muzzle velocity: c.1312fps (400mps)
(data: MP5A3)
Length, stock extended: 26.00in (660mm)
Length, stock retracted: 19.29in (490mm)
Weight unloaded: 5lb 10oz (2.55kg)
Barrel: 8.85in (225mm), 4 grooves, right-hand twist
Magazine: 10, 15 or 30-round detachable box
Cyclic rate: 650rpm
Muzzle velocity: c.1312fps (400mps)

MASCHINENPISTOLE HK53
Federal Republic of Germany
Heckler & Koch GmbH, Oberndorf-am-Neckar
5.56mm x 45mm (0.223in)

The HK53 is virtually the same weapon as the MP5, but chambered for the 5.56 mm cartridge. The idea of a submachine-gun in this calibre may at first seem strange, as until now pistol ammunition has been almost exclusively used in this class of weapon. The 5.56mm bullet has, however, a lethality and stopping power disproportionate to its size and the round might well prove successful in this role —and, of course, if the rifles, machine-guns and submachine-guns of an army are all chambered for the same round, logistics are greatly simplified.

The HK53 has yet to be adopted by any military force, but time will tell. The sights are graduated to 400m and are fully adjustable for windage and elevation, and there is a distinct possibility that the HK53 (though classified by its makers as a submachine-gun) could become a very useful assault rifle.

Length, stock extended: 30.11in (765mm)
Length, stock retracted: 22.00in (560mm)
Weight unloaded: 7lb 6oz (3.35kg)
Barrel: 8.85in (225mm),
Magazine: 40-round detachable box
Cyclic rate: 600rpm
Muzzle velocity: c.2460fps (760mps)

◁ The Hungarian 39M, designed by Kiraly. The weapon is chambered for the powerful 9mm 'Mauser Export' cartridge, and the magazine folds forward into the stock (RSAF).

◁ The Hungarian 43M, a modification of the earlier 1939 design. The magazine can again fold forward (RSAF).

◁ The current Hungarian 'submachine-gun'—a much-shortened version of the standard AKM assault rifle (RSAF).

◁ The Israeli-designed 9mm Uzi, as manufactured in Belgium by Fabrique Nationale (authors' collection).

GEPISZTOLY 39M, GEPISZTOLY 43M
Hungary
Fegyver és Löserdyár, Budapest
9mm töltény 39M ('9mm cartridge M39')

The 43M was developed from the earlier 39M (designed by Pal Kiraly), few of which were made. The 43M is a sound design incorporating some unusual features; it fires the powerful 9mm Mauser round and, in order to reduce the jump and 'climb' when firing with a light weapon, it uses a form of retarded blowback as the bolt is in two parts, the smaller of which forces the larger backwards at a suitable mechanical disadvantage. The long wooden forestock has a slot into which the magazine can be folded and, when this is done, a cover snaps over the feed port. The magazine holds 40 rounds, a number infrequently encountered, and the rearsight is graduated to 600 metres—which seems a little optimistic. The 43M is very well made, incorporating many machined components. It served the Hungarian Army through the latter stages of World War 2 until finally replaced in the postwar era by Soviet weapons.

(data: 39M)
Length: 41.00in (1041mm)
Weight unloaded: 9lb 0oz (4.08kg)
Barrel: 17.75in (450mm), 6 grooves, right-hand twist
Magazine: 20 or 40-round detachable box
Cyclic rate: 730rpm
Muzzle velocity: c.1480fps (450mps)

(data: 43M)
Length, stock extended: 37.50in (953mm)
Length, stock folded: 29.50in (749mm)
Weight unloaded: 8lb 0oz (3.64kg)
Barrel: 16.75in (425mm), 6 grooves, right-hand twist
Magazine: 40-round detachable box
Cyclic rate: 750rpm
Muzzle velocity: c.1475fps (450mps)

SUBMACHINE-GUN 9MM UZI
Israel
Israeli Metal Industries, Tel Aviv, and Fabrique Nationale d'Armes de Guerre, Herstal-lèz-Liège
9mm Parabellum

First designed in the early 1950s and based on the Czechoslovakian vz/23 series, the Uzi is one of the best and most satisfactory submachine-guns in service today. As soon as Israel became independent in 1948 urgent steps were taken to develop a national arms industry, and the Uzi was one of the first products. It has been extensively used in the border clashes between Israel and her neighbours, as well as in the various desert wars. It is an extremely compact weapon, achieving its short length by having the bolt recessed to take the face of the breech and so having the main mass of the bolt forward of the breech; the idea was not entirely novel when the Uzi was designed, but it was amongst the first guns to use the principle so successfully. The magazine housing forms the pistol grip and the whole gun balances so well that

single-handed firing is perfectly possible. Early models had a wooden butt stock, but all of current production are fitted with a neat and strong folding stock which enables the gun to be carried by vehicle crews. West Germany has adopted the Uzi (as has the Netherlands) and it is made in Belgium under licence by Fabrique Nationale d'Armes de Guerre of Herstal, who have supplied small quantities to many South American armies. One unusual feature of the gun is a grip safety, which ensures that it will not fire if dropped

Length, stock extended: 25.00in (635mm)
Length, stock folded: 17.00in (432mm)
Weight unloaded: 7lb 10oz (3.51kg)
Barrel: 10.25in (260mm), 4 grooves, right-hand twist
Magazine: 25, 32 or 40-round detachable box
Cyclic rate: 600rpm
Muzzle velocity: c.1250fps (381mps)

MITRIAGLICE LEGGERA VILLAR PEROSA M15 or PISTOLA MITRIAGLICE RIV MODELLO 1915
Italy
Officine Villar Perosa, Villar Perosa; FIAT SpA, Torino; Canadian General Electric Company Limited, Toronto
9mm cartucchia pallottola modello 10 ('Glisenti')

This venerable gun perhaps has the distinction of being the first submachine-gun ever made; while not appearing in the form in which subsequent guns were made, it nevertheless incorporated most if not all of the features apparent in more modern weapons. It was always made as a double-barrelled gun and in the early stages of its life was used as a normal light machine-gun—a role for which, of course, it was ill suited. The first models appeared in 1915 and were immediately brought into service in the Italian Army as a light machine-gun, but after two years of war its proper potential was appreciated and it was then used very much as all submachine-guns have been since: as highly mobile, short-range firepower for foot infantry. The gun was made by a variety of Italian factories and also in Canada, and is often called either by the name of the designer (Revelli) or by the name of FIAT (one of the manufacturers) thus adding a certain amount of confusion. A form of retarded blowback was used, and a light bolt and strong spring return gave the combination a high rate of fire. The Villar Perosa appeared on a number of mountings, including tripods, fixed shields, on bicycles, and occasionally in armoured vehicles (all of which added further date designations), and the gunner was provided with a large number of spare magazines. Although the weapon did not itself have a particularly long or distinguished life, it clearly pointed the way for those that followed, and it was a notable milestone in the history of smallarms.

Many of the original Villar Perosa

weapons were later converted by the firm of Pietro Beretta SpA to provide the Beretta modello 1918.
Length: 21.00in (533mm)
Weight unloaded: 14lb 6oz (6.52kg)
Barrel: 12.50in (318mm), 6 grooves, right-hand twist
Magazine: 25-round detachable box
Cyclic rate: 1200rpm (each barrel)
Muzzle velocity: c.1200fps (365mps)

MOSCHETTO AUTOMATICO OVP
Italy
Officine Villar Perosa, Villar Perosa
9mm cartucchia pallottola modello 10 ('9mm Glisenti')

The OVP was derived from the Villar Perosa of 1915 and was produced in small numbers—in the 1920s—for the Italian Army. It uses exactly the same method of operation as the Villar Perosa and the same magazine and feed mechanism. Selective fire is possible using the two triggers; the front one gives automatic fire and the rear one gives semi-automatic fire. The bolt handle is an oddity, taking the form of a cylinder over the receiver with a slot to clear the trigger mechanism. To cock the gun the cylinder is pulled back and then returned forward. The most notable improvement over the Villar Perosa lies in the addition of a wooden stock of conventional design, and the barrel jacket acts as a forward hand guard. An aperture rearsight is fitted, but it is rather too far forward, lying just in front of the magazine housing. The OVP was still in use to a small extent at the beginning of World War 2.

Length: 35.50in (901mm)
Weight unloaded: 8lb 1oz (3.67kg)
Barrel: 11.00in (279mm), 6 grooves, right-hand twist
Magazine: 25-round detachable box
Cyclic rate: 900rpm
Muzzle velocity: c.1250fps (381mps)

MOSCHETTO AUTOMATICO BERETTA MODELLO 1918
Italy
Pietro Beretta SpA, Brescia
9mm cartucchia pallottola modello 10 ('9mm Glisenti')

The Beretta of 1918 is another of the modified versions of the original Villar Perosa (see also MOSCHETTO AUTOMATICO OVP). The action, the receiver, the feed and the barrel of the Villar Perosa were united with a new trigger mechanism and a wooden one-piece stock; a folding bayonet was also provided. The resulting gun was a great success, and so many Villar Perosa submachine-guns were converted into Berettas that the original is now scarce.

Two versions of the Beretta gun are known, one with *due grilletti* (two triggers) and one with a single trigger. The double-trigger version was capable of both semi-automatic and fully-automatic fire, the triggers acting as the selector device, but the single-trigger gun was really a semi-automatic carbine in which the fully-automatic mechanism was deleted. Both worked by a system of retarded blowback utilising two inclined planes machined in the receiver walls, whose resistance had to be

▲The Pistola Mitriaglice RIV Modello 1915—the 'Villar Perosa'—held by some to have been the first successful submachine-gun, although the Italians' tactical doctrines really prevented it being used in such a manner (RSAF).
▷The OVP, a conversion of the original Villar Perosa to provide a true submachine-gun. The gun is cocked by pushing the knurled sleeve (behind the magazine) to the rear; the weapon in the photograph has the sleeve at the limit of the cocking stroke (RSAF).
▷The Beretta modello 1918, another modification of the Villar Perosa; the double trigger mechanism gives both automatic and self-loading fire (Beretta).
▷A version of the Beretta modello 18 intended solely as a self-loading carbine (Beretta).

overcome before the bolt unit could reciprocate. This slowed the rate of fire compared to the Villar Perosa, which nonetheless used a similar type of retarding mechanism, but the automatic Beretta must have been difficult to hold.

Guns of this pattern were still in use in World War 2.

Length: 33.50in (776mm)
Weight unloaded: 7lb 3oz (3.30kg)
Barrel: 12.00in (305mm), 6 grooves, right-hand twist
Magazine: 25-round top-mounted detachable box
Cyclic rate: 900rpm
Muzzle velocity: c.1250fps (381mps)

MOSCHETTO BERETTA MODELLO 1918/30
Italy
Pietro Beretta SpA, Gardone-val-Trompia
9mm cartucchia Parabellum
The Beretta semi-automatic carbine of 1930 was based closely on the previous models of 1918, which themselves owed much to the old Villar Perosa. The principal differences were the calibre, 9mm Parabellum instead of the 9mm modello 10 Glisenti round (which of course necessitated stronger recoil springs owing to the more powerful round), and the substitution of a 25-round under-

action box magazine instead of the former top-feeding pattern. The modello 1918/30 was issued to the Italians' Milizia Forestale and also saw sales to South America.

PISTOLA MITRIAGLICE BERETTA MODELLO 38A (or 'Moschetto automatico modello 38A')
Italy
Pietro Beretta SpA, Gardone-val-Trompia
9mm Parabellum, 9mm cartucchia pallottola modello 38A
The modello 38A Beretta design was derived from a series of submachine-

◁The Beretta modello 1918/30 semi-automatic carbine; note the upward feed, which replaced the top-mounted box magazine of the earlier models (Beretta).

◁The Moschetto Automatico Beretta (MAB) modello 38A. This is the prototype with a one-port compensator (Beretta).

◁The production version of the MAB 38A, with lateral ejection (note the shape of the ejection slot) and a four-slot compensator (Beretta).

◁The MAB 38A fitted with the standard modello 38 bayonet (Beretta).

◁A wartime version of the MAB 38A. Note the shape of the stock, altered in an attempt to restrict muzzle climb, and the reversion to a large-port muzzle brake. The ejection port is also different (Beretta).

▲An experimental MAB 38A with an aluminium cooling jacket, made c.1941 (Beretta).

▲The MAB 38/42; note the large-diameter barrel, longitudinally grooved, and the two-port muzzle brake. The ejection port has been returned to the left side of the receiver (Beretta).

guns dating back to the 1918 type. It was an excellent design, very well made, and long lasting: it went into mass production from the start and continued to be made in quite large numbers until 1950. The modello 38A equipped the Italian Army throughout World War 2 and was also supplied to the German and Romanian armies. Although fairly large and heavy—a legacy of its ancestry—the gun was popular with those who used it and has survived in many parts of the world. Early models were expensively made from machined steel and carried both a bayonet and a muzzle compensator. These refinements were dropped in later wartime versions and, by 1941, a certain amount of sheet-steel had found its way into the construction and the bolt had been modified slightly. Apart from these, the gun remained the same to the end of its life. A special high velocity 9mm cartridge was developed for this gun, called the 9mm cartucchia pallottola modello 38A, and this round gave some credence to the rearsight adjustment which went up to 500 metres. This ammunition was separately and distinctly packed from the other 9mm

varieties used in the Italian services. Beretta produced a variety of magazines for this gun, varying in size from 10 to 40 rounds, and in two types. A distinctive feature of this Beretta lies in the provision of twin triggers, the forward one giving semi-automatic fire and the rear one providing fully automatic operation.

Length: 37.50in (953mm)
Weight unloaded: 9lb 4oz (4.26kg)
Barrel: 12.50in (318mm), 6 grooves, right-hand twist
Magazine: 10, 20, 30 or 40-round detachable box
Cyclic rate: 600rpm
Muzzle velocity: c.1370fps (417mps)

PISTOLA MITRIAGLICE BERETTA MODELLO 38/42
Italy
Pietro Beretta SpA, Gardone-val-Trompia
9mm Parabellum
Beretta's modello 38A proved to be too expensive and too difficult to produce in the quantities necessary in wartime, and it soon became necessary to look for a simpler model. The modello 38/42

◁The MAB 38/42, production type, with a slimmer tapered barrel not found on the prototype (Beretta).
◁The MAB 38/44, basically a slightly modified version of the 38/42 and 38/43 (Beretta).
◁The folding stock version of the MAB 38/49, known as the MAB modello 49 di Regia Marina (1949 Navy model) (Beretta).
◁The 1956 series of the MAB modello 49 di Regia Marina, characterised by the addition of the muzzle of a folding bayonet (Beretta).
▼A version of the MAB 38/49 with a folding—as opposed to telescoping—stock (Beretta).

is a modified version incorporating a number of changes, the most noticeable of which are the shortening of the barrel and the removal of the barrel jacket. The receiver is made from sheet steel, and so are several of the other parts; the wooden stock is cut square at the front and the sights, trigger guard, and other minor parts are much simplified. A new bolt handle was designed with a form of dust cover incorporated, which undoubtedly stemmed from the experiences of the Italian Army in the Western Desert. However, the 38/42 is still the same weapon as the modello 38A and, despite the simplifications, is still made to high standards. The rate of fire was slightly reduced and only 9mm Parabellum ammunition was used, as it was found to be impractical in wartime to issue a separate round for submachine-guns. The German and Romanian Armies also took delivery of this model, and it may still be found either in service or in reserve stocks elsewhere.
Length: 31.50in (798mm)
Weight unloaded: 7lb 3oz (3.30kg)
Barrel: 8.50in (216mm), 6 grooves, right-hand twist
Magazine: 20 or 40-round detachable box
Cyclic rate: 550rpm
Muzzle velocity: c.1250fps (381mps)

MOSCHETTI AUTOMATICHI BERETTA, MODELLO 38/43 and MODELLO 38/44
Italy
Pietro Beretta SpA, Gardone-val-Trompia
9mm Parabellum
The 38/43 and 38/44 were minor variations of the earlier 38/42, and hence of the original Moschetto Automatico Beretta Modello 1938A. The 38/43 was an intermediate production stage between the 1942 and 1944 patterns, making use of a stamped receiver which was married to the bolt components of the 38/42. The external surface of the barrels of these weapons, together with the quality of the rifling, were of indifferent execution; like the 38/42, the external surface was longitudinally grooved.

The moschetto modello 38/44, production of which began at the beginning of the year, was a simplified version of the 1943 type making use of a stamped receiver and some redesigned internal components—which resulted in a lower cyclic rate of approximately 600rpm.
Length: 31.50in (798mm)
Weight unloaded: 7lb 3oz (3.30kg)
Barrel: 8.50in (216mm), 6 grooves, right-hand twist
Magazine: 20 or 40-round detachable box
Cyclic rate: 550rpm
Muzzle velocity: c.1250fps (381mps)

PISTOLA MITRIAGLICE BERETTA MODELLO 38/49
Italy
Pietro Beretta SpA, Gardone-val-Trompia
9mm Parabellum
The modello 38/49, as its name suggests, is yet another version of the remarkably successful 38A and differs little from the modello 38/42, simply being a postwar version of the latter intended for sale to any country who would buy it. Minor modifications such as bayonet fittings were added to the whim of the customer, and the resultant sales were considerable. The countries who bought the weapon were mostly those too small to have arms industries of their own, which means that this weapon is to be found in Asia, North Africa and South America. At least two versions were made with folding stocks, one in which the unit folded forward on a swivel behind the triggers and another in which a wire stock telescoped. Both these models had wooden pistol grips for the trigger hand. All were similar in operation and, although one model had only a grip safety—which is unusual for submachine-guns—it does not appear to have been produced in very large numbers. These guns were the last to be produced with the well-known double trigger, and with the end of the series in about 1961 it went out altogether. All these versions of the 1938A had been the work of one brilliant designer, Tullio Marengoni, and his practices were not continued after his death.

△The MAB 38/49, folding stock type, with the stock folded forward under the gun (Beretta).

△The MAB 38/49 modello 5 (Beretta).

△The MAB 38/49 modello 4 (Beretta).

▽The FNAB modello 1943 (RSAF).

▷An example of the FNAB modello 43, with the stock folded and the magazine unit folded forward (RSAF).

▷A wood-stocked Franchi submachine-gun, c.1955; a prototype of the LF57 (RSAF).

PISTOLA MITRIAGLICE FNAB MODELLO 1943
Italy
Fabbrica Nazionale d'Armi, Brescia
9mm Parabellum

The FNAB was manufactured in small numbers during World War 2 and is an interesting and unusual design. Expensively produced by traditional methods of milling and machining, it would today be an economic impossibility. The butt and magazine housing fold to make an extremely compact unit and the barrel jacket incorporates a compensator.

The operation of the gun is also unusual, for it is a delayed blowback using a two-piece bolt unit with a combined accelerator/retarder lever separating the units. When fired, this lever first retards the opening of the breech by engaging with the receiver, then—after unlocking—it pivots to act as an accelerator and force the bolt body rearwards. On the return stroke the front section of the bolt chambers the round, the lever rotates to lock, and the rear section of the bolt is driven by the recoil spring to operate the firing pin.

Length, stock extended: 31.15in (790mm)
Length, stock retracted: 20.75in (527mm)
Weight unloaded: 7lb 2oz (3.25kg)
Barrel: 7.80in (198mm), 6 grooves, right-hand twist
Magazine: 20 or 40-round detachable box
Cyclic rate: 400rpm
Muzzle velocity: c.1250fps (381mps)

PISTOLA MITRIAGLICE TZ45
Italy (Burma)

Tonon e Zorzoli, Gardone-val-Trompia
9mm Parabellum

This weapon was developed in Italy in 1944 and a small number were produced during the last months of World War 2. It is a conventional blowback weapon, typical of its era, with the addition of a simple grip safety on the magazine housing which locks the bolt in a similar manner to the later and better-known Madsen. The telescoping butt is held in the closed position by an index plate beneath the barrel casing.

The weapon was briefly evaluated by various Allied agencies after the war, but the general opinion seems to have been unfavourable: most reports speak of the TZ45's unreliability in prolonged use and its poor standard of manufacture. In spite of this, the designers managed to sell it to the Burmese Army c.1950 and —as the BA52—it was produced in Burma for some years.

Length, stock extended: 33.50in (851mm)
Length, stock retracted: 21.50in (546mm)
Weight unloaded: 7lb 3oz (3.26kg)
Barrel: 9.00in (229mm), 6 grooves, right-hand twist
Magazine: 40-round detachable box
Cyclic rate: 550rpm
Muzzle velocity: c.1250fps (381mps)

PISTOLA MITRIAGLICE FRANCHI MODELLO LF-57
Italy
Luigi Franchi SpA, Brescia
9mm Parabellum

The Franchi was first produced in 1956 and, when modified in the following year, became the modello 57. It was the first complete gun produced by the firm of Luigi Franchi of Brescia and although interesting and well made it was not a commercial success. Small numbers were ordered for the Italian Navy in the early 1960s. The LF-57 uses the principle of the recessed bolt head to reduce the length of the weapon, much in the same way as the Beretta modello 12. The difference lies in the fact that the Franchi carries the mass of the bolt above the barrel rather than around it as in the Beretta, thus simplifying manufacture to some extent. In fact, the Franchi is well designed and the great majority of the parts are made from stampings and pressings: the entire sides of the gun are made in one piece and the two are joined by one long seam. The weapon dismantles very easily as the barrel, for instance, is held by a single barrel nut. There is no furniture in the accepted sense, the pistol grip being entirely of steel, and the sights are rather crude fixtures. The tubular stock folds sideways on to the right side of the receiver. The Franchi was a neat weapon, but it was not significantly better than any of the many others being produced at the same time and it failed to make an impact.

Length, stock extended: 27.00in (686mm)
Length, stock folded: 16.50in (419mm)
Weight unloaded: 7lb 0oz (3.22kg)
Barrel: 8.00in (203mm), 6 grooves, right-hand twist
Magazine: 20 or 40-round detachable box
Cyclic rate: 500rpm
Muzzle velocity: c.1200fps (365mps)

PISTOLA MITRIAGLICE BERETTA MODELLO 12
Italy
Pietro Beretta SpA, Gardone-val-Trompia
9mm Parabellum

The modello 12 is another of Beretta's postwar designs, produced in the late 1950s and offered for sale for a few years into the early 1960s. It is a modern design and owes little to the previous varieties from the same factory. It is small, compact, very well made, and amongst the first to use the idea of recessing the barrel into the bolt head. This system allows the overall length of the weapon to be much reduced without sacrificing barrel length or bolt weight. The principle has become a general practice in recent designs and it is claimed, with some justice, that it greatly reduces the tendency of the muzzle to climb in fully-automatic fire. The modello 12 was designed for rapid and simple manufacture and is largely constructed of steel stampings and pressings welded together. It can be fitted with either a folding metal stock or a removable wooden one, the latter being slightly heavier.

Length, stock extended: 25.40in (645mm)
Length, stock folded: 16.40in (416mm)
Weight unloaded: 6lb 8oz (2.95kg)
Barrel: 8.00in (203mm), 6 grooves, right-hand twist
Magazine: 20, 30 or 40-round detachable box
Cyclic rate: 550rpm
Muzzle velocity: c.1250fps (381mps)

◀The stages in the design of a submachine-gun, in this case of the Beretta modello 12. The first step, top, bears a distinct family resemblance to the MAB series from which it was obviously derived. The second gun, step two, incorporates lessons learned from the Czech vz/23—especially the use of a bolt partially shrouding the barrel, and with the bulk of the reciprocating mechanism forward of the breech. The third gun represents an attempt to streamline and refine the second. It is noticeable that all the guns have a grip safety on the rear of the pistol grip. The fourth and fifth guns are closer in appearance to the final modello 12, and in the last the grip safety has been moved to the grip's front surface. (All Beretta.)
▷The final modello 12 (Beretta).
▷The Japanese Type 100 submachine-gun of 1940, showing the peculiar auxiliary bayonet bar on the underside of the barrel casing (RSAF).

**100 SHIKI KIKANSHOJU (Type 100
    submachine-gun)**
Japan
State arsenals (see text)
8mm Taisho 14

Japan was surprisingly slow to adopt
submachine-guns, although they are the
ideal jungle weapon and the intention of
dominating the Pacific had been germi-
nating for several years. Sensible weapon
development was not, however, a feature
of the pre-World War 2 Japanese High
Command and, apart from a few Berg-

mann and MP28/II guns bought in the
1930s, it was 1940 before a native design
appeared; the Type 100, which used the
weak 8mm Japanese automatic pistol
cartridge, was well-made and of reasonably conventional design. About 10,000
of the original Type 100, with perhaps
another 7,500 of the folding-butt parachutist's model were made in the years
before 1943. The former were manufactured by Kokura Army Arsenal and
the latter at Nagoya. The guns were not
really successful, largely because little

factory space could be spared for a
continuous development programme and
hence little effort was given to improving
the weapons; another drawback lay in
the poor quality of the ammunition
which gave frequent jams.

In 1944 the Japanese introduced an
improved model, which differed only in
minor respects, and again only about
8,000 were produced at one of Nagoya
Arsenal's subplants before the end of the
war. The manufacture of the Type 100's
1944 version was much simplified to

eliminate as far as possible the valuable machine time which would be otherwise wasted on non-essentials: this consequently meant the appearance of much rough welding, the sights were fixed, and the firing pin could be replaced if it fractured. The rate of fire of the 1944 variety was considerably greater than that of the original 1940 gun.

Length: 35.00in (889mm)
Weight unloaded: 8lb 8oz (3.83kg)
Barrel: 9.00in (228mm), 6 grooves, right-hand twist
Magazine: 30-round detachable box
Cyclic rate: 450 rpm (1940), 800 rpm (1944)
Muzzle velocity: c.1100fps (335mps)

MITRAILETTES 'SOLA-SUPER' and 'SOLA-LEGER'
Luxembourg
Société Luxembourgeoise d'Armes SA, Ettelbruck
9mm Parabellum

The rise of the submachine-gun during World War 2, together with the inferior character of many of the weapons adopted, led to a vast number of designs being marketed in the years immediately following the war in the hope of landing a military contract to replace the wartime weapons. The 'Sola-Super' was manufactured in small quantities in 1954–7 and marketed with some success in North Africa and South America. It

was evaluated by several other countries but was never adopted by any major power.

The Sola is a conventional blowback weapon capable either of firing single shots or fully automatic operation. The gun was obviously designed with an eye to cheapness and simplicity of production, for there is considerable use of stamped components and the design is pared to the point of having no more than thirty-eight components. It is for its class a long and cumbersome weapon, though the long barrel with an integral compensator gives a reasonable degree of accuracy and an above-average velocity. There is, however, nothing in the

◁Two views of the 1944-pattern Type 100 submachine-gun. Note the asymmetric slots in the compensator, which were intended to counteract the gun's inclination to climb upwards and to the right (Tom Nelson).
◁The Sola-Legér (RSAF).

design which has not been done as well (if not better) elsewhere and this was probably why the Sola failed to gain wide acceptance.

In an attempt to make it a commercial success the makers redesigned the weapon, doing away with the bulky trigger mechanism housing and shortening the barrel. The resulting 'Light Model' was put on the market in 1957 but met with even less success than the original 'Super'; with this, the company decided to quit the armaments field.

(data: Sola-Super)
Length, stock extended: 35.00in (889mm)
Length, stock retracted: 24.00in (610mm)
Weight unloaded: 6lb 6oz (2.90kg)
Barrel: 12.00in (305mm), 6 grooves, right-hand twist
Magazine: 32-round detachable box
Cyclic rate: 550rpm
Muzzle velocity: c.1400fps (425mps)

KARABIN MASZYNOWY WZ/43–52
Poland
Fabryka Broni w Warszawie, Warszawa
7.62mm Soviet M30

The Polish Army was supplied with the usual armoury of Soviet weapons after World War 2, and among them were some submachine-guns of the PPS43 type. In this the Poles were fortunate since there are few instances of this weapon being sent anywhere else in the Communist bloc, and a variant of the PPS43 was developed and made in Poland under the designation wz/43-52. Basically it is the same gun fitted with a wooden stock and a few small production alterations to suit the Warsaw Arsenal machinery. It employs the same steel stamping processes for its manufacture and the only marked difference between the Soviet and Polish versions is that the latter is capable of single shot fire as well as fully automatic fire.

PISTOLA AMETRALLADORA STAR SI35
Spain
Bonifacio Echeverria SA, Eibar
9mm cartucho Largo

The Echeverria company of Eibar undertook a great deal of experimentation with submachine-gun designs during the 1930s, and the SI35 is representative of their efforts—perhaps the most involved of the models. Stemming from a self-loader, the series stayed much the same in appearance and mechanism until c.1942, when the company changed to more simple designs, broadly copying contemporary German models.

The SI35 incorporated delayed blowback operation performed by a cam plate engaging in the receiver body; a hold-open device indicated when the magazine was empty, and, most unusual of all, a switch was provided to adjust the rate of fire to either 300rpm or 700rpm.

While the weapon functioned well, it was unnecessarily complicated in design and difficult and expensive to mass-produce. A slightly altered version was tested in 1942 by the United States Army, under the name 'Atlantic', and the SI35 was itself tested by the British Army at about the same time. Neither country considered the design suited to wartime production and the gun was rejected.

Length: 35.45in (900mm)
Weight unloaded: 8lb 4oz (3.74kg)
Barrel: 10.60in (269mm), 6 grooves, right-hand twist
Magazine: 10, 30 or 40-round detachable box
Cyclic rate: 300rpm or 700rpm
Muzzle velocity: c.1350fps (412mps)

PISTOLA AMETRALLADORA 'LABORA', 1938–9
Spain
Industrio de Guerra do Cataluña, Cataluña
9mm cartucho Largo

This weapon was manufactured in the last few months of the Spanish Civil War (1936–9) and, in view of this, is remarkable in being a most expensively machined design rather than the inferior weapon one might expect in such circumstances. This was probably due to the availability of skilled gunsmiths and traditional machinery and the general

▼The Star S135 (RSAF).

absence of facilities for mass-production.

Of uncomplicated blowback design, the Labora is of interest because it is not a direct copy of any existing weapon, though the bolt has obvious affinities with early Schmeisser designs. The recoil spring is much stronger than average, which was probably necessitated by the combination of a powerful cartridge and an unusually light bolt.

Few examples of the Labora remain; with the end of the Spanish Civil War production ceased, and it was unlikely that such a costly weapon would ever again be put into production.

Length: 31.75in (806mm)
Weight unloaded: 9lb 6oz (4.25kg)
Barrel: 10.25in (262mm), 4 grooves, right-hand twist
Magazine: 36-round detachable box
Cyclic rate: 750rpm
Muzzle velocity: c.1300fps (397mps)

PISTOLA AMETRALLADORA STAR MODELO Z45

Spain
Bonifacio Echeverria y Compania SA, Guernica
9mm cartucho Largo, 9mm Parabellum

The Z45 is a Spanish adaptation of the German MP40 with the addition of some minor improvements. It was manufactured in Spain for several years from 1944 onwards and was adopted in the late 1940s by the Spanish police and armed forces. The Echeverria firm used the original German drawings for their basic design but added some extra safety features such as a bolt lock to prevent accidental discharges. Selective fire was introduced, controlled by means of a two-position trigger, the initial movement of which gave semi-automatic fire and further pressure gave full automatic fire. A muzzle compensator was also used as a

barrel lock and, by rotating it, the barrel is very easily removed. While interesting, this feature is not one which is particularly necessary on a submachine-gun although it was claimed (by the manufacturers) that simply by changing the barrel another calibre could be used. The military version of the Z45 was fitted with the same type of folding stock as the original MP40, but another version was made with a full length wooden stock. This permitted more accuracy and to some extent prevented the gun from climbing in automatic fire. Several South American and a few Middle Eastern countries are said to have bought the Z45, but precise numbers are not known.

Length, stock extended: 33.10in (841mm)
Length, stock folded: 22.85in (580mm)
Weight unloaded: 8lb 8oz (3.87kg)

◁ An example of the Labora gun, made in Cataluña during the Spanish Civil War (1936-9); this gun is missing its magazine (RSAF).

◁ The Swedish Kulspruta pistol m/45, generally known as the 'Carl Gustav' after the manufacturers. This gun is fitted with a silencer (RSAF).

◁ The Swedish m/45B (RSAF).

Barrel: 7.75in (196mm), 6 grooves, right-
hand twist
Magazine: 10 or 30-round detachable box
Cyclic rate: 450rpm
Muzzle velocity: c.1250fps (381mps)

KULSPRUTA PISTOL M/45
Sweden
Carl Gustafs Stads Gevärfactori, Eskil-stuna
9mm patron m/39 (9mm Parabellum), 9mm patron m/39B

Sweden found herself in an uneasily neutral position during World War 2, supplying material to both sides yet without any submachine-guns for its forces. As a stop-gap some Finnish Suomi were made under licence by Husqvarna Vapenfabrik but, by 1945, a native design had emerged which was cheap and simple to produce. This, the KP m/45, is still in production and service, and has passed through several minor modifications while retaining all of its essential original characteristics. The current service weapon, the Kulspruta pistol m/45B, has a non-removable magazine housing. It is a well made gun, of conventional design and operation, although it is only capable of automatic fire. It has been sold to Egypt on a large scale (in fact, a factory was converted in Egypt to make it as the 'Port Said') and it was used by the Egyptian Army in the 1957 war with Israel. Large numbers are in service with the Swedish Army, it has also been used by Indonesia and may now be found in many other countries in varying quantities. A special high-velocity round called the 9mm patron m/39B has been developed in Sweden for this gun and, by virtue of a heavier jacket, it is claimed to have greater penetration and range than any other type of submachine-gun ammunition.

Length, stock extended: 31.75in (806mm)
Length, stock folded: 21.75in (552mm)
Weight unloaded: 7lb 9oz (3.48kg)
Barrel: 8.00in (203mm), 6 grooves, right-
hand twist
Magazine: 36 or 50-round detachable box
Cyclic rate: 600rpm
Muzzle velocity: c.1250fps (381mps)

MASCHINENPISTOLE S1–100 ('Steyr-Solothurn')
Switzerland
Waffenfabrik Solothurn AG, Solothurn
7.63mm Mauser, 7.65mm Parabellum, 9mm Parabellum, 9mm Steyr, 9mm Mauser Export

The Solothurn was widely used by the German Army during World War 2 and is often taken to be a German weapon. In fact, it was originally designed by a German—and perhaps a prototype was made in Germany in the 1920s—but the manufacture was undertaken in 1930 by the Swiss firm of Solothurn (who were then owned by Rheinische Metallwaaren- und Maschinenfabrik of Düsseldorf). It was also made in Austria by Oster-reichische Waffenfabrik-Gesellschaft at Steyr and so is often known as the Steyr-Solothurn. Worldwide sales were enjoyed until manufacture stopped in 1940 and the gun was offered in a variety of calibres to suit the user. Other variations could be obtained, including long barrels, bayonet lugs, and even a tripod mounting. Much of the general design of the Solothurn quite obviously came direct from the MP18/I and MP28/II, both of which were then current in Germany. The manufacture of the Solothurn also follows the contemporary practice, with the majority of the parts machined from solid and bearing a very high standard of finish. The resulting weapon is therefore robust and reliable. Although the official submachine-gun of the German Army was the MP40, the Solothurn was issued in quite large numbers as the Maschinenpistole 34(ö) and remained in service until 1945. Many remain in various parts of the world, although becoming steadily scarcer.

Length: 33.50in (851mm)
Weight unloaded: 8lb 8oz (3.87kg)
Barrel: 7.75in (196mm), 6 grooves, right-
hand twist
Magazine: 32-round detachable box
Cyclic rate: 500rpm
Muzzle velocity: c.1250fps (381mps)

▼An example of the beautifully-made 'Steyr-Solothurn' submachine-gun.

MASCHINENPISTOLE FURRER 41/44 (MP41/44)
Switzerland
Waffenfabrik Bern, Bern
9mm Parabellum

The MP41/44 was one of the most expensive submachine-guns ever made and a military failure in consequence: it was unnecessarily complicated and involved and should never have been accepted for service. Nevertheless, in the frightening days of 1940 when war seemed imminent, the Swiss Military Command was panicked into making the decision to take this gun. In three years only 5,000 or so complete guns were produced, largely owing to the difficulty of manufacture and the time required to make the many components. The basic trouble was the Fürrer action which, rather than a simple blowback, was recoil-actuated using a toggle system similar in principle to the Maxim gun. Thus the breech was actually locked at firing, and the toggle linkage opened sideways to the left, where a special housing was provided to cover it. Such complication is totally unnecessary on a submachine-gun, as the Swiss Army soon discovered. It was complex and heavy, and one can wonder not only at the mentality which designed it but also at those who accepted it at a time when many better and cheaper weapons could be obtained. In outline and general shape the MP41 followed the fashion of the day, adding a pistol grip for the trigger hand and a small folding handle for the forward hold. The rate of fire was high and the magazine held the rather large number of 40 rounds.

Length: 30.50in (775mm)
Weight unloaded: 11lb 7oz (5.22kg)
Barrel: 9.75in (247mm), 6 grooves, right-hand twist
Magazine: 40-round detachable box
Cyclic rate: 900rpm
Muzzle velocity: c.1300fps (396mps)

MASCHINENPISTOLE 43/44 (MP43/44)
Switzerland
Société Anonyme Suisse Hispano-Suiza, Genève
9mm Parabellum

Although credited here as a product of Hispano-Suiza, this is actually the Finnish Suomi made under licence in Switzerland. It was hurriedly bought when it was realised that the MP41 would not be forthcoming in sufficient numbers to equip the Swiss Army within the time allowed. The Suomi design was bought from Finland as one of the few good designs commercially available in 1943 and was made in quite large numbers by the end of the war. It is little different from the original Finnish model, although some have bayonet lugs to carry the standard Swiss rifle bayonet and the sights were simplified. The Suomi 71-round drum magazine was not adopted and a 50-round double-row box was used instead. This excellent gun remained in service in Switzerland until long after the end of the war and is still believed to be held in reserve stocks.

Length: 34.00in (863mm)
Weight unloaded: 10lb 8oz (4.79kg)
Barrel: 12.50in (318mm), 6 grooves, right-hand twist
Magazine: 50-round detachable box
Cyclic rate: 800rpm
Muzzle velocity: c.1300fps (396mps)

MASCHINENPISTOLE 48 (MP48)
Switzerland
Schweizerische Industrie-Gesellschaft (SIG), Neuhausen-am-Rheinfalls
9mm Parabellum

The MP48 was among the first submachine-gun to be completely designed by Schweizerische Industrie-Gesellschaft (SIG), although they had been famous international arms manufacturers for many years. Their previous weapons had been noted for excellent finish and careful machining, but they were often relatively heavy. The MP48 was unusual in using precision castings for many parts and not the more normal stampings or pressings. If properly made, precision castings do not require machining, and this was what SIG were anxious to avoid in order to keep the price down. The MP48 followed two other models, the MP44 and the MP46, both of which generally resembled the MP48 and shared the folding magazine. This was a SIG innovation in the early 1930s and was continued for some years despite little success in the sales field. No mechanical safety was provided on the MP48 and it was taken that this would be applied by folding the magazine forwards under the barrel, so cutting off the ammunition supply. A spring-loaded shutter closed the feed opening when the magazine was folded and, of course, the weapon was easier to carry. A tubular steel stock could be retracted to reduce the overall length. Despite its novelties, the MP48 offered very little that other cheaper guns did not also offer and only a few sales were made, mostly outside Europe.

Length, stock extended: 28.00in (711mm)
Length, stock folded: 22.50in (570mm)
Weight unloaded: 6lb 7oz (2.96kg)
Barrel: 7.75in (196mm), 6 grooves, right-hand twist
Magazine: 40-round detachable box
Cyclic rate: 700rpm
Muzzle velocity: c.1250fps (381mps)

MASCHINENPISTOLE 310 (MP310)
Switzerland
Schweizerische Industrie-Gesellschaft, Neuhausen-am-Rheinfalls
9mm Parabellum

Developed by SIG in the early 1950s (from the MP48) the MP310 was a standard pattern of blowback-operated submachine-gun, although several unusual features were incorporated in the design. The magazine was a folding pattern, released by a spring-catch on the left side of the magazine housing to

◁◁ Two versions of the SIG-designed MP41 submachine-gun, which competed in the 1941 trials without success: the Fürrer weapon was adopted instead. The SIG gun was based on the earlier MK33 (or MKMO), a delayed blowback gun, and on the MK37 (MKMS), a standard blowback pattern. Although not adopted by the Swiss, the SIG-MP41 provided the basis for the postwar MP46, MP48 and MP310 (SIG).

◁ The SIG Maschinenpistole 310, developed in the early 1950s from the MP48 (SIG).

◁ Another view of the MP310, this time with the magazine folded forward (SIG).

fold forward underneath the barrel: in fact SIG often made use of this feature on their weapons of this class, claiming for it safety and the fact that the folding unit gave the soldier 'a remarkable mobility in combat'. The MP310 trigger mechanism was constructed to give a two-stage pull, the first of which was used to fire single shots and the latter full automatic fire. A drum-type rearsight was used with settings for 50, 100, 200 and 300m. Despite the attractive features of the MP310, and the substitution by SIG of plastics and precision castings for some of their earlier weapons' expensive machined components, the gun failed to sell in large numbers; it is probably true to say that there were war-surplus guns to be had at far cheaper prices, and that this conspired against the SIG weapon.

Length, stock extended: 28.95in (735mm)
Length, stock folded: 24.00in (610mm)
Weight unloaded: 7lb 0oz (3.15kg)
Barrel: 7.83in (200mm), 6 grooves, right-hand twist
Magazine: 40-round detachable box
Cyclic rate: 900 rpm
Muzzle velocity: c.1200fps (365mps)

MASCHINENPISTOLE 'REXIM-FAVOR'
Switzerland
Société Anonyme Suisse Rexim, Genève
9mm Parabellum
The Rexim Company entered the arms business in the 1950s with a design which some aver was stolen from the French, although whether or not there is anything in that tale is of little consequence; the subsequent development of the weapon, however, was just as involved. Although Rexim were set up in Switzerland the weapons were made for them in Spain, and samples were hawked round the world with little success until the company failed in 1957. After this, the Spanish manufacturers marketed the gun under their own name, La Coruña, with equally little success.

The version shown here is the 'Favor' —the first model to be offered. It was later slightly simplified for manufacture and the production model, which has a perforated barrel jacket, was known as the 'FV Mark IV'. A variety of stock patterns and barrel lengths were produced as alternative models during prototype development and offered in the company's somewhat optimistic brochures, but the basic configuration of the weapon remained the same.

The operation of the Rexim was unnecessarily complicated, firing as it did from a closed bolt by allowing an independent annular hammer to be released by the trigger to operate the firing pin. It is possible that a few of these weapons may still remain in the Middle East, but they are now uncommon.

Length, stock extended: 34.35in (873mm)
Length, stock retracted: 24.35in (617mm)
Weight unloaded: 10lb 5oz (4.67kg)
Barrel: 13.35in (339mm), 6 grooves, right-hand twist
Magazine: 32-round detachable box (German MP40 magazine)
Cyclic rate: 600rpm
Muzzle velocity: c.1400fps (427mps)

PISTOLET-PULEMET DEGTYAREVA OBRAZETS 1934/38G ('Degtyarev machine pistol, model of the year 1938')
Union of Soviet Socialist Republics
State factories
7.62mm patron o30g
The PPD is really a series of several similar weapons produced in the Soviet Union during the period 1934–40. The model illustrated was a standard issue to the army, produced until 1940—when it was supplemented by the PPD40 and then replaced by the PPSh41. It is a fairly conventional gun for its time, although it looks as though it drew much inspiration from the German MP28/II and the Finnish Suomi. The mechanism is quite straightforward but must have been somewhat expensive to manufacture as the components are machined from high-quality steel; there are no stampings. The 25-round box magazine feeds from the underside, and an unusual pattern of drum could also be supplied. This was the first Soviet weapon to utilise the drum magazine which later became a regular feature of all but two of the entire series of Soviet submachine-guns. The 7.62mm round was, of course, the standard Soviet pistol round, firing a comparatively light bullet at a high muzzle velocity: this increased velocity, however, did not give it any greater effectiveness than that of the 9mm Parabellum or any more range. One feature of this gun, and all the remainder of the series, was that the barrel was chromed: an expensive process but popular with the Soviet designers as it considerably extended barrel life.

Length: 30.50in (775mm)
Weight unloaded: 8lb 4oz (3.76kg)
Barrel: 10.75in (272mm), 4 grooves, right-hand twist
Magazine: 25-round detachable box or 71-round drum
Cyclic rate: 800rpm
Muzzle velocity: c.1640fps (500mps)

PISTOLET-PULEMET DEGTYAREVA OBRAZETS 1940G
Union of Soviet Socialist Republics
State manufacture
7.62mm patron o30g
The Red Army began experimenting with submachine-guns as early as 1926, but early designs of Tokarev and Korovin were manufactured in token numbers only, and it was not until the middle 1930s that Degtyarev produced a serviceable weapon. This, the PPD34/38, was largely based on the original Bergmann MP18, differing mainly in the use of a drum magazine which had a peculiar 'extended lip' which fitted into a maga-

▷The Rexim-Favor FV Mark 4, designed by the Swiss Colonel Favier after whom it was named. The tubular bayonet is missing from its housing under the barrel. It was normally carried on the gun, backwards in the housing with the blade underneath the barrel casing (RSAF).
▷The Russian PPD submachine-gun of 1940 (RSAF).
▷The PPSh 1941, one of the crudest-made guns ever issued on a large scale—but undeniably effective and reliable (RSAF).

zine housing in a similar fashion to a box magazine.

This was replaced in 1940 by the PPD40—a better weapon in most respects; it was designed with more of an eye to manufacturing processes, and the peculiar drum magazine was replaced by a model based on the Finns' Suomi drum—an open-topped pattern which slid into a recess in the fore-end of the gun. The PPD40 was well made of good material and was obviously a peacetime product; when the war ensnared the Soviets the PPD was abandoned for those of even simpler make.

Length: 30.60in (777mm)
Weight unloaded: 8lb 2oz (3.70kg)
Barrel: 10.60in (269mm), 4 grooves,
*　right-hand twist*
Magazine: 71-round drum
Cyclic rate: 800rpm
Muzzle velocity: c.1640fps (500mps)

PISTOLET-PULEMET SHPAGINA OBRAZETS 1941G
Union of Soviet Socialist Republics State factories
7.62mm patron o30g

Two national catastrophes contributed to the Soviet enthusiasm for submachine-guns. The first was the Winter War with Finland in 1939–40 when the Finns used submachine-guns with devastating effect during close combat in the forests, and the second was the German invasion of 1941 when the Russians lost in the retreats both huge quantities of small arms and much of their engineering capability. There then arose an urgent demand for a light and simple weapon capable of a high volume of fire, and the answer to this was the PPSh41, designed by Georgii Shpagin. It was much cheaper and quicker to make than the preceding models and was finished roughly; the

barrel was still chromed, however, and there was never any doubt about the weapon's effectiveness. Stripping was simplicity itself, as the receiver hinged open to reveal the bolt and spring. There was no selector lever on some of the late models, when the gun was capable only of automatic fire, and the magazine was the proved and tried 71-round Suomi drum. The rate of fire was high, but a rudimentary compensator helped to steady the climb of the muzzle. About five million PPSh guns had been made by 1945, and the Soviets adapted their infantry tactics to take full advantage of such huge numbers: often complete units were armed with nothing else. In Russia the PPSh went out of service in the late 1950s but it has been supplied in enormous quantities to the satellite and pro-Communist countries, so that it will still be seen for many years. It has

◁The PPS of 1943, with its stock folded forwards over the top of the receiver (RSAF).

◁The PPS43 with the stock extended and the magazine removed (SIM).

◁The British Lanchester submachine-gun Mark 1, a copy of the German MP28 with a Lee-Enfield type stock and a bayonet lug for the Bayonet Number 1 Mark 1 (RSAF).

◁A comparison between the Sten Mark 1 (top) and the Sten Mark 2 (bottom) (RSAF).

been made in various Communist countries, and there is a multitude of variants. At one time the German Army converted a few captured guns to 9mm by changing the barrel and magazine housing—a policy of desperation.

Length: 33.00in (838mm)
Weight unloaded: 8lb 0oz (3.64kg)
Barrel: 10.50in (266mm), 4 grooves, right-hand twist
Magazine: 35-round detachable box or 71-round drum
Cyclic rate: 900rpm
Muzzle velocity: c.1600fps (488mps)

PISTOLET-PULEMET SUDAYEVA OBRAZETS 1942G, PISTOLET-PULEMET SUDAYEVA OBRAZETS 1943G
Union of Soviet Socialist Republics
State factories
7.62mm patron o30g

The PPS guns are to some extent an oddity in the Soviet armoury since the policy during World War 2 was one of rigid concentration upon one model for each type of weapon. During the siege of Leningrad, however, the supply of guns ran very low, and the PPS42 was hurriedly manufactured in a local factory to a design best suited to the equipment available. Quite naturally it was simple in the extreme, but it proved surprisingly effective and continued to be made after the siege was raised; it was then improved to the PPS43, which differed only in the design of the folding stock, the form of the safety catch and in the barrel casing (which, in the PPS42, had a vertical joint in front of the magazine housing). In all about one million of the PPS were made, and they continued in service after the war for a few years. Unusually for a Soviet gun, the PPS used a box magazine holding 35 rounds and, so far as is known, it was never adapted to take the more popular drum. Despite its extreme simplicity bordering on crudity, the PPS was highly effective. It has now disappeared, having been rarely offered to other Communist countries. The Finnish m/44 and m/44-46 series, and the Spanish/German DUX guns, were derived from the PPS.

(data: PPS42)
Length, stock extended: 35.00in (889mm)
Length, stock folded: 25.00in (635mm)
Weight unloaded: 6lb 8oz (2.99kg)
Barrel: 10.75in (272mm), 4 grooves, right-hand twist
Magazine: 35-round detachable box
Cyclic rate: 700rpm
Muzzle velocity: c.1600fps (488mps)

(data: PPS43)
Length: 32.25in (820mm)
Weight unloaded: 7lb 6oz (3.39kg)
Barrel: 10.00in (254mm), 4 grooves, right-hand twist
Magazine: 35-round detachable box
Cyclic rate: 700rpm
Muzzle velocity: c.1600fps (488mps)

MACHINE CARBINE, 9MM LANCHESTER MARK 1 and MARK 1*
United Kingdom
Sterling Engineering Company, Dagenham, Essex
9mm SAA Ball (9mm Parabellum)

The Lanchester was made in 1941 and is memorable not for any oddity in its design nor feature in its manufacture but for the fact that it was ever made in the form that it was. It was nothing more than a direct copy of the German MP28/II designed by Hugo Schmeisser and the only visible differences were minor and not readily distinguishable. The gun was conceived in haste and whatever may be said against the principle of copying one's adversaries' weapons, the MP28 was a proven design of known reliability. So too was the Lanchester. It took its name from its designer and was made by the Sterling Engineering Company exclusively—and somewhat unusually—for the Royal Navy. But 1941 was not a normal time in the United Kingdom and expediency was the order of the day: the Lanchester did all that was required of it until it was ultimately replaced in the early 1960s by the Sterling, emanating from the same factory. One change from the MP28/II was that the stock of the Lanchester was of similar pattern to that of the Rifle Number 1 (SMLE), and it had a bayonet lug to take the long bayonet (Pattern 1907 or Bayonet Number 1). Other differences lay in the design of the receiver lock catch and the magazine housing: the latter component was of solid brass, fully in the naval tradition but hardly appropriate in time of war. The magazine (again a derivation from the MP28/II) held 50 rounds, although the 32-round Sten magazine could be inserted in some weapons.

There were two versions of the Lanchester carbine; the original had a large Rifle Number 1 type of rearsight, and a selector switch on the front portion of the trigger-guard. The later Mark 1*, which was only capable of automatic fire, had a much simplified rearsight and, of course, lacked a selector switch. Most Mark 1 guns were later converted to Mark 1* standards.

Length: 33.50in (851mm)
Weight unloaded: 9lb 9oz (4.34kg)
Barrel: 8.00in (203mm), 6 grooves, right-hand twist
Magazine: 50-round detachable box
Cyclic rate: 600rpm
Muzzle velocity: c.1250fps (381mps)

MACHINE CARBINE, 9MM STEN, MARK 1
United Kingdom
Birmingham Small Arms Company Limited, Birmingham; Royal Small Arms Factory, Fazakerly, Liverpool (chief contractors)
9mm SAA Ball (9mm Parabellum)

The Sten took its name from the initials of its designers (Sheppard and Turpin)

and the Royal Small Arms Factory at Enfield, although much of the wartime production was subcontracted to other manufacturers, particularly the Birmingham Small Arms Company Limited (BSA) and other Royal Ordnance factories. It was a weapon conceived in an air of haste and extreme emergency. The United Kingdom entered World War 2 without a submachine-gun of any kind, despite the clear warnings of the Spanish Civil War, and the Blitzkreig not only caught the British Army unawares but also seriously ill-equipped. The threat of invasion by air and sea in the summer of 1940 led to a panic expansion of the arms industry and a frantic search for a submachine-gun. The first Sten appeared in the summer of 1941 and by 1945 nearly four million had been made, in several different marks and variants. The basic Sten was very simple and its principle of manufacture—the extensive use of subcomponents — was copied from the MP40. Cheapness and simplicity were paramount in the design and, despite some shortcomings, the Sten was one of the outstanding war-winning weapons in the Allied armoury; early versions cost about £2.50 to make, later ones slightly more. The Sten was never an entirely popular gun with British troops largely because its single feed magazine, again taken from the MP40, jammed frequently; the Sten survived, however, to equip many thousands of Allied soldiers, guerillas and partisans in Occupied Europe. The gun illustrated is one of the very first of the Mark 1 guns. About 100,000 Mark 1 Stens were made in all.
Length: 35.25in (895mm)
Weight unloaded: 7lb 3oz (3.30kg)
Barrel: 7.75in (196mm), 6 grooves, right-hand twist
Magazine: 32-round detachable box
Cyclic rate: 550rpm
Muzzle velocity: c.1250fps (381mps)

MACHINE CARBINE, 9MM STEN, MARK 2
United Kingdom
See Sten, Mark 1
9mm SAA Ball (9mm Parabellum)
The Sten Mark 2 was the work-horse of the type and over two million were made in three years. Even within the mark classification there were variations and not all were officially noted with a separate variation number, although most of the divergences concerned the stock and forward handgrip and were not changes to the basic layout. In general the Mark 2 was smaller, neater and handier than the Mark 1; the barrel was often a drawn steel tube held on by a screwed jacket, the stock was skeletal in the extreme and the magazine housing rotated to close the opening when it was not in use. The gun easily dismantled into its component parts and so was ideal for the clandestine operations of the underground forces in Europe and elsewhere. The mechanism was simplicity

itself, being little more than a bolt and spring with the most basic trigger and fire selector equipment. Sights were fixed for 100yd and they could not be adjusted for zero. The magazine held 32 rounds, although generally loaded with 30 to minimise strain on the magazine spring and hence reduce jams, and had to be filled with a special filler.
Length: 30.00in (762mm)
Weight unloaded: 6lb 8oz (2.99kg)
Barrel: 7.75in (196mm), 2 or 6 grooves, right-hand twist
Magazine: 32-round detachable box
Cyclic rate: 550rpm
Muzzle velocity: c.1250fps (381mps)

MACHINE CARBINE, 9MM STEN, MARK 2 (SILENCER)
United Kingdom
See Sten, Mark 1
9mm SAA Ball (9mm Parabellum)
The Mark 2(S) is one of the few submachine-guns to be produced as a separate variant with an integral silencer: in fact, it is not common to find silencers on submachine-guns at all. The Mark 2(S) differs from the standard Mark 2 firstly in respect of the silencer itself, which is a long cylinder of the same diameter as the receiver and containing baffles to trap the gas. The silencer threads on to the receiver in the same way as the normal barrel, but the actual barrel inside it is very short and the bullet emerges at a speed below that of sound. It is almost inaudible at a few yards, although its effective range is reduced considerably. The greatest noise comes from the mechanical movement of the bolt which, in this version, was reduced in weight and fitted with a weaker return spring to compensate for the lower breech pressure resulting from the shortened barrel. The gun was intended to be fired in single shots only, as automatic fire quickly wore out the baffles and was also inclined to detach the end cap of the silencer. The Mark 2(S) was made for special forces and continued in service until after the Korean War. Several thousand were made, although none now remain in service use. The life of the silencer was comparatively short, but it was an effective device and quite widely used.
Length: 35.75in (908mm)
Weight unloaded: 7lb 12oz (3.56kg)
Barrel: 3.50in (87mm), 6 grooves, right-hand twist
Magazine: 32-round detachable box
Cyclic rate: 450rpm
Muzzle velocity: c.1000fps (305mps)

MACHINE CARBINE, 9MM STEN, MARK 3
United Kingdom
See Sten, Mark 1
9mm SAA Ball (9mm Parabellum)
The Sten Mark 3 was the second of the series to be made in large numbers and, together with the Mark 2, is the one which was most frequently found in service with the British Forces. It is really

▷An example of the Sten Mark 2(S) fitted with an integral silencer. Note the design of the stock, and the sleeve around the silencer casing (RSAF).
▷A Danish copy of the Sten, made by the country's resistance fighters during World War 2 (SIM).
▷The Sten Mark 4A, a prototype made in an attempt to devise a smaller and more compact gun for—amongst other things—paratroop use (RSAF).
▷An example of the Sten Mark 5, a 'prestige' version of the basic design intended to give the troops more confidence in their weapons. Guns of early production were fitted with a second grip in front of the magazine housing (RSAF).
▷The Sten Mark 6, a silenced version of the Mark 5 and intended as a replacement for the Mark 2(S). Note the wooden butt and the pistol grip (RSAF).

a variation of the basic Mark 1 for manufacture by alternative methods; the receiver and barrel jacket are in one piece, made from a formed sheet-steel tube which extends almost to the muzzle. The barrel is a fixture inside this jacket and so the easy dismantling of the Mark 2 is not repeated in the Mark 3. The magazine housing is also fixed. One small feature of the Mark 3 which does not appear on any others is the finger guard in front of the ejection opening—a projecting lug riveted to the receiver which prevents the firer's finger from straying into the opening. Internally the Mark 3 was identical with the Mark 1 and it would accept all the varieties of stock which were made, although it was usually supplied with the simple tubular butt similar to the Mark 2. The Mark 3 first appeared in 1943 and was made until 1944, both in the United Kingdom and Canada.
Length: 30.00in (762mm)
Weight unloaded: 7lb 0oz (3.22kg)
Barrel: 7.75in (196mm), 6 grooves, right-hand twist
Magazine: 32-round detachable box
Cyclic rate: 550rpm
Muzzle velocity: c.1250fps (381mps)

MACHINE CARBINES, 9MM STEN, MARK 4A and MARK 4B
United Kingdom
See Sten, Mark 1
9mm SAA Ball (9mm Parabellum)
The Mark 4 Sten was a most interesting gun which was only made in prototype in 1943 and never saw service. It was an attempt to produce a smaller and more compact submachine-gun for particular use by parachute troops. The Mark 2 Sten was used as the basis and the barrel was cut until it was roughly half the original length, but it was mounted in a jacket similar to the Mark 2 and retained by the same magazine housing. A flash-hider was fitted to the muzzle and a curious folding butt stock swivelled on the rear of the receiver so that it stowed forward under the gun. A catch on the stock engaged in a recess on the bottom of the pistol grip and locked it in either position: two types were made, the differences lying in the pistol grip and trigger mechanism. Neither represented a really worthwhile submachine-gun and it was probably a wise decision not to pursue the design. The additional manufacturing effort required to produce such a major alteration to the original would certainly not have been regained in any increase in performance or utility, and the Mark 5 was introduced instead.
Length, stock extended: 27.50in (698mm)
Length, stock folded: 17.50in (443mm)
Weight unloaded: 7lb 8oz (3.45kg)
Barrel: 3.75in (95mm), 6 grooves, right-hand twist
Magazine: 32-round detachable box
Cyclic rate: 570rpm
Muzzle velocity: c.1250fps (381mps)

MACHINE CARBINE, 9MM STEN, MARKS 5 and 6
United Kingdom
See Sten, Mark 1
9mm SAA Ball (9mm Parabellum)
The Sten was never really popular with British troops mainly because its single-feed magazine gave so many jams, and—whenever possible—some other gun was used. The Thompson design was a particular favourite of the parachute troops, for whom submachine-guns were a vital weapon. In 1944 an attempt was made to overcome the opposition to the Sten by producing a better version with a more robust and expensive appearance. Rather more care was taken in machining and assembly and the finish was improved, a wooden stock and pistol grip were fitted (which required the trigger mechanism to be moved forward along the receiver) and the foresight from the Number 4 rifle was adapted to the barrel. The rifle bayonet could be fitted to the muzzle and the butt plate had a trap for cleaning materials. The first Mark 5s guns had a fore pistol grip but this broke easily and was abandoned after a few months. In all other respects the model was similar to the Mark 2 and, in fact, represented only a limited improvement over it. The magazine still jammed on occasion and the wooden furniture meant extra weight. It survived, however, until the early 1960s although replacement by the Sterling had begun in 1953.
The Mark 6 Sten may be conveniently considered here as it was simply the Mark 5 with the addition of a silencer functioning in the same fashion as the Mark 2(S), although the actual internal arrangements and construction were rather different.
(data: Mark 5)
Length: 30.00in (762mm)
Weight unloaded: 8lb 9oz (3.90kg)
Barrel: 7.75in (196mm), 6 grooves, right-hand twist
Magazine: 32-round detachable box
Cyclic rate: 600rpm
Muzzle velocity: c.1250fps (381mps)

MACHINE CARBINE, 9MM, VESELY EXPERIMENTAL (or V42), 1942
United Kingdom
Birmingham Small Arms Company Limited, Birmingham
9mm SAA Ball (9mm Parabellum)
The V42 was one of a number of designs developed by Vesely and made in prototype by the BSA company during World War 2 for submission to the British Army. This particular model was put forward in 1942, but by that time production of the Sten gun was well under way and, while the army were quite willing to try out the design and evaluate it for future reference, it was made plain that regardless of the trials' results there could be no hope of official adoption.
The V42 was designed with production in mind and used a large amount of stamped components in its assembly. It was rather unusual in that it did not rely on differential locking, as the bolt was seated and stopped at the moment of firing. To compensate for this the recoil spring was larger than normal and concealed in the wooden butt. The magazine was also of unusual type, having two columns of rounds in tandem. The front column was fired first, and when this was empty the rear column automatically came into use. In trials this refinement proved a source of trouble at first, but it was eventually perfected although it has never been used since.
Regardless of the performance of the gun—which was quite impressive—the V42 appeared at an inopportune moment and was never likely of real success.
Length: 32.00in (813mm)
Weight unloaded: 9lb 3oz (4.17kg)
Barrel: 10.00in (254mm), 6 grooves, right-hand twist
Magazine: 60-round detachable box
Cyclic rate: c.750rpm
Muzzle velocity: c.1350fps (412mps)

MACHINE CARBINE, 9MM WELGUN, MARK 1
United Kingdom
Birmingham Small Arms Company Limited, Birmingham
9mm SAA Ball (9mm Parabellum)
The Welgun was another example of an attempt to make a smaller type of submachine-gun for parachutists. Although never put into production, it is included because it shows a sensible and original approach to the problem of reducing size. The design was developed during World War 2, and 1943 can be taken as a good representative date for it. A Sten barrel, magazine and operating spring were used, but the spring was wrapped around the barrel and pulled the bolt forwards instead of pushing it, and the magazine fed vertically upwards. The bolt was exposed on both sides by two wide slots in the receiver and was cocked by being grasped by the fingers and pulled back; there was no other cocking handle and it is arguable that such large openings would allow mud and dirt to jam the mechanism. The firing pin was not fixed as in the Sten but was forced forward by a rocking bar pivoted inside the bolt, which was in turn tripped back by a plunger engaging on the breech-face as the bolt closed. This afforded a mechanical safety ignored in other designs of the time. A folding butt hinged over the top of the receiver. A possible weakness of the Welgun lay in the position of the spring, since it rapidly absorbed heat from the barrel—which might ultimately have led to spring failures. However, the Welgun was a well made weapon typical of the advanced thinking of the firm which introduced it, and it might easily have been a great success.
Length, stock extended: 27.50in (700mm)
Length, stock folded: 17.00in (432mm)

Weight unloaded: 6lb 13oz (3.09kg)
Barrel: 7.75in (196mm), 6 grooves, right-hand twist
Magazine: 32-round detachable box
Cyclic rate: 650rpm
Muzzle velocity: c.1250fps (381mps)

MACHINE CARBINE, BSA EXPERI-MENTAL, 1949
United Kingdom
Birmingham Small Arms Company Limited, Birmingham
9mm SAA Ball (9mm Parabellum)
The 1949 design of BSA was produced in prototype form as one of the contenders for the replacement for the Sten submachine-gun in the British service. It was an interesting and novel design which followed the general trend set by

its predecessor, the Welgun. The mainspring was returned to its more usual place behind the bolt and large openings in the receiver were abandoned, but there was once again no retracting handle and the bolt was pulled to the rear by a forward handgrip. This item was initially pushed forward and then pulled back: the latter movement engaged a bar with the bolt and conveyed the push. Slight rotation of the handgrip freed the bar and the bolt could then move freely on firing. The only openings to the receiver were the ejection port and the magazine housing and, when the bolt was forward, these were also covered. The magazine housing swung to the rear on a hinge to allow a jam to be cleared without removing the

▲The Veselý V42 made by BSA. The wide magazine held two columns.
▲The Welgun (RSAF).
▲The BSA of 1949 (RSAF).

magazine, which also facilitated cleaning. The furniture was plastic and the stock folded forwards under the receiver. Although quite successful, the BSA was thought to be unduly complicated for a submachine-gun and was not adopted.
Length, stock extended: 28.00in (711mm)
Length, stock folded: 19.00in (481mm)
Weight unloaded: 6lb 9oz (3.00kg)
Barrel: 8.00in (203mm), 6 grooves, right-hand twist
Magazine: 32-round detachable box
Cyclic rate: 600rpm
Muzzle velocity: c.1250fps (381mps)

▲The Patchett submachine-gun of 1943, the prototype of the later Sterling (RSAF).
▼The silenced Sterling, known to the British Army as the L34A1 (authors' collection).
▼The L2A3 Sterling shown with the stock folded forward around the receiver.

MACHINE CARBINE, 9MM STERLING, L2A1, L2A2, L2A3, and L34A1
United Kingdom
Sterling Engineering Company, Dagenham, Essex
9mm SAA Ball (9mm Parabellum)

The L2A3 is the militarised current service version of the original Patchett machine carbine produced in the 1940s by the Sterling Engineering Company of Dagenham. It has been in service in British and Canadian forces since 1953. There have been some minor alterations to the L2A1 in the seventeen years that it has been in service, but it is still substantially the same. In outline it is a conventionally modern submachine-gun, made entirely from steel and plastic with a side-feeding box magazine and a folding stock. There is rather more machin-ing in the design than appears in other submachine-guns and this leads to a higher cost than many contemporaries. It is, however, extremely reliable and performs outstandingly well in adverse conditions. The bolt has four special clearance ribs machined on its body, and these push any dirt or fouling into special vent holes. There is a separate firing pin and a means of ensuring that it lines up with the primer only at the moment of firing, which is a useful safety measure. The curved magazine holds 34 rounds and has rollers instead of the more usual platform follower. A bayonet can be attached, the foresight can be adjusted for zero, and the rearsight has a 'flip' setting for 100 and 200 yards. The present version appears to be perfectly satisfactory and, as far as is known, no further modifications are contemplated. A version of the basic design with an integral silencer, intended to replace the Mark 6 Sten, is known to the British Army as the L34A1.

Length, stock extended: 28.00in (711mm)
Length, stock folded: 19.00in (481mm)
Weight unloaded: 7lb 9oz (3.48kg)
Barrel: 7.75in (196mm), 6 grooves, right-hand twist
Magazine: 34-round detachable box
Cyclic rate: 550rpm
Muzzle velocity: c.1250fps (381mps)

US SUBMACHINE-GUN, CALIBER .45, M1928A1 ('Thompson')
United States of America
Manufactured by Colt's Patent Firearms Manufacturing Corporation, Hartford, Connecticut, and by Savage Arms

▲▲The Thompson M1928, shown fitted with a 20-round box magazine: a drum was also available (RSAF).
▲The Hyde Model 35 (RSAF). A modified version, the Hyde 109, was submitted to the US authorities in 1939. It differed from the Model 35 in the positioning of the cocking handle, which was on the right side of the receiver.

Company Corporation, Utica, New York, for Auto-Ordnance Corporation, Bridgeport, Connecticut
.45 M1911 (0.45in ACP)
This was the first model of the Thompson submachine-gun to be definitely used by the military, although several models were offered in the 1920s as 'Military Models'. The 1928 version was undoubtedly used by United States Marine Corps in Nicaragua and also by the United States Coast Guard. It was directly derived from the 1921 model, which it closely resembled, and some 1928 models appear to have been 1921 models modified and overstamped with the new date. The so-called 'Navy' model has the horizontal foregrip, sling swivels and muzzle compensator, whereas the civilian model of the same year has the

more familiar vertical foregrip with the finger notches. Very few were taken into service, despite the lessons of the Spanish Civil War, and serious manufacture did not start until 1939. Some of these pre-war Thompsons still survive in the hands of the American police forces.

The early Thompson submachine-guns made use of the much-disputed Blish principle, a method of slowing down the opening of the breech by the frictional forces created by the action of two blocks of metal sliding over each other. Although the weight of the unit, as much as anything else, helped to slow the cyclic rate of the guns manufactured prior to 1942, the efficiency of the locking mechanism is questionable.
Length: 33.75in (857mm)
Weight unloaded: 10lb 12oz (4.90kg)

Barrel: 10.50in (266mm), 6 grooves, right-hand twist
Magazine: 18, 20 or 30-round detachable box or 50 or 100-round drum
Cyclic rate: 800rpm
Muzzle velocity: c.910fps (277mps)

HYDE SUBMACHINE-GUN MODEL 35, 1935
United States of America
Marlin Firearms Corporation, New Haven, Connecticut
.45 M1911 (0.45in ACP)
George J Hyde developed a number of submachine-gun designs during the period 1935–43 and the Model 35 was one of the best. Although bearing obvious affinities in shape with the Thompson, it differed mechanically in that it was a plain blowback firing from

an open bolt. The principal fault was purely psychological—the cocking handle protruded from the rear of the receiver and oscillated in front of the firer's eye as the gun fired.

Tested by the United States Army late in 1939, the Hyde was found to be a reliable and effective weapon in most respects, but there were a number of design deficiencies in the firing mechanism and magazine which caused it to be rejected. The British Army tested the Model 35 shortly afterwards and the same defects were noted. Hyde was by this time working on newer designs and the Model 35 was abandoned without further development.

Length: 35.00in (888mm)
Weight unloaded: 9lb 9oz (4.34kg)
Barrel: 11.25in (286mm) 7 grooves, right-hand twist
Magazine: 20-round detachable box
Cyclic rate: c.750rpm
Muzzle velocity: c.900fps (275mps)

◁The Reising Model 50 (RSAF).
◁The folding-stock Reising Model 55 (RSAF).
◁The M1A1 submachine-gun, a modified version of the basic Thompson design in which the much-disputed locking system was discarded in favour of blowback operation (RSAF).
◁The UD Model 42 (RSAF).

REISING SUBMACHINE-GUN MODEL 50
United States of America
Harrington & Richardson Arms Company, Worcester Massachusetts
.45 M1911 (0.45in ACP)
This interesting gun was designed just before World War 2, and about 100,000 of this model and the later Model 55 were made between 1941 and 1945. Harrington & Richardson contracted to make them and most of the production went to the United States Marine Corps, although a few were sold to Allied countries. Mechanically, the Reising is ingenious and unusual in that it fires from a closed bolt—not in itself a necessarily advantageous feature of an automatic weapon. The internal mechanism is fairly complicated, and the operation of the trigger tripped a series of related operations leading to the striking of the primer, quite unlike the simplicity of the open-bolt systems.

Automatic fire was really a rapid series of semi-automatic shots in sequence, since the mechanism performed the same functions each time. Another unusual feature is the fact that the bolt was 'semi-locked' on firing by being cammed upwards into a recess in the receiver. The magazine was out of the ordinary, being supplied in sizes of 12 and 20 rounds. The former was intended only for semi-automatic firing and was probably meant for training. In favour of the Reising it must be said that it was light and pleasant to shoot, but it was hopelessly prone to jamming from dirt and dust and suffered from radical weaknesses in the design of the magazine. Attempts were made to improve the weapon, but the drawbacks were inherent to the design and the Reising was not popular with its users.
Length: 35.75in (907mm)
Weight unloaded: 6lb 12oz (3.10kg)
Barrel: 11.00in (279mm), 6 grooves, right-hand twist
Magazine: 12 or 20-round detachable box
Cyclic rate: 550rpm
Muzzle velocity: c.920fps (280mps)

REISING SUBMACHINE-GUN MODEL 55
United States of America
Harrington & Richardson Arms Company, Worcester, Massachusetts
.45 M1911 (0.45in ACP)
The Model 55 was an attempt to produce a slightly lighter version of the Model 50 and was a more militarised-looking weapon. It unfortunately retained the exact mechanism of the Model 50 and thus all its many faults. The changes were to cut down the wooden stock and substitute a folding wire butt, to add a wooden pistol grip, and to eliminate the muzzle compensator. It was no more successful than its predecessor.
Length, stock extended: 31.00in (787mm)
Length, stock folded: 22.50in (570mm)
Weight unloaded: 6lb 4oz (2.89kg)
Barrel: 10.50in (266mm), 6 grooves, right-hand twist
Magazine: 12 or 20-round detachable box
Cyclic rate: 500rpm
Muzzle velocity: c.920fps (280mps)

US SUBMACHINE-GUNS, CALIBER .45, M1 AND M1A1 ('Thompson')
United States of America
Manufactured by Savage Arms Corporation, Utica, New York, for Auto-Ordnance Corporation, Bridgeport, Connecticut
.45 M1911 (0.45in ACP)
When the Thompson gun was required in large numbers during the early years of World War 2, it was soon found that the manufacturing processes were not well suited to mass production. By 1942, when Lease-Lend was getting into full swing, it became imperative to simplify the weapon in order to keep up the supplies. The United States Government therefore undertook to modify the design and the result was the M1, which functioned by simple blowback principles rather than by the delayed blowback of the previous models, and the bolt was slightly heavier as a result. The bolt handle was moved to the right-hand side, and the sights were considerably simplified. The drum magazine was dropped in favour of the 20 and 30-round boxes, and the muzzle compensator disappeared. The M1A1 further simplified the design by introducing a fixed firing pin in place of the previous hammer.

The Thompson in all its various forms was a popular gun, and it frequently found favour in place of the Sten and M3 which replaced it. It continued in production until 1945, reappeared in the Korean War and was still being offered to Asian countries under the Offshore Program as late as 1960. It is now only in first line use in the smaller armies of the world, but the design will be seen in service for many years to come.
Length: 32.00in (813mm)
Weight unloaded: 10lb 9oz (4.82kg)
Barrel: 10.50in (266mm), 6 grooves, right-hand twist
Magazine: 20 or 30-round detachable box
Cyclic rate: 700rpm
Muzzle velocity: c.910fps (277mps)

SUBMACHINE-GUN UD M42 ('United Defense')
United States of America
High Standard Manufacturing Company Hamden, Connecticut; Marlin Firearms Company, New Haven, Connecticut
9mm Parabellum, .45 M1911 (0.45in ACP)
The UD M42 was designed prior to American involvement in World War 2 by Carl Swebilius of High Standard but was not made until late 1941 or early 1942, and so became the Model 42. Apparently the prototypes and early models were made by High Standard and the production run of just about 15,000 by the Marlin Firearms Company. The Marlin output was bought by the

United States Government and is believed to have been sold to various Allied countries. It appears that none was taken into service in the regular American Forces, although some were used by the Office of Strategic Services (OSS).

The UD M42 was rather more complicated than the normal submachine-gun but it was very well made from expensive machined parts and it performed well in mud and dirt. It was unfortunate in appearing just after the Thompson had been accepted, thus never gaining a large contract. The gun fired from an open bolt and the firing pin was operated by a hammer as the bolt closed. The bolt handle was unusual in that it was a slide which did not move with the bolt and kept the boltway clear of dirt. A 0.45in version was made, but there was no call for it although it shot well, and apparently had few vices.

Length: 32.25in (820mm)
Weight unloaded: 9lb 1oz (4.17kg)
Barrel: 11.00in (279mm), 6 grooves, right-hand twist
Magazine: 20-round detachable box
Cyclic rate: 700rpm
Muzzle velocity: c.1310fps (399mps)

US SUBMACHINE-GUN, CALIBER .45, M2 ('Hyde')
United States of America
Marlin Firearms Company, New Haven, Connecticut
.45 M1911 (0.45in ACP)
Designed by George Hyde, this is another of the many weapons submitted to Aberdeen Proving Ground in the early years of World War 2 when there was an urgent demand for submachine-guns and no fixed notions of how best to make

them. The M2 was a relatively simple and straightforward design, although it was not easy to make. The Marlin Firearms Company were given a contract to manufacture the M2, but they encountered so many difficulties that the order was cancelled when only about 400 had been made. The gun had performed well in tests and was easy to shoot; it was reasonably reliable and at least the equal of the Thompson in general performance.

The bolt was comparatively massive and made in two diameters, the larger being at the rear and providing the weight. The recoil spring was rather weak and some guns jolted on firing, but the M2 was accepted in 1942 and only the difficulty of manufacturing it prevented it from being a service issue. It was accurate, but rather heavy. The magazines were of box type and held 20 or 30 rounds, the 30-round version being the same as that supplied for the Thompson.

Length: 32.00in (813mm)
Weight unloaded: 9lb 4oz (4.26kg)
Barrel: 12.00in (305mm), 6 grooves, right-hand twist
Magazine: 20 or 30-round detachable box
Cyclic rate: 500rpm
Muzzle velocity: c.960fps (292mps)

INGRAM SUBMACHINE-GUN MODEL 6
United States of America
Police Ordnance Company, Los Angeles, California
9mm Parabellum, 0.38in Super, and .45 M1911 (0.45in ACP)
The Ingram is not a particularly inspired design, but it is one of the very few which have reached any sort of quantity

production in the United States since the end of World War 2. The Model 6 appeared in the early 1950s and was sold in limited numbers to various police forces, the Cuban Navy, the Peruvian Army and the Thailand forces. It was a simple design and its main feature was that it had no selector lever. Semi-automatic fire was produced by pulling the trigger back to an intermediate position. Fully automatic fire occurred when the trigger was pulled fully back. The system was reliable and straightforward, although unusual.

Much trouble was taken to ensure that the Ingram could be made with the minimum of special tools and the receiver, barrel, and magazine were all made from steel tubing. There was little machining and· no need for expensive stamping machinery.

The Ingram failed because no real market existed for it on the American Continent, and in Europe the market was flooded with cheap weapons from the war. Ingram was probably lucky to sell as many as he did.

Length: 30.00in (762mm)
Weight unloaded: 7lb 4oz (3.34kg)
Barrel: 9.00in (228mm), 6 grooves, right-hand twist
Magazine: 30-round detachable box
Cyclic rate: 600rpm
Muzzle velocity: c.900fps (274mps)

US SUBMACHINE-GUN, CALIBER .45, M3
United States of America
Guide Lamp Division of General Motors, Detroit, Michigan
.45 M1911, 9mm Parabellum
In the early years of World War 2 the

◁ The Ingram Model 6 (RSAF).
◁ The M3. Note the cocking arrangements (RSAF).
▲ The standard M3, left side, with the stock extended and the magazine removed (SIM).
▲ A silenced version of the M3 (RSAF).

United States Government was engaged in testing a large number of privately produced submachine-guns, few of which showed any sign of fulfilling the army's specification. A design team at the Aberdeen Proving Ground was formed to produce such a weapon and within two years it was in production. This was the M3—a simple, robust, cheap and entirely adequate gun which fulfilled the specification in every way, although it was later found to have certain defects, particularly in the magazine. As a first try at designing a submachine-gun it was nevertheless a remarkable effort. It was passed for service in December 1942 and remained in first line service until 1960. The M3 is still on the inventory of many smaller armies in the world. It was designed for mass production and the construction is mainly of stampings and pressings; there are few machining operations, and the barrel was swaged in a single process. The rate of fire was unusually low, but this allowed single shots to be fired by snatching the trigger (as no change lever was incorporated) and it also made for steadiness when firing bursts as the gun recoil was controllable.

Inevitably, some minor mistakes were made. One was in the magazine, which gave constant feed troubles throughout

the gun's life. Another was in the choice of materials for some of the earlier models, whose components broke too easily. But for all this the M3 was practical and cheap, which was all that was asked of it. It had one interesting feature in that it could be converted to fire 9mm Parabellum merely by changing the bolt and the barrel, and by inserting a magazine adaptor thus allowing the Sten magazine to be used. All this could be done without tools. Very few were so modified and almost all of M3 type fired the .45 M1911 cartridge.

Length, stock extended: 30.00in (762mm)
Length, stock folded: 22.75in (577mm)
Weight unloaded: 8lb 15oz (4.05kg)
Barrel: 8.00in (203mm), 4 grooves, right-hand twist
Magazine: 30-round detachable box
Cyclic rate: 450rpm
Muzzle velocity: c.900fps (274mps)

US SUBMACHINE-GUN, CALIBER .45, M3A1
United States of America
Guide Lamp Division of General Motors, Detroit, Michigan; Ithaca Gun Company, Ithaca, New York
.45 M1911 (0.45in ACP)
Although the M3 appeared to be simple to produce, it was found that still further improvement could be made and, at the

same time, some of the deficiencies and faults of the original design could be corrected. In December 1944 the M3A1 was accepted for service. It differed from the M3 by eliminating the bolt retracting mechanism altogether, and the firer pulled back the bolt by the unusual method of inserting his finger into a recess in the bolt and simply pulling. For this to happen the ejection opening was enlarged, an oil reservoir was placed in the pistol grip and a variety of minor improvements were incorporated, as well as some ingenious ways of using various parts as tools to strip other parts. The troublesome magazine remained, but the frequency of jamming was reduced to some extent by fitting it with a plastic dust cap. Even so, it never achieved any great popularity and it was usually referred to in rather disparaging terms. The 0.30in calibre M1 carbine was more sought after, and so the M3 played only a minor role in World War 2 and in Korea. About 700,000 were made in the United States and many more have been produced in other countries who either made it under licence or simply copied it.

Length, stock extended: 29.75in (756mm)
Length, stock folded: 22.75in (577mm)
Weight unloaded: 8lb 3oz (3.71kg)
Barrel: 8.00in (203mm), 4 grooves, right-hand twist
Magazine: 30-round detachable box
Cyclic rate: 400rpm
Muzzle velocity: c.910fps (277mps)

MACHINE CARBINE MODEL 49, MACHINE CARBINE MODEL 56
Yugoslavia
Crvená Zastava, Kragujevač
7.62mm Soviet M30

As with all the Communist inclined countries of Eastern Europe, Yugoslavia was equipped with generous quantities of Soviet weapons when World War 2 ended, but in keeping with their intransigent attitude to the political parent, the Yugoslavs elected to make indigenous versions of some of them. The PPSh41 was modified for Yugoslavian manufacture and was adopted as the M49 in the early months of 1949. The PPSh41 ancestry was quite clear, except for the box magazine: the Yugoslavs had elected to discard the 71-round drum. The 35-round box was almost the same as the

one made for the PPSh41, and was said to be interchangeable with it. The general outline of the M49 is very similar to the PPSh and it looks to be little more than a neater version of the Soviet weapon; it is in fact more than that, as it has an improved bolt and spring apparently borrowed from the Beretta modello 38A and there is also a better buffer. The furniture is well finished, in common with most of the construction. The gun was still made primarily from steel stampings, but probably more care was taken in the final assembly. The M49 has been improved, simplified and fitted with a folding stock similar to that found on the German MP40, and—with some other minor changes—is still in service as the M56.

(data: M49)
Length: 34.40in (870mm)
Weight unloaded: 8lb 9oz (3.91kg)
Barrel: 10.50in (267mm), 4 grooves, right-hand twist
Magazine: 32-round detachable box
Cyclic rate: 750rpm
Muzzle velocity: c.1700fps (518mps)
(additional data: M56)
Length, stock extended: 34.25in (870mm)

▲The M3A1; note the revised method of cocking by inserting a finger in the bolt and pulling it to the rear (USMC).

Bolt-action rifles

By 1900 the major nations had all adopted rifles that were of bolt-action, straight-pull or turn-bolt types with box or rotary magazines below the bolt. The guns were fully-stocked, issued with bayonets, and sighted to some distance in the order of 2,000m. In general, they weighed something in the order of 8 or 9lb.

The emergence of this pattern can be laid at the door of the rifle enthusiasts, both military and civil, of the late nineteenth and early twentieth centuries. Their god had two heads—*height of trajectory* and *muzzle velocity*. Their ideal rifle was one which had such a high muzzle velocity that the trajectory was, to all intents and purposes, flat to the maximum range. This ideal was, however, ballistically improbable and practically impossible in view of excessive recoil or excessive length and weight. The usual compromise had consequently to be made. This inevitably led to similar weapons being adopted everywhere and thus the magazine rifle of 1900 fired a projectile of between 6 and 8mm calibre (0.236–0.315in), at about 600–700mps (1970–2295fps) through a long and heavy barrel. Moveover the long range capability was demanded as a result of experience in colonial wars where the ability to shoot an opponent at long range, before he got near enough to return fire, was paramount.

The rifle bullet issued at this time was a direct descendant of Rubin's Swiss army cartridge's jacketed bullet of 1889, blunt of nose and with a squared-off base. In the early years of the century some basic ballistic phenomena were discovered with the aid of spark-gap photography and the German army introduced a *spitzer* ·or pointed bullet. This, with a sharply-tapered nose and a square-cut base, was a better form to travel through the air at supersonic velocities and within a year or two every army had scrambled on the bandwagon by designing and adopting similar bullets. Thus the muzzle velocity was raised and the trajectory lowered to the point where the soldier had no need to adjust the sights on his rifle when firing at closer distances than 300m (330yd); the bullet also stood a good chance of causing serious casualties for quite a long portion of its flight.

It was ultimately discovered that spitzer bullets were less effective and accurate at long ranges than the earlier round-nosed type, and further experiments discovered that the base of the bullet had a greater effect than the nose when the velocity dropped below that of sound (approximately 1100 fps/335mps); at long ranges this meant the greater part of the trajectory, and so the last improvement in rifle bullets came within the adoption of the "boat-tailed" or streamlined bullet. Although such bullets are more difficult to manufacture, since they tend to be difficult to seal in the barrel and thus promote severe wear, their accuracy while the gun barrel lasts is superior and they have since remained the preferred form.

Although the majority of the combat during World War 1 was of the trench-to-trench variety, the magic of the long-range rifle stayed with the world's armies until the middle of World War 2. The German army then reached the conclusion that since the majority of fire seemed to be at short ranges, it might pay to design the cartridge/weapon combination to have optimum performance at an intermediate range. The rounds would weigh less, and the soldier could therefore carry more, and the weapons could be made lighter and more comfortable to fire. In the case of semi-automatic weapons the action could be more compact, since the new cartridge would be shorter; the weapons could be less strong, and this making manufacture less exacting and less wasteful of raw material. The result was the 7.92mm Pist Patr 43, an idea rapidly taken up by the Soviets; after the war much work was done by other nations, but by this time the semi-automatic rifle was gaining universal acceptance.

During the life of the magazine rifle there had been little change, and a soldier trained on Lee-Enfield or Gewehr 98 in 1900 would have had little difficulty in adapting himself to the modified designs of the same rifles which were being manufactured in 1945. The only concessions to modernity which made themselves apparent were the simplification of the sights, a reduction in barrel and overall length, and the redesign of the rifles to suit them to mass-production techniques.

The magazine rifle is not yet dead, for it lingers on wherever there is a need for real accuracy. In the Korean War some of the United States forces still fielded the M1903A4 (Springfield) as their sniper rifle, and as recently as 1970 the British Army announced that the Lee-Enfield is to be rebarrelled to 7.62mm NATO calibre for use as a sniper rifle.

ARISAKA (MAUSER) SYSTEM
Japan, United Kingdom, Russia, Siam (Thailand)
State arsenals
6.5mm Meiji 30, 7.7mm Type 99

During the Sino-Japanese War of 1894, the Japanese army was principally armed with the 8mm Murata rifle (Meiji 20) of 1887—a turnbolt design with an under-barrel tube magazine. This was generally considered outdated and unsatisfactory, and since all western nations were beginning to rearm with small-calibre magazine rifles the Imperial authorities followed suit and appointed a commission, headed by Colonel Arisaka, to devise a suitable replacement for the old Murata guns. The commission considered various designs and finally settled upon a 6.5mm rifle based for the most part on Mauser principles, which was adopted in 1897 as the Meiji 30; a carbine was introduced at the same time. Although the weapons made use of Mauser features, particularly noticeable in the design of the magazine, the bolt unit was an odd combination of Mauser and Mannlicher ideas in that it was fitted with a separate bolt head and a bolt-mounted ejector. The Russo-Japanese War (1904-5) showed that the Meiji 30 was in need of severe modification, and so a modified rifle was devised and placed in production at the war's end. The Meiji 38, so named because 1905 was the 38th year of the reign of Emperor Meiji, was based on the Gewehr 98 then in the hands of the German army. The firing mechanism was redesigned, and the Mauser 'flag safety' was replaced by a large mushroom head on the end of the bolt which was pushed in and turned to the left. An internal difference was that the Arisaka rifle cocked on the closing of the bolt instead of, as is more usual with Mauser designs, on the opening stroke.

Various Japanese rifles and carbines exist as follows.

6.5mm rifle, Meiji 30th year type (1897). The 1897 rifle design was the original pattern, and was immediately recognisable by the unusual safety lever protruding from the cocking piece—which earned for the gun the sobriquet 'hook safety'. The Meiji 30 was fitted with a bolt-mounted ejector and extractor, and the internal box magazine was loaded through the action by means of a five-round charger of Mauser type.
6.5mm carbine, Meiji 30th year type (1897). The 1897 carbine, introduced at the same time as the rifle, shared the rifle action with the bolt-mounted ejector and extractor and the five-round magazine, but was otherwise much smaller.
6.5mm rifle, Meiji 38th year type (1905). The 1905 design was a considerable improvement on that of 1897, with a different bolt more closely based on Mauser's work and a receiver-mounted ejector. The mushroom-head safety device replaced the earlier hook type and the bolt handle was enlarged

Length: 50.25in (1275mm)
Weight unloaded: 9lb 8oz (4.26kg)
Barrel: 31.45in (798mm), 6 grooves, right-hand twist
Magazine: 5-round internal box
Muzzle velocity: c.2400fps (730mps)
6.5mm carbine, Meiji 38th year type (1905). This was the standard carbine version of the 1905 rifle, of which it was a much-shortened derivative. The Meiji 38 carbine could be fitted with the standard Meiji 30 infantry bayonet.
6.5mm carbine, Meiji 44th year type (1911). The 1911 carbine pattern was intended as an arm for the cavalry, although otherwise essentially similar to the 1905 carbine; it was fitted with a folding bayonet attached under the muzzle.
Length: 38.50in (978mm), bayonet retracted
Weight unloaded: 8lb 13oz (4.01kg)
Barrel: 18.50in (469mm), 6 grooves, right-hand twist
Magazine: 5-round internal box
Muzzle velocity: c.2250fps (685mps)
6.5mm sniper's rifle, Type 97 (1937). This rifle fired the standard 6.5mm cartridge, and was given a bipod and a telescope sight offset to the left side of the gun so that it could still be loaded by a charger. The bolt handle was turned down to clear the scope when open.

Experiences in the Sino-Japanese fighting in Manchuria, in the 1930s, led to the opinion that the 6.5mm bullet was insufficiently lethal and that a heavier cartridge was therefore desirable. In 1932 a machine-gun had been introduced firing a semi-rimmed round called the Type 92, and this cartridge was promptly redesigned in a rimless form known as the Type 99. A modified form of the Meiji 38 rifle was introduced to accompany it.
7.7mm rifle, Type 99 (1939). The 1939 rifle pattern was little more than a re-chambered version of the earlier Meiji 38, although the opportunity was taken to produce a 'short rifle' in line with the weapons of contemporary armies abroad and to redesign the components to make manufacture less exacting. The Type 99 rifle was remarkable for being fitted with a flimsy wire monopod and a most optimistic sighting device (consisting of folding lead bars on the rearsight) intended for use against aircraft. This reflects the concern at the time for air attack, but it was more in the nature of a psychological crutch for the soldiers than a serious anti-aircraft threat.
Length: 45.00in (1143mm)
Weight unloaded: 9lb 2oz (4.19kg)
Barrel: 25.75in (654mm), 4 grooves, right-hand twist
Magazine: 5-round internal box
Muzzle velocity: c.2400fps (730mps)
7.7mm parachutist's rifle, Type 99 (c.1940-1). The Type 99 rifle was modified for airborne use by the addition of a joint between the barrel and the action which, in this pattern, took the form of an interrupted-screw joint in the fashion

▲The open action of the Meiji 30th year carbine, showing the 'hook' safety on the end of the cocking piece (RSAF).
▲The action of the Meiji 35th year (M1902) naval rifle, showing the light pressed-steel bolt cover. This did not reciprocate with the bolt, and is shown pushed forward to allow spent cases to be ejected (RSAF).
▲The action of the Meiji 38th year (M1905) rifle, which was usually found with a permanently-attached bolt cover which reciprocated as the action was worked (RSAF).
▲The open action of the Meiji 44th year (M1911) cavalry carbine, here without the cover (RSAF).
▲The action of the Type 2 parachutist's rifle, but applicable to all weapons of the 1939 system (RSAF).
▷Meiji 30th year carbine (RSAF).
▷Meiji 30th year rifle, in the guise of the British Rifle, Magazine 0.256in P1900; a sealed pattern label dangles from the trigger-guard (RSAF).
▷Meiji 38th year rifle (RSAF).
▷Meiji 38th year carbine (SIM).
▷Meiji 44th year cavalry carbine (RSAF).
▷Type 99 rifle with the monopod extended (RSAF).

of a small artillery piece. The design of the joint distinguishes the design of the Type 99 from the later Type 2, and it was not a success.

7.7mm parachutist's rifle, Type 2 (1942-3). The Type 2 was introduced as an attempt to improve upon the abortive Type 99; the screw joint was replaced by a sliding horizontal wedge which mated with a cut-out in the top surface of the barrel. The result was quite serviceable, but relatively few were ever made.

It is as well to note that, towards the end of the war, the quality of the Japanese rifles rapidly decayed owing to the universal shortage of raw materials and the lack of available machine time. Various production short-cuts were used. The result was rifles in which the leaf rearsights were eliminated in favour of 300m standing blocks, monopods were discarded, and the finish was generally ignored until the rifles were covered in machine marks. Inferior substitute steels were also used towards the end of the war, which made firing some of the rifles a distinctly hazardous business.

A little-known and unusual fact about the Arisaka rifle is that for a period of time it was an official British weapon. In 1914 the British Army needed vast numbers of rifles for training and arming its rapidly-expanding army, and so a quantity of Arisaka rifles were purchased from Japan and used for training purposes. They were given official British nomenclature as follows.

Rifle, Magazine, 0.256in Pattern 1900 (introduced on 24th February 1915). This was the 6.5mm Meiji 30 rifle, the model developed by the Imperial commission.

Rifle, Magazine, 0.256in Pattern 1907 (introduced on 24th February 1915). This was the same as the Japanese Meiji 38.

Carbine, Magazine, 0.256in Pattern 1907 (introduced on 24th February 1915). This was the Carbine Meiji 38.

The terminology '1907' is of interest; the British *Textbook of Small Arms, 1909* quotes the rifle Meiji 38 as having been introduced in 1907, and presumably this is from where it was derived. All three 0.256in weapons were declared obsolete for British service on 25th October 1921.

As well as the British and Japanese guns, Arisaka-system rifles were also supplied by Britain (guns which had originally been supplied as training weapons from Japan) and Japan to Tsarist Russia; it seems that 763,400 were supplied in the period 1914–16. Mexico also used a small quantity of Arisaka guns, in 7mm calibre and using the Mexican knife bayonet, and guns in 8mm were supplied to Siam (Thailand).

BERTHIER SYSTEM
France
Various State arsenals, including those of Chatellerault, St. Etienne and Tulle
8mm Cartouche Mle 86, 7.5mm
Cartouche Mle 29

With the adoption by Germany of the Gewehr 88, and the issue in Austria-Hungary of the various weapons on the Mannlicher system, the French quickly realised that the Lebel guns were inferior to those of their neighbours and likely enemies.

As a result of deliberations, therefore, they sanctioned the issue of small quantities of a cavalry carbine designed by a committee headed by André Berthier, amongst the most competent of the designers to come from France. The carbine continued to use the well-tried (but somewhat complicated) bolt-action used on the Fusil Mle 86 and its derivatives, but it allied the action to a magazine very similar to those of Mannlicher. The Carabine Mle 90 was loaded through the action with a clip containing three cartridges which were then forced up and into the loading position by a spring-loaded follower, and after the last round had been chambered the clip fell through a slot in the magazine floorplate.

A modified pattern of the carbine followed in 1892 in which a slight modification was made to the design of the clip,

▼The Mousqueton d'Artillerie Mle 1892 (RSAF).
▼The Mousqueton d'Artillerie Mle 1892, modified in 1916 by the addition of a five-round magazine which can be seen protruding beneath the stock (RSAF).
▼A specimen of the Mousqueton d'Artillerie Mle 1892 with fixed bayonet (SIM).

▲The Fusil d'Infanterie Mle 07/15 (Remington).
▲The Fusil d'Infanterie Mle 16 (SIM).

and the shape of the rifle stock was considerably altered; apart from detail difference in the action components, the carbines manufactured to the system of 1892 were otherwise identical to that of 1890. Various rifles followed, similar in action to the carbines and differing only in dimension, amongst them the patterns of 1902 and 1907. Experience in World War 1 convinced the French authorities that the three-round clip of their rifles and carbines placed the French troops at a disadvantage, as the German Gewehr 98 magazine held 5 rounds and that of the British Lee-system rifles held 10, so in 1915 it was decided to introduce a five-round clip (known as the Chargeur Mle 16). A modified rifle pattern, that of 1916, was introduced to make use of the increased magazine capacity although it was structurally little different from the model of 1907. At a later date many of the 1892 carbines were altered to take the five-round clip, and in 1916 the opportunity was also taken to produce new carbines to the modified system.

Little changed until 1934 when, as a result of trials involving modified ammunition, the French introduced a new rifle firing the 7.5mm cartridge Mle 29, although the rifle was still in reality a Berthier. The chance was also taken of replacing the Mannlicher magazine, in which the clip was an integral part, with a staggered-row Mauser magazine into which five rounds were stripped from a charger.

Carabine de Cavallerie Modèle 1890. A distinctive pattern of carbine with a combless stock, the Mle 90 cavalry type had a turned-down bolt handle and a sling ring attached to the left side of the stock. There was neither handguard nor bayonet, although a cleaning rod was contained within the stock.
Length: 37.20in (945mm)
Weight unloaded: 6lb 11oz (3.02kg)

Barrel: 17.85in (453mm), 4 grooves, left-hand twist
Magazine: 3-round integral clip-loaded box
Muzzle velocity: c.2000fps (609mps)
Carabine de Cuirassiers Modèle 1890. Essentially similar to the cavalry carbine, the pattern intended for the Cuirassiers had a leather butt-plate fixed to the butt by means of two screws.
Carabine de Gendarmerie Modèle 1890. Similar to the other two guns on the 1890 system, the Gendarmerie design was adapted for an épée bayonet—similar to that of the Fusil d'Infanterie Mle 86—which required a special nosecap.
Mousqueton d'Artillerie Modèle 1892. The 1892 system was very similar to that of 1890, although the guns are readily recognisable by the combed stock which gives them an altogether conventional appearance. The Artillerie 'musketoon' —in reality a carbine—carried a cleaning rod in a channel hollowed out in the left side of the forestock. A knife bayonet was supplied with the gun, whose three-round magazine was entirely contained within the stock.
Length: 36.90in (937mm)
Weight unloaded: 6lb 12oz (3.10kg)
Barrel: 17.50in (434mm), 4 grooves, left-hand twist
Magazine: 3-round integral clip-loaded box
Muzzle velocity: c.2000fps (609mps)
Mousqueton de Gendarmerie Modèle 1892. Identical to the artillery model of the same year.
Mousqueton Modèle 1892 Transformé 1927 (Mle 92/27). A conversion of the 1892 system guns—applied to either Artillerie or Gendarmerie weapons —in which the action was suitably modified to use the five-round Chargeur Mle 16. Apart from various detail alterations mainly concerning the removal of the cleaning rod and the filling-in of the stock channel, the Mle 92/27 was recognisable from the Mle 16 or the Mle 16/27 by the absence of an over-barrel handguard.

Fusil des Tirailleurs Indo-Chinois Modèle 1902. The first rifle to be manufactured on the Berthier system, the Mle 02 was no more than a rifle-length version of the Mle 92 carbines. The gun was not issued on a large scale, except to native levies in French Indo-China, and served essentially as a prototype for the succeeding designs of 1907 and 1915.
Fusil des Tirailleurs Sénégalais Modèle 1907 (sometimes called 'Fusil Modèle 1907 dit Coloniel'). As a result of the trials in Indo-China of the Mle 02, a modified rifle was issued to colonial troops in 1907 although the two patterns only differed in minor respects. The three-round clip of the Mousquetons Mle 92 was used and the rifle had a one-piece stock without a handguard. The calibre of the Mle 07, like all the rifles and carbines before it of similar system, was 8mm.
Fusil d'Infanterie Modèle 1907 Transformé 1915 (Mle 07/15). After the advent of World War 1, the French authorities soon realised that the Berthier rifles were much superior to the Lebel patterns then in the hands of the Line infantry; the 'colonial' Mle 07 rifle was seized upon as a replacement and entered into production—with only minor variations to the sights and action—as the Fusil Mle 07/15. As well as the native production, some of the rifles were manufactured in the United States of America by the Remington Arms-Union Metallic Cartridge Company of Ilion in New York State.
Length: 51.24in (1303mm)
Weight unloaded: 8lb 6oz (3.79kg)
Barrel: 31.40in (798mm), 4 grooves, left-hand twist
Magazine: 3-round integral clip-loaded box
Muzzle velocity: c.2350fps (716mps)
Fusil d'Infanterie Modèle 1916. It was soon realised that the three-round Chargeur Mle 92 had insufficient capacity for the trenches and so a modified pattern— the Chargeur Mle 15—was issued in 1916 to hold five; as a result, the Fusil

Mle 07/15 was redesigned to use the enlarged clip and became the Mle 16. The weapon is easily recognised by the full-length one-piece stock—with a handguard—and the protruding magazine unit. The calibre was 8mm.
Length: 51.24in (1303mm)
Weight unloaded: 9lb 3oz (4.15kg)
Barrel: 31.40in (798mm), 4 grooves, left-hand twist
Magazine: 5-round integral clip-loaded box
Muzzle velocity: c.2350fps (716mps)
Mousqueton Modèle 1916. A carbine version of the Fusil Mle 16 built around the five-shot clip, the Mousqueton Mle 16 could again be recognised from the earlier 1892 system by the presence of a handguard and the protruding magazine housing. A cleaning rod was carried in a channel in left side of the stock, and the butt had a sling bar.
Mousqueton Modèle 1916 Transformé 1927 (Mle 16/27). A conversion of the basic five-shot Mle 16 to approximate to the Mle 92/27 conversion, executed by the removal of the cleaning rod (and the filling of the stock channel) and the addition to the nosecap of a stacking 'prong'.
Fusil d'Infanterie Modèle 1907, Transformé 1915 et Modifié 1934 (Mle 07/15 M34—or 'Fusil Mle 34'). A much-modified and shortened form of the basic rifle Mle 07/15 in which the Mannlicher pattern magazine was discarded in favour of a staggered-row box of Mauser type. The old 8mm 'Lebel' cartridge was replaced in the French service by two of

7.5mm: the 7.5mm Cartouche Mle 24—an experimental issue—and its successor the 7.5mm Cartouche Mle 29. The Fusil Mle 07/15 M34 was chambered for the latter round.
Length: 42.70in (1084mm)
Weight unloaded: 7lb 13oz (3.53kg)
Barrel: 22.62in (575mm), 4 grooves, left-hand twist
Magazine: 5-round integral box
Muzzle velocity: c.2600fps (792mps)
Fusil de Cavallerie Modèle 1907, Transformé 1915 et Modifié 1934. Identical to the infantry rifle of the same pattern, but with the bolt handle turned down so that it lay along the stock.

DE LISLE SYSTEM
United Kingdom
Royal Small Arms Factory, Enfield Lock, Middlesex.
0.45in SAA ball (0.45in ACP)
The De Lisle carbine is an unusual weapon, produced in Britain in small numbers during World War 2 for use by Commando and other clandestine forces. It is based on the standard Lee bolt action but it is fitted with a 0.45in calibre barrel forming part of a large and extremely efficient silencer. The calibre was selected in order to overcome the greatest obstacle to silent weapon design—the problem of silencing not the explosion of the charge but the sound wave which precedes the bullet: in other words, the sonic 'bang'. To counter this, it is necessary to propel the bullet through the air at subsonic velocity, and there are three ways of achieving this. Firstly, gas

can be tapped from the barrel in such a way that the time the bullet reaches the muzzle it is subsonic; this, the most common technique, represents a considerable waste of propellant. The second method requires the production of a special round of ammunition loaded either with a reduced charge or a heavier bullet; this was tried at various times both by the Germans and by the British, but it introduces a further logistic complication. The third system—the most simple—is to begin with a subsonic cartridge around which a weapon can be designed. This is the De Lisle system; the American .45 M1911 Auto pistol cartridge, barely subsonic, is used.

The De Lisle is undoubtedly among the most silent weapons ever developed, and the only noise audible on firing is the striker falling on the cap. Unfortunately, this is somewhat negated by the appalling clatter as the bolt is worked to chamber the next round. The gun is also vastly superior to most silenced weapons in matters of range and accuracy; although the 0.45in bullet is generally accepted as a short-range pistol cartridge, this assumption is drawn from its use in short-barrelled pistols and submachine-guns. The barrel of the De Lisle is one of the longest of its calibre in military use, and owing to this it shoots with remarkable accuracy up to three or four hundred yards.

▼▼Two versions of the De Lisle carbine, the folding version above (SIM) and the wood-stocked version below (RSAF)

ENFIELD (MAUSER) SYSTEM
United Kingdom, United States of America.
Various manufacturers (see text)
0.303in SAA Ball (British), .30 M1906 (USA)

When the Short Magazine Lee-Enfield was introduced into British service, it met with a storm of criticism—though little of it came from the soldiers. A typical example, from *Arms and Explosives* magazine for November 1908, states:

'The rifle was always bad, its defects always notorious . . . and the propagation of badness will doubtless continue for several more generations to come'. Whether or not this campaign of calumny had any effect, the War Office

▼The Rifle P1914 (Remington).
▼A specimen of the Rifle P1914 with an experimental muzzle-brake (SIM). In 1926 these rifles were renamed Number 3 Mark 1 in accordance with the new system of nomenclature.
▼The Rifle P1914, left side, showing the long range sight behind the rear barrel band. (RSAF).
▼The Fusil Modelo 1934, a conversion by Remington of the Rifle Pattern 1914 supplied in the 1930s to Honduras; alterations are evident to the receiver bridge and a new rearsight has been added (Remington).

began developing a rifle more in keeping with the critics' ideas of what a military weapon ought to be. The result was based on the Mauser action and was of 0.276in (7mm) calibre; after extensive experimentation, both in theory and in practice, it was approved for issue on a trial basis in 1913. The cartridge was roughly based on the Ross 0.280in and was exceptionally powerful; loaded with cordite, amongst the results were excessive muzzle flash and blast, barrel overheating, severe erosive wear, irregular chamber pressures and premature ignition owing to barrel heat. Before these problems could be resolved the outbreak of war caused the whole idea to be indefinitely shelved.

When in 1914 the demands of the war raised problems in mass-producing rifles, high-speed production of the Lee-Enfield was out of the question. The 0.276 in rifle had, however, been designed with

an eye to rapid production, so the design was taken out and rapidly converted to the standard 0.303in chambering; in 1915 manufacturing contracts were placed with American companies, amongst them Remington and Winchester, and the rifles entered British service as the 'Pattern 1914'.

Rifle, Magazine, 0.303in Pattern 1914 Mark 1E (introduced on 21st June 1916). These rifles can be recognised by the long exposed muzzle and prominent 'wings' protecting the foresight, and also by the fact that the magazine is concealed within the body. Although they may have been designed to the specifications of the target shots, they were not liked by the brutal and licentious soldiery: the P14 was too long, badly balanced, and cumbersome to handle in combat—particularly when garlanded by a long bayonet. The 'e' models were made by the Remington Arms-Union Metallic Cartridge Company at their plant at Eddystone Arsenal, Pennsylvania, and were distinctively marked: on the front top of the body appeared RE, on the right side of the stock IR, and on all the principal components 'e'. The guns survived World War 2, when they were principally used for Home Guard issue, and were finally declared obsolete in July 1947.

Rifle, Magazine, 0.303in Pattern 1914 Mark 1R (introduced on 21st June 1916). Identical to the 'e' model, these were made by the Remington Arms-Union Metallic Cartridge Company at their Bridgeport, Connecticut plant. They were marked ERA, IE and 'r' in the places noted above.

Rifle, Magazine 0.303in Pattern 1914 Mark 1W (introduced on 21st June 1916) As the previous models, these were made by the Winchester Repeating Arms Company plant at New Haven (Connecticut) and marked W, IW and 'w' on the various parts.

Rifle, Magazine, 0.303in Pattern 1914 Mark 1E*; Rifle, Magazine, 0.303in Pattern 1914 Mark 1R*; Rifle, Magazine, 0.303in Pattern 1914 Mark 1W*. These three weapons were all introduced in February 1917. They were basically the same as the previous models, differing only in minor manufacturing details.

▶The US Magazine Rifle, M1917—a Rifle P1914 modified to accept the standard American 0.30in cartridge. Apart from minor modifications for the different cartridge, the two rifles are identical (Remington).

FUSIL MAS36, FUSIL MAS36 CR39
France
Manufacture d'Armes de Saint-Etienne, Saint-Etienne
7.5mm Cartouche Mle 29

French experience in World War 1 convinced them that the 8mm Mle 86 cartridge had outlived its usefulness; it was a very inconvenient shape, with a wide rim and a sharp taper to the bottleneck, and it would not stand comparison with the better-proportioned rimless rounds used by other nations. Owing to its peculiar proportions it was exceptionally difficult to design a good automatic weapon to function with the Mle 86 cartridge and in the 1920s a good deal of experimentation was undertaken, which culminated in the adoption in 1924 of a new 7.5mm rimless cartridge based on the 7.92mm Mauser. A modified version of the Mle 24 cartridge—slightly shorter—was introduced in 1929. The first priority was to develop a machine-gun to suit, and once this had been accomplished a magazine rifle was the next item on the list.

The result was known as the MAS36, in general design a modified Mauser but with the bolt so altered to lock into the

▼The MAS36 action (RSAF).
▷The MAS36 (RSAF).
▷The folding-stock MAS36CR39 shown with the butt folded forward around the trigger guard and fore-end (SIM).
▷The MAS36 with bayonet fixed (RSAF).

body of the weapon behind the magazine rather than into the breech aperture. This allows a shorter bolt stroke but is, of course, less strong than the original Mauser design, and owing to this design it proved necessary to bend the bolt

When in 1917 the United States entered World War 1, it too had a rifle shortage and—since production facilities for the British rifle existed in some quantity—the Pattern 1914 was quickly redesigned to accept the standard American .30 M1906 rimless cartridge. The gun entered American service as the *US Rifle, caliber .30 Model 1917*, though commonly called the 'Enfield' as a tribute to its birthplace.

The M1917 is identical in appearance with the British Pattern 1914 rifle, so much so that during World War 2 (when a million or so Model 1917 rifles were sold to Britain for the Home Guard)

they were marked around the butt with a two-inch stripe of red paint to draw attention to their calibre. Many units were also armed with P14 rifles, and while attempting to load a British rimmed 0.303in cartridge into an American chamber led to nothing more serious than a minor jam, the reverse case usually demanded the services of an armourer to remove it.

Length: 46.25in (1175mm)
Weight unloaded: 9lb 10oz (4.36kg)
Barrel: 26.00in (661mm), 5 grooves, left-hand twist
Magazine: 5-round integral box
Muzzle velocity: c.2800fps (853mps)

Rifle, Magazine, 0.303in Pattern 1914 Mark 1*W(T) (introduced on 11th April 1918). The Mark 1W* with the addition of an Aldis sniping telescope and a cheekpiece on the butt.

The Pattern 1914 rifles were removed from service after World War 1 and were placed in store. In 1940 they were again issued, but in 1926 the system of rifle nomenclature had changed and they were reintroduced as **Rifles Number 3 Mark 1** or **1*** (the 'e', 'r' and 'w' suffixes being no longer distinguished). The sniping version became the **Mark 1*(T)A,** the 'A' indicating the use of an Aldis telescope.

handle forward (in a very awkward fashion) to bring it into a convenient position for the firer's hand. Like its predecessors in French service, the MAS36 had no safety catch. It was the last bolt-action rifle ever to be adopted

by a major military power, though a short-barrelled version for use by paratroops was later made in small numbers; this, the MAS36 CR39, was basically the same weapon with the substitution of a folding butt of hollow aluminium.

Length: 40.15in (1020mm)
Weight unloaded: 8lb 5oz (3.78kg)
Barrel: 22.60in (573mm), 4 grooves, left-hand twist
Magazine: 5-round integral box
Muzzle velocity: c.2700fps (823mps)

FUSIL 1, or FUSIL MODELE F1
France
Manufacture Nationale d'Armes de Saint-Etienne, Saint-Etienne
7.5mm Cartouche Mle 29, 7.62mm NATO

The Modèle F1 is a bolt-action magazine rifle of modern design and considerable precision. It is offered in three versions: Modèle A for sniping, Modèle B for competition shooting and Modèle C for big-game hunting. The Modèle A is in service with the French Army in small numbers and so, too, is the Modèle B, as it was used by the victorious French Army team in the 1966 Prix Leclerc NATO shooting competition. In design the rifle is of no great novelty, but it is undoubtedly carefully constructed, and much effort goes into the machining of the components and the setting up of the whole weapon; it is not cheap. Butt length can be adjusted by a series of extension pieces (which is a sensible and easy method) and the sniping version has a folding bipod which makes for steadier aiming. A night sight to aid shooting in poor light is available, and the rifle is normally fitted with a telescope sight for daylight use. The trigger pull can be adjusted by a micrometer screw and a number of different foresight fittings are supplied. The weapon is really a specialised competition rifle which has been militarised for the sniping role, and this might be a better approach than the more usual one of attempting to improve the accuracy of a standard military rifle which was never meant to shoot to such fine limits.

Length: 44.70in (1138mm)
Weight unloaded: 8lb 2oz (3.70kg)
Barrel: 21.70in (552mm)
Magazine: 10-round
Muzzle velocity: c.2800fps (853mps)

GODSAL SYSTEM, 1902
United Kingdom
Webley and Scott Limited, Birmingham
0.303in SAA Ball

The experimental Godsal rifle appeared in 1902, the design of Major P T Godsal, an enthusiastic and expert shot who had on many occasions represented England at international rifle meetings. He maintained that the Lee series of British rifles had many failings and he spent much time and effort trying to persuade the War Office to accept his ideas. About five rifles were made to his designs by Webley and Scott at his own expense, but the rifle got no further than that.

The idea behind the Godsal was to produce a lighter and more accurate rifle using a travelling block instead of a bolt, although the 'travelling block' was really only a very short (4.50in long) bolt with forward locking lugs engaging in a barrel extension in a similar way to the Mauser. The breech was further back than on conventional rifles, so allowing a longer barrel, but this brought the magazine above the position of right-hand grip, which so restricted its depth that it could only accept five rounds. The bolt travelled slightly downhill on opening, which was claimed to assist extraction, but the action was nowhere near as smooth as the Lee-Enfield. It must be admitted, in fairness, that the rifles were only experimental and that improvements could have been effected.

The Godsal was a courageous attempt to produce a worthwhile bolt-action rifle, and for an amateur designer it represented a remarkable feat, but it offered too few advantages over the contemporary service weapons to be considered as a rival and the design passed quickly into history.

Length: 45.00in (1143mm)
Weight unloaded: 7lb 2oz (3.20kg)
Barrel: 29.75in (756mm), 4 grooves, right-hand twist
Magazine: 5-round integral box
Muzzle velocity: c.2450fps (747mps)

◁The Fusil Modèle 1, type A, sniper's rifle (authors' collection).
◁The Godsal rifle (RSAF).
▲A Danish Krag-Jørgensen rifle, the Gevaer m/89-10 (SIM).

◁The open action of the Godsal rifle, at full stroke (RSAF).

KRAG-JORGENSEN SYSTEM
Denmark and Norway
State arsenals
8mm patron m/89 (Denmark), 6.5mm Patron M94 (Norway)

The Krag - Jørgensen system was developed in the late 1880s by Captain Ole Krag of the Royal Norwegian Artillery and Erik Jørgensen, an engineer at the Norwegian State arsenal of which Ole Krag later became superintendent. The rifles were first adopted in 1889 by Denmark and in 1892, in a modified version, by the United States of America

After various improvements had been carried out to the desires of the Board of Officers supervising the United States Army trials, Krag and Jørgensen patented an improved version of the rifle in 1893; this was later adopted by the army of Norway, whose first rifle pattern appeared in the following year.

The turnbolt action makes use of a single locking lug at the front of the bolt unit, although the bolt handle turns down into a recess in the receiver body to act as an auxiliary lock; the design of the locking system has in the past been the subject of much criticism but, with the relatively low-powered cartridges for which it was originally conceived, the gun is unquestionably safe. The most remarkable feature of the design lies, however, in the pattern of the magazine, which loads laterally under the bolt through a hinged trapdoor. On the door's inner face is a leaf spring and the magazine follower, and with the trap open, loose cartridges can be dropped into the loading slot. Closing the trap brings the spring and follower to bear upon the last cartridge, pushing the rounds across the magazine, under the bolt and up to the left side of the action where the round rests against the bolt. When the bolt is operated, the closing stroke pushes against the rim of the first cartridge, easing it forward to an enlargement of the feed slot at which point the rim can pass through; the round can then enter the feedway and into the chamber.

The original Danish Krag-Jørgensen was given a loading trap vertically hinged at the front, which meant that it swung forward for loading: it also meant that the rifle had to be canted towards the left when loading as the cartridges would otherwise fall to the ground. The 1892 American design, and the later Norwegian pattern, replaced the Danish gate with a type having a horizontal hinge at the bottom of the receiver, which meant that the open trap also served as a loading platform.

DENMARK
8mm Gevaer m/89. The pattern of 1889 was the first of a series of similar weapons; a long, somewhat clumsy rifle instantly recognisable by the barrel jacket—a feature possessed by few other guns—and the side-loading gate was hinged at the front of the receiver.
Length: 52.35in (1330mm)
Weight unloaded: 9lb 12oz (4.42kg)
Barrel: 32.75in (832mm), 6 grooves, right-hand twist
Magazine: 5-round internal 'tray'
Muzzle velocity: c.1985fps (602mps)
8mm Gevaer m/89–08. In 1908 it was decided to modify the rifle design to incorporate a new type of safety catch designed by Barry, which appeared on the cocking piece.
8mm Gevaer m/89–10. In 1910 a second set of minor modifications were made, the most important being the regradation of the rearsight from 2000m to 2100m. Most of the earlier rifles then in service were altered to the new system, just as they had been in 1908, which means that original 1889-type rifles are now very scarce indeed.
8mm Rytterkarabin m/89. This was the cavalry carbine version of the 1889 rifle, a shortened and lightened rifle with a wooden handguard and sling swivels on the left side of the stock and on the left side of the top band. The original leaf sight was replaced by one of tangent pattern. The carbine was adopted in 1912, which leads to an alternative designation 'Rytterkarabin m/89–12'.
8mm Rytterkarabin m/89–23. The basic cavalry carbine was modified in 1923 to accept the light sword bayonet of 1915, which necessitated the addition of a suitable bayonet bar to the muzzle. All carbines of the type then in service were so altered.
8mm Ingeniørkarabin m/89–24. This variation of the carbines was intended for the use of the engineers; the m/89–24 was fitted with sling swivels under the butt, the barrel band and the nosecap. A bayonet bar was fitted to the underside of the muzzle, and a wooden handguard appeared over the barrel.
8mm Fodfolkskarabin m/89–24. The infantry's carbine, this was basically a short version of the rifle m/89, even to the fitting of a steel barrel-jacket. There was no handguard and the stock was fitted with grasping grooves—one to each side—below the rearsight. A bayonet bar was fitted to the barrel jacket at the muzzle.
8mm Artilleriekarabin m/89–24. This was essentially similar to the infantry carbine

of the same year, except that the bolt handle was turned downwards towards the stock.

NORWAY
6.5mm Gevaer M/1894. The original Norwegian Krag, the M/1894 rifle, was quickly recognised by the semi-pistol grip stock and the wooden handguard which only covered the rear portion of the barrel between the breech and the rearmost barrel band. The loading gate, on the right side of the receiver below the bolt guideway, had a side-hinging trap. A tangent-leaf rearsight was fitted and a bayonet bar appeared below the foresight.
Length: 50.00in (1270mm)
Weight unloaded: 8lb 15oz (4.05kg)
Barrel: 30.07in (765mm), 4 grooves, left-hand twist
Magazine: 5-round internal 'tray'
Muzzle velocity: c.2400fps (731mps)
6.5mm Karabin for kavaleriet M/1895. A short version of the rifle M/94 was introduced in 1895 for the cavalry, easily distinguishable by the half-stock which gave it the appearance of a sporting gun. A tangent sight was used with a very small wooden handguard between the receiver ring and the rearsight: no bayonet was provided for the carbine.
6.5mm Karabin for bergartilleriet og ingeniørvapnet M/1897. The 'carbine for mountain artillery and engineers' of 1897 was no more than the cavalry pattern of 1895 with a repositioned butt swivel, which was moved to a position 10cm from the heel of the butt.

6.5mm Karabin for ingeniørvapnet M/1904. A variation of the 1895 cavalry pattern with a full stock and a full-length handguard over the barrel. No bayonet was used on this gun, which was intended for the use of the engineers' corps.
6.5mm Karabin for feltartilleriet M/1907. A version of the M/1904 engineers' carbine, from which it differed primarily in the positioning of the swivels (one on the top band and one on the underside of the butt).
6.5mm Karabin M/1912. The final version of the Norwegian carbines, the first production of the M/1912 were fitted with down-turned bolt handles although later examples reverted to straight ones. The barrel of the carbine was some 9cm longer than that of the preceding types, and the gun appeared with a full-length stock with a handguard above the complete barrel. A bayonet bar was provided underneath the top-band/nosecap assembly.
6.5mm Karabin M/1912, modified 1916. A strengthening band was added to the forestock, immediately to the rear of the bayonet bar. The gun was otherwise the same as the original M/1912, and the modification was retrogressively applied to all service weapons of this pattern.
6.5mm Skarpskyttergevaer M/1923. This was the first of the Norwegian snipers' rifles, with an aperture rearsight and a hooded foresight. The pistol-grip was chequered and the barrel was covered by a handguard.
6.5mm Skarpskyttergevaer M/1925. A version of the M/1923 using the forestock

▲The Norwegian 6.5mm Gevaer m/1894 (RSAF).
▲Krag and Jørgensen's Karabin for Kavaleriet M/1895 (SIM).
▲The Norwegian Karabin M/1912 with the 1916-type strengthening band added to the gun's muzzle (RSAF).

Apart from Denmark and Norway, the USA also used the Krag-system rifles, which were adopted in 1892 (at a time when better systems were available). The adoption of the Mauser-system 'Springfield' M1903 rifle meant that the Krags were little used in the twentieth century; there were, however, several variants. Amongst them were the rifles of 1892, 1896 and 1898, and carbines of 1896, 1898 and 1899.
▷The US Rifle Model 1896 (SIM).
▷The US Carbine Model 1896 (SIM).
▷The French Fusil d'Infanterie Mle. 86/93, generally known as the 'Lebel', fired a small-calibre smokeless cartridge which made obsolete overnight the rifles of other nations (RSAF).

—with a half-handguard—of the Gevaer M/1894, it was otherwise identical to the preceding model.
6.5mm Skarpskyttergevaer M/1930. This rifle was fitted with a halfstock, which gave it the appearance of a sporting gun. The heavy barrel was provided with a hooded foresight and an aperture rearsight and, unlike the previous snipers' rifles, the M/1930 had no provision for a bayonet. These rifles were ultimately replaced in the Norwegian Army by weapons on the Mauser system.

LEBEL SYSTEM
France
Various State arsenals, including those at Chatellerault, St. Etienne and Tulle
8mm Cartouche Mle 86

In 1886 the French Army replaced their single-shot 'Gras' rifles (Fusil d'Infanterie Modèle 1874) with a weapon which, for a short time, put them ahead of the world. The new weapon, ultimately known as the Fusil d'Infanterie Modèle 1886—or the Lebel, after the senior officer on the committee—was notable in that it introduced a smokeless cartridge firing a small-calibre jacketed bullet.

The gun itself was a strange combination of ideas and, in view of contemporary advances elsewhere, it could well be described as mechanically backward (indeed, improved weapons became widespread within a couple of years) utilising as it did the magazine system of the Austrian Kropatschek: a tube-fed mechanism dating back to the 1870s. The bolt was a variation of that found on the Gras of 1874, incorporating modifications made when the French adopted the Kropatschek in 1878.

The turnbolt action of the Mle 86 employed a magazine tube running forward beneath the barrel, and as the bolt was withdrawn so a lifting mechanism brought a fresh round in line with the chamber. When the bolt was closed, this round was swept into the chamber and the lifter moved down to be supplied with a new cartridge pushed backwards by the pressure of the magazine spring. The result was a long and heavy weapon

which retained its superiority for a very short time before being overtaken by the mechanically more perfect—and aesthetically more pleasing—patterns of Mauser and Mannlicher. The Mle 86, however, continued in service until the end of World War 2; many had been greatly shortened in 1935, but others survived unmodified in the hands of the reserve. The Mle 86 and its various derivations were never entirely supplanted by the later weapons of the Berthier system.

From time to time various minor improvements were effected: in 1898 the French authorities replaced the round-nosed Balle M with the boat-tailed spitzer Balle D, but the days of the tubular-magazine rifles, in which there was always a danger of jarring two cartridges together tip-to-nose with attendant chances of an explosion, were numbered by the advent of the clip-loaded Berthier weapons.

Fusil d'Infanterie Modèle 1886. The original production variant of the basic pattern, it could be easily recognised by the unusual receiver and the two-piece stock. The under-barrel tubular magazine held eight rounds, and a long cruciform-bayonet could be fixed underneath the protruding muzzle.
Length: 51.00in (1295mm)
Weight unloaded: 9lb 5oz (4.28kg)
Barrel: 31.50in (800mm), 4 grooves, left-hand twist
Magazine: 8-round under-barrel tube
Muzzle velocity: c.2350fps (716mps)
Fusil d'Infanterie Modèle 1886 Transformé 1893 (Mle 86/93). After the

original rifles had seen service in the hands of the troops, several deficiencies were discovered; the entire machining of the receiver was revised to eliminate weakness caused by insufficient torsional rigidity, a hole was bored in the bolt-head to enable gas to escape from a ruptured cartridge, the rearsight underwent minor modifications, and a stacking 'prong' was added to the muzzle cap.

Fusil Modèle 1886 Racroché 1935 (Mle 86R35). A much-shortened version of either the Mle 86 or the Mle 86/93 intended to make a much more handy weapon, the conversion was executed by reducing the barrel and the forestock, fitting a middle band similar to that of the Mousqueton Mle16, and replacing the original rearsight with the pattern of the Mousqueton Mle 16—which had to be suitably modified to enable it to fit the contours of the Lebel barrel.
Length: 37.20in (944mm)
Weight unloaded: 6lb 12oz (3.10kg)
Barrel: 17.75in (451mm), 4 grooves, left-hand twist
Magazine: 3-round under-barrel tube
Muzzle velocity: c.2000fps (609mps)

LEE STRAIGHT-PULL SYSTEM
United States of America
Winchester Repeating Arms Company, New Haven, Connecticut
6mm (.236 M1895)

James Paris Lee (1831–1904) was a talented inventor who worked in the second half of the nineteenth century. His greatest triumph was the box magazine which subsequently appeared

▲The M1895 Lee straight-pull (RSAF).
▼The action of the Lee straight-pull rifle (RSAF).

in different forms on practically every military rifle in the world, but he also designed and developed many other projects. In the early 1890s he produced his design for a straight-pull bolt-action, thus circumventing the existing patents and offering what—or so it was hoped—would be a better and faster action. The United States Navy adopted the idea in 1895 in the calibre of 0.236in (6mm) and the manufacturing contract was awarded to Winchester, who had to go to the Lee Arms Company for the patent rights.

US Navy Rifle, calibre .236, 6mm M1895. The bolt on the 1895 Lee pattern does not rotate; it is locked by cam action into the receiver and is operated by a small movement of the cam handle, which lies downward along the right-hand side and looks very much like a conventional bolt handle. By pulling the handle to the rear the cams unlock from the recess, permitting the bolt to move slightly up-hill—it is not an altogether easy motion to work. No doubt the United States Navy found the same thing, for their original order for 10,000 rifles was not extended, and Winchester discovered that private sales (allowed by their contract with Lee) were sluggish. A sporting rifle was tried, but when the final clearance was made in 1916 only 1,700 sporters out of a total of 20,000 made had been sold. The best feature of the Lee was the magazine, which is said to have been the first made commercially in the United States of America with clip loading.

The Lee rifle is pleasant to handle and was probably good to shoot, except for the slightly awkward mechanism; but it failed to catch on as a rival to the almost universal turnbolt system, and it passed from sight very quickly.

Length: 47.00in (1194mm)
Weight unloaded: 8lb 0oz (3.63kg)
Barrel: 27.25in (692mm), 5 grooves, left-hand twist
Magazine: 5-round integral box
Muzzle velocity: c.2400fps (732mps)

LEE TURNBOLT SYSTEM
United Kingdom
State ordnance factories
0.303in
During the 1880s the British Army busied itself with the study of various rifle systems in an endeavour to determine which might best suit their requirements, and their deliberations ended with the adoption in 1888 of the Lee-Metford rifle, under the official designation of *Rifle,*

Magazine, Mark 1. This utilised the turn-bolt action and magazine attributable to James Lee, the Scots-born American inventor, together with the rifling and barrel designed by William Metford specifically to combat the fouling inherent in the gunpowder propelling charges of the time.

Rifle, Magazine, Mark 1 (introduced on 2nd December 1888). A bolt-action rifle with dust-cover, and with a box magazine holding eight rounds of 0.303in cartridge in a single column; barrel length 30.20in (767mm), rifle length 49.50in (1257mm), weight 9lb 8oz (4.37kg). It was rifled on Metford's system, with 7 grooves 0.004in deep and lands 0.023in wide. The left-hand twist was uniform, with one turn in 10in (or 33 calibres). The foresight was

a square block with a vertical slot in it, and the rearsight was a square notch, fixed in its lowest place at 300yd and graduated to 1900yd. On the side of the stock were a set of 'Extreme Range Sights' graduated from 1800yd to 3500yd. The muzzle velocity, using the compressed black-powder cartridge, was about 2200fps (670mps). In August 1891 the designation of this rifle was officially changed to *Rifle, Magazine, Lee-Metford Mark 1.*

Rifle, Magazine, Lee-Metford Mark 1* (introduced on 19th January 1892). The design was sealed to govern future manufacture and also to govern the conversion of stocks of the Mark 1 Rifle. The safety catch on the cocking piece was omitted, the handguard was modified and a brass

▲The rifle, Magazine, Mark 1—later known as the Mark 1 Lee-Metford (RSAF).
▲The Rifle, Magazine, Lee-Enfield Mark 1 of 1895; note the cleaning rod, removed in later marks (RSAF).
▲The Rifle, Magazine, Lee-Enfield Mark 1**(1899) which was no more than a Mark 1* with the cleaning rod deleted from the design. A sealed pattern tag hangs from the fore sling-swivel (RSAF).
▲An example of the Rifle, Charger Loading, Magazine Lee-Enfield Mark 1*. Note the charger guide on the receiver (RSAF).

disc for regimental numbering was let into the butt, the piling swivel was strengthened, the bolt mainspring was of 32 coils of 0.049in wire instead of 39 coils of 0.040in wire (with a length of 3.25in instead of 5.00in), the magazine spring had four coils instead of three, a blade front sight was fitted—in converted rifles it was pinned into the original front sight block—and the sight graduations were altered to take account of new ammunition having a velocity of 2000fps (609 mps). The long range sight was consequently graduated from 1600yd to 2900 yd.

Rifle, Magazine, Lee-Metford Mark 2 (introduced on 30th January 1892). The principal difference between this and the previous models was that the magazine

was changed to a pattern holding ten rounds in two columns, and as a result the body was somewhat modified in contour. The magazine spring was of 'C' shape instead of a coil, the barrel was lighter, and there were minor variations in the construction of the bolt and magazine cut-off. The weight was now 9lb 4oz (4.25kg). A number were re-barrelled in 1902 with Enfield rifling, and had 'E' stamped on the Knox-form, though the nomenclature remained unchanged.

Rifle, Magazine, Lee-Metford Mark 2* (introduced on 22nd April 1895). This differed from the Mark 2 in that the bolt was lengthened by 1.00in (25.40mm) and fitted with two grooves for a safety catch, and the cocking piece was also lengthened and fitted with the safety catch. In 1903, some rifles were rebarrelled with Enfield rifling and marked E on the Knox-form, the designation being changed to *Rifle, Magazine, Lee-Enfield Mark 1* if fitted with the original pattern of nose-cap, or *Mark 1** if fitted with the later pattern of solid fore-end and nose-cap.

Rifle, Charger-Loading, Magazine, Lee-Metford Mark 2 (introduced on 1st July 1907). This is a conversion from the Mark 2 achieved by fitting a bridge charger guide across the bolt way and a new magazine; the rifle also had an adjustable blade foresight with a fixed protector and a new rearsight graduated for smokeless powder ammunition.

Carbine, Magazine, Lee-Metford Mark 1 (introduced on 29th September 1894). The carbine was based on the Rifle Mark 2 but differed in a number of small ways as well as in major dimensions; the total length was a mere 39.94in (1014mm), the barrel length was 20.75in (527mm), and the weight 7lb 7oz (3.42kg). The carbine's rifling was identical to that of the rifle.

LEE-ENFIELD SYSTEM

With the adoption of cordite as the standard military propellant, a change in rifling was made. Because cordite left virtually no residue in the bore after firing, the principal advantage of Metford rifling no longer existed and it was possible to adopt a more efficient pattern of rifling which was more suited to a high-velocity rifle. This was the Enfield rifling—named from its development at the Royal Small Arms Factory, Enfield Lock—and the marriage of this to the Lee action produced the Lee-Enfield rifle. A carbine model was also produced, and there were a number of modified weapons derived from earlier patterns which were modernised by rebarrelling with 'Enfield' barrels.

Rifle, Magazine, Lee-Enfield Mark 1 (introduced on 11th November 1895). This was much the same as the Lee-Metford Mark 2*, differing only in the rifling which had 5 grooves, 0.005in deep, with a left-hand twist pitched to make one turn in 10in. The foresight was positioned 0.05in left of the bore axis to compensate for the drift of the bullet. The rifle's length was 49.50in (1257mm), the barrel length 30.22in (767mm) and the weight 9lb 4oz (4.25kg).

Rifle, Magazine, Lee-Enfield Mark 1* (introduced on 19th May 1899). Converted from the Mark 3 Martini-Henry rifle by fitting a 0.303in Enfield-rifled

barrel. The sights were central to the axis of the bore. The rifle's length was 46.50in (1181mm), the barrel length was 30.19in (767mm) and the weight 8lb 5oz (3.78kg). Its most obvious feature was the all-embracing furniture and the snub nose. The rearsight was half way down the barrel, at a time when advanced thought was turning to aperture rearsights under the shooter's eyelids, and the familiar Lee magazine protruded through the bottom. The original introduction was cancelled, and the design was slightly altered by the addition of a wind-gauge to the rearsight and the substitution of screws for rivets in one or two minor places, after which it was reintroduced on 14th September 1903.

Length: 44.57in (1132mm)
Weight unloaded: 8lb 2oz (3.71kg)
Barrel: 25.19in (640mm), 5 grooves, left-hand twist [1]
Magazine: 10-round detachable box
Muzzle velocity: c.2200fps (670mps)

Rifle, Magazine, Lee-Enfield Mark 1** (introduced on 19th May 1899). This is simply the Mark 1 without the attached cleaning rod and its fittings.

Rifle, Short, Magazine, Lee-Enfield Mark 1 (introduced on 1st July 1903). With the intention of developing one rifle which would serve the infantryman as a rifle and everybody else as a carbine, the 'Short Lee-Enfield' was designed. Universally execrated by every self-styled expert in the Western world when it was introduced, the rifle was held to be too short to be a target-shooter's arm and too long to be a cavalryman's companion—and that, in fact, it was an abortionate device developed by unscrupulous Government technicians by robbing wherever possible every good feature from other rifles and then ruining them. In spite of this chorus of woe the 'SMLE' survived, to become in its later versions probably the finest combat bolt-action rifle ever developed.

Rifle, Short, Magazine, Lee-Enfield Mark 1* (introduced on 2nd July 1906). This was a version of the Mark 1 incorporating several small improvements suggested after the originals had passed into the hands of the troops. The old butt plate was replaced by one of gunmetal and incorporated a butt-trap for cleaning materials and an oil-bottle, a Number 2 pattern magazine and spring were substituted (being slightly deeper at the

▲An example of the first pattern (July 1903) Rifle, short, Magazine Lee-Enfield Mark 1. Note the design of the barrel handguard and the protecting 'wings' of the rearsight (RSAF).

▷The Rifle, Short, Magazine Lee-Enfield Converted Mark 2, of 1903. A sealed pattern label hangs from the small of the stock (RSAF).

▷A Rifle, Short, Magazine Lee-Enfield Mark 1* (introduced in 1906), made at Enfield in 1911 (RSAF).

▷The Rifle, Short, Magazine Lee-Enfield Mark 3 of 1907. The sights differed from previous marks (RSAF).

▷An example of the Rifle, Short, Magazine Lee-Enfield Converted Mark 4, introduced in 1907 (RSAF).

▷The Rifle, Short, Magazine Lee-Enfield Mark 3* was a wartime pattern which incorporated several manufacturing concessions to ease mass-production troubles (RSAF).

▷This example of the SMLE Mark 3* is a pattern sealed as a guide to the manufacture of a grenade launching attachment intended to project the Number 23 grenade (seen here) and to use a cut-down Pattern 1907 bayonet as a means of securing the projector to the rifle (RSAF).

---

1. Groove depth 0.005in to 14in from muzzle, where they became 0.0065in.

front), the striker was retained by a keeper screw which had a slot big enough to be turned by a coin, and the sharp corners on various components were rounded.

Rifle, Short, Magazine, Lee-Enfield Converted Mark 1 (introduced on 2nd November 1903). A conversion of the *Rifle, Magazine, Lee-Metford Mark 1** by fitting new sights, shorter and lighter barrels, and adapting them for charger loading. The original announcement stated that the design was sealed to govern such conversion as may be ordered, but none except the sealed pattern was ever made and the design was declared obsolete in 1906.

Rifle, Short, Magazine, Lee-Enfield Converted Mark 2 (introduced on 6th November 1903). A conversion of the *Rifles, Lee-Enfield Marks 1 and 1** and *Rifles, Lee-Metford Marks 2 and 2** achieved by fitting new sights, shorter and lighter barrels and modifying the action-bodies to permit charger loading.

Rifle, Short, Magazine, Lee-Enfield Converted Mark 2* (introduced on 2nd July 1906). A conversion similar to the Converted Mark 2, from which it differed in having the butt recessed for the sling swivel, provision for a butt trap, and a Number 2 magazine.

Rifle, Short, Magazine, Lee-Enfield Mark 3 (introduced on 26th January 1907). The principal change in the Mark 3 lay in the sights: it was otherwise the same as the Mark 1 or 1*. The foresight was a simple blade instead of a barleycorn (an 'inverted V') and was supplied in five heights. The rearsight bed was wider, and the sight leaf—graduated on the left and right sides to 2000yd—had a fine adjustment worm wheel. A 'U' notch replaced the former 'V' notch. The body was fitted with a bridge charger-guide shaped so that the closing movement of the bolt would automatically eject the

charger; and the charger guide on the bolt head was omitted. The weight was 8lb 10.5oz (3.94kg).

In 1916, as a wartime concession to the manufacturers, it was agreed that rifles might embody any of the following modifications: omission of the long-range sights, replacement of the rearsight wind gauge by a fixed cap, alteration of the contours of the striker, and omission of the piling swivel lugs.

Rifle, Short, Magazine, Lee-Enfield Converted Mark 4 (introduced on 17th June 1907). This differed from the Converted Mark 2* insofar as it embodied the various special features of the SMLE Mark 3. Weight 8lb 14.5oz (4.13kg).

Rifle, Charger Loading, Magazine, Lee-Enfield Mark 1* (introduced on 1st July 1907). A conversion of Lee-Enfield Marks 1 and 1* or Lee-Metford Mark 2* by the addition of a bridge charger guide, a new magazine and a new rearsight.

Rifle, Short, Magazine, Lee-Enfield Mark 1** (introduced on 22nd October 1909). This weapon was issued only to the Royal Navy and was a conversion from SMLE Mark 1 rifles carried out in naval ordnance depots at Chatham, Portsmouth and Plymouth. It consisted of fitting a SMLE Mark 3 foresight and a rearsight wind-gauge with a 'U' notch to suit.

Rifle, Short, Magazine, Lee-Enfield Converted Mark 2** (introduced on 22nd October 1909). Another naval conversion, the same as the Mark 1** but performed on the SMLE Mark 2 rifle.

Rifle, Short, Magazine, Lee-Enfield Converted Mark 2*** (introduced on 22nd October 1909). The third naval conversion, as before but applied to the SMLE Converted Mark 2*.

Rifle, Short, Magazine, Lee-Enfield Mark 1*** (introduced on 22nd April 1914). A conversion from the SMLE Mark 1* achieved by fitting a wind-gauge with 'U' notch to the rearsight and a new blade foresight to suit Mark 7 ball ammunition.

▲The Rifle Number 4 Mark 1 (RSAF).
▷An example of the Rifle Number 1 Mark 5, 1927/33, with an experimental rearsight graduated to 1400yd (SIM).
▷The Rifle Number 1 Mark 6 of 1930. Note the rearsight folded down on top of the receiver (RSAF).
▷The Rifle Number 4 Mark 1 of 1939; this particular rifle was one of the first batch made (SIM).
▷A Rifle Number 4 Mark 1, manufactured in 1941, with the Bayonet Number 9 Mark 1 fitted (SIM).

This marked the adoption of the Mark 7 pointed bullet, which superseded the Mark 6 blunt-nosed bullet.

Rifle, Short, Magazine, Lee-Enfield Mark 3* (introduced on 2nd January 1916). This was a wartime model differing from the Mark 3 in having the magazine cut-off omitted during manufacture.

Carbine, Magazine, Lee-Enfield Mark 1 (introduced on 13th January 1902). To quote the official paragraph: 'When Carbines Magazine Lee-Metford Mark 1 are fitted with Lee-Enfield barrels and have the wings of the nosecaps drawn out to the same height as that on the Lee-Enfield Carbines, they will be described as above. The barrels will be marked by the manufacturer on the Knox-form with the letter "E" . . .'.

Carbine, Magazine, Lee-Enfield Cavalry Mark 1 (introduced on 6th December 1907). The first purpose-built Enfield-rifled carbine, it was basically the Lee-Metford carbine Mark 1 with Enfield rifling, improved sights, the sling fittings omitted and an attached leather cover for the rearsight. The weight and dimensions remained the same as the earlier gun.

Between the wars the British Army decided to change the system of nomenclature of its rifles. The foregoing examples have shown how cumbrous the titles had become, and in the interests of brevity and accuracy the rifles were now listed in a numbered series, so that the *Rifle, Short, Magazine, Lee-Enfield Mark 3* now became the *Rifle Number 1 Mark 3*, although nobody but quartermasters and armourers ever called it that. Since the last mark issued under the old system was the Converted Mark 4, the first under the new system was the **Rifle Number 1 Mark 5.** This was made in limited numbers in the early 1920s but was never accepted as a service weapon. The principal difference between it and the Mark 3 was the moving of the rearsight back to the

body bridge in an endeavour to improve shooting by making a longer sight base. This model led to the **Rifle Number 1 Mark 6,** which was a further simplification of the Mark 5 and a step on the way to the design of the Rifle Number 4. The Mark 6 was never issued.

The object of all this redesign was to produce a rifle which would retain the general characteristics of the Mark 3 but which would be easier to produce in wartime. This aim was attained in the Rifle Number 4.

Rifle Number 4 Mark 1 (introduced on 13th February 1941). The Number 4 was similar to the Short Magazine Lee-Enfield but with an aperture rearsight hinged at the rear of the body, the nosecap abolished and the muzzle exposed for about three inches. All screw threads were to standard specifications instead of being 'gunmaker's specials'. The length was 44.43in (1128mm) and the weight 9lb 1oz (4.17kg).

Rifle Number 4 Mark 1(T) (introduced on 12th February 1942). This was the Mark 1 fitted with a tangent rearsight and prepared for a telescopic sight; the butt was fitted with a cheek rest.

Rifle Number 4 Mark 1* (introduced on 15th June 1941). This was similar to the Mark 1 pattern but with the following exceptions: the cutting of a slot and the omission of machining for the breech bolt-head catch, the omission of the breech bolt-head catch (with the attendant spring and plate), and the addition of a new pattern bridge piece to permit more ready removal of the bolt. The magazine catch screw was replaced by a pin, and the sear pin was increased in length. In other words, a simpler method of bolt removal was devised and instigated. Most of these Mark 1* rifles were made in the United States of America or Canada.

Rifle Number 4 Mark 2 (introduced on 31st March 1949). Similar to the Mark 1,

▲An experimental version of the Rifle Number 4 Mark 2 with an all-steel stock (RSAF).

▲A lightweight version of the Rifle Number 4 developed at the Canadian Long Branch (Toronto) arsenal. The sporting-style buttplate, necessary to reduce the effect of the violent recoil expected in such a light (6lb 12oz) gun, is worthy of note (SIM).

▷The Rifle Number 5 Mark 1, the so-called 'Jungle carbine', developed in 1944/45 for the Pacific Theatre of operations (SIM).

▷An example of the Austro-Hungarian Repetier-Gewehr Modell 1886, a straight-pull Mannlicher design firing an 11mm blackpowder cartridge (RSAF).

the Mark 2 was provided with a new design of trigger mechanism in which the trigger was hinged about a pin located in a bracket forged integrally with the body, instead of being hinged to the trigger guard as hitherto.

Rifle Number 4 Mark 1/2 (introduced on 31st March 1949). A Number 4 Mark 1 modified to approximate to Mark 2 by having the trigger rebuilt.

Rifle Number 4 Mark 1/3 (introduced on 31st March 1949). A Number 4 Mark 1* with trigger modified to approximate to Mark 2.

Rifle Number 5 Mark 1 (introduced on 23rd May 1945). This was the famous 'Jungle Carbine'—virtually a Rifle Number 4 Mark 1 shortened by about 5in (126mm). The other distinctive features were the belled-out flash-hider on the muzzle, a single hand-guard, a short fore-end stock and a rubber recoil pad on the butt. The rearsight was graduated to 800yd and set by a screw. Whilst dashing in appearance and light and handy to carry, the gun's recoil was excessive and few soldiers were sorry to see it go.

The remaining 'numbered' rifles were Numbers 2, 8, and 9. Numbers 2 and 8 were 0.22in calibre training rifles, but the Number 9 was a self-loader.

Rifle 7mm Number 9 Mark 1 (introduced 'for record' and declared obsolete on 30th May 1960). This was the weapon better known as the 'EM2' and discussed under that name in the section on self-loading rifles.

When the British Army converted to 7.62mm NATO calibre the FN FAL self-loading rifle was adopted, but—as a reserve—it was decided to rebuild numbers of bolt action rifles to accept the new cartridge. When this was done, the nomenclature was also revised in keeping with a system which was adopted in 1954. In this an initial letter denotes the service developing the weapon, thus 'L'

for Land Service (Army), 'N' for Naval Service, and 'A' for Air Service. This is followed by a model number, the letter 'A', and another number indicating the model variant. Thus where an earlier system might have labelled a weapon as Marks 1, 2 and 3, the new system would label it L65A1, A2 and A3. The model designations applied to the conversions were: Rifle Number 4 Mark 1 (0.303in) when converted to 7.62mm became **Rifle 7.62mm L8A4.** Rifle Number 4 Mark 1* (0.303in) when converted to 7.62mm became **Rifle 7.62mm L8A5.** Rifle Number 4 Mark 1/2 (0.303in) when converted to 7.62mm became **Rifle 7.62mm L8A2.** Rifle Number 4 Mark 1/3 (0.303in) when converted to 7.62mm became **Rifle 7.62mm L8A3.** Rifle Number 4 Mark 2 (0.303in) when converted to 7.62mm became **Rifle 7.62mm L8A1.**

MANNLICHER SYSTEM (STRAIGHT-PULL)
Austria-Hungary, Bulgaria, Switzerland
Osterreichische Waffenfabrik-Gesell-
schaft, Steyr
various calibres

Although Mauser's name is probably the most widely-known in military rifle design, Ferdinand von Mannlicher (1848–1903) deserves the palm as the more prolific designer. Mannlicher's experiments with manual-operation rifles had all but finished by the turn of the century, for from then until his death in 1903 he was mainly concerned with trying to perfect an automatic rifle. His fame, however, rests on his straight-pull rifle designs (especially the 1895 Austro-Hungarian service pattern) described by one of his obituaries as 'known the world over not only for its ingenuity of principle but mainly for the fact that it reproduces the essential requirements of a magazine rifle—construction with the minimum complication of parts and a directness of purpose which at once

stamps it as an ideal weapon to place in the hands of the soldier'. Despite this eulogy, it is apparent that the Mannlicher rifle suffered their share of drawbacks (a stricture which applies in varying degree to all military rifles) not least amongst them the difficulties of a clip-loading system and the lack of primary extraction inherent in the straight-pull bolt.

The early Mannlicher clip-loaded rifles used fixed magazine housings in which a complete five-round clip was placed, although later developments included the rotary magazines of Antonin Spitálsky and Otto Schönauer (see MANNLICHER-SCHONAUER SYSTEM). The clip magazines, which were used by all of the native Austro-Hungarian weapons, generally ejected the clip through a hole in the magazine floorplate.

11mm Repetier-Gewehr 'Osterreichische Vörlage', 1884. This early design, which never attained commercial or military success, deserves mention as the first of Mannlicher's perfected straight-pull action rifles, laying the foundations for others of similar principle which were later accepted as service weapons.

The bolt handle was part of a sleeve surrounding the true bolt, and with helical ribs mating in corresponding tracks cut into the bolt; pulling the bolt handle then revolved locking lugs— midway along the bolt assembly—into an out of their locking recesses. The gun's magazine was a top mounted gravity pattern, mounted in a position offset to the left side of the receiver where it did not interfere with the line of sight, and a mechanical linkage thrust the cartridges into the feedway as the bolt was operated. The rifle was chambered for the standard Austro-Hungarian cartridge, the 11mm Patrone M1877.

11mm Repetier-Gewehr Modell 1885. This straight-pull design represented a considerable improvement over the 1884 pattern. The bolt action was completely revised and used a vertically-hinged block which was cammed up and down by the bolt action to lock into a recess in the receiver under the bolt. The top-mounted magazine was abandoned in favour of a clip-loading box pattern in which the empty clip was ejected upwards through the action after the last round had been fired and the spent case ejected.

11mm Repetier-Gewehr Modell 1886.
This weapon was very similar to the M1885 but introduced a modified form of the clip system in which the spent clip dropped through the magazine floorplate after the last round had been chambered. This overcame one of the most important objections to the experimental rifles of the previous year.
Length: 52.00in (1320mm)
Weight unloaded: 9lb 15oz (4.50kg)
Barrel: 31.70in (805mm), 6 grooves, right-hand twist
Magazine: 5-round integral box
Muzzle velocity: c.1600fps (488mps)

8mm Repetier-Gewehr Modell 1888.
When the move towards smaller calibres was begun by the French with their adoption in 1886 of the 'Lebel' cartridge, the Austro-Hungarians were forced to reconsider their adoption of the Mannlicher-system rifle of 1886 which had fired an 11mm blackpowder cartridge. As a result they introduced an 8mm round using a steel-jacketed lead-cored bullet with a blackpowder charge owing to the lack of a suitable smokeless propellant.

The M1888 rifle was little more than the 1886 type redesigned to handle the smaller cartridge. It made use of the same type of cammed-block locking mechanism, which was one of the design's unfortunate features, for the locking block was under the rear of the bolt behind the magazine well. When the rifle was fired, it meant that the majority of the bolt was put under stress and—although perfectly satisfactory with a relatively low-powered cartridge—the action was not suited to the use of overloaded cartridges or those of greater power; this led to the development of the improved 1890 system.
Length: 50.39in (1280mm)
Weight unloaded: 9lb 14oz (4.49kg)
Barrel: 31.89in (810mm), 6 grooves, right-hand twist
Magazine: 5-round integral box
Muzzle velocity: c.1750fps (533mps)

8mm Repetier-Gewehr Modell 1888/90.
The M88/90 was identical to the M1888 except for the addition of a new rearsight leaf calibrated for the M1890 smokeless cartridge, for which the opportunity was also taken of strengthening some of the action's components.

8mm Repetier-Gewehr Modell 1886/90.
At the same time as the alteration of the 1888 rifle to fire the smokeless cartridge, it was decided to rebarrel as many of the surviving 11mm Modell 1886 guns as possible, in order both to provide a quick supply for the troops and to ensure that the weapons' useful life was extended. The conversion was applied to approximately 75,000 of the 93,000 1886-

type rifles manufactured.

8mm Repetier-Karabiner Modell 1890.
Defects had arisen as a result of the rear-locking feature of the 1886 and 1888 rifles, and so Mannlicher determined to produce an improved design which appeared in April 1889 and was promptly issued in 1890 as a cavalry carbine—almost so that the opportunity could be taken of subjecting the carbine's action to a long and leisurely trial. The gun reverted to the earlier straight-pull system in which revolving lugs were used, although they had been moved to the front of the bolt. The clip-loading feature was used and the carbine, like most of its day, carried sling swivels on the furniture.
Length: 39.37in (1000mm)
Weight unloaded: 7lb 2oz (3.25kg)
Barrel: 19.51in (495mm), 6 grooves, right-hand twist
Magazine: 5-round integral box
Muzzle velocity: c.1900fps (580mps) (smokeless charge)

8mm Repetier-Gewehr Modell 1895
This became the official Austro-Hungarian service rifle to the exclusion of the various other rifle patterns, most of which were quickly relegated to the Landwehr. The M95 was used throughout the Habsburg empire and was adopted c.1897 by Bulgaria; many survived until World War 2, including many in the hands of the Italian army who had received them in 1919–20 as war reparation. The 1895 rifle is mechanically the same as the 1890 carbine, using a straight-pull bolt with rotary locking and

◁The Repetier-Gewehr Modell 1888, basically a modified version of the original Modell 1886 to accept the 8mm smokeless cartridge. Note the smaller magazine and the generally slimmer appearance of the M1888 when compared to the M1886 (RSAF).

◁An example of the 8mm Repetier-Gewehr Modell 1895, used throughout World War 1 by the troops of Austria-Hungary. This specimen bears Bulgarian markings (SIM).

◁The Repetier-Stutzen-Gewehr Modell 1895, a 'carbine' form of the M1895 rifle issued to artillerymen and mountain troops (RSAF).

▼The Romanian Mannlicher rifle of 1893, and the carbine design of the same year (RSAF).

a clip-loaded magazine. The rifle was of conventional appearance, recognisable by the prominent spur of the cocking piece and the side-mounted piling hook alongside the exposed muzzle.

Length: 50.00in (1270mm)
Weight unloaded: 8lb 5oz (3.78kg)
Barrel: 30.12in (765mm), 4 grooves, right-hand twist
Magazine: 5-round integral box
Muzzle velocity: c.2000fps (610mps)

8mm Repetier-Kavallerie-Karabiner Modell 1895. This was the cavalry carbine derivation of the basic rifle designs and exists in two forms, varying only in minor respects. The same rotary-locking straight-pull action and clip-loaded magazine were used, and the carbine was fitted with sling swivels. One version was fitted for a bayonet and the other was not.

8mm Repetier-Stutzen-Gewehr Modell 1895. This was a short version of the 1895 rifle very similar in design to the cavalry carbine of the same year. The stutzen, issued to artillerymen, engineers and others to whom its handiness was an advantage, was fitted with a special knife bayonet with a foresight atop the muzzle ring. This was intended to compensate for the altered impact of the bullets when the rifle was fired with a fixed bayonet.

Length: 39.37in (1000mm)
Weight unloaded: 7lb 14oz (3.57kg)
Barrel: 19.00in (482mm), 4 grooves, right-hand twist
Magazine: 5-round integral box
Muzzle velocity: c.1750fps (533mps)

MANNLICHER SYSTEM (TURN-BOLT)
Austria-Hungary, Romania, Holland, Hungary and others
Osterreichische Waffenfabrik-Gesellschaft, Steyr
various calibres

Mannlicher's perfected turning-bolt action was developed in 1890 after some years of experimental work, and was of 'split-bridge receiver' type in which the bolt handle locked down in front of the bridge to form an additional safety feature; the bolt handle acted as an

auxiliary locking lug. Mannlicher also incorporated a removable bolt head which allowed the bolt to be hollowed from the front and left only the tiny firing-pin hole at the rear. The result was a strong and simple rifle adopted in 1893 by Romania and in 1895 by Holland; the Austro-Hungarians were, however, quite satisfied with the performance of their straight-pull rifles and so Mannlicher's turn bolt designs met with little success in his native land.

ROMANIA

6.5mm Rifle Model 1892. This was the first of the Romanian rifles and served as a prototype for the definitive pattern of 1893 which followed. The ejector of the 1892 rifle was mounted on the bolt itself, and there was no stacking hook on the top band, features which distinguished the two guns. The weapon was clip-loaded using a standard Mannlicher clip and the magazine held five 6.5mm rimless rounds.

6.5mm Rifle Model 1893. The rifle of 1893 was officially adopted as the service weapon of the Romanian army; in reality little different from the earlier 1892 semi-prototype, the ejector was moved from the bolt to position at the left rear of the receiver, and a stacking hook was added to the muzzle. The gun used a split receiver bridge giving a third locking surface when the bolt handle was turned down ahead of the bridge; the usual Mannlicher clip-loaded magazine was used and the rifle was chambered for the rimless 6.5mm cartridge. In appearance the gun differed from most contemporary Mannlicher designs in a slimmer magazine, owing to the use of a smaller cartridge; an offset piling hook and a side-mounted bayonet bar appeared on the nosecap.

Length: 48.50in (1232mm)
Weight unloaded: 8lb 13oz (4.00kg)
Barrel: 28.56in (725mm), 4 grooves, right-hand twist
Magazine: 5-round integral box
Muzzle velocity: c.2400fps (730mps)

6.5mm Carbine Model 1893. This was no more than a much-shortened version of the rifle of the same year, introduced for the use of mounted troops. The bolt-handle was turned down closer to the stock and the bayonet bar and stacking hook were eliminated.

HOLLAND
6.5mm Geweer model 1895. The Dutch rifle was a slightly modified version of the Romanians' 1893 design, firing a similar 6.5mm cartridge. As a result the rearsight of the Dutch guns was different; apart from the different graduations owing to the slightly-different loading, the Dutch authorities adopted a tangent sight similar to the contemporary Italian pattern which replaced the Romanian leaf-sight. The M1895 rifle could also be recognised by the positioning of the bayonet bar on the nosecap, for the Dutch had used an unusual type of bayonet fitting adapted from the British type used on the Lee-Metford and Lee-Enfield rifles; this meant that the bayonet bar protruded from the lower part of the nosecap and slotted into the underside of the pommel, and resulted in the bayonet lying directly underneath the barrel—although this was not immediately obvious at first sight.
Length: 51.00in (1295mm)
Weight unloaded: 9lb 11oz (4.38kg)
Barrel: 31.13in (790mm), 4 grooves, right-hand twist
Magazine: 5-round integral box
Muzzle velocity: c.2400fps (730mps)
6.5mm Karabijn model 1895 aantal 1 OM ('carbine number 1, old model'). The old model number 1 carbine was a short form of the rifle, with a short sporting-type stock, a straight bolt handle, and sling swivels on the left side of the butt and the barrel band. A socket bayonet, taken from the old Beaumont rifle of 1871, was used with the carbine.
6.5mm Karabijn model 1895 aantal 1 NM. The new model number 1 carbine was a modification of the old model, with similar sling swivels and bolt handle, but with more conventional stock and nosecap, to which could be fitted a short-bladed knife bayonet. The number 1 carbines were intended for the Dutch cavalry. A wooden magazine extension was pinned and glued to the left side of the magazine.
6.5mm Karabijn model 1895 aantal 1. The 'Colonial' model carbine was essentially similar to the new model number 1, but with the deletion of the handguard and a new turned-down bolt handle. The wooden magazine extension was used on this gun.
6.5mm Karabijn model 1895 aantal 2 OM. The old model number 2 carbine, issued to the Dutch Gendarmerie, was distinguished by the addition to the muzzle of a cruciform-bladed folding bayonet. The bolt handle was straight, and the sling swivels were fitted to the side of the forestock and the underside of the butt.
6.5mm Karabijn model 1895 aantal 2 NM. The new model number 2 carbine

was essentially similar to the preceding old model, but the wooden magazine extension, pinned and glued to the stock, was added to the left side of the action. The folding bayonet was retained on this gun.
6.5mm Karabijn model 1895 aantal 3 OM. The old model number 3 carbine was distinguished by the unusual handguard which protruded forward of the nosecap and forestock. The carbine was otherwise fitted with swivels on the underside of the nosecap and the butt, and a straight bolt handle.
6.5mm Karabijn model 1895 aantal 3 NM. The new model carbine was the same as the preceding old model, with the addition to the left side of the magazine of the wooden protective extension. This was not found on the previous model. Both number 3 carbines made use of the long carbine bayonet, which had a 19in (483mm) blade.
6.5mm Karabijn model 1895 aantal 3 gewijzigd ('number 3 carbine modified'). This was no more than the number 3 carbine modified by the removal of the swivels to positions on the side of the forestock and butt.
6.5mm Karabijn model 1895 aantal 4 OM. The old model number 4 carbine was recognisable by the standard handguard and forestock assembly, which distinguished it from the number 3 carbines' overhanging handguard. The sling swivels were on the side of the butt and forestock.
6.5mm Karabijn model 1895 aantal 4 NM. The new model carbine was the same as the old model with the addition to the magazine of the wooden extension, and the long carbine bayonet was still used.
6.5mm Karabijn 1895 aantal 5. Manufactured from shortened Geweer 1895 infantry rifles, this carbine is said to have been issued to personnel of the Dutch airforce. The bolt handle was straight, the magazine unprotected, and the sling swivels under the butt and on the left side of the forestock. The handguard and forestock assembly resembled that of the number 4 carbines, and the standard infantry bayonet was apparently used.
7.92mm Geweer model 1917. This rifle was developed during World War 1 to capitalise upon the common ammunition supply possible with the Schwarzlose and Lewis machine-guns then in Dutch service. The rifle was rebarrelled and resighted to use the 7.92mm rimmed cartridge, but it is unlikely that more than a few were so treated.

HUNGARY
After the dissolution of the Habsburg empire in 1918, Austria and Hungary went their separate ways. After developing a modified version of the standard 1895 model straight-pull short rifle, chambered for the Hungarian 8mm 31M cartridge which had the same base diameter as the old Austro-Hungarian

M1893 type, the Hungarians developed their own turn-bolt rifle based on the Mannlicher system.
8mm Huzagol 35M (8mm rifle model 35). This was the last Mannlicher to be adopted as a service weapon, and was basically the Romanian 1893 rifle redesigned in Hungary to fire the improved 31M rimmed cartridge, and shortened to more handy proportions. The result was a serviceable rifle using the protruding Mannlicher clip-loaded magazine, a two-piece stock, and a bolt handle which locked down ahead of the receiver bridge.
Length: 43.75in (1110mm)
Weight unloaded: 8lb 14oz (4.04kg)
Barrel: 23.60in (600mm), 4 grooves, right-hand twist
Magazine: 5-round integral box
Muzzle velocity: c.2400fps (730mps)
7.92mm Gewehr 98/40. This was not really a Hungarian service rifle, for it was manufactured in the Hungarian factories under German supervision. The Germans decided that they were in need of rifles, and so in 1940 they redesigned the 35M rifle to accept the standard 7.92mm Modell 98 service cartridge. They also deleted the Mannlicher clip-loading feature in favour of the Mauser charger type. The resulting Gew 98/40 was stocked in German fashion and used the German service bayonet.
7.92mm Huzagol 43M. The Hungarians were so impressed by the German improvements to the 35M rifle that they adopted the Gew 98/40 as the 43M rifle, although the stock and fittings reverted to standard Hungarian pattern. The Mannlicher bolt mechanism was all that remained of the original designs of the 1890s.

MANNLICHER-PARRAVICINO-CARCANO SYSTEM
Italy
State arsenals
6.5mm cartuccia pallottola modello 1895 and others
The Italian rifle design was developed at Torino arsenal in the period 1890–91 and was adopted by the authorities on 29th March 1892; the names of Parravicino, the general who was president of the commission studying the rifle's adoption, and of Salvatore Carcano, a technician at Torino who was instrumental in developing the gun, are often linked to the results which were little used outside Italy, though some chambered for the Japanese 6.5mm cartridge were supplied to the Japanese government, c.1905.

The only Mannlicher feature to be retained by the designing committee was the clip-loaded magazine, as the turnbolt action was adapted from Mauser's 1889 Belgian design with the addition of Carcano's bolt-sleeve safety mechanism. Various designs of rifles and carbines existed:
6.5mm Fucile modello 91. This was the original pattern of the rifle, adopted on

29th March 1892, and distinguishable by the full length stock, the box magazine, the split-bridge receiver and the tangent rearsight. A wooden handguard covered the barrel between the front of the rearsight and the first barrel band.
Length: 50.79in (1290mm)
Weight unloaded: 8lb 6oz (3.80kg)
Barrel: 30.71in (780mm), 4 grooves, right-hand twist
Magazine: 6-round integral box
Muzzle velocity: c.2400fps (730mps)
6.5mm Moschetto modello 91, per cavalleria. The cavalry carbine version of the basic rifle, adopted during the course of 1893, the gun was half-stocked with a folding bayonet under the exposed muzzle.
6.5mm Moschetto modello 91, per truppe speciali (Mod 91 TS). Another of the short derivations of the rifle design of 1891, the Moschetto 91 TS existed in two forms, the first of which was provided with a peculiar bayonet with a transverse fixing slot across the back of the pommel. This mated with a transverse lug underneath the moschetto's nosecap. It is thought that this particular feature was introduced by the Italians in an attempt to overcome the problem—which rarely arose anyway—of an opponent snatching the bayonet from the muzzle of the rifle during combat. The later version of the Moschetto 91 TS reverted to a standard pattern of nosecap and utilised the normal modello 91 bayonet. A third version of the Moschetto, the **Moschetto modello 91 per truppe speciali modificato,** was an alteration of the first pattern to approximate to the second; it can be recognised by a barrel band immediately behind the nosecap.
6.5mm Moschetto modello 91/24. This was a shortened version of the original rifles, which were cut down after World War 1. The gun, which was otherwise similar to the Moschetto modello 91 per truppe speciali modificato, could be recognised by the large rifle-type rearsight in place of the smaller carbine type.
6.5mm Fucile modello 91/38. This was a shortened and modified version of the 1891 rifle intended to approximate in dimension to the 7.35mm rifle of 1938.
7.35mm Fucile modello 38. The Italians found as a result of their campaign in Abyssinia that their 6.5mm cartridge was insufficiently lethal, and so an enlarged 7.35mm round was introduced in 1938 along with a modified version

of the 1891 rifle. Apart from the calibre, the Fucile modello 38 had a fixed 300m rearsight in place of the earlier weapons' tangent sight.
7.35mm Moschetto modello 38, per cavalleria. This was the cavalry carbine version of the Fucile modello 38, with a fixed rearsight and a folding bayonet under the carbine's muzzle.
7.35mm Moschetto modello 38, per truppe speciali (Mod 38 TS). This was the truppe speciali version of the Fucile 38.

At the close of World War 2, somebody—perhaps the Germans—modified quantities of the Italian rifles and moschetti to 7.92mm calibre. The results were somewhat dangerous owing to the increased chamber pressures, and although some later appeared in Syria and Israel few now exist.

MANNLICHER-SCHONAUER SYSTEM
Austria-Hungary and Greece
Osterreichische Waffenfabrik- Gesellschaft, Steyr; Societa Industria Ernesto Breda, Brescia
6.5mm
Towards the end of the nineteenth century many inventors attempted to design and perfect rotary magazines, in an effort to eliminate some of the less desirable feeding characteristics of rimmed cartridges when in a box magazine. Amongst the Austrians and Hungarians who produced rifles were Antonin Spitálsky, Otto Schönauer, and Josef Schulhof; Mannlicher himself produced two rifles using rotary or 'spool' magazines, one in 1887 (which had been designed c.1885) and a straight-pull turn-bolt rifle in 1888.

Few of the weapons had met with success, and it was not until Schönauer perfected his design in the 1890s that a chance arose of military adoption of such a magazine. Schönauer's magazine was allied to a bolt-action designed by Mannlicher, and in c.1900 the rifle was offered to the Austro-Hungarian authorities who promptly rejected it on the grounds that full-scale production of the 1895 straight-pull rifle. design had begun; they did not wish to involve themselves in expensive retooling. But the Greek army adopted the Mannlicher-Schönauer rifle in 1903 and many were supplied for the Portuguese trials of 1901–4, where the Mauser-Vergueiro was eventually declared acceptable.

The Schönauer magazine, also extensively employed for sporting purposes, used a spring-tensioned rotary spool into which five rounds were loaded from a Mauser-type charger. While ingenious and neat, the spool magazine conferred little advantage over the simpler and cheaper box magazine when rimless cartridges were used, though the design did permit surer feeding of rimmed rounds.

GREECE
6.5mm Rifle Model 1903. The Greek rifle was the only rotary magazine rifle ever to achieve service issue (apart from the Johnson autoloading rifle of 1941) and was easily recognised by the lack of a protruding magazine, unique amongst Mannlicher-type rifles. The gun was otherwise similar to the Romanian rifle of 1893 with a split-bridge receiver in which the bolt handle locked down in front of the bridge to supplement the dual locking lugs on the bolthead. Unlike many of the other Mannlichers, the Greek rifle could be cocked simply by raising and lowering the bolt handle, an idea taken from the Mauser system used by the Gew 98.

Although the prewar guns had been supplied by Osterreichische Waffenfabrik-Gesellschaft AG of Steyr, the onset of World War 1 obviously stopped deliveries as Greece declared for the Alliés. The Greek army soldiered on until the middle 1920s when, owing to the number of weapons lost by attrition, fresh supplies of M1903 rifles were ordered from the Italian Breda firm—deliveries of which commenced in 1927; it seems, however, that the rifles were still known as 'M1903' although they incorporated a small number of manufacturing improvements.
Length: 48.25in (1225mm)
Weight unloaded: 8lb 5oz (3.78kg)
Barrel: 28.55in (725mm), 4 grooves, right-hand twist
Magazine: 5-round revolving pattern, charger loaded
Muzzle velocity: c.2200fps (670mps)
6.5mm Carbine Model 1903. The 1903 carbine was simply a shortened full-stocked version of the rifle of the same year. Unlike the later carbine of 1914, the 1903 type was not fitted for a bayonet.
6.5mm Carbine Model 1914. This was another carbine version of the 1903 rifle, of which it was merely a much-shortened form. The 1914 carbine pattern was fitted for a bayonet.

▼The Greek rifle M1903, made by Osterreichische Waffenfabrik at Steyr (RSAF).

▲The 6.5mm Geweer m/1895 used by the Dutch armed forces (RSAF).
▲The Gewehr 98/40, a German derivative of the Hungarian rifle pattern of 1935. The Hungarian army later adopted a modified version of the Gew 98/40 as the rifle model of 1943 (RSAF).
▲An example of the Italian Moschetto modello 91 per truppe speciali — M91 TS — fitted with a grenade projector (in this case the annesso trombonico modello 1928) (RSAF).

MAUSER SYSTEM
Germany (originally)
Various manufacturers—see text
Various calibres—see text
The Mauser-system rifles were manufactured by a wide variety of firms and government arsenals; most of the first Prussian weapons were produced by the Königlich Gewehr- und Munitionsfabrik at Spandau, the government plant close to Berlin. After c.1874, guns began to flow from Gebrüder Mauser & Cie at Oberndorf-am-Neckar, a company renamed Waffenfabrik Mauser AG in 1884 and Mauser-Werke AG in 1922. Some of the Gew 71/84 rifles are known marked by the Königlich Bayerische Gewehr- und Munitionsfabrik at Amberg, the state arsenal of Bavaria.

The later Gew 98 weapons were produced by the Prussian government plant at Erfurt, Deutsche Waffen- und Munitionsfabriken AG of Berlin (who in 1896–7 received the Waffenfabrik Mauser shares held by Ludwig Loewe & Cie—of Berlin—who had themselves made Mauser-system rifles). Other manufacturers will be mentioned as and when they arise in the text.

Peter-Paul Mauser, born in 1838, was the son of a master gunsmith working at the Württemberg state's arsenal at Oberndorf; after an apprenticeship, Mauser himself took up work at the plant until he was conscripted into the artillery, for whom he designed a breech-loading field-gun.

In the middle 1860s he began work on improving the Dreyse bolt-action needle-fire rifle which was then in widespread service; his first improvement was the invention of a separate bolt mechanism which featured a self-cocking action (with the Dreyse it was necessary to cock the action manually before the action could be opened). After a brief and unsavoury skirmish with an American entrepreneur named Norris, Mauser began to manufacture small numbers of rifles; his first real success, however, was the adoption by the Prussian authorities of the Infanteriegewehr Modell 1871—thereafter issued to the forces of the Deutsches Reich. A number of Gew 71 rifles and carbines were purchased in 1876 by China, Mauser's first export order. In 1881 the Serbian army placed orders for 100,000 rifles, and from then Mauser's success was ensured. In the same year Mauser first demonstrated his under-barrel tubular-magazine repeater, later adopted by the Prussians in 1884 as the Infanterie-Repetier-Gewehr Modell 1871/84—although, owing to the advent in France of the small-calibre smokeless-propellant cartridge, the Modell 71/84 was doomed to obsolescence after a few short years.

In 1888 the Germans adopted the Reichs-Commissions-Gewehr Modell 1888, an amalgam of Mauser, Mannlicher and other ideas which sorely tried Mauser's patience (it is however arguable that at the time Mauser had little better to offer). But enough orders flowed into the Oberndorf factory, notably an order for 550,000 rifles and carbines placed on behalf of the Sultanate of Turkey, to keep the plant at full stretch for several years: indeed, it was found necessary to subcontract manufacture of the Gew 88, and so Mauser passed all such contracts to Ludwig Loewe & Cie's Berlin plant.

At the same time work began on a rifle to utilise the new small-calibre smokeless propellant and Mauser's first essay into the field was a 7.65mm rifle, which was adopted in 1889 by the Armée Belge and manufactured in the Belgian plants of Fabrique Nationale d'Armes de Guerre and Fabrique d'Armes de l'Etat, both of whom operated within or in the environs of Liège.

In 1892 the Spanish authorities were supplied in small quantities with a box magazine rifle which incorporated Mauser's newest ideas of bolt design, an improvement of the Belgian weapon of three years before; 1893 brought with it Mauser's internal magazine rifle, the first of which were supplied to Spain in the same year. After further refinement, the Spanish Fusil Modelo 1893 led to the Germans' Gew 98, arguably the most famous rifle ever developed. Indeed the action of the Gew 98 (although later modified in certain minor respects) remains the zenith of Mauser design, since all which came later were but improvements in detail to suit the purchasers' whims; the Mauser of 1895 (the year in which the action of the Gew 98 received its German patent) has become the standard to which is referred every other action of similar type. It is without doubt a strong action with excellent mechanical features—guaranteed to commend it to the troops on grounds of morale alone—and one which by virtue of its front-locking lugs contributes materially to the strength and accuracy of any arm employing it. There are, it is true, several minor faults—but none more than other designs, and there have been more rifles manufactured on the Mauser system than any other; that cannot be entirely attributable to good salesmanship.

1871 SYSTEM (Germany)
This was the first Mauser design to be placed in extensive production and to be adopted by the military forces. A single-shot weapon, the Gew 71 was instantly identifiable by the presence of a large slotted-head screw on the side of the bolt. Unlike the majority of Mauser designs, the bolt locking lug was at the rear and locked against the split receiver bridge. The two-piece bolt carried the safety catch on the rear of the cocking piece, as in all later designs.

Infanterie-Gewehr Modell 1871. This was the original German weapon, of full length with two barrel bands, a

nosecap adapted for a sword bayonet, and a plain trigger-guard. The rifle fired a large 11.15mm calibre cartridge loaded with a charge of blackpowder.
Length: 52.75in (1240mm)
Weight unloaded: 10lb 4oz (4.68kg)
Barrel: 33.46in (850mm), 4 grooves, right-hand twist
Magazine: None, single-shot
Muzzle velocity: c.1400fps (425mps)

Jäger-Gewehr Modell 1871 or Jäger-büchse Modell 1871. This was a slightly-shortened version of the basic Gew 71, and the weapon of the Jäger (rifleman) troops; the gun had a single barrel band, a nosecap adapted for a sword bayonet; and a trigger-guard with a rearward spur (intended as a finger-rest). The 11.15mm cartridge was shared with the infantry rifle.

Karabiner Modell 1871. The carbine was really a much-shortened and lightened version of the rifle, with a single barrel band and a nosecap to which a bayonet could not be fitted. The full-power rifle cartridge was used in the carbine, leading to an unpleasant and violent recoil, and it is thought that a special carbine cartridge (with correspondingly less propellant) was developed during the 1870s.

1878 SYSTEM (Serbia)
Puská 1878/80. This was a single-shot version of the Gew 71, and could be instantly recognised by a rearward projection of the action which acted as a platform for the open bolt. In 10.15mm calibre, most of the rifles were converted in the 1880s to take an 8-round tubular magazine.
Length: 50.70in (1290mm)
Weight unloaded: 9lb 14oz (4.53kg)
Barrel: 31.50in (800mm), 4 grooves, right-hand twist
Magazine: None, single-shot (original)
Muzzle velocity: c.1550fps (470mps)

Karabin vzor 1878/80. This was no more than a version of the rifle of the same designation—shorter and lighter, and with no provision for a bayonet. Most were converted to tubular-magazine repeaters c.1886–8; 7 rounds were carried in the magazine.

The Serbian rifles were officially known as the 'Mauser-Koká' system after the president of the trials commission, but they were more often called 'Mauser-Milanovič', after a Serbian engineer who had been responsible for some of the mechanical features.

1884 SYSTEM (Germany)
This was basically an improvement over the old 1871 system by the addition to the rifle of an under-barrel tubular magazine. The revisions were known as the *Infanterie-Repetier-Gewehr Modell 1871/84* and the *Jäger-Repetier-Gewehr Modell 1871/84*; in 11.15mm calibre, their recognition features were practically the same as the original rifle types of 1871.
Length: 51.00in (1295mm)

Weight unloaded: 10lb 2oz (4.62kg)
Barrel: 31.50in (800mm), 4 grooves, right-hand twist
Magazine: 8-round under-barrel tube
Muzzle velocity: c.1400fps (426mps)

1887 SYSTEM (Turkey)
This represented the last and most efficient of Mauser's rifles of large calibre, designed to fire a cartridge loaded with blackpowder; the selection of 9.5mm was necessitated by a desire to extract the last grains of performance from the propellant. The Turkish authorities ordered more than one half-million of the rifles, but the order was curtailed after Waffenfabrik Mauser had delivered approximately 220,000. Most of the 9.5mm guns were relegated to the reserve after Turkey had taken delivery of the improved 1890 pattern rifles firing a small-calibre smokeless cartridge; anxious of events in Europe, Turkey's sultan had ensured that his troops' weapons were the equals of those in the hands of the European powers.

Rifle Model 1887. This was essentially the same as the German Modell 1871/84, of which it was but a slight variant. The calibre of 9.5mm clearly distinguished the Turkish gun from its German counterpart (which was of 11.15mm calibre).
Length: 49.50in (1255mm)
Weight unloaded: 9lb 5oz (4.28kg)
Barrel: 30.35in (770mm), 4 grooves, right-hand twist
Magazine: 8-round under-barrel tube
Muzzle velocity: c.1750fps (535mps)

1889 SYSTEM (Belgium, Turkey, Spain, Argentina)
The rifles on the 1889 system introduced the box magazine to the Mauser weapons, using a detachable pattern with a front-mounted sprung follower arm which forced the cartridge upwards to be chambered; this accounted for the projection on the magazine, as the arm's pivot point protruded at the bottom front. The other significant advance in design was the adoption in these weapons of the one-piece bolt with dual frontal locking lugs, which has since become a major Mauser design feature.

BELGIUM
Fusil d'Infanterie Modèle 1889. This was the first of the Belgian weapons, adopted in 1890 and manufactured by Fabrique Nationale d'Armes de Guerre of Herstal; FN, as they have since become widely known, was specifically founded to manufacture Mauser rifles. The guns were, however, also made by the government plant (Fabrique d'Armes de l'Etat) in Liège and—during World War 1—both in England and in the United States. The Mle 89 rifle could be recognised by the prominent barrel jacket and fired a 7.65mm cartridge using a smokeless charge.
Length: 50.50in (1295mm)

Weight unloaded: 8lb 13oz (4.01kg)
Barrel: 30.67in (780mm), 4 grooves, right-hand twist
Magazine: 5-round box
Muzzle velocity: c.2000fps (610mps)

Fusil pour les Corps Spéciaux de Garde Civique Modèle 1889. This was not more than a slight modification to the basic rifle pattern, in which the bolt handle was turned down. A different type of knife bayonet was used—with a different blade length—but the nosecap and bayonet bar were unchanged.

Carabine pour le Gendarmerie à Pied et de l'Artillerie de Fortresse Modèle 1889. The carbine was a shortened version of the rifle with a turned-down bolt handle and issued with a long-bladed sword bayonet (which used the same hilt as the infantry and Garde Civique rifles' types).

Carabine de Cavallerie Modèle 1889. This was a lightened carbine which could be recognised by the almost half-stocked appearance; a long section of the barrel jacket protruded beyond the stock and there was no provision for a bayonet.

Carabine pour Gendarmerie à Cheval Modèle 1889. Intended for the use of the horsed police units, this was similar to the cavalry carbine although the stock was continued nearer to the muzzle and an extra barrel band was used. A knife or sabre bayonet could be used with the gun.

Fusil Modèle 1936. This was a modified version of the 1889 rifles incorporating some of the features of the 1898 system. It was only issued in small quantities.

TURKEY

Rifle Model 1890. This was a modified pattern of the Belgian 1889 rifle, again in 7.65mm calibre, but without the barrel jacket; instead of being manufactured from thin steel, surrounded by an external jacket, the barrel was of heavy tapered steel.

Length: 48.62in (1235mm)
Weight unloaded: 9lb 1oz (4.17kg)
Barrel: 29.13in (740mm), 4 grooves, right-hand twist
Magazine: 5-round box
Muzzle velocity: c.2000fps (625mps) using original round-nosed ammunition

SPAIN

Rifles and carbines were supplied to Spain in 1890 on a trial basis; virtually identical to the Turkish rifles of 1890 (and in 7.65mm instead of the later 7mm Spanish) they could be recognised by the appearance above the chamber of the Spanish coat-of-arms.

ARGENTINA

Fusil Mauser modelo Argentino 1891. The Argentine's rifle of 1891 was no more than the Turkish type of 1890 with a slightly modified bolt and a strengthened extractor. A 7.65mm cartridge similar to that of Belgium and Turkey was used.

Carabina Mauser de Caballeria modelo Argentino 1891. A short derivative of the rifle of the same year, the carbine could not be fitted with a bayonet.

Fusil Mauser modelo Argentino 1891 modificado para Bala 'S' modelo 1909. This was a version of the original 1891 rifle with a regraduated sight to handle

▲The Belgian Fusil d'Infanterie Mle 89 as manufactured by Fabrique Nationale; note the protruding magazine and the barrel jacket (FN).

▲The Belgian Fusil d'Infanterie Mle 89 cut to carbine length, c.1922-4; the barrel jacket has been deleted and a new barrel handguard added (FN).

▲The Swedish Gevär m/1896, a 6.5mm calibre rifle with an internal 5-round magazine. This specimen was made by Carl Gustafs Stads Gevärsfactori in 1902 (SIM).

▷The German Gewehr 98, in its original form with the unusual tangent rearsight (authors' collection).

▷An original Kar 98, showing the very distinctive shape of the pistol-grip stock, the muzzle-band, the piling hook, and the bayonet bar. This gun has a muzzle protector fitted, which also blocks the foresight until it is removed prior to firing (RSAF).

▷A late example of the Kar 98k, with stamped buttplate and barrel bands (authors' collection).

▷A Kar 98k with grenade launcher and grenade sights (which are on the left side of the fore-end; only the sight clamp is visible behind the rearsight) (RSAF).

▷The Kar 98k, here fitted with an Ajack 4× telescope sight (RSAF).

▷A specimen of the Kar 98k with the small 1.5× Zf42 telescope sight (SIM).

the 'spitzer' (pointed-nose) ammunition of 1909.

Carabina de Caballeria modelo Argentino 1891 modificado para Bala 'S' modelo 1909. A similar conversion executed to the old 1891 carbines. The adoption of the ammunition coincided with the purchase of a new rifle design (the modelo 1909 on the 1898 system).

1892/1893 SYSTEM (various countries)
In 1892 Waffenfabrik Mauser supplied the first of a new rifle design to Spain; known as the Fusil modelo 1892, a new pattern of bolt was used. A modified version, the rifle of 1893, also introduced Mauser's internal staggered-round magazine containing 5 rounds within the line of the stock.

SPAIN
Fusil del Ejército Español modelo 1892. The first issue Mauser rifle, although few were purchased before the design was superseded by the 1893 guns. The modelo 92 introduced the 7mm cartridge to the Spanish services and was immediately recognisable by the protruding in-line magazine of similar type to that of the Belgian 1889 and Turkish 1890 rifles.
Fusil del Ejército Español modelo 1893. This rifle, the first of a long line of similar weapons which attained worldwide dispersal, fired a 7mm cartridge and differed from the earlier modelo 92 primarily in the internal magazine.
Length: 48.62in (1235mm)
Weight unloaded: 9lb 7oz (4.30kg)
Barrel: 29.03in (704mm), 4 grooves, right-hand twist
Magazine: 5-round internal box
Muzzle velocity: c.2300fps (700mps) with original round-nosed ammunition
Mosqueton del Ejército Español modelo 1893. The mosqueton was no more than a shortened version of the rifle, with an overall length of approximately 41in (1040mm); it was consequently an intermediate step between the rifle and the carbine of 1895. It is probable that the guns date from c.1894–5. Unlike the carbine, this mosqueton used the rifle's knife bayonet.
Carabina de Caballeria del Ejército Español modelo 1895. The cavalry carbine version of the modelo 93 rifle could be recognised by the short length; stocked to the muzzle, no bayonet fitted the carbine.
Length: 37.00in (920mm)
Weight unloaded: 7lb 7oz (3.42kg)
Barrel: 17.60in (435mm), 4 grooves, right-hand twist
Magazine: 5-round internal box
Muzzle velocity: c.2000fps (610mps) with original round-nosed ammunition
Mosqueton para Artilleria del Ejército Español modelo 1916. The 1916 design of short rifle, issued to the Spanish artillery with a sword bayonet, was

similar to the 1893 type although longer. (The barrel band and nosecap were also more widely spaced.) An improved gas-escape system was incorporated on guns made after c.1925.

In addition to the guns purchased from Waffenfabrik Mauser AG and Ludwig Loewe & Cie, the guns were made in Spain by the arsenal at Oviedo (Industrias Nacional de Oviedo) and by Industrias de Guerra de Cataluñă.

TURKEY
Rifle Model 1893. This was little more than a slightly altered version of the Spanish modelo 93 rifle, in 7.65mm calibre in place of 7mm and with alterations to the action to accommodate the different round. A magazine cut-off was incorporated in the Turkish guns, something absent in the original Spanish issue.

SWEDEN
The Swedish guns were slight modifications of the 1893 system in which the shape of the bolt was changed (in the Swedish weapons the bolt face was round) and a guide rib added to the bolt body.
6.5mm Mauser-Karbin m/1894. The carbine of 1894, purchased from Waffenfabrik Mauser AG, was the first of the Swedish rifles and carbines. It was bought in the nature of an experiment to see how superior the magazine carbines were to the obsolescent Jarmann-type weapons then in service. The carbines were not fitted for bayonets.
6.5mm Mauser-Karbin m/1894/17. In 1917 all surviving carbines of m/94 type were modified to take a tubular-hilted all-steel bayonet.
6.5mm Mauser-Gevär m/1896. The rifle of 1896, firing the Scandinavian 6.5mm cartridge, was the Swedes' official infantry rifle—adopted after the authorities had realised just how obsolete the antiquated Jarmann rifles actually were. Many of the m/96 rifles were manufactured in Sweden by Husqvarna Våpenfabrik and by the state-owned Carl Gustavs Stads Gevärsfactori.
Length: 49.50in (1255mm)
Weight unloaded: 8lb 12oz (3.98kg)
Barrel: 29.03in (740mm), 4 grooves, right-hand twist
Magazine: 5-round internal box
Muzzle velocity: c.2400fps (730mps) with 156-grain round-nosed ammunition
6.5mm Mauser-Gevär m/1938. The original m/96 rifle ultimately proved too clumsy, and so in 1938 the authorities shortened some of the rifles' barrels to approximately 24in (610mm), reducing the rifles' overall length by some 5.5in (140mm).
6.5mm Mauser-Gevär m/1941. In 1941 it was found necessary to fit some of the m/96 rifles with telescope sights; special sights in two ring mounts were fitted to specially-selected rifles, and the result was extremely accurate snipers' weapons.

OTHER COUNTRIES
The 1893 rifle pattern was also adopted by Brazil in 1894, in 1895 by Mexico, and in the same year by Chile (whose rifles, short rifles and carbines had an auxiliary locking lug behind the bolt handle which locked into a recess in the receiver). Uruguay and China also adopted the rifles in 1895, and similar rifles were supplied to Transvaal and the Orange Free State. The last rifle of this pattern was adopted in 1899 by Serbia.

1895/1898 SYSTEM
The adoption by the Germans of the Gewehr 98 followed upon two years' trials in which the authorities had experimented with rifles of various calibres, including 6mm and 6.5mm; the rifles' action had been patented by Mauser in 1895.
Infanteriegewehr Modell 1898. Together with the Spanish model of 1893, the system typified by the Gew 98 was the most widely adopted of Mauser's rifles.

The Gew 98 introduced an improved bolt which incorporated a third locking lug at the rear of the action behind the bolt handle (something which had been used on the Chilean rifles of 1895), engaging in a recess on the action body; a gas diverting flange was also added to the bolt plug. The German rifle was otherwise recognisable by the pistol-grip stock, an unusual tangent rearsight, the exposed barrel, the under-barrel bayonet bar, and the horizontal bolt handle. The special and elaborate rearsight was not continued in later production.
Length: 49.40in (1255mm)
Weight unloaded: 9lb 0oz (4.14kg)
Barrel: 29.15in (740mm), 4 grooves, right-hand twist
Magazine: 5-round internal box
Muzzle velocity: c.2850fps (870mps) with S-munition
Karabiner Modell 1898. This designation was applied to two weapons; the first was a genuine short carbine version of the Gew 98, stocked to the muzzle and with a bayonet bar under the forestock at the position of the barrel band. The carbine was only manufactured in the period 1899–1903.

The second gun, also known as the **Kar 98** was a short rifle developed c.1904 after consideration of the British Lee-Enfield and American Springfield short 'universal' guns, both of which were designed for issue to all branches of the forces. (It must be noted, however, that although the arsenal at Erfurt received machinery to manufacture the Kar 98 in 1905 the weapon was not officially accepted for issue until 1908, whereupon deliveries of the rifle were made to the cavalry.) The bolt handles of both Kar 98 guns were turned down, but in the 1904-type gun a recess was cut in the stock to allow the firer to grasp the handle with greater ease. The gun had a prominent piling hook under the muzzle, and the

▲An example of the Modèle 1922 rifle made by Fabrique Nationale. Note the unusual muzzle band, which distinguishes these guns from the later models (especially that of 1924) (FN).

▲The Modèle 1922 Fusil Court, the short rifle version of the basic Mle 22 design (FN).

▲The Czechoslovakian vz/24 rifle, which provided the inspiration for the Germans' Kar 98k (SIM).

▲The Modell 1931 Mauser-system rifle made by Osterreichische Waffenfabrik of Steyr; this particular specimen was made in 1939 for the German Luftwaffe, by whom the rifles were used as Gewehre 29/40 (ö) (RSAF).

▲Fabrique Nationale's Fusil Modèle 35, also marketed as the 'Carbine pour Gendarmerie sans baionette'—a police carbine without a bayonet—and offered in a variety of calibres (FN).

stock of the second Kar 98 had less drop than that of either the preceding carbine or of the Gew 98 itself—probably to counteract a tendency for the gun to 'jump' violently upon firing by providing what might now be termed a 'straight line' stock. The muzzle blast of the Kar 98, which used the same ammunition as the Gew 98, was more unpleasant than that of the rifle owing to the carbine's shorter barrel.

(data: Kar 98, 1904 type)
Length: 43.30in (1100mm)
Weight unloaded: 8lb 0oz (3.63kg)
Barrel: 23.62in (600mm), 4 grooves, right-hand twist
Magazine: 5-round internal box
Muzzle velocity: c.2750fps (840mps) with S-munition

In 1904 the German army caused the rest of the world to reconsider their ammunition by the adoption in Germany of a pointed ('spitzer') bullet; all had previously used round-nosed types. The pointed bullet was of slightly larger dimensions and the new shape and diameter, plus an improved and heavier propellant charge, gave a considerable increase in muzzle velocity. The flatter trajectory thus achieved simplified sighting and fire control. Needless to say, every other nation eventually produced a similar design of bullet for their forces even if, as happened in some cases, the accuracy of the new design was inferior to that of the old round-nosed bullets.

The '1898' Mauser system has never been improved, except in detail, and in the years that followed upon its adoption many millions of rifles and carbines were made. All were derivatives of a basic pattern, with few alterations to the original patent of 1895. The Germans recognised the following major variants in their service, all of 7.92mm calibre.

Infanteriegewehr Modell 1898 (Gew 98).
Karabiner Modell 1898 (Kar 98), 1899 type.
Karabiner Modell 1898 (Kar 98), 1904 type.
Gewehr Modell 1898a (Gew 98a). This was slight post-World War 1 variation of the Gew 98 with a lighter pattern of leaf rearsight.
Karabiner Modell 1898a (Kar 98a). This was the post-1920 designation of the original Kar 98, 1904 type.

Karabiner Modell 1898b (Kar 98b). Although titled *karabiner,* this was no more than the old Gew 98 with simplified sights and the bolt handle turned down. A post-1920 variant.
Karabiner Modell 1898k (Kar 98k). The 'k' indicated *kurz* (short), which showed that this was a short rifle derived from the old Kar 98a. The Kar 98k was introduced to the German army in 1935, although commercial guns of identical type had been first produced in 1933—some had gone to Ethiopia and Paraguay before the Germans took their first deliveries. The Kar 98k was the standard rifle of the Wehrmacht throughout World War 2.
Length: 43.60in (1110mm)
Weight unloaded: 8lb 9oz (3.90kg)
Barrel: 23.60in (600mm), 4 grooves, right-hand twist
Magazine: 5-round internal box
Muzzle velocity: c.2450fps (745mps)
Gewehr Modell 29/40(ö). This was the German service version of the Austrian-manufactured Modell 31 commercial rifle, made at Steyr by Osterreichische Waffenfabrik; most were delivered into the hands of the Luftwaffe.
Gewehr Modell 33/40, sometimes known as **Gew 33/40(t).** The Gew 33/40 was a German-adopted variation of a Czechoslovak carbine, vz/33, with modifications made to shorten and lighten it. The result was a short lightweight carbine issued to mountain troops; like all such guns firing a full-powered cartridge, the Gew 33/40 had a violent recoil and an excessive muzzle blast.
Length: 39.37in (1000mm)
Weight unloaded: 7lb 15oz (3.65kg)
Barrel: 19.30in (490mm), 4 grooves, right-hand twist
Magazine: 5-round internal box
Muzzle velocity: c.2350fps (715mps)

After World War 1 there were sufficient surplus Mauser rifles to equip most of the emergent nations, and subsequent developments of the Mauser 98 system were few. The principal post-war developments were the Belgian Modèles 1922, 1924 and 1930 (produced at Herstal by Fabrique Nationale), the Polish Karabin wz/29, and the Czechoslovakian Puská vz/24—all of which were precursors of the later German Kar 98k, developed by Mauser-Werke AG from the Belgian and Czechoslovak guns.

▼The Mauser-Vergueiro rifle of 1904; note the split-bridge receiver and the position of the bolt handle in relation to that of most other Mauser rifles. (SIM).
▷An example of the Russian M1891 rifle with the old 1891-type rearsight graduated for the 1891 ball ammunition (SIM).
▷This version of the M1891 has a newer 1908-type rearsight, with a curved leaf and a different set of graduations, intended for use with the 1908 type L light ball ammunition (SIM).
▷The 1910 cavalry carbine (John Walter).

MOSIN-NAGANT SYSTEM
Russia
Tulskii Oruzheinyi Zavod, Sestroretskii Orzheinyi Zavod, Izhesvskii Oruzheinyi Zavod and various other plants
7.62mm patron o91g

The Mosin-Nagant was the first Russian rifle to incorporate the ideas of a small-calibre high-velocity magazine rifle, and replaced the earlier single-shot Berdan rifle in the hands of the Tsarist troops.

The first models were introduced in 1891, after a year's trials in which the Russians had sought to combine the features of a series of rifles designed by the Belgians Emile and Léon Nagant with those of one designed by Sergei Ivanovitch Mosin—a colonel in the Tsarist artillery. Upon their introduction the rifles were known as the **Russkaya 3-lineinaya vintovka obrazets 1891 goda** ('Russian 3-line rifle, model of the year 1891'). It will be noted that the Russians failed to include either of the inventors' names in the designation, and this has in the past led to accusations that the Tsarist government deliberately played down the part played in the rifle by Sergei Mosin: in view of the Germans' omission of Mauser's name in the designation of the Gew 98, and France's treatment of Lebel, further comment need not be made.

The weapons were known as the 'three-line' rifles as a result of their calibre; a line was a now-obsolete measurement approximating to 0.10in (2.54mm) which indicated that the rifles were of 0.30in (7.62mm) calibre. With the adoption by the Soviets of the metric system, after the 1917 revolution, the rifles were renamed '7.62mm'.

The rifles were in general appearance of straightforward turnbolt magazine pattern, charged through the action by means of a five-round charger. The bolt, it was usually conceded, bore a resemblance to contemporary French designs and was unnecessarily complicated, but this apart the rifles were serviceable enough.

The magazine was unusual in that it used a control latch which secured the second and lower rounds in the magazine and thus relieved the top round of pressure during the loading movement. Once the bolt was closed the latch moved clear and allowed the magazine spring to force the cartridge against the under-side of the bolt ready for the next reloading stroke.

Russkaya 3-lineinaya vintovka o1891g. This was the basic model, fully stocked except for a few inches of the muzzle to which a socket bayonet could be fitted. Although obsolete elsewhere, the Russian placed great reliance upon the socket bayonet, which was intended to be carried in a permanently-fixed attitude: indeed, alterations were incorporated in the sights to allow for the altered point of impact owing to the effect of the bayonet on the barrel vibrations. The bayonet blade ended in a screwdriver point with which the rifle could be dismantled and the cleaning rod, which was carried in the forestock, protruded beneath the muzzle where it acted as a piling hook. A leaf sight was fitted, graduated to 2700 arshins (an arshin being a native measurement equivalent to approximately 28in/ (711mm), although most rifles' sights were regraduated after 1908 to allow for the then-new Type L cartridge, whose lighter bullet had a different trajectory.
Length: 51.25in (1304mm)
Weight unloaded: 9lb 10oz (4.43kg)
Barrel: 31.60in (802mm), 4 grooves, right-hand twist
Magazine: 5-round integral box
Muzzle velocity: c.2650fps (805mps)
Russkaya 3-lineinaya dragunskaya vintovka o1891g. This, originally issued to the Russian dragoons, was identical to the rifle with the exception of a shorter barrel 28.8in (732mm). It was produced in place of a carbine, probably owing to a belief prevalent at the time that the new smokeless powders could not develop reasonable ballistics in a short barrel—a theory which was soon proved wrong.
Length: 48.75in (1240mm)
Weight unloaded: 8lb 12oz (3.98kg)
Barrel: 28.75in (730mm), 4 grooves, right-hand twist
Magazine: 5-round integral box
Muzzle velocity: c.2600fps (790mps)
Russkaya 3-lineinaya kazach'ya vintovka o1891g. A near-identical variant of the dragoon rifle, the Cossack (kazak) rifle was also intended as a weapon for mounted troops; few of this pattern were ever manufactured. It is thought that, unlike the dragoon rifle, they were stocked virtually to the muzzle and issued without a bayonet.
Russkaya 3-lineinaya karabin o1910g (sometimes called **karabin o1891g**). The

dragoon and Cossack rifles were neither true carbines nor true rifles, and as such they fell between two requirements; it was therefore found necessary to introduce a genuine carbine, some 10in (254mm) shorter than the guns it replaced, and consequently much more handy. The carbine's action was identical to that of the rifles. After the October Revolution, the Russians adopted the metric system and—after c.1922—many of the infantry and dragoon rifles' sights were replaced by those graduated in metres; none of the 1910 carbines were apparently so treated.

Length: 40.00in (1016mm)
Weight unloaded: 7lb 8oz (3.45kg)
Barrel: 20.00in (510mm), 4 grooves,
*　right-hand twist*
Magazine: 5-round integral box
Muzzle velocity: c.2500fps (760mps)

SSSR 7.62-milimetr'ya vintovka o1930g (also called 'o1891/30g'). This was the first of the Soviet developments, a modified version of the 1891 rifle pattern shortened to approximate to the dragoon rifle and with the receiver body changed from hexagonal to cylindrical (a change which simplified manufacture). At the same time an opportunity was taken to alter the archaic sights from the leaf pattern to a tangent-leaf type, and to

change the foresight from an open barleycorn (an inverted V) to a tapered post hooded by a cylindrical guard.

SSSR 7.62-milimetr'ya karabin o1938g. This resembled the preceding 1910 design, upon which it was based, although it incorporated the changes made on the 1930 rifle; the receiver was changed to a plain cylinder and the foresight was hooded.

Length: 40.00in (1016mm)
Weight unloaded: 8lb 14oz (4.04kg)
Barrel: 20.45in (520mm), 4 grooves,
*　right-hand twist*
Magazine: 5-round integral box
Muzzle velocity: c.2500fps (760mps)

SSSR 7.62-milimetr'ya vintovka o1930g with telescope sights. These were issued from c.1937/8 as sniper's weapons. The original was fitted with a telescope sight known as the PU, which was held to the rifle by a single block mount dovetailed into the left side of the receiver. Owing to the short length of the unit, which meant that the firer had to crane forward to adjust his sights each time he fired, the PU telescope was often replaced by the larger and heavier PE sight in two ring mounts, which meant that the windage and elevation controls were in a more convenient place. The rifles were still issued with conventional iron sights: indeed, apart from the special sight

▲The Soviets' M1930 rifle (RSAF).
▲The M1930 rifle fitted with a PU telescopic sight (RSAF).
▲An example of the carbine model of 1944, shown with the bayonet (which folded backward along the right side of the barrel) extended and locked. into position (RSAF).

▷The Reichs-Commissions-Infanterie-Gewehr Modell 1888. This particular rifle has been modified for the addition of a 4.5mm sub-calibre training device, loaded through a port visible behind the muzzle band (RSAF)
▷The Remington Model 700, military version, fitted with a Redfield variable-power telescope sight (Remington).

blocks, the guns were no different from the standard pattern.

SSSR 7.62-milimetr'ya karabin o1944g. The 1944 carbine design was no more than the 1938 type with the addition to the muzzle of a folding, cruciform-bladed bayonet. One is at a loss to explain the adoption of such an archaic design at such a late date.

REICHS-COMMISSIONS-SYSTEM
(Hybrid Mauser-Mannlicher)
Germany
Various manufacturers
7.92mm Gew Patr 88 (originally)

The Commission rifle was adopted by the German army in 1888. Committees in general design poor weapons, as they are prone to attempt adding too many desirable features, resulting in an over-complicated or inefficient weapon; in the case of this rifle, however, and of the revolvers fathered by a similar commission of 1879–83, the result was a strong and workable design in no way inferior to the weapons of other contemporary armies (although the rifle became obsolescent within a few years). Probably the best and longest-lasting result of the 1888 committee's work was the adoption of the 7.92mm cartridge which has continued, with periodic improvements, to the present day, and which has become so inseparably linked with the Mauser rifle that it has become popularly known as the '7.92mm Mauser'.

While Mauser's bolt action was recognised by the commission as the best then available, they preferred the speed of the Mannlicher clip-loaded magazine to either Mauser's contemporary tubular magazines or his first attempts at designing a box magazine. The commission's weapon allied the Mauser bolt to a magazine of Mannlicher's design, although the bolt was actually changed from Mauser's original conception by the addition of a removable bolthead, with the locking lugs on the bolt body—

a piece of gratuitous modification which, if it did nothing else, made the rifle more difficult to clean. But the Gew 88 also served as an inspiration to Mauser to develop the first of his frontal locking lug systems, exemplified by the Belgian Mauser rifle of 1889, whose appearance made the Gew 88 obsolescent.

The Reichs-Commissions-Gewehr had a short life. While mechanically sound (many thousands survive to this day, converted to fire various commercial cartridges), its downfall was caused by the limitation imposed by the clip-loading system which prevented the rifle being use as a single-loader and also prevented the firer topping up the magazine with loose rounds. Other nations were content with the Mannlicher system, but the Germans—being more combat-oriented than most—turned quickly to something better. The result was the Gew 98.

Several versions of the Gew 88 were issued:

Reichs-Commissions-Infanterie-Gewehr Modell 1888. The original variant, the rifle had a barrel jacket in the manner of the later Belgian Mauser of 1889, a straight or 'English' style stock, a protruding box magazine formed as a graceful continuation of the trigger guard, and a split-bridge receiver in front of which the bolt handle locked down. A bar for the sword or knife bayonet appeared on the right side of the nosecap.

Length: 48.80in (1240mm)
Weight unloaded: 8lb 7oz (3.82kg)
Barrel: 29.15in (740mm), 4 grooves, right-hand twist
Magazine: 5-round clip-loaded box
Muzzle velocity: c.2100fps (640mps)

Reichs-Commissions-Karabiner Modell 1888. The carbine was of similar action to the rifle, with a turned down spatulate bolt handle and a full stock; no bayonet was used.

Reichs-Commissions-Artillerie-Gewehr Modell 1891. Although termed a rifle, the

Gew 91 was of identical length to the carbine of 1888. It could be immediately distinguished from the carbine by the piling hook protruding underneath the nosecap.

Prior to World War 1, many of the Gew 88 rifles were converted for the 'spitzer' S-munition (and renamed **Gewehr 88S**), and these could be distinguished by the appearance over the breech chamber of a large 'S'. Many others (**Gewehr 88/14**) had a clip permanently fixed into the magazine so that the rifles could be charger-loaded (for which modifications were required to the bridge of the receiver) or loaded by single loose rounds.

The various versions of the Gewehr 88 saw wide service in World War 1, particularly in the hands of the German army's second-line, garrison and line of communication troops.

REMINGTON MODEL 700
United States of America
Remington Arms Company, Ilion, New York State
7.62mm NATO

This rifle is a current military version of the Remington Model 700 'Varmint' rifle offered for commercial sale. The only real differences lie in the adoption of a military grade of finish rather than the more polished finish demanded in the civilian market and the factory fitting of a Redfield variable power (3–9×) telescopic sight. The calibre is commercially known as .308 Winchester, so there is no change in the actual chambering.

These rifles have been supplied to the United States Marine Corps in small numbers for snipers' use.

Length: 41.50in (1055mm)
Weight unloaded: 6lb 12oz (3.10kg), without sights
Barrel: 22.00in (558mm), 4 grooves, right-hand twist
Magazine: 5-round integral box
Muzzle velocity: c.2800fps (853mps)

ROSS SYSTEM
Ross Rifle Company, Quebec (Ross's first rifles were assembled in Hartford, Connecticut, from parts manufactured elsewhere)
0.303in SAA
Sir Charles Ross designed his straight-pull action rifle in 1896 and first patented it in the following year. After several sporting and target models had been produced in the period 1897–1902, the Ross rifle was adopted in April 1902 by the Department of Militia and Defence as an official weapon of the Royal Northwest Mounted Police. The first deliveries of the rifle were made in 1905, though manufacture had begun in 1903.

Ross's original design made use of an unusual locking system based on the Austro-Hungarian Mannlicher rifles, although undeniably using features of Ross's conception; the bolt locked on an interrupted-thread in the original 1897 designs, although in 1900 Ross changed the pattern to a rotating lug system. A cam track was used to unlock the bolt when the handle was pulled to the rear, but it is interesting to note that Ross reverted to a thread system on his 'perfected' 1910 design with inconspicuous results.

The Ross was extensively tested in Britain between 1900 and 1912 but on each occasion it was rejected as a possible service weapon. The Commandant of the Small Arms School, at Hythe, summed up military opinion in his 1910 report on the Ross Mark 2**: 'It seems clear that this rifle is designed as a target rifle pure and simple, without regard to the requirements of active service or of the training of large bodies of men of average attainment'.

In spite of this opinion, the Canadian Army of 1914 went to war with the Ross, but, by 1915, it was found that the troops had lost confidence in the weapon, and were abandoning them in favour of Lee-Enfield rifles gleaned from the battlefields.

Official investigations revealed that the muddy conditions of trench warfare prevalent in Flanders were ill-suited to the bolt design, and that there was insufficient primary extraction which caused difficulties with cartridges of indifferent wartime manufacture. It was also found that much of the trouble arose by virtue of the position of the bolt-stop, which bore against the rearmost of the three locking 'screw-lugs': the result was that the massive steel stop butted against the lug every time the breech was opened, damaging it to the extent that it became all but impossible to force the bolt into a locked position. The Ross was consequently withdrawn from combat and relegated to a training role, but it was revived for a short time during World War 2 when numbers were shipped to Britain to arm the Home Guard.

There were innumerable minor variants of the Ross rifles, largely as Ross was constantly attending to minor difficulties in the design (it is said that one

▲The Rifle, Ross Mark 2, with Harris' controlled platform magazine; this gun has the Sight, Ross Mark 2 (RSAF)
▲The Rifle, Ross Mark 2, with Harris' magazine and the Sight, Ross Mark 2 (RSAF).
▲An example of the Rifle, Ross Mark 3 (RSAF).

authority recognises no fewer than 85 distinct models) and the picture is further confused by the periodic changes both in the rearsight and magazine design and by the changes in nomenclature; it is hoped that the following list will clarify the most important variants.

Rifle, Ross, Mark 1. This was the first of the service weapons, fitted with an unusual pattern of magazine known as the 'Harris Controlled Platform Magazine', in which the platform could be depressed by hand through an external thumb-lever. This allowed five loose rounds to be quickly loaded, after which release of the lever then placed the cartridges under compression. The Rifle, Ross, Mark 1 has been seen listed as the GP Model. Various sights were used with the Rifle Mark 1, leading to the appearance of a confusing number of subvarieties. It was originally intended to make use of the Sight, Ross Mark 1—a large leaf sight—but this proved too fragile for service use and was replaced before the rifles and carbines were actually issued by the Sight, Ross, Mark 2, a tangent sight based upon that of the German Gewehr 98 type (a Mauser design). A modified version of the Mark 2 sight, known as the Sight, Ross, Mark 3, was later found necessary.

Carbine, Ross, Mark 1. A short version of the basic Mark 1 rifle, the carbine could be recognised by the forestock extending to the muzzle. Unlike the rifle, the carbine could not be fitted with a bayonet.

Rifle, Ross, Mark 2. As a result of the trials and tribulations centred on the Mark 1, it was found necessary for Ross to devise an improved model in an attempt to stem the criticism. The Mark 2 had a slightly modified bolt mechanism which compressed the striker spring during the opening of the bolt, rather than the closing-stroke compression of the Mark 1. The chamber dimensions of the Mark 2 were also changed so that the rifles could be used with standard British service ammunition.

Rifle, Short, Ross, Mark 1. In April 1912 it was found necessary to change the nomenclature of the Ross rifles in an attempt to camouflage the number of modifications that had been made to the basic design. The Short Mark 1 was the new name for the Rifle, Ross, Mark 2.

Rifle, Ross, Mark 2*. The Mark 2* was the same rifle as the Mark 2, with the substitution of the Mark 3 sight for the Mark 2 of the earlier rifle. Some modifications were also made to internal components both to rectify deficiencies and to simplify manufacture.

Rifle, Ross, Mark 2**. The Mark 2**, similar to its predecessors, was fitted with a Sutherland rearsight in place of the various Ross types.

Rifle, Ross, Mark 2***, and **Rifle, Ross, Mark 2****.** These were minor variations of the Mark 2*, using the Sutherland rearsight, incorporating minor manufacturing modifications: neither

saw much service. The barrels of the Mark 2*** and 2**** were 28in (701mm) long.

Rifle, Ross, Mark 2*****. By the time five major modifications—discounting the innumerable minor ones—had been made to the Ross design, the Canadian authorities realised that something had to be done to further camouflage the amount of modifications and so in April 1912 they renamed the rifles 'Short Mark 2' (although they were still no more than variants of the basic Ross Mark 2 pattern). The Mark 2***** was otherwise similar to its predecessors, with a Sutherland rearsight, although a change was made to the shape of the wooden handguard over the chamber. The extractor was also modified and a 28in (701mm) barrel was used.

Rifle, Short, Ross, Mark 2. The Short Mark 2 was the result of the revised 1912 naming system; it was originally the Mark 2*****.

Rifle, Ross, Mark 2. This designation arose as the result of the 1912 programmes, and was not the same thing as the earlier Mark 2 rifle of c.1906. The '1912' Mark 2 was the new name for the old Rifle, Ross, Mark 2**.

Rifle, Ross, Mark 3. The Mark 3 was the first of the rifles manufactured to Ross's improved 1910 design, in which the solid locking lugs of the earlier service weapons were replaced by a form of triple-thread interrupted-screw system. A double-pressure trigger unit was fitted, and charger guides were added to the action body so that the guns could be loaded from the standard British 0.303in charger. The standard model weighed 9lb 12oz (4.32kg), but a lighter version weighing 9lb 1oz (4.11kg) was made for trials in 1911.

Rifle, Ross, Mark 3*. This is thought to have been a modification of the basic Mark 3 in which alterations were made to the action body and the bolt head to improve the efficiency of the lock. This designation is uncertain. A different foresight and muzzle-band were also apparently fitted.

Rifle, Magazine, Ross, 0.303in Mark 3B. This was the only rifle in the Ross series to have been adopted by the British Army, in October of 1915. It was the same as the standard Mark 3/Mark 3* with the addition to the action of a Lee-Enfield type cut-off, added above the magazine so that the rifle could be used as a single-loader while keeping a full magazine in reserve. The Mark 3B was declared obsolete in November 1921.
Length: 50.56in (1285mm)
Weight unloaded: 9lb 14oz (4.48kg)
Barrel: 30.15in (775mm), 4 grooves, left-hand twist
Magazine: 5-round detachable box
Muzzle velocity: c.2600fps (790mps)

Rifle, Ross, Mark 3 (Sniper's). A standard Ross rifle fitted with a telescope sight manufactured by the Warner and Swasey Company of Cleveland in Ohio. The telescope sight, which was offset to the

left side so that the action could still be loaded from a charger, was a 5.2× type similar to the US Army's Telescopic Musket Sight Model 1913. The Ross snipers' rifles were much loved by those to whom they were issued on account of their undoubted accuracy, helped by the 30.53in (833mm) barrel, and many were retained after the standard service rifles had been recalled. The snipers' weapons, of course, were not subject to the severe conditions suffered by the line weapons.

Approximately 419,130 Ross military rifles were manufactured in the period 1903–15, 342,040 of which were delivered to the Canadian military authorities and 67,090 to Britain.

SCHMIDT SYSTEM
Switzerland
Schweizerische Industrie-Gesellschaft, Neuhausen-am-Rheinfalls and others
7.5mm patrone M90 and M11

This, the national rifle of Switzerland, is a straight-pull bolt-action rifle, one of the few such designs which ever prospered although it is arguable that the deficiencies would have been shown more clearly under service conditions: the Swiss have fought few wars. The weapons are usually known by the soubriquet 'Schmidt-Rubin', from the names of the two designers; Colonel Rudolf Schmidt was one of the foremost firearms experts of his day, and to him is due the design of the rifle. Colonel Rubin was responsible for the development of the jacketed small-calibre bullet and the general conception of the small-calibre high-velocity military rifle.

It is difficult to understand why a straight-pull mechanism was selected, especially as Schmidt could draw upon the ideas of many of Europe's top designers, but it may be that there was in the design more than a hint of national pride—with an attendant desire to produce something that was different. It could also have been a way of avoiding existing patents, which could sometimes be costly to infringe. The principal drawback of the 1889 system lay in its inordinate length, something which was to an extent solved by the later 1931 system, devised long after Schmidt's death, and it can be seen from the illustration that there is a considerable length of receiver behind the magazine.

The operation of the Schmidt action is relatively simple; but what appears to be the bolt handle is actually attached to an operating rod sliding in its own groove in the action body. This carries a lug which engages in a helical groove on the bolt carrier. When the rifle has been fired, a rearward pull on the handle causes the lug to travel along the helical groove, at the same time rotating the bolt assembly to unlock the lugs; further movement of the handle then withdraws the bolt to the rear. The return stroke moves the bolt forward to chamber the round, after which further movement of the operating handle drives the lug through the helical groove and rotates the bolt lugs into the locked position. The ring which protrudes from the rear is a combination safety device and recocking handle.

The complication of the Schmidt action is not favourably comparable to the more widespread manual-turning bolt designs (*ie:* those in which the bolt lugs are disengaged by manual rotation of the

bolt handle—in the Schmidt this is accomplished by the translation of the linear movement into one of rotation). Straight-pull systems are usually more difficult to manufacture, and there are more moving and bearing surfaces involved: the action, as a result, is usually more difficult to operate and it is often particularly difficult to unseat a tight-

▲The Swiss rifle model of 1889 (RSAF).
▲The Swiss carbine Modell 1911 (RSAF).
▲▲Two views of the Infanterie-Gewehr Modell 1911 (SIG).
▲A left-side view of the Karabiner Modell 1931. Note the position of the magazine in relation to the trigger-guard (SIG).
▲The Karabiner Modell 1931 (RSAF).

fitting cartridge case. There is of course no primary camming extraction in a straight-pull system. Most straight-pull enthusiasts claim that the action's speed is superior to that of any manual turnbolt type, but it is open to considerable doubt whether the Schmidt designs can be operated any more quickly than a Lee-Enfield. It is interesting to note the fate of the only other straight-pull rifles adopted for military service: the Ross and the Lee were failures, and even Austria-Hungary—for long the champion of straight-pull operation—had decided by 1914 that her Mannlicher rifles would be replaced by Mausers. It is also possible that the Schmidt would not have been retained for long by a combatant power, as it is thought that the deficiencies would have shown more clearly in trench warfare conditions.

Repetiergewehr system Schmidt Modell 1889 (sometimes known as the **Infanteriegewehr M1889** or **IG 89**). This was the first of the Schmidt weapons, making use of Rubin's first perfected cartridge with a rimless case 2.11in (53.5mm) long. The rifle used a bolt with rear locking lugs and an exceptionally long receiver to accommodate the bolt stroke. The box magazine was abruptly rectangular and especially prominent as it was designed to hold twelve rounds. Most of the original 1889 rifles were later converted to fire modified ammunition; 212,000 Modell 1889 rifles were manufactured.
Length: 51.25in (1302mm)
Weight unloaded: 9lb 13oz (4.44kg)
Barrel: 30.75in (780mm), 4 grooves, right-hand twist
Magazine: 12-round detachable box
Muzzle velocity: c.2000fps (609mps)

Repetiergewehr system Schmidt Modell 1889/96. This was a modified version of the original 1889 type in which the receiver and bolt mechanism were slightly shortened to provide a shorter action. The 1896 action was readily recognisable by the lenticular cuts on the top rear of the receiver: on the M1889 they appeared at the front, immediately behind the loading port. 137,000 of the 1896-type rifles were manufactured.

Kadettengewehr system Schmidt Modell 1897. The cadet rifle was a much-lightened derivative of the M1889/96 rifle, intended for cadets whose stature was smaller than that of the regular infantry. The rifle introduced a peculiar spike bayonet to the Swiss service; 7000 were manufactured.

Kurzgewehr system Schmidt Model 1889/00. The 1900 pattern of short rifle, intended to be issued to bicyclists and machine-gunners, was really a hybrid of the M1889/96 rifle and the 1897 Kadettengewehr. Also intended to be issued to fortress artillery and other ancillary troops, it had a 6-round box magazine and weighed about 7lb 15oz (3.60kg). Eidegenössische Waffenfabrik, of Bern, made 18,750 rifles in the period 1900–4.

Kavalleriekarabiner system Schmidt

Modell 1905. The 1905 cavalry carbine was immediately recognisable by the full-stock, the 6-round magazine and the action of the 1900 short rifle. No bayonet was used. The carbine, 7,900 of which were manufactured by Eidegenössische Waffenfabrik, weighed approximately 7lb 15oz (3.60kg) and was 42.10in (1070mm) long.

Infanteriegewehr Modell 1911 (IG 11). In order to improve the ballistics of the M1890 and M1890/03 cartridges, a new round was designed to use a streamlined and pointed bullet, a more powerful charge, and a redesigned cartridge case 2.183in (54.45mm) long. To accommodate the additional chamber pressures, and to lessen strain on the bolt, the action was redesigned using lugs placed at the front of the bolt sleeve while the action was itself generally strengthened. The magazine capacity was reduced from 12 rounds to 6, a pistol grip replaced the straight-line butt, and a new pattern of tangent-leaf rearsight replaced the old tangent type of the M1889 and M1889/96 rifles. 133,000 M1911 rifles were made.
Length: 51.65in (1312mm)
Weight unloaded: 10lb 2oz (4.62kg)
Barrel: 30.75in (780mm), 4 grooves, right-hand twist
Magazine: 6-round detachable box
Muzzle velocity: c.2600fps (790mps)

Karabiner Modell 1911. The carbine of 1911 was the short version of the 1911 rifle design, making use of the same modified action. It was issued to all for whom the short length was advantageous—cavalry, artillery, engineers, etc. Eidegenössische Waffenfabrik, of Bern, made 185,000 of the Karabiner Modell 1911.
Length: 43.40in (1100mm)
Weight unloaded: 8lb 10oz (3.93kg)
Barrel: 23.30in (590mm), 4 grooves, right-hand twist
Magazine: 6-round detachable box
Muzzle velocity: c.2500fps (760mps)

Infanteriegewehr Modell 1896/11. This was a conversion of the original 1889/96 rifle to make use of the 1911 cartridge. The original 12-round magazine was replaced by the 6-round pattern of the 1911 rifle, a pistol-grip stock was added, and the old barrel was replaced by a modified one with a new design of rearsight similar to that of the Infanteriegewehr Modell 1911.

Karabiner Modell 1900/11. This was a modified version of the original Kurzgewehr Modell 1889/00 to handle the modified cartridge: alterations included the provision of a new barrel with a modified design of chamber, and the magazine pattern of 1911.

Karabiner Modell 1905/11. The opportunity was also taken to modify surviving cavalry carbines to handle the 1911 type of cartridge. The barrels were changed and the magazine modified.

Karabiner Modell 1931 (Kar 31). The carbine—or short rifle—of 1931 was the first radical change in the Schmidt action. The principal objection to the earlier

models had been the inordinate length of the action owing to the design of the bolt mechanism, and so the unit was redesigned to operate in half its length although still clinging to the basic ideas. The 1931 gun, issued to replace all the previous rifles and carbines, was undoubtedly the best of the Schmidt types and remained in service until replaced after 1957 by the StG 57; quantities of the Kar 31, however, are still retained as reserve. 528,180 were manufactured.
Length: 43.50in (1105mm)
Weight unloaded: 8lb 13oz (4.01kg)
Barrel: 25.70in (655mm), 4 grooves, right-hand twist
Magazine: 6-round detachable box
Muzzle velocity: c.2550fps (775mps)

Karabiner Modell 1931/42 (Kar 31/42). The M31/42 was a version of the basic 1931 carbine fitted with a peculiar form of telescope sight (1.8×) permanently fixed on the left side of the receiver. The head of the sight could be folded out of use, in which position it lay down alongside the stock.

Karabiner Modell 1931/43 (Kar 31/43). This was a second telescope-sighted rifle, of similar pattern to the preceding Kar 31/42 but with a 2.8× sight—the Swiss had found the lower-powered M42 scope insufficient.

Scharfschützengewehr Modell 1955 (S Gew 55). This was the last of the Schmidt-Rubin designs to be introduced to the Swiss forces; based on the Kar 31, and M55 was fitted with a pistol-grip half-stock, a muzzle brake, a bipod, and a conventional sporting-pattern telescope sight mounted above the receiver.

SPRINGFIELD SYSTEM
United States of America
Springfield Arsenal, Rock Island Arsenal, and private contractors
Cartridges .30, M1903 and M1906
For reasons which no doubt seemed good at the time the US Army had adopted the Krag-Jorgensen rifle in 1892, at the beginning of the smokeless powder era, but within a very short space of time, however, the Krag's limitations were realised and the Ordnance Department were forced to look into the question of replacing the guns with something more advanced. It has to be admitted that this step must have taken a great deal of courage, considering the large sums of money which had been laid out for tooling up and producing the Krag. Be that as it may, after considerable investigation of contemporary rifle designs and the painful lessons of the Spanish-American War, the Ordnance Department decided that the Mauser system had the most to offer and entered into arrangements with the Mauser company to build a modified Mauser under licence in the United States.

Since it was first manufactured at the Springfield Arsenal, the rifle came to be widely known as the 'Springfield Rifle', although correctly titled the *US Magazine Rifle, Caliber .30, Model of 1903.* As originally designed it was built round a blunt-nosed bullet of 220grains weight (Caliber .30 M1903), but while troop trials were in progress with this model the German army introduced its 'spitzer' (pointed) bullet, and the rest of the world hurried to follow suit. A 150grain pointed bullet was adopted by the USA to replace the earlier model and the rifle was re-designed to suit it. The cartridge with this bullet entered service as the *Cartridge, Ball, Caliber .30, Model of 1906,* and inevitably both rifle and cartridge have come to be known as the '.30–06'. As has already been indicated the rifle is basically a Mauser, but it is interesting to see that the American designers appreciated the waste of effort that went into the contemporary practice of designing a rifle for infantry and a carbine for the rest; in similar fashion to the designers of the Short Lee-Enfield in Britain they produced a short rifle which successfully filled both roles, sufficiently long to be accurate as an infantry weapon and short enough to be carried in a saddle bucket as a cavalry weapon.

The 'Springfield' survives to this day in the hands of private owners and survived for military use until the Korean War (1950–3), in which it was used as a sniping rifle and during this long career there have been surprisingly few varia-tions, and the following list summarises the military or 'service' models; it must be noted that a variety of match rifles also existed.

US Magazine Rifle, Caliber .30, M1903. This was the original version of the design, first supplied with a rod bayonet and chambered for the M1903 cartridge with a 220grain roundnose bullet; altera-tions were made to the barrel's chamber in 1905 and, with the introduction in 1906 of the 150grain 'spitzer' bullet, the rifles were fitted with regraduated rearsight leaves. The M1903 was easily recognised by the straight or 'English' style stock in which no pistol grip appeared. The rod bayonet had disappeared abruptly when President Theodore Roosevelt personally had the system suppressed.

Length: 43.20in (1097mm)
Weight unloaded: 8lb 11oz (3.94kg)
Barrel: 24.00in (610mm), 4 grooves, left-hand twist
Magazine: 5-round internal box
Muzzle velocity: c.2800fps (853mps)

US Rifle, Caliber .30, M1903, Mark 1. The Mark 1 was identical to the service M1903 with the exception of a few modifications made to accept the ill-fated Pedersen Device (see '*US Automatic Pistol, Caliber .30, M1918*') Changes were made to the sear mechanism, the cut-off was discarded, and an ejection port was cut through the left wall of the receiver—to the rear of the chamber—to permit the passage of spent cases. It is recorded that 101,775 of these rifles were produced in the period 1918-20, after which time the Devices were scrapped and the rifles reconverted to M1903 specifications; they can, of course, be recognised by the ejection port.

US Rifle, Caliber .30, M1903, Special Target. This was a specially-assembled and finished version of the standard M1903 intended for use in the National Matches' shooting competitions. Com-petitors were given the option of pur-chasing their weapons, but those who did not returned them to the military authorities by whom the guns were classified as 'Special Target'. These rifles were renamed in 1928.

US Rifle, Caliber .30, M1903A1, Special Target. This was the new name applied in 1928 to weapons of 'Special Target' class.

US Rifle, Caliber .30, M1903A1. This, introduced to the US Army on 5th December 1929, was no more than a standard M1903 fitted with a Type C semi-pistol grip stock.

Length: 43.50in (1105mm)
Weight unloaded: 8lb 0oz (3.64kg)
Barrel: 24.00in (610mm), 2 or 4 grooves, left-hand twist

Magazine: 5-round internal box
Muzzle velocity: c.2800fps (853mps)

US Rifle, Caliber .30, M1903A2. This was not a personal weapon but instead the barrel and action of an M1903 rifle carried in mounting blocks, which enabled it to be mounted in the breech of an artillery piece to allow the parent weapon to be used for training at restricted ranges and at low cost. Originally produced for the 3in Sea Coast Gun, the M1903A2 was later supplied with a variety of other weapons.

US Rifle, Caliber .30, M1903A3. This, introduced on 21st May, 1942, was a re-design of the M1903A1 devised to facilitate mass-production. The principal and most obvious differences lay in the adoption of an aperture sight—adjustable for windage and elevation—mounted at the rear of the receiver, in which position it replaced the leaf sight of the earlier rifles placed on top of the barrel. Various minor components, amongst them the trigger-guard, were fabricated from sheet-steel stampings.

US Rifle, Caliber .30, M1903A4 (Sniper's). The standard sniper's rifle derivative of the M1903, the M1903A4 was fitted with permanently - mounted telescope sight blocks. The Telescope Sight M73B1 (commercially known as the Model 330C) manufactured by the W R Weaver Company of El Paso, Texas, was chosen as the standard although various alternatives were accepted to offset supply difficulties. The M1903A4 weighed 9lb 6oz (4.34kg) with the optical sight. No conventional iron sights were used.

THORNEYCROFT SYSTEM, 1901
United Kingdom
Manufacturer unknown
0.303in SAA Ball

The Thorneycroft carbine was another private venture which, it was hoped, would be accepted as a military arm. It appeared in 1901 and few records remain to explain its background. The action is very similar to the Godsal (*qv*) and it is more than likely that there was some collusion between the two designers. The action is a little smoother, and a wooden guard on the rear of the bolt provides a better right-hand grip than is possible on the Godsal. Once again the magazine holds only five rounds, but the design could probably have been varied to accept more. The rearsight is quite an elaborate aperture pattern with elevation and windage screw settings, and the fore-sight is a simple barleycorn.

The remaining example of the Thorneycroft offers no clue as to its maker (although it might have been Webley and Scott) and so it is assumed that it must have been put out to one of the well-known manufacturers under private contract. The weapon handles well and is comfortable to hold and sight. It has been said that this was the last weapon to be specifically designed for use by the cavalry, but as it was never accepted there is no justification for this opinion. Notwithstanding the several useful features, the Thorneycroft was too late to influence the pattern of smallarms design.

Length: 39.12in (993mm)
Weight unloaded: 7lb 8oz (3.40kg)
Barrel: 25.00in (635mm), 4 grooves, right-hand twist
Magazine: 5-round integral box
Muzzle velocity: c.2450fps (745mps)

▲The US Rifle Model 1903 (Remington).
▲The US Rifle Model 1903A3; note the bridge-mounted aperture rearsight and the stamped trigger-guard and barrel bands (Remington).
▲The US Rifle M1903A4, together with the Telescopic Sight M73B1. There are no fixed sights on this pattern of rifle (Remington).
▲The Thorneycroft carbine, 1901 (RSAF).

Self-loading rifles

The story of the self-loading rifle—essentially a weapon of the twentieth century—is long and complex, punctuated by official disapproval, conservative military opinion and the insuperable technical difficulties encountered by many of the early inventors.

Regardless of claims forwarded by many, anxious to claim for themselves the honour of having produced the first semi-automatic rifle, the first service pattern was a Madsen recoil-operated gun issued in 1896 to the Royal Danish navy and coastguard; in advance of its time, this rifle was not issued to the Danish army and so its potential largely passed unnoticed.

The turn of the century saw various inventors striving to make practical propositions of their brainchildren, hampered as much as anything by the inconsistent quality of the ammunition upon which so much depended: the variable pressures so developed made it at times impossible to obtain reliable and consistent operation from the automatic mechanisms. Their efforts were also hindered by two further factors; the era's military authorities were reluctant to regard the rifles with much more than contempt for something little more than a means of wasting stocks of ammunition, and at that an unreliable way in which to do it. The second problem was one of metallurgy, a science still then in its infancy, which led to difficulties in manufacturing parts both sufficiently light and sufficiently strong. Most of the rifle designs proposed by Mauser and Mannlicher—most of which were recoil-operated—failed because the often brilliant design concepts were not matched in practice by the manufacture.

Gas-operation offered an alternative, discarding the complex metal-to-metal bearing surfaces of the recoil guns at the expense of greater reliability upon the comparatively unreliable ammunition. Rifles of this type, exemplified by the Mexican/Swiss Mondragon of c.1907 (although a design claimed to have originated in 1893), were used during World War 1 to no great effect. Mud so clogged the various guns tried in World War 1's trenches, including the French RSC which probably emerged with most credit, to justify whatever doubts existed in the military's mind.

The malaise unfortunately lasted through the interwar years and, despite extensive tests in several countries, only the USA and the USSR had by 1939 issued self-loading weapons to their troops (although the guns were widespread in neither army). The American Rifle M1 Garand, despite its failings, was the outstanding weapon of its class in the early war years. The 1943 development by the Germans of the 7.92mm intermediate round, together with the MP43 *sturmgewehr* (the first gun in a class now termed 'assault rifles') influenced further development.

Self-loading rifles design has now, perhaps, reached its zenith in such weapons as the AKM, the M16, the SIG SG510, and the various Stoner and Armalite designs. What future improvement there will be must be centred—once the argument of ideal calibre and bullet weight has been finally resolved—on providing lighter guns without sacrificing strength, which means (amongst other things) that improvements must be sought in metallurgy.

▶A field conversion of the Rifle No 1 Mk 3 (SMLE Mk 3) made at an unknown base workshop during World War 2. This is an interesting example of a severly-impractical idea—a conversion of a service bolt-action rifle to automatic fire (RSAF).

▼An example what could have been, and yet was not: the unfortunate Farquhar-Hill self-loading rifle. Submitted to various trials in Britain in the period 1908-30, this—but for ill-fortune and the attitude of the testing commissions—could perhaps have served the British well in World War 1. The guns were submitted in various calibres including the 7.65mm and 7.92mm Mauser cartridges, and a peculiar 'wildcat' made by enlarging the neck of a 7.65mm case to take a standard British 0.303in bullet. The weapons shown here are, (top) 7.92mm of c.1908, (middle) 0.303in of c.1914, and (bottom) 0.303in of 1915.

FUSIL AUTOMATIQUE MODELE 1930 (or 'FUSIL MITRAILLEUR MLE 30')
Belgium
Fabrique Nationale d'Armes de Guerre, Herstal-lèz-Liège
Various calibres

The Belgian Mle 1930 rifle is an FN-manufactured Browning Automatic Rifle, originally based on the United States Army's M1918 type. There are some small differences—notably in the design of the magazine, the ejection port covers, and the gas regulator—and the barrel is ribbed as a gesture towards solving the cooling problem.

In addition to being a standard Belgian Army weapon (in 7.65mm), the Mle 1930 was offered commercially and can be met in a variety of calibres. Some were provided with quick-change barrels. Guns are known to have been supplied by FN to Chile, China, Poland and Sweden—all of whom received deliveries prior to 1939. Sweden also developed and manufactured indigenous guns, made by the state-owned Carl Gustafs Stads Gevärsfactori at Eskilstuna.

FUSIL AUTOMATIQUE BROWNING TYPE D
Belgium
Fabrique Nationale d'Armes de Guerre, Herstal-lèz-Liège
7.92mm, 0.30in (US Model 1906)

The Type D automatic rifle is a modernised version of the venerable Browning Automatic Rifle (or BAR) first designed in 1917, and of Fabrique Nationale's Modèle 30. After World War 2 Fabrique Nationale saw a market for an improved model of this gun, which would provide a light machine-gun lighter than those current at the time. It was bought in small numbers by the Belgian and Egyptian armies, by the latter after their defeat in the 1947 Israeli War when they set about rearming and replacing their rather antiquated equipment. Two significant improvements over the original Browning design are incorporated in the Type D. The first is the fact that the barrel can be easily and quickly changed, so allowing the gunner the capability of continuous fire provided that he has other barrels. The other is a simplification of the assembly of the receiver and trigger mechanism so that these components can be more easily removed, replaced, or cleaned. These changes made the Type D a much better light machine-gun—but it came too late and could not compete with others that were appearing at the same time. One drawback was the 20-round magazine which, owing to an upward feed, could not easily be enlarged. However, the Type D served the Egyptian Army well enough for several years until the Soviets replaced it with their patterns.
Length: 45.00in (1143mm)
Weight unloaded: 20lb 4oz (9.18kg)
Barrel: 20.00in (508mm), 4 grooves, right-hand twist
Magazine: 20-round detachable box
Muzzle velocity: c.2400fps (730mps)

FUSIL AUTOMATIQUE MODELE 49 (often known as the 'Saive', SAFN or ABL)
Belgium
Fabrique Nationale d'Armes de Guerre, Herstal-lèz-Liège
7mm, 7.65mm, 7.92mm, 0.30in

The Modèle 49—offered in standard (selective-fire), automatic only, and sniper versions—was designed before World War 2 and was shelved during the German occupation, appearing to catch the immediate postwar market for self-loading rifles which became surprisingly large and lucrative. As the range of calibres shows, every effort was made to please the customer and the rifle was sold in large numbers in Egypt, Europe and South America. The bolt system is similar to the Russian Tokarev as the action is locked by the bolt tilting under the influence of cams in the receiver sides. The action is operated by gas, with a long cylinder and tappet above the barrel. The firing pin is struck by a hammer and the 10-round magazine can be loaded either by chargers or with individual rounds. The whole construction of the rifle is of a very high standard, making it expensive to produce, and the Mle 49 was taken as a basis for the development of the later FAL—which is an undeniable improvement on it.

Amongst the users of the Mle 49 were Colombia (0.30in), Venezuela (7mm), Egypt (7.92mm), and Indonesia (0.30in).
Length: 44.00in (1116mm)
Weight unloaded: 9lb 8oz (4.31kg)
Barrel: 23.25in (590mm), 4 grooves, right-hand twist
Magazine: 10-round detachable box
Muzzle velocity: c.2400fps (730mps)

FUSIL AUTOMATIQUE LEGER (FAL)
Belgium
Fabrique Nationale d'Armes de Guerre, Herstal-lèz-Liège
7.62mm NATO

Probably the most successful of the many designs produced by Fabrique Nationale, the FAL (Fusil Automatique Léger) has been sold to thirty-six countries at the time of writing, but the number continues to grow rapidly. The FAL has been made under licence in many countries all over the world and the design is the equipment of most of the NATO partners. Such enormous success stems partly from political and economic factors, but these would be of little influence if the original weapon was not sound and practical. This it is in every way. Developed from the Modèle 49, the FAL first appeared in 1950, and large orders were first placed in 1953. Changes in the trigger mechanism make the rifle capable of automatic fire, but it

◁FN's Fusil Automatique Mle 30 (RSAF).
◁The Fusil Automatique Type D, a slightly modernised version of the preceding Mle 30, and hence of the old Browning automatic rifle of World War 1 (FN).
◁A specimen of the SLEM self-loading rifle, manufactured at RSAF Enfield Lock c.1945-6 ('SLEM'—'self-loading experimental model') and designed by Dieudonné Saive. Saive fled Belgium at the time of the German invasion in 1940 and landed in Britain, where he was able to further develop his rifle designs. The SLEM, tested by the British and ultimately rejected, was made in postwar years by Fabrique Nationale under the title 'Modele 1949' (SIM).

◁An Egyptian version of the SAFN, bought from FN in the early 1950s; this gun is chambered for the 7.92mm round (SIM).
◁The SAFN, ABL or Modèle 1949 (FN)
▲An experimental version of the Belgian FAL—probably c.1952/3—made for tests in Britain. This later led to the Rifle L1A1 (RSAF).

is a little light and climbs excessively, even when fitted with a light bipod. A version with a heavier barrel and a robust bipod is intended to be a squad light automatic gun and is used by several armies for this purpose. All versions are outwardly similar, although there are some changes in furniture and such smaller items as flash-hiders and bayonet fixings. The cocking handle is on the left-hand side—so leaving the right-hand on the trigger when cocking—and there is a folding carrying handle.

Robust, reliable, and simple to maintain and operate, the FAL set a new standard when it appeared and it has continued as a leading design for over twenty years. Many countries have adopted the FAL, among them Austria, Belgium, Canada, Chile, Ecuador, Ireland, Israel, Libya, Netherlands, Paraguay, Peru, Portugal, South Africa, the United Kingdom, West Germany and Venezuela.

Length: 41.50in (1053mm)
Weight unloaded: 9lb 8oz (4.31kg)
Barrel: 21.00in (533mm), 4 grooves, right-hand twist
Magazine: 20-round detachable box
Muzzle velocity: c.2800fps (853mps)

◁The T48 rifle, FN's competitor in the US trials which ultimately led to the adoption in 1957 of the M14. In addition to the weapons purchased direct from FN, a small number were also made in the USA by Harrington & Richardson (authors' collection).
◁The Fusil Automatique Legér—FAL or LAR (light automatic rifle)—as marketed by Fabrique Nationale (FN).
◁The folding stock version of the FAL (FN).
◁The heavy-barrel version of the FAL (marketed in English-speaking countries as the LAR HB) with a bipod, for use as a light machine-gun and capable of a measure of sustained fire (FN).
▲The Carabine Automatique Legér, a 5.56mm version of the 7.62mm FAL although using a different locking system (FN).
▼The Holek-designed vz/29 self-loading rifle, tested by several countries in the 1930s (including the USA) but not adopted (RSAF).

CARABINE AUTOMATIQUE LEGERE (CAL)
Belgium
Fabrique Nationale d'Armes de Guerre, Herstal-lèz-Liège
5.56mm × 45mm (0.223in)
The Vietnam war has brought about a new family of smallarms, just as previous wars have done, and in this case it is the 5.56mm series. The success of this calibre has prompted several manufacturers to make their own weapons in 5.56mm and the CAL (Carabine Automatique Légère) is the one first produced by Fabrique Nationale. It much resembles a scaled-down version of the FAL although the system of operation uses a rotating bolt. Early models had a 3-round selector system, an integral part of the trigger, which permitted three consecutive rounds to be fired with one trigger pull. There is also provision for fully automatic and semi-automatic fire. The barrel is held to the receiver by a single large threaded nut and, once the hand guard has been removed, dismounting the barrel is simple. The magazine holds 20 rounds and the entire weapon is neat and workmanlike. It has yet to sell in significant numbers, but this may be due to the fact that it is only ten or so years since the major countries in Europe changed to the 7.62mm NATO round and the cost of a further change of calibre is too high until the 7.62mm type has become outdated.
Length: 38.50in (978mm)
Weight unloaded: 6lb 8oz (2.99kg)
Barrel: 18.50in (469mm), 6 grooves, right-hand twist
Magazine: 20-round detachable box
Cyclic rate: 850rpm
Muzzle velocity: c.3200fps (975mps)

ZCASTA SAMOCINNA PUSKA HOLEK VZ/29
Czechoslovakia
Ceská Zbrojovká Holek, Brno
7.92mm Gew Patr 98 (German)
Designed by Emanuel Holek of the Brno factory in the middle 1920s, the ZH-vz/29 was widely tested by many countries in the 1930s but few ever found their way into military service. Operation was by a gas piston upon the principle later perfected in the various ZB machine-guns, although the vz/29 made use of a locking bolt cammed into a recess in one side of the receiver. The design necessitated a chamber which was eccentric to the axis of the barrel blank—an expensive item to machine accurately.

Long and heavy, the vz/29 was nevertheless reliable and was obviously designed to provide a weapon capable of sustained fire, as shown by the unusual ribbed handguard of light alloy intended to prevent barrel heat from blistering the firer's fingers. The guns were made in single-shot or selective single-shot/automatic patterns, the customers' demands being as readily met in this respect as they were in the matter of calibre and barrel length.
Length: 45.50in (1155mm)
Weight unloaded: 10lb 0oz (4.54kg)
Barrel: 21.50in (545mm), 4 grooves, right-hand twist
Magazine: 10 or 25-round detachable box
Muzzle velocity: c.2700fps (823mps)

ZCASTA SAMOCINNA PUSKA ZK VZ/420, ZCASTA SAMOCINNA PUSKA VZ/420S
Czechoslovakia
Ceskoslovenská Zbrojovká Koucky, Brno
7.92mm Gew Patr 98 (German)

The ZK vz/420 was one of several designs by the talented pair Josef and Frantizek Koucky (hence the 'K' in ZK) and first appeared in 1942: there was progressive improvement on the original prototype until the final version of 1946. This had a short forestock and a prominent gas cylinder projecting from it. The one-piece bolt is inside a bolt carrier and is rotated into and out of lock by a stud and cam cut in the carrier; locking is achieved by rotating the forward lugs into recesses immediately behind the breech. The construction relies heavily on milling and similar time-consuming and expensive processes, so that the rifle was too expensive and rather heavy to compete in the postwar markets. It was not adopted by the Czech Army, which did not help its potential sales, although it was offered in several calibres including 7mm, 7.5mm and 0.30in. The ZK was tried in many European countries but does not appear to have been bought in any quantity.

The design was improved in certain respects and renamed the ZK vz/420S, but it met with no better success and passed out of production when the vz/52 was adopted by the Czech Army. There were no real faults in either the 420 or the 420S; their only trouble was that by the time that they were perfected there were too many self-loading rifles from which to choose, and after World War 2 any new design had to contend with the huge numbers of surplus arms which were to be had comparatively cheaply and easily. Unless a design was unusually radical or advanced it simply stood no chance, and the 420 was no more than a well-made (but undistinguished) derivation from a series which had been in existence for some years.

(data: ZK vz/420)
Length: 41.25in (1047mm)
Weight unloaded: 10lb 0oz (4.54kg)
Barrel: 21.00in (533mm), 4 grooves, right-hand twist
Magazine: 10-round detachable box
Muzzle velocity: c.2700fps (822mps)

(data: ZK vz/420S)
Length: 40.00in (1016mm)
Weight unloaded: 9lb. 0oz (4.08kg)
Barrel: 20.50in (520mm), 4 grooves, right-hand twist
Magazine: 10-round detachable box
Muzzle velocity: c.2450fps (746mps)

▲The Czechoslovakian vz/420S rifle (John Walter).
▲The vz/52 (SIM).
▲The vz/52-57; note the side-swinging bayonet and the magazine shape (RSAF).

ZCASTA SAMOCINNA PUSKA VZ/52, ZCASTA SAMOCINNA PUSKA VZ/52-57
Czechoslovakia
Ceskoslovenská Zbrojovká, Strakonice
7.62mm náboj vz/52 (vz/52), 7.62mm náboj vz/43 (Soviet) (vz/52-57)

This rifle is chambered for the Czech 7.62mm round known as the náboj vz/52. It is an unremarkable weapon which relied heavily on other designs for its ideas; no longer in service in the Czech Army, it was not made in large numbers. The system of operation was an adaptation of that found in the wartime German MKb42(W) and this was linked to a trigger mechanism which owed much to the M1 Garand. However, the locking of the bolt was probably original, as it was achieved by locking lugs at the front of the bolt engaged by tipping the unit. This is a most unusual way of doing it and makes the vz/52 interesting for that reason alone. It is not a satisfactory way of locking and has only ever been used in isolated instances. The magazine was loaded by chargers and another rather outdated idea was the attachment of a folding bayonet. A later model of the vz/52, called the vz/52-57, was chambered for the Soviet 7.62mm short cartridge; it did not survive in service for very long and both models are now obsolete.

Length: 40.00in (1015mm)
Weight unloaded: 9lb. 0oz (4.08kg)
Barrel: 20.50in (520mm), 4 grooves, right-hand twist
Magazine: 10-round detachable box
Muzzle velocity: c.2440fps (743mps)

ZCASTA SAMOCINNA PUSKA Vz/58P, ZCASTA SAMOCINNA PUSKA Vz/58V
Ceskoslovenská Zbrojovká, Strakoniče
7.62mm M43 (Soviet), 7.62 x 45mm (Czech)

The Vz/58 is a Czech-designed and produced assault rifle which is the standard service rifle of the Czech army as well as being sold in other countries. Two versions exist--the Vz/58P, with a conventional wooden stock, and the Vz/58V, fitted with a folding metal stock. The dimensions of both are the same. Early models had natural wood furniture, but this has now been replaced with a plastic-impregnated wood-fibre compound and some may even be found with all-plastic fittings. Superficially the Vz/58 resembles the AK47 but internally the two are quite different; the Czech weapon has a tilting bolt and an axial hammer,

whereas the AK47 has a rotating bolt and a swinging hammer. The Vz/58 is very slightly shorter than the AK and uses a shorter barrel, but its overall weight is roughly the same as the AKM. The Vz/58 gun is well made and finished and one interesting feature is the simplicity of the trigger mechanism, which is better than that of the AK series. There are several ancillary items that can be fitted to the weapon, among them a light bipod which clamps to the barrel immediately behind the foresight and in so doing prevents a bayonet being fitted. Whether the changes in design have produced a better weapon than the original AK is difficult to say, since the Vz/58 has not seen the same amount of use as has the AK series. It is safe to say that it is an extremely workmanlike, robust and smooth rifle based on sound engineering principles.

Length: 33.20in (843mm)
Weight unloaded: 6lb 14oz (3.13kg)
Barrel: 15.80in (420mm), 4 grooves, right-hand twist
Magazine: 30-round detachable box
Muzzle velocity: c.2330fps (710mps)

BANG-GEVAER
Denmark
Manufactured by various companies
Supplied in various calibres

Soren H. Bang, an inventive Dane, was greatly taken with the prospects of putting a neglected Maxim idea to some

practical use. This—an idea which Maxim had patented in the 1880s—concerned tapping the muzzle blast and making it actuate a loading mechanism. Bang developed a number of rifles and machine-guns which used muzzle-cones to trap the gas blast, which were consequently pulled forward taking an operating rod with them. By various linkages this rod was made to unlock and retract the breechblock, the whole cycle then being completed by the usual type of return spring.

The weapons were extensively tested by several nations prior to World War 1 and again, in improved forms, in the 1920s; none was adopted. Their principal drawbacks were a lack of robustness in their construction (especially in the barrel, which readily overheated) and high manufacturing costs.

The principle was later revived by Walther and Mauser during the development of the Gew 41(W) and Gew 41(M) designs produced for the German Army.

No data is given since virtually every Bang weapon was unique; the dimensions and calibre were largely dependent upon Bang's contemporary ideas and the market for which he was designing the gun.

▼▼Two views of the vz/58 rifle; the vz/58V, top, and the vz/58P, below (RSAF).
▼The Bang self-loading rifle, 1927 type, made in 1930 for trials in Britain

▲The Danish Madsen LAR (RSAF).

LET AUTOMAT GEVAER ('Light Automatic Rifle' or m/62)
Denmark
Dansk Industri Syndikat AS 'Madsen', København
7.62mm NATO

The much-respected firm of Madsen has now ceased to make smallarms, but for many years after World War 2 they adapted existing designs and manufactured a wide variety of infantry weapons which all displayed the same high standards maintained by the firm for over a century. In the early 1960s a light automatic rifle was produced in NATO calibre and offered for sale to interested nations. Unfortunately, it came a little late into the arena and most countries had by that time already made their selections. The m/62 was extremely well made and exhibited several good design features, the most notable of which was the extensive use of light alloys in the general construction. The return spring was above the barrel and around the piston rod, so that it pulled the bolt forward instead of the more usual push action. There were similarities, no doubt unintentional, to the Soviet Kalashnikov—particularly in the action and design of the bolt, but in all other respects it appears to be quite original. It was intended to be remarkably versatile and could be fitted with a telescope and a bipod, the latter being of value when the gun was used in fully automatic fire. Two types of stock were offered: a fixed wooden one and a folding metal one which telescoped alongside the receiver. There is no doubt that it was an excellent design and the remaining examples are beautifully made, but it was too expensive and too late. The weapon was the last big effort of the Madsen company and they then turned to more dependable products of a less warlike nature.
Length: 42.50in (1080mm)
Weight unloaded: 10lb 9oz (4.80kg)
Barrel: 21.00in (533mm)
Magazine: 20-round detachable box
Cyclic rate: 600rpm
Muzzle velocity: c.2650fps (807mps)

RYNNAKKOKIVAARI MALLI 60, RYNNAKKOKIVAARI MALLI 62 ('Assault Rifles, m/60 and m/62')
Finland
Valtion Kiväärithedas, Jyväskylä, and others
7.62mm patruuna m/60 (Soviet M43)

The Finnish Army uses a variety of weapons of basically Soviet origin and the m/60 is one of them; it is no more than a copy of the AK47 modified in some minor respects. The fore handgrip is made of plastic instead of wood, the stock is of tubular steel and the rearsight is placed on the sliding cover of the receiver. The only other obvious differences are the trigger-guard—which is virtually non-existent—and the bayonet, which is more of a knife than a conventional bayonet. A later version, designated m/62, has also been produced and the changes in design are little more than some slight changes in the handguard and the introduction of a trigger-guard. Nevertheless, the Finnish version of the AK47 is fairly distinctive and, on the surface, looks to be an improvement.
Length: 36.00in (914mm)
Barrel: 16.50in (419mm), 4 grooves, right-hand twist
Magazine: 30-round detachable box
Cyclic rate: 650rpm
Muzzle velocity: c.2400fps (730mps)

FUSIL MITRAILLEUR RSC MODELE 1917, FUSIL MITRAILLEUR RSC MODELE 1918
France
Manufacture d'Armes de Saint-Etienne
8mm Cartouche Mle 86

This semi-automatic rifle, properly known as the Modèle 1917 or RSC (from the designers Ribeyrolle, Sutter and Chauchat), takes its common name of 'Saint-Etienne' from the place of manufacture. It was the end product of a number of experimental weapons which had been developed in the early years of the century and was issued in great haste during World War 1. Better designs were available, but the Modèle 1917 was the only one which used the standard French 8mm rimmed 'Lebel' cartridge, and it was thus selected in order not to disrupt ammunition production or complicate supply.

It seems to have been beyond the power of early French firearms designers to produce an aesthetically acceptable weapon and the RSC is no exception to this rule, an ugly and awkward-looking weapon whose length and weight go a long way to support this impression. It is gas operated through a piston and a bolt carrier, and it feeds from a clip unique to the design and holding five rounds. The Modèle 1918 was an attempt to improve matters by shortening and lightening the weapon and altering the feed system to take the standard cartridge clip, the Chargeur Mle 16. The Modèle 1917 rifle was used in limited numbers during World War 1, but the 1918 design did not appear until after the Armistice. A transitional form of the Fusil Mitrailleur Mle 17 is known to exist; this is basically a Mle 17 shortened to approximate the length of the Mle 18, probably a retrospective alteration.

In 1935, the surviving rifles were altered to a type of manual straight-pull bolt action, achieved simply by blocking the gas port. It is thought that these were then issued to colonial troops in French Equatorial Africa.
(data: Modèle 1917)
Length: 52.40in (1331mm)
Weight unloaded: 11lb 9oz (5.25kg)
Barrel: 31.40in (798mm), 4 grooves, right-hand twist
Magazine: 5-round internal box
Muzzle velocity: c.2350fps (716mps)
(data: Modèle 1918)
Length: 43.10in (1095mm)
Weight unloaded: 10lb 8oz (4.79kg)
Barrel: 23.10in (586mm), 4 grooves, right-hand twist
Magazine: 5-round internal box
Muzzle velocity: c.2200fps (670mps)

FUSIL MITRAILLEUR MODELE 49 (MAS 49)
France
Manufacture d'Armes de Saint-Etienne, Saint-Etienne
7.5mm Cartouche Mle 29

France was early in the field in Europe

with a semi-automatic rifle for her infantry and the MAS 49 was first issued—as its title suggests—in 1949, at a time when most of the other European countries were still using prewar bolt-action weapons. In many ways the MAS 49 resembles the earlier MAS 36, for it uses the same two-piece stock and sights and is generally similar in outline. In fact, it is not an automatic version of the MAS 36 but a new design which incorporates some of the earlier fittings to reduce costs. It is a rather heavy, very strong, and highly reliable gas-operated rifle. The gas system uses no piston or cylinder: the gas is conducted through a pipe to blow directly on to the face of the bolt and force it backwards. This

arrangement has not proved popular with other designers, largely owing to rapid accumulation of fouling, but it seems to work well enough in this rifle. A grenade launcher is fitted as an integral part of the muzzle, and the MAS 49 was one of the first weapons to be produced with such a fitting. There are also permanent grenade-launching sights on the left side of the rifle and the foresight near the end of the stock moves the grenade stop up or down the barrel according to the range set on the sight. This shift alters the muzzle velocity and so the range. Unusually, the Modèle 49 was not intended for a bayonet, but a few were adapted for the small 'spike' of the Modèle 36. The breech was

locked by tilting the breechblock in the same way as the Tokarev designs and the 'SAFN' produced by Fabrique Nationale, a simple and reliable arrangement. The MAS 49 and its derivatives have been in service with the French Army for over twenty years; they have fought in Indo-China, Algeria and Egypt with complete success.
Length: 43.50in (1105mm)
Weight unloaded: 10lb 0oz (4.54kg)
Barrel: 22.75in (577mm), 4 grooves, left-hand twist
Magazine: 10-round detachable box
Muzzle velocity: c.2425fps (740mps)

▼The Fusil RSC Modele 1917 (RSAF).
▼The Fusil MAS Modele 1949 (SIM).

MAUSER-SELBSTLADEGEWEHRE, 1898-1918
Germany
Waffenfabrik Mauser AG, Oberndorf-am-Neckar
7.92mm Gewehr Patrone 98

The first self-loading rifle patents were granted to Peter-Paul Mauser in February 1898, although it is possible that some of his employees—notably the Feederle brothers—were in some way responsible for the developments: it was company policy that all patents should be granted in Mauser's name, sometimes with total disregard to the actual designers.

Mauser seems to have been fascinated by recoil operation, as all of his rifle designs (and all of the pistols produced prior to 1918 with the exception of the 1910 and 1914 pocket patterns) utilised the recoil forces in some way.
Gewehr Construction 98 (Gew C98) (Short recoil operation). This was the first of the rifles, based on a block of five patents granted late in February of 1898. The barrel and bolt were securely

locked together by two flaps—one on either side of the breech—which were positioned in a housing built around the chamber. When the rifle was fired, recoil of the barrel cammed the locking flaps out of engagement with the bolt, which was then allowed to continue rearwards; it was then returned to battery by the recoil spring and the return of the barrel once again forced the locking flaps into the recesses cut in the bolt. A drawback of the design was that the locking mechanism was not totally enclosed and the flaps protruded behind the flap housing during the unlocking and reloading cycle which, although providing a positive means by which the firer could tell whether or not the bolt was locked, also allowed the ingress of dirt and mud, with the resultant derangement of the somewhat delicate mechanism. Although an entire infantry regiment was armed in 1901 with the C98, extensive field trials failed to impress the military authorities and the design was abandoned.
Gewehr Construction 02 (Gew C02) (Long recoil operation). The patents for

this design were granted to Mauser in November 1902 and covered another recoil-operated rifle in which locking was achieved by a two-piece rotating bolt. Barrel recoil was used to force the back part of the bolt unit towards the rear, which turned the two bolt-lugs from the barrel recesses by means of a screw joint between the two parts of the bolt. Production weapons of C02 pattern also incorporated a separate cocking lever which could either be used to cock the mechanism for self-loading fire, when the handle was turned downwards to disengage it from the bolt, or for single-shot bolt-action operation, when the handle was left in a horizontal attitude. Although issued on a small scale for troop trials, the C02 was relatively heavy and rather too long; it was quickly abandoned in favour of the C06/08.
Gewehr Construction 06/08 (Gewehr C06/08) (Short recoil operation). The designation C06/08 covered three rifles of basically similar operation cycles but with different forms of lock mechanism. The most popular type used a form of

locking flap similar to the Friberg-Kjellman system, which had been revived in 1904 and was later successfully used in the gas-operated Russian Degtyarev light machine-gun; two rear-pivoted locking flaps supported the rear of the bolt in the Mauser design and barrel recoil cammed the flaps in and out of recesses cut in the receiver, by means of two studs sliding in suitably-cut channels. The bolt unit was then allowed to recoil along a guide rod, compressing the recoil spring as it did so. The return of the block to battery was then accomplished by the spring and the return of the barrel once more cammed the flaps behind the breechblock. Two variants of this system, patents for which were granted in June and November 1906, discarded the locking flaps and instead substituted a block in the form of a saddle; the breechblock slid backwards within the 'saddle', which was cammed in and out

of a recess cut in the top of the receiver by the recoil of the barrel unit.

The German Army tested the C06/08 until the beginning of World War 1, although they never sanctioned the widespread issue of the rifles.

Flieger-Selbstladekarabiner Modell 15. The only use for the Mauser-designed self-loading rifles was in arming aircraft observers and balloon crews before the advent of sufficient flexible machine-guns. Once production of the latter weapons was of a sufficient volume the rifles were removed from service, although a few later appeared on the Western Front as infantry weapons—by which time they had been fitted with full-length stocks and bayonet attachments—where they had little success. The aircraft weapon was developed from the 'flap-locking' version of the C06/08.

In retrospect, it is hard to say why the Mauser rifles were such dismal

failures in view of the care with which they were made: perhaps the single-mindedness with which Mauser pursued recoil operation blinded him to the possible use of gas, although it must be admitted that the recoil-operated rifles were no less successful than most of the contemporary gas-operated types. One important factor might well have been the standard of contemporary metallurgy, as the Mauser rifles were all relatively complex and relied heavily on the precise metal-to-metal fit of the cam surfaces and the various bearings: despite the care taken to ensure the smooth motion of the barrel (itself the subject of several patents), wear often rendered the too-delicate mechanism inoperative. It is interesting to note that some of the operating principles of these weapons later appeared in others, with degrees of success ranging from complete failure to considerable usefulness.

GEWEHR 41 (WALTHER) ('GEW 41[W]')
Germany
Carl Walther Waffenfabrik AG, Zella-Mehlis
7.92mm Gewehr Patrone 98
Germany had issued self-loading rifles of one sort or another in World War 1, but only in small numbers and not all were of her own design or manufacture. An experimental programme was started in 1940 as a matter of urgency to produce a semi-automatic rifle, and the Gew 41 weapons were the ultimate result. Two designs were made, a Mauser—the Gew 41(M)—and the Walther-designed Gew 41(W), but the Mauser type was soon dropped. The Walther Gew 41(W) was adopted, a gas-operated rifle using a variation of the rather crude Bang system in which gas was deflected by a muzzle cup to turn back and strike an annular piston around the barrel and so a long piston rod. Locking was by hinged flaps similar to the Russian Degtyarev machine-gun design. The 10-shot magazine was

integral with the action and so was slow to load. Manufacture was expensive as much machining was involved and the gas system—in particular—was complicated. The rifle was not a great success as it was heavy and ill-balanced. It was noticeably muzzle-heavy to hold and, although tens of thousands were made, it was only issued to special units principally stationed on the Russian Front. When the Gew 43 appeared, all production of the Gew 41 stopped, although it never completely passed from service: Germany was too short of equipment to allow that to happen.
Length: 44.50in (1130mm)
Weight unloaded: 11lb 0oz (5.02kg)
Barrel: 21.50in (545mm), 4 grooves, right-hand twist
Magazine: 10-round internal box
Muzzle velocity: c.2550fps (776mps)

FALLSCHIRMJÄGERGEWEHR 42 ('FG42' or 'FjG42')
Germany
Rheinmetall-Borsig AG, Düsseldorf
7.92mm Gewehr Patrone 98

▲▲Mauser-Selbstlade Gewehr pre-1915; Gewehr 41(W) (both RSAF).

The Fallschirmjägergewehr 42 was one of the outstanding smallarms designs of World War 2 and it was very nearly a complete success. In the event, a combination of circumstances militated against it and it was made only in small numbers; probably no more than 7,000 were produced. This remarkable weapon nearly achieved the impossible feat of being a serviceable selective-fire design using the old-style full power ammunition. It was one of the notable forerunners of the now-fashionable assault rifles, all of which use ammunition of lower power and are thus more easily controlled. The FG42 was produced for the Luftwaffe parachute troops, and was first used in the dramatic circumstances of the rescue of Mussolini; it later appeared in Italy and France. Many were captured by the Allies, which gave the impression that more were in service than was actually the case. The FG42 is a gas-operated rifle with several novel

features: it fired from an open breech when set at automatic fire, in order to avoid 'cook offs' (premature discharges caused by heating the round in the chamber) and from a closed breech, to improve accuracy, when set for semi-automatic operation. The FG42 was one of the first service rifles to be made in the now-fashionable 'straight line' configuration, and it had a light bipod and an integral bayonet: all of this in a weapon weighing less than ten pounds (4.54kg). The magazine, rather awkwardly, fed from the left side and while most of the ideas embodied in the FG42 have been subsequently copied this has not, as it tends to unbalance the gun. The FG42 was unfortunately expensive and time-consuming to make, and as a result it was not favoured by the Oberkommando der Wehrmacht (armed forces high command). The parachute arm of the Luftwaffe declined in importance as the war progressed and the rifle was never properly developed.
Length: 37.00in (940mm)
Weight unloaded: 9lb 15oz (4.53kg)

Barrel: 20.00in (508mm), 4 grooves, right-hand twist
Magazine: 20-round detachable box
Cyclic rate: c.750rpm
Muzzle velocity: c.2500fps (761mps)

MASCHINENKARABINER 42(H) (MKb42[H])
Germany
C G Haenel Waffen- und Fahrradfabrik AG, Suhl
7.92mm pist patr 43
The MKb42(H) was produced by Haenel to the same specification that inspired the MKb42(W); the Haenel weapon was designed by Louis Schmeisser in the period 1940–1, and fifty specimens had been produced by mid-1942. A gas-operated tipping-bolt type, the MKb42 (H) was more conventional in design than its Walther competitor, with a standard form of gas tube and piston. When the tapped gas impinged on the piston—which was attached to the bolt carrier—it drove the carrier rearwards until the carrier unlocked the bolt by moving it back and down from the lock-

▲FG42, Krieghoff (SIM). FG42, Rheinmetall (RSAF). MKb42(H)(RSAF).

ing recesses; the bolt, the carrier and the piston continued to travel until halted by the recoil spring from which position the components were returned to battery. The MKb42(H) was externally similar to the later MP43 (for which it served as a prototype), except for the visible gas tube above the barrel, the attachment of a bayonet lug, and a slightly different trigger and pistolgrip assembly.

Approximately 8,000 of the MKb42 (H) were produced in the period November 1942 to April 1943 and, after trials on the Russian Front, it was decided to place the weapon in production once Schmeisser had attended to a few minor details. It then became the MP43.
Length: 37.00in (940mm)
Weight unloaded: 10lb 13oz (4.90kg)
Barrel: 14.37in (364mm), 4 grooves, right-hand twist
Magazine: 30-round detachable box
Cyclic rate: 500rpm
Muzzle velocity: c.2100fps (640mps)

▲The MKb42(W), Walther's unsuccessful competitor of the MKb42(H) (RSAF).

MASCHINENKARABINER 42(W) (MKb42[W])
Germany
Carl Walther Waffenfabrik AG, Zella-Mehlis
7.92mm pist patr 43

The MKb42(W) was produced by the Walther concern in response to a specification calling for an 'assault rifle' chambered for the 7.92mm 'intermediate' round then being produced on an experimental basis by Polte-Werke of Magdeburg. Development was instigated in 1940 and the first prototype was produced in July 1942. Like the competing design emanating from the workshops of Haenel, the MKb42(W) was designed for uncomplicated production in the simplest possible manner, and using as little as practical of the valuable raw material; much use was made of pressings and stampings which were riveted or welded together. The MKb42(W) was a gas-operated locked-breech design with a tipping bolt locked by frontal lugs; an unusual gas assembly was used in the form of an annular piston which surrounded the barrel and which reciprocated within a cylindrical housing. Gas impinged upon the piston and pushed it back within the housing, and a sleeve attached to the piston unlocked the bolt. The gun was externally recognisable by the circular forestock, and by the lack of a separate gas tube; a bayonet lug was fitted and there was a larger gap between the magazine and trigger assembly than in the MKb42(H).

Approximately 3,000-5,000 guns were made for trials on the Russian Front, from which it was decided to place the MKb42(H) in volume production. The MKb42(W) was dropped.

Length: 36.68in (931mm)
Weight unloaded: 9lb 11oz (4.40kg)
Barrel: 16.00in (406mm), 4 grooves, right-hand twist
Magazine: 30-round detachable box
Cyclic rate: 600rpm
Muzzle velocity: c.2125fps (646mps)

GEWEHR 43, KARABINER 43 (Gew 43, Kar 43)
Germany
Carl Walther Waffenfabrik AG, Zella-Mehlis; Berliner-Lübecker Maschinenfabrik AG, Lübeck; Gustloff-Werk, Weimar
7.92mm Gewehr Patrone 98

The Gew 43 was the logical development of the Gew 41(W), applying the experience of war to the design. It incorporated the same bolt locking system but radically altered the gas system. The gas cylinder was placed on top of the barrel in the same way as the Russian Tokarev designs, a simple gas nozzle and cup were used, and the magazine was made detachable. More significantly, a dovetail was machined on the receiver to take a telescopic sight and the rifle was generally used for sniping. The Gew 43 was probably first used on the Russian Front in late 1943, although encountered fairly generally on all fronts—always in small numbers and always as a specialist's weapon. A definite improvement on the Gew 41(W), the Gew 43 was much easier to make; most were found with laminated wooden furniture but, towards the end of the war, plastic was also used. Owing to the economic situation there was ultimately a further simplification of manufacture which gives some of the remaining models a very rough external appearance. The Gew 43 remained in production until the end of the war and, after 1945, was adopted in small numbers by the Czechoslovak Army as a sniper's rifle. The Karabiner 43 differed from the Gewehr 43 only in the substitution of a large trigger-guard, although it was also some 2in (51mm) shorter.

(data: Gew 43)
Length: 44.00in (1117mm)
Weight unloaded: 9lb 9oz (4.40kg)
Barrel: 22.00in (558mm), 4 grooves, right-hand twist
Magazine: 10-round detachable box
Muzzle velocity: c.2450fps (746mps)

▼The breech of the Gew 43, showing the Zf4 sight (RSAF).

▲▲▲The Gew 43, the MP43/1, and the MP43 mit Krummlauf (all RSAF).

MASCHINENPISTOLE 43, MASCHINENPISTOLE 43/1, MASCHINENPISTOLE 44, STURMGEWEHR 44 (MP43, MP43/1, MP44, StG44)
Germany
C G Haenel Waffen- und Fahrradfabrik AG, Suhl; Erfurter Maschinenfabrik B Geipel GmbH, Erfurt; Mauser-Werke AG, Oberndorf-am-Neckar, and others
7.92mm pist patr 43

The MP43 was the developed version of the MKb42(H) with certain modifications made in the light of combat experience on the Russian Front; the first deliveries of the weapon were made in July 1943 and production continued until the first months of 1945. In late 1943 a variation of the basic MP43 was manufactured, under the designation MP43/1, in which the clamp-on grenade launcher was replaced by one of screw-on pattern: a short threaded section appeared at the muzzle of the MP43/1 to allow the grenade launcher to be attached. A mounting bracket for optical sights was also fitted, something which never appeared on the original MP43. In April 1944 the nomenclature was advanced—for some undetermined reason—to MP44, which was otherwise identical to the MP43 although some weapons were fitted with the sight bracket. Towards the end of 1944 a further term was given to the weapon; this, StG44 (for Sturmgewehr—'assault rifle'—44), is said to have been bestowed upon the rifles by a well-satisfied Adolf Hitler. At any rate, it more adequately describes the rifles' role.

Versions of the StG were developed with suitably curved barrels; they are described in the next entry.

Length: 37.00in (940mm)
Weight unloaded: 11lb 4oz (5.12kg)
Barrel: 16.50in (418mm), 4 grooves, right-hand twist
Magazine: 30-round detachable box
Cyclic rate: 500rpm
Muzzle velocity: c.2125fps (647mps)

MASCHINENPISTOLE MIT VORSATZ J, MASCHINENPISTOLE MIT VORSATZ P, MASCHINENPISTOLE MIT VORSATZ V ('Maschinenpistole 44 mit Krummlauf')
Germany
Manufacturer unknown
7.92mm pist patr 43

The curved-barrel Maschinenpistolen were a remarkable wartime development which, however, well illustrates the gusto with which the German High Command entered into futile projects which promised relatively little and diverted valuable production time from more conventional weapons of war.

The base for the Krummlauf device was an MP44 to which was fitted a curved-barrel unit with suitable mirror sights attached to the muzzle. It has been said, though never satisfactorily proved, that the idea was to provide a means for firing around corners without exposing the operator to hostile fire; and another version tells of the necessity for dislodging hostile Russians from tanks. A third story, however, tells that the curved-barrel was an unexpected by-product from a project originally intended to provide a device by which firing trials could be satisfactorily accomplished without recourse to conventional firing ranges: it is said that from this it was thought that other, more useful purposes could be served—and it may also be that the last tale is the most likely of the three.

Three versions of the Krummlauf were envisaged: one which turned the bullet through 30°, MP44 mit Vorsatz J (usually called the MP44(P) or the MP44 K/30°—the latter term for 'Krummlauf 30°'); another which was intended to turn it through 90°, MP44 mit Vorsatz P (MP44(P) or MP44 K/90°) and a final design, no more than a paper exercise, the MP44 mit Vorsatz V—capable of a 40° deflection. Only the first type, 10,000 of which are said to have been ordered in 1944, was ever properly developed. The principle was to have the curved barrel pierced with a number of ports through which gas could be progressively expelled, thereby decreasing the pressure behind the bullet as each successive port was passed and ensuring that the barrel remained in one piece, but this also reduced the velocity substantially and the bullet—initial muzzle velocity c.2100fps (640mps) in an unmodified specimen—emerged from the curved barrel at a subsonic velocity of c.900-1000fps (275-305mps). It is plainly evident from this that the effectiveness of the rifle was greatly diminished as a result of the much-reduced exit velocity: the Krummlauf-MP44 was, however, envisaged solely as ultra-short-range equipment.

VERSUCHS-GERAT 1–5 or VOLKS-STURM-GEWEHR 1–5
Germany
Designed by Gustloff-Werke, Suhl, and made in Suhl by unknown manufacturers
7.92mm pist patr 43

The VG 1–5 was a self-loading 'assault rifle' hurriedly developed by the Suhl-based Gustloff-Werke concern as part of the Primitiv-Waffen-Programm of 1944; the weapons were intended for issue to the Volkssturm ('home guard') and sundry last-ditch organisations which ultimately came to nothing.

The rifle was designed by Barnitzke, Gustloff-Werke's chief designer, who had developed the operating principles in 1943 taking an MP43 as his base. The VG 1–5 is remarkable as the mechanism incorporates a textbook case of delayed-blowback operation; the barrel is surrounded by a hollow sleeve, which can reciprocate and carries with it the bolt which is attached to the rear of the sleeve. Some 2.5in (6.4mm) from the muzzle are four gas ports and, when the gun is fired, the gas passes through the ports and into the annular space between the barrel and the slide. The pressure thus generated is sufficient to hold the breech closed until the bullet has passed from the muzzle, by which time the pressure has dropped sufficiently to allow the breechblock to move rearwards in normal blowback manner. The breechblock takes with it the gas sleeve and, in doing so, vents the gas into the atmosphere; the recoil spring then returns the breech mechanism to battery.

One drawback of the design was that the bearing surfaces of gas-sleeve, and the barrel surfaces on which they slid, had to be machined to relatively close tolerances; gas residue soon fouled the surfaces unless they were carefully greased, and barrel expansion sometimes jammed the weapon completely.

The VG 1–5 was designed to fire the 7.92mm 'Intermediate' round, and the 30-round magazine of the MP43 series was utilised to simplify both manufacture and supply.

Length: 34.85in (885mm)
Weight: 10lb 2oz (4.62kg)
Barrel: 14.90in (378mm), 4 grooves, right-hand twist
Magazine: 30-round detachable box
Muzzle velocity: c.2150fps (655mps)

GEWEHR 3 (G3)
Federal Republic of Germany (Bundesrepublik Deutschland)
Heckler & Koch GmbH, Oberndorf-am-Neckar (originally); Rheinmetall GmbH, Düsseldorf
7.62mm NATO

Although classed as a State-produced rifle, the G3 is made by Heckler & Koch of Oberndorf and Rheinmetall of Düsseldorf under contract to the West German government. It is also either made under licence in other countries in Europe or bought direct from Germany by other armies. The rifle is a modification and development of the original Spanish CETME and, since the CETME was itself founded on a wartime German rifle, the wheel has turned full circle and the design has once again come home—though it would no longer be recognisable when compared to the original. As in the CETME, the G3 uses the principle of blowback with delay by rollers, and it is known to be sensitive to variations in the load of the cartridges it fires. Since the NATO round is made in slightly different ways in different countries, the G3 cannot be said to perform consistently with all kinds of ammunition, but it is undoubtedly reliable and robust. It is made from sheet metal stampings, with plastic furniture, and there have been several variations including one with a folding bipod and stock (although the standard German weapon has none of these). A rifle grenade launcher is incorporated in the muzzle and the standard magazine holds 20 rounds; the rearsight rotates to provide elevation and the foresight is a thick post. The G3 is hardly an attractive rifle, but it is functional and effective and, as a result, it has sold widely in Europe. It is also in service with the armies of Portugal and Pakistan.

7.62mm Gewehr 3. The first rifle design produced by Heckler & Koch, the G3 has a 'flip-over' rearsight and a wooden butt unit.

7.62mm Gewehr 3A1. A variant of the G3 in which the wooden butt is replaced

▲Barnetske's VG1-5, firing the 7.92mm Pist Patr 43 'intermediate' round, and locked by a type of delayed blowback (RSAF).

▲The G3A3 (Heckler & Koch).
▲The G3A3Z (Heckler & Koch).
▲The G3A4 (Heckler & Koch).
▲The G3SG/1, a sniper's version of the basic G3 rifle (SG—Scharfschützen Gewehr, sniper rifle) fitted with a specially-selected barrel and a new trigger mechanism (Heckler & Koch).

by a folding stock hinging to the left. The 'flip-over' rearsight of the G3 is retained.
7.62mm Gewehr 3A2. The G3A2 is a version of the basic G3 in which the original rearsight is replaced by a unit of rotary pattern.
7.62mm Gewehr 3A3. The current production variant of the G3, the G3A3 has the rearsight of the G3A2 but the foresight design has been modified and a prong-type flash-suppressor has been added to the muzzle.
7.62mm Gewehr 3A3Z. A version of the G3A3 fitted with a telescopic sight on suitable mounts, the 'Z' in the designation represents *zielfernrohr*—'telescope'.
7.62mm Gewehr 3A4. Another folding stock variant, this time of the G3A3, and fitted with a retractable stock which slides in channels cut along the receiver sides.

(data: G3A3)
Length: 40.00in (1016mm)
Weight unloaded: 9lb 6oz (4.25kg)
Barrel: 17.75in (450mm), 4 grooves, right-hand twist
Magazine: 20-round detachable box
Cyclic rate: 550rpm
Muzzle velocity: c.2650fps (807mps)

GEWEHRE HK33A2, HK33A3 and HK33KA1
Federal Republic of Germany
Heckler & Koch GmbH, Oberndorf-am-Neckar
5.56mm × 45mm (0.223in)

The HK33 series are 0.223in calibre derivatives of the original G3 design, using the same roller-locked delayed blowback operating system. All are capable of fully automatic fire and, because of the light cartridge, they are surprisingly controllable in this role.

Three versions of the rifle are currently offered by the manufacturers, alike in action but differing in appearance and external fittings. The standard weapon is the HK33A2, developed from the original HK33 by way of the HK33A1, which is offered with a permanently-attached plastic stock; the HK33A3, although otherwise similar, is marketed with a telescopic metal skeleton stock; and the HK33KA1 (in which the 'K' represents *kurz*—'short') is no more than a shorter version of the HK33A3. The two longer models are capable of launching spigot-type grenades from their exposed barrels without recourse to a separate launching attachment.

▲The 4.56mm HK36 rifle, an experimental military rifle which awaits a change in adoption policy.
◁The HK33 series: HK33, HK33A2, HK33Z with telescope sight, and the HK33A3 (Heckler & Koch).

(data: HK33A2)
Length: 36.22in (920mm)
Weight unloaded: 7lb 12oz (3.50kg)
Barrel: 15.35in (390mm), 6 grooves, right-hand twist

Magazine: 20, 30 or 40-round detachable box
Cyclic rate: 600rpm
Muzzle velocity: c.3150fps (957mps)
(data: HK33A3)
Length, stock extended: 37.00in (940mm)
Length, stock retracted: 28.70in (730mm)
Weight unloaded: 8lb 7oz (3.85kg)
Barrel: 15.35in (390mm), 6 grooves, right-hand twist
Magazine: 20, 30 or 40-round detachable box

Cyclic rate: 600rpm
Muzzle velocity: c.3150fps (957mps)
(data: HK33KA1)
Length, stock extended: 34.05in (865mm)
Length, stock retracted: 26.37in (670mm)
Weight unloaded: 8lb 6oz (3.80kg)
Barrel: 12.67in (322mm), 6 grooves, right-hand twist
Magazine: 20, 30 or 40-round detachable box
Cyclic rate: 650rpm
Muzzle velocity: c.3018fps (917mps)

▲
FUCILE MITRIAGLICE CEI-RIGOTTI
Italy
Officine Glisenti, Bettoni
6.5mm cartucchia pallottola modello 95
In 1900 Captain Cei-Rigotti of the Bersaglieri invented and constructed a gas-operated selective-fire carbine which temporarily attracted considerable interest in European military circles. Gas was led into a cylinder about halfway down the barrel and operated a short-stroke piston from which a tappet curved up to the right-hand side of the barrel. This tappet struck a long operating rod connected to the bolt, and a lug on the rod ran in a cam track cut in the bolt; the reciprocating movement of the rod rotated the bolt, drew it to the rear, pulled it forward again and locked it by final rotation. Locking was achieved by engaging two lugs on the bolt-head in corresponding barrel recesses. The system is very similar to that later used on the American M1 carbine and many other designs. A simple change lever gave single shot or fully automatic fire and there were different sizes of magazine as large as 50 rounds.

The few remaining examples show that the design had several failings and contemporary reports speak of frequent jams and erratic shooting, although some of these troubles may well have stemmed from the ammunition. The Cei-Rigotti must be numbered almost the earliest workable selective-fire rifle and it was unfortunate that no army could be found to take an interest in it, for—with a little development work—it would probably have been quite successful. Despite efforts by the Glisenti firm to find buyers, the Cei-Rigotti had to be ultimately abandoned without hope of revival.
Length: 39.37in (1000mm)
Weight unloaded: 9lb 9oz (4.30kg)
Barrel: 19.00in (483mm), 4 grooves, right-hand twist
Magazine: 10, 20 or 50-round detachable box
Cyclic rate: not known
Muzzle velocity: c.2400fps (730mps)

FUCILE AUTOMATICO BERETTA MODELLO 59 (BM59)
Italy
Pietro Beretta SpA, Gardone-val-Trompia
7.62mm cartucchia pallottola NATO
Since 1945 Italy has had to rely on variants of the US Garand for her infantry rifles. When the NATO cartridge made the original 0.30in cartridge obsolete, it was decided to bring the original design up to date rather than to build a completely new series. Beretta took the basic Garand, and from it produced a modern, lightweight weapon capable of both automatic and semi-automatic fire.

The BM59 incorporates the basic features of the well-proved Garand with various improvements, producing a greatly improved and more versatile rifle. It is the official service rifle of the Italian armed forces and is in service in three versions—a standard infantry version, a version for Alpine troops (*Alpini*) and special units, and a version for paratroops (*Paracadutisti*).

All versions incorporate the same modifications from the original Garand. Apart from a barrel of 7.62mm calibre, the main modification is to the receiver and its associated mechanism; a 20-round magazine is fitted, which can be loaded from chargers while on the rifle. The trigger is altered to accept the new firing mechanism, and a new trigger group is installed. The remaining changes relate to the operating springs, the gas cylinder, change levers and the stock. A combined grenade launcher/flash-hider is fitted to all versions, but it is detachable in the parachutist's version to reduce the overall length.

The standard gun (BM59 Mark 1) has a full-length wooden stock, a rubber butt-plate, and an optional light bipod fitted to the gas cylinder. The Alpini version has a cut-down stock, a pistol-grip, a bipod and a folding skeleton butt. The parachutist's rifle is very similar except that the flash hider can be removed. A more elaborate edition of the standard version (BM59 Mark 4) has a heavier bipod, a pistol-grip and a hinged butt-plate, all intended to steady the gun in automatic fire.

The modifications to the Garand are comparatively straightforward and the resulting BM59 is a rugged and reliable weapon. It is a high-quality product—though it is claimed to be reasonably priced—and appears to be a most effective way of producing a modern rifle without going to the cost of introducing a completely new design. The only possible criticism of the guns is that they are slightly heavier than their contemporaries

(data: BM59 Mark 1)
Length: 43.00in (1095mm)
Weight unloaded: 9lb 9oz (4.40kg)
Barrel: 19.30in (491mm), 4 grooves, right-hand twist
Magazine: 20-round detachable box
Cyclic rate: 800rpm
Muzzle velocity: c.2700fps (823mps)

(data: BM59 Alpini)
Length: 48.20in (1225mm)
Weight unloaded: 10lb 1oz (4.56kg)
Barrel: 19.30in (491mm), 4 grooves, right-hand twist
Magazine: 20-round detachable box
Cyclic rate: 800rpm
Muzzle velocity: c.2700fps (823mps)

(data: BM59 Paracadutisti)
Length: 43.70in (1110mm)
Weight unloaded: 9lb 10oz (4.46kg)
Barrel: 18.4in (468mm), 4 grooves, right-hand twist
Magazine: 20-round detachable box
Cyclic rate: 810rpm
Muzzle velocity: c.2625fps (800mps)

◁ The open action of the BM59 (RSAF).
◁ BM59 Mark 1 (Beretta).
◁ BM59 Mark 1 with a bipod and grenade launcher similar to those of the Mark 1 Ital (RSAF).
◁ BM59 Mark 1 Ital (Beretta).
▲ BM59 Paracuditisti, with a bipod, a folding stock and a removable grenade launcher (Beretta).
▲ BM59 Mark 4 (Beretta).
▲ BM59 Alpini, essentially similar to the Paracuditisti version but with a fixed grenade launcher (Beretta).

FUCILE AUTOMATICO BERETTA MODELLO 70
Italy
Pietro Beretta SpA, Gardone-val-Trompia
5.56mm x 45mm

The modello 70 is a lightweight air-cooled gas-operated magazine-fed rifle designed for both full and semi-automatic firing. It is offered in two forms, the Assault Rifle (*Fucile d'Assalto*) designated as the AR70 and the Special Troops' Carbine (*Carabina per Truppe Speciali*) known as the SC70.

The AR70 resembles many other similar rifles in its outline, and it is made from steel stampings and pressings with plastic furniture. Extensive use is made of spot welding for the main components, and the removable items are held by pins and spring catches. The whole standard of manufacture is very high—as with all Beretta products—and it is claimed that the functioning is highly reliable. An optional light bipod can be fitted, and the muzzle has a combination flash-hider/grenade launcher. An ingenious flip-up device on the fore and rearsights not only raises the sight line for grenade firing, but at the same time reduces the gas supply to the cylinder and so ensures that the full force of the cartridge is used to drive the grenade.

The SC70 is very similar in all general respects to the AR70 except that it has a folding skeleton butt.

The grenade that is fired is the 40mm Mecar, which generally is issued in both HE (high explosive) and anti-tank versions. A bayonet can be fitted to the

▲AR70 (Beretta).
▲SC70 (Beretta).

muzzle of the rifle, and a small knife bayonet of light construction is usually provided. There is also a blank-firing attachment which blocks the muzzle and permits the force of the blank cartridge to operate the mechanism.

The system of operation is by conventional gas action, using a top-mounted gas cylinder. The piston works against the breechblock which carries a light-weight bolt. The bolt locks by rotating and engaging two forward-mounted lugs, the rotation being accomplished by a cam and cam slot in the bolt and breechblock. The number of parts has been kept to the minimum and as little machining as possible is used.

The modello 70 represents a typical modern high-class 5.56mm rifle. It is certainly as good as the many others that are being produced in the world, and may well be better than most.

(data: AR70)
Length: 37.60in (955mm)
Weight unloaded: 7lb 10oz (3.50kg)
Barrel: 17.80in (450mm), 4 or 6 grooves, right-hand twist
Magazine: 30-round detachable box
Cyclic rate: 700rpm
Muzzle velocity: c.3150fps (960mps)
(data: SC70)
Length: 37.80in (960mm) (stock extended)
Weight unloaded: 7lb 12oz (3.55kg)
Barrel: 17.80in (450mm), 4 or 6 grooves, right-hand twist
Magazine: 30-round detachable box
Cyclic rate: 700rpm
Muzzle velocity: c.3150fps (960mps)

64 SHIKI JIDOJU (Type 64 Self-acting gun)
Japan
Howa Kogyo Kyokai, Tokyo
7.62mm NATO (see also text)
Although this rifle is a purely government undertaking, it was actually designed and manufactured by Howa Kogyo Kyokai. The Japanese Defence Force have found that the NATO round is too powerful for their needs and have introduced a reduced-charge round, using the same bullet and case: this is a perfectly adequate round and it compares well with the full-power version. The Type 64 rifle is intended to be used with the reduced-power Japanese round, but it can also take the normal one if necessary as there is an adjustment in the gas regulator to allow for the greater gas flow from the more powerful cartridge. The gas regulator can also be closed entirely to allow grenades to be launched from the muzzle, where there is an integral launcher. The rifle is fitted with a bipod which folds under the forward handguard, and the Japanese soldier is taught to use it whenever possible. Another aid to good shooting is a folding strap on top of the butt which prevents the butt slipping down out of the shoulder. In all other respects the Type 64 is a fairly normal gas-operated selective-fire rifle, with a rather low cyclic rate and a reasonably low weight. The bolt-locking system is slightly old-fashioned in that it employs a tipping bolt controlled by a cam on the bolt carrier, an arrangement also used by the Russian Simonov-designed rifle.
Length: 39.00in (990mm)
Weight unloaded: 9lb 8oz (4.37kg)
Barrel: 17.75in (450mm), 6 grooves,
right-hand twist
Magazine: 20-round detachable box
Cyclic rate: c.500rpm
Muzzle velocity: c.2650fps (807mps) (2350fps [716mps] with the reduced-charge round)

FUSIL PORFIRIO DIAZ SYSTEMA MONDRAGON MODELO 1908
Mexico (Germany/Switzerland)
Schweizerische Industrie - Gesellschaft, Neuhausen-am-Rheinfalls
7mm Mauser
The Mexican-designed Mondragon, first conceived in the early 1890s, was one of the earliest semi-automatic rifles to be taken into military service, although in 1896 the Danes had issued their Navy with limited quantities of a Madsen self-loading rifle. Manuel Mondragon, granted a patent in 1907 by the United States Patent Office, was forced to seek a European manufacturer for his rifle as there were no production facilities in Mexico and the principal US manufacturers had plenty of work; as a result the weapons were produced in Switzerland by SIG.

The Mondragon utilises gas tapped from the barrel to drive an actuating piston to the rear and open the bolt—a fairly standard pattern. Locking is achieved by rotating the bolt lugs by means of projections on the bolt/operating handle, which engage in helical cam tracks cut into the bolt body: indeed, one wonders whether or not Mondragon drew any ideas from the Swiss Schmidt-system straight-pull rifles. It is also possible to disconnect the bolt from the gas mechanism and thus turn the gun into a manual-operation rifle—a straight-pull bolt-action design. This particular provision was invariably requested by contemporary government specifications, demonstrating the lack of trust in which the self-loading operation was genuinely held.

As befits Swiss produce, the guns themselves are beautifully made of the finest materials and there are known to be several separate models. Apart from the development models, which seem to have been manufactured in a variety of calibres including 7mm (Mauser) and 7.5mm Swiss ordnance, the basic model adopted by Mexico in 1908 (as the *Fusil Porfirio Diaz Systema Mondragon Modelo 1908*) was in 7mm calibre and fitted with a box magazine into which an 8-round clip could be fitted. At the same time, however, SIG are known to have

marketed a version with a 20-round detachable box magazine and a rather spindly bipod—with which it was intended to serve as a rudimentary light machine-gun — although it seems that sales were not forthcoming in large enough quantities to merit the production of large numbers.

With the outbreak of war in 1914, some of the Mondragon rifles then in SIG's hands were purchased on behalf of the government of Germany, where they were used as the *Mondragon-Flieger-selbstladekarabiner Modell 1915*. Most of the German weapons were fitted with a 30-round helical 'snail' magazine invented by Tatarek and von Benkö and also used (in a slightly different form, of course)

on the Parabellum pistol. At the same time the Germans experimented with the rifles for infantry use, but the muddy conditions of the Western front soon clogged the rifles' somewhat delicate action, and the survivors were withdrawn from front-line use.

(data: Mexican model)
Length: 43.50in (1105mm)
Weight unloaded: 9lb 4oz (4.18kg)
Barrel: 22.75in (577mm), 4 grooves, right-hand twist
Magazine: 8-round clip-loaded box
Muzzle velocity: c.2500fps (760mps)

▼▼▼Three Mondragon rifles; the Mexican model 1908 (RSAF), the German of 1915 (RSAF) and the Swiss (SIG).

FUSIL D'ASSALTO CETME MODELO 58 and variants
Spain
Centro de Estudios Técnicos de Materiales Especiales (CETME), Madrid
7.62mm NATO special (see text)

Although firing a cartridge of the same physical dimensions as the NATO round and originally designed for a special 7.92mm round with a short case, the latest models of the CETME will also fire the normal NATO ammunition and a reduced-charge/lighter bullet cartridge called the CSP003. It was one of the first successful rifle designs to fire a full-powered round from an unlocked breech and this in itself makes it a remarkable weapon. It originated directly from the World War 2 Mauser-produced Gerät 06(M) or StG45(M) of 1945, whose designers moved to Spain at the end of the war. In practice the CETME uses only the basic layout and principles of the StG45, and the shape and construction of the two rifles is not strikingly similar. It is the standard rifle of the Spanish Forces and has been produced in quantity in Spain for some other countries.

It is made from low grade steel, using stampings, formings, drawings and welding as a means of reducing the complexity of manufacture and the cost of the plant needed to make it. The operating system is blowback with delay, the delay being provided by projecting rollers in the bolt which engage in recesses in the receiver. The chamber has to be fluted

to prevent the cartridge case sticking to the walls on extraction and some gas leaks round the case to enter the action as the bolt begins to move back. As a result, the mechanism is fouled to a black colour after firing, but there is said to be sufficient power in the design to overcome any tendency to jam.

Automatic fire is done from an open bolt, and single shots are fired from a closed bolt. A light bipod is permanently fitted to the fore-end by means of a collar, and it folds back to provide a carrying handguard on the early model. Later examples have tubular bipods, or wood handguards without bipods. There are also models designed specifically for competition target shooting ('modelo Deportivo'—semi-automatic operation only) and a sporting model (modelo S); these variants have different fittings and are offered in a variety of calibres.
Length: 40.00in (1015mm)
Weight unloaded: 9lb 15oz (4.50kg)
Barrel: 17.70in (450mm), 4 grooves, right-hand twist
Magazine: 20-round detachable box
Cyclic rate: 550-650rpm
Muzzle velocity: c.2580fps (786mps)

AUTOMAT GEVAR MODEL 37 (Browning 'BAR')
Sweden
Carl Gustafs Stads Gevärsfactori, Eskilstuna
6.5mm patron m/96

The Automat gevär m/37 is a modifica-

▲The CETME assault rifle, the original pattern of c.1957/8 (RSAF).
▲The CETME assault rifle Modelo C
▷The Egyptian 'Hakim' version of the AG42, again in 7.92mm calibre (RSAF).
▷The Madsen (Danish) version of the Swedish AG42, in 7.92mm (RSAF).
▷The SKS46 (SIG).

tion of the Browning Automatic Rifle developed at the Carl Gustafs Stads Gevärsfactori before World War 2. The chief differences lie in the calibre and in the fact that the barrel can be easily changed. The barrel is held by a simple latch on the front of the receiver and, when this is unlocked, the barrel can be lifted clear by a carrying handle. To allow for this, the usual large fore handgrip of the Browning has disappeared and the gun has to be carried by grasping the folded bipod legs. The m/37 is far more of a light machine-gun than its parent Browning, although the 20-round magazine detracts from its tactical value as it does with all the Browning conversions. The m/37 has now been phased out of first line service with the Swedish Army, but it is still held on the inventory of the reserve forces.
Length: 46.00in (1168mm)
Weight unloaded: 21lb 0oz (9.53kg)
Barrel: 24.00in (610mm), 6 grooves, right-hand twist
Magazine: 20-round detachable box
Cyclic rate: 500rpm
Muzzle velocity: c.2450fps (746mps)

HALVAUTOMATISKT GEVAR 42, HALVAUTOMATISKT GEVAR 42B (Eklund-Ljungmann system)
Sweden
Carl Gustafs Stads Gevärsfactori, Eskilstuna
6.5mm patron m/96

The AG42 was designed in Sweden by Erik Eklund and was introduced to the Swedish Army less than one year after having left the drawing board, an extraordinary feat by any standards.

The basic feature of the Eklund-Ljungmann system was unusual when first introduced, although it has since gained more widespread acceptance: the usual gas piston assembly has been discarded in favour of a simple direct-gas system in which the gases themselves impinge upon the bolt, thus doing away with the usual piston and rod devices used to convert the gas pressure into mechanical action. The gas strikes the face of the bolt carrier, which is then blown back and rotates the bolt by virtue of suitably-shaped cam tracks; the recoil spring then returns the bolt which strips a cartridge from the magazine in the process. The direct-gas system has since been used with success on the Stoner-designed AR10 and AR15 rifles.

After having adopted the AG42, the Swedes found deficiencies in their rifle—which is none too surprising in view of the haste with which it was adopted—and so a modified pattern, the AG42B, was introduced in 1953. The trigger mechanism and the extractor were revised, the foresight strengthened, the magazine modified, and stainless steel was used in the manufacture of the gas tube.

Apart from the Swedish patterns, the rifle was also manufactured in Denmark by Dansk Industri Syndikat 'Madsen'; the Madsen version had a longer gas tube coiled around the barrel and, although thereby lessening the fouling generation rate, the tube was difficult to clean. Largely owing to the inability of Madsen to persuade the Danish Army to adopt the rifle, it quickly passed from production. The Egyptians have also manufactured the Ljungmann rifle in 7.92mm Gew Patr 98 ('7.92mm Mauser'); it is known by them as the 'Hakim'.

Length: 47.80in (1215mm)
Weight unloaded: 10lb 6oz (4.74kg)
Barrel: 24.50in (623mm), 6 grooves, right-hand twist
Magazine: 10-round box
Muzzle velocity: c.2450fps (745mps) with Swedish ammunition

SELBSTLADEKARABINER MODELL 46 (SK46)
Switzerland
Schweizerische Industrie-Gesellschaft, Neuhausen-am-Rheinfalls
7.92mm Gew Patr 98 (German) and others

The SIG concern developed some self-loading rifles during World War 2 and, shortly after the war ended, the SK46 was produced and offered for sale in a variety of calibres. It was a simple weapon which showed marked Schmidt-Rubin influence both in outline and in the design of the receiver. Gas was tapped from a port on the right-hand side just forward of the breech and operated a fairly conventional tilting breechblock. The semi-automatic system could be disconnected by turning the cocking handle upright, and the rifle could then be fired as a conventional bolt-action weapon; by fitting a discharger, the rifle could be used for firing grenades. A telescopic sight of 2.2 × magnification was fitted as standard, adding 13.50oz. (0.38kg) to an already heavy rifle. Placing the gas port close to the breech is not a popular method of tapping gas as the pressure is very high at that point in the barrel and also very hot; erosion of the gas port is far less if the port is further from the point of ignition, and it also allows a longer delay before starting to operate the breech mechanism. The SK46 did not sell, as too many war surplus weapons were to be had cheaply to allow new designs much of a chance on the market.

Length: 44.25in (1125mm)
Weight unloaded: 10lb 0oz (4.54kg)
Barrel: 23.63in (600mm), 4 grooves, right-hand twist
Magazine: 5 or 10-round detachable box
Muzzle velocity: c.2700fps (823mps)

AUTOMATISCHEKARABINER MODELL 53 (AK53)
Switzerland
Schweizerische Industrie-Gesellschaft, Neuhausen-am-Rheinfalls
7.5mm Patrone M11

Another postwar design from SIG was the AK53, an attempt to make an easily manufactured selective-fire weapon. The 7.5mm calibre was chosen for the initial models because it was already in use among certain countries — particularly Switzerland—who might have been a potential market. The rifle worked on the entirely novel principle of moving the barrel forward and leaving a stationary bolt. This offers the advantages of a short overall length but compensates with some severe disadvantages, among them maintenance of accuracy from the moving barrel and the difficulty of preventing jamming when the barrel heats and expands. The rate of fire is also very low. Another drawback is that the AK53 fired from a closed breech, and so there was always a danger, after several bursts, of heat igniting the round in the breech. No doubt these points presented themselves to potential buyers, because this interesting weapon never sold and it remains one of the more unusual rifles of recent years.

Length: 39.37in (1000mm)
Weight unloaded: 10lb 12oz (4.90kg)
Barrel: 23.63in (600mm), 4 grooves, left-hand twist
Magazine: 30-round detachable box
Cyclic rate: 300rpm
Muzzle velocity: c.2450fps (750mps)

▲The AK53, a SIG design operating on blow-forward principles—unusual in a rifle, although the idea had been tried in several pistol designs (SIG).
▷The StuG57 (or SG57) manufactured at Neuhausen for the Swiss army. Note the similarity of the SG57 to the SG510 series' early models, in reality no more than service and export versions of the same gun (SIG).
○The SG510 weapons: the SG510-1 was almost identical to the StuG57, the SG510 2 was a lightened version and the SG510-3 (otherwise similar) was chambered for the 7.62mm × 39mm cartridge.
▷SG510-1 (SIG).
▷SG510-2 (SIG).
▷SG510-3 (SIG).

STURMGEWEHR MODELL 57 (StuG57)
Switzerland
Schweizerische Industrie-Gesellschaft, Neuhausen-am-Rheinfalls
7.5mm Patrone M11

The early history of the M57 is not entirely clear, but it is probable that it was originally inspired by the CETME; certainly there are similarities, particularly in the blowback action, the delay by rollers, and the general 'straight line' layout. As in the CETME and the G3 the locking rollers are in the head of the bolt, which is far lighter than the main portion, and on retracting they force the heavier bolt to the rear with a mechanical disadvantage. In an attempt to prevent sticking cases, the M57 uses a fluted chamber —another feature of the CETME. A major difference between the two weapons is that the M57 fires from a closed bolt on automatic fire, whereas the CETME fires from an open bolt.

The M57 followed closely the AM55, and this weapon had some relationship to another called the Direx. These earlier guns were marketed in a variety of calibres, but mainly in the Swiss army's 7.5mm chambering. The family likeness is readily apparent when they are compared.

The M57 has a number of modern features; a bipod is permanently fitted and it can be moved to any position along the barrel to suit the firer. There is an integral grenade-launcher on the muzzle and a rubber butt to absorb recoil. SIG now call this weapon the SIG Type 510, and the 510-1 is virtually the same as the M57.

Length: 43.50in (1105mm)
Weight unloaded: 12lb 4oz (5.63kg)
Barrel: 23.00in (583mm), 4 grooves, right-hand twist
Magazine: 24-round detachable box
Cyclic rate: 450-500rpm
Muzzle velocity: c.2500fps (761mps)

▲The guns here (from top to bottom) are: an SG510-4 with a light bipod folded back above the barrel, a standard SG510-4 version with upper and lower handguards, an SG510-4 with a telescope sight, and an SG510-4 with sight and bipod (all SIG).

STURMGEWEHR MODELL 510 Series (SG510)
Switzerland
Schweizerische Industrie-Gesellschaft, Neuhausen-am-Rheinfalls

7.62mm NATO-Patrone; 7.62 x 39mm

The SG510 series of selective-fire rifles is a direct descendant of the StG57 and all share the same system of delayed-blow-back operation. With the change of calibre to the 7.62mm round, the opportunity was taken to improve the weapon in several minor respects and it has now attained a very high standard indeed. From a technical standpoint the SG510 is probably the best selective-fire rifle in Europe and, as with all other products of SIG, the finish and standard of manufacture is beyond reproach. The rifles are consequently expensive and the design also came late into the field, so that sales have been limited to the Swiss army and a few African and South American

countries. It is now unlikely that the SG510 will appear in quantity as the NATO nations are already beginning to look at the next generation of smallarms with which to replace their current models, and the existing 7.62mm weapons will be made to last out the intervening period.

There are a number of variants in the 510 series. The 510-1 was the standard commercially-available weapon, and the 510-2 a lightened version. More important are the 510-3, chambered for the 7.62 x 39mm cartridge, and the 510-4, chambered for the standard NATO round. The 510-3 is, owing to the lighter cartridge, a smaller and lighter weapon and has a more capacious magazine.

Both the 510-3 and 510-4 show several interesting features. They can be fitted with light bipods which fold on top of the barrel when not in use, there is an indicator on the magazine to show the

ammunition state, a sniping telescope can be fitted, and a large winter trigger folds down alongside the trigger guard. The experience gained from the SG510 series has been put to good use by the company in the development of their 5.56mm rifle, the SG530.

(data: SG510–3)
Length: 35.00in (889mm)
Weight unloaded: 8lb 4oz (3.75kg)
Barrel: 16.50in (419mm), 4 grooves, right-hand twist
Magazine: 30-round detachable box
Cyclic rate: 450-600rpm
Muzzle velocity: c.2300fps (700mps)

(data: SG510–4)
Length: 40.00in (1015mm)
Weight unloaded: 9lb 6oz (4.25kg)
Barrel: 19.80in (505mm), 4 grooves, right-hand twist
Magazine: 20-round detachable box
Cyclic rate: 500-650rpm
Muzzle velocity: c.2635 (790mps)

▲The SG530 guns: standard, with a bayonet and with a telescope sight (SIG).

STURMGEWEHR MODELL 530–1 (SG530–1)
Switzerland
Schweizerische Industrie-Gesellschaft, Neuhausen-am-Rheinfalls
5.56mm x 45mm (0.223in).

The SG530-1 started as a scaled-down SG510 chambered for the 5.56mm round, but it was soon realised that this round does not easily lend itself to blowback action and a change was therefore made to gas operation. The breechblock was converted to take a piston extension to a piston running in a cylinder above the barrel, with a gas port about two-thirds of the way to the muzzle. The locking rollers are retained and are withdrawn by the gas action; blowback plays virtually no part in the operation. The rifle is neat and well made, and—in common with all SIG products—there are several optional extras. A light bipod is available and so is a special light bayonet; another swersion of the rifle has a folding skeleton butt which swings about a hinge on the rear of the receiver and lies alongside the right-hand side. Stripping is simple and no tools are required for normal field dismantling and cleaning. So far, this excellent rifle has not enjoyed large sales since the NATO nations, as has been previously said, are waiting to see what will be the next calibre; the SG530-1 is one of the European contenders for any future equipment and the latest model can be fitted, if required, with provision for a 3-round controlled burst.

Length: 37.00in (940mm)
Weight unloaded: 7lb 8oz (3.45kg)

▼▼▼Three views of the SG540/SG542 assault rifle manufactured by SIG. These weapons are examples of the prototype and preproduction guns, which explains why the finish is not comparable to that of the company's usual products (SIG)

Barrel: 15.50in (394mm), 4 grooves, right-hand twist
Magazine: 30-round detachable box
Cyclic rate: 600rpm
Muzzle velocity: c.3000fps (912mps)

STURMGEWEHR MODELLE 540 and 542 (SG540, SG542)
Switzerland
Schweizerische Industrie-Gesellschaft, Neuhausen-am-Rheinfalls
5.56mm (SG540), 7.62mm NATO (SG542)

SIG's SG540 series represents the company's latest venture into the self-loading rifle market and an improved version of the 5.56mm SG530, whose commercial success was unspectacular. The SG540 series is a good example of a modern rifle designed with a regard for simplicity and intended for uncomplicated manufacture: stampings and pressings are used wherever possible in an attempt to cut the unit cost, a drawback which has existed in the past with some SIG products.

The SG540 is a gas-operated selective-fire rifle firing from a closed breech, locked by virtue of lugs on the rotating bolt. Provision is also made for the attachment of a 3-round automatic burst device, but in this weapon it is a separate component and not an integral part of the gun; the device can be fitted by the

▲Another view of the SG540/SG542
prototype assault rifle (SIG).
▲The AVF of 1916 (John Walter).

firer without recourse to special tools
and the rifle needs no modification to
accept it.

Various accessories are supplied for
the rifles, including telescope sights,
bipods and bayonets (of tubular or conventional type), and an integral flash-
suppressor / compensator / grenade
launcher appears at the muzzle. The
launcher is capable of either direct or
indirect projection of the grenades.

It is—of course—too early to predict
what success awaits the SG540 and the
SG542, and indeed the weapons shown
here are prototypes: production guns
will have the high standard of finish
expected of their manufacturers.

(data: SG540, fixed stock)
Length: 37.50in (953mm)
Weight unloaded: 6lb 13oz (3.03kg)
Barrel: 19.29in (490mm) with flash-hider,
4 grooves, right-hand twist
Magazine: 20 or 30-round detachable box
Cyclic rate: 650-800rpm
Muzzle velocity: 3215fps (980mps)

(data: SG542, fixed stock)
Length: 38.83in (987mm)
Weight unloaded: 7lb 13oz (3.54kg)

Barrel: 19.50in (495mm) with flash-hider,
4 grooves, right-hand twist
Magazine: 20-round detachable box
Cyclic rate: 650-800rpm
Muzzle velocity: 2690fps (820mps)

AVTOMATICHESKAIA VINTOVKA FEDEROVA, 1916
Russia
Imperatorskiĭ Oruzheinyi Zav'od Sestroretskiĭ, Sestroretsk
6.5mm Meiji 30 (Japanese)

The Federov selective-fire rifle can
probably lay claim to being the ancestor
of the present generation of assault rifles,
although it falls into that category perhaps more by chance than by design.

Vasiliy Federov was a prominent
Tsarist arms designer who later continued
in the service of the Soviets, to become
the author of many official textbooks.
Prior to World War 1, however, he had
produced a number of experimental rifles
with varying degrees of success. One of
his major problems lay in the ammunition with which he was forced to work;
the standard rifle cartridge of the Russian
Army was a fat, awkward, rimmed-case

▷▷▷ The AVS36 (SIM), SVT38
(RSAF) and the SVT40 (SIM).

round which did not easily lend itself to automation—and many of the rounds, particularly those of indigenous make, were of inferior and inconsistent quality. Furthermore, it was typical of its period —a powerful round which demanded a heavy and robust weapon. After the Russo-Japanese War of 1904–5, for reasons concealed in history, the Russians produced a number of designs chambered for the Japanese 6.5mm Meiji 30 ('Arisaka') cartridge, most of which remained no more than paper exercises.

In 1916, Federov developed a selective-fire rifle around the Japanese round, using short-recoil of the barrel to operate the mechanism; the rifle had a forward pistol-grip, a curved magazine, and weighed some 9lb 8oz (4.37kg). The Avtomat could well have been as decisive in battle as the Russian submachine-guns of World War 2, but the October Revolution stopped production of the Federov design after rather less than 5,000 had been made.

Length: 41.15in (1045mm)
Weight unloaded: 9lb 8oz (4.38kg)
Barrel:
Magazine: 25-round detachable box
Cyclic rate: 600-650rpm
Muzzle velocity: c.2400fps (730mps)

AVTOMATICHESKAIA VINTOVKA SIMONOVA OBRAZETS 1936G (AVS or AVS36)
Union of Soviet Socialist Republics
State factories
7.62mm patron o1891g (7.62mm M91 Russian)
The Simonov was the first automatic rifle

to be adopted in quantity by the Red Army, who accepted it in 1936. It is a gas-operated weapon using a piston mounted above the barrel to unlock and retract the bolt; the locking system is itself rather unusual, relying on a vertically-moving block to lock the bolt and the carrier securely to the receiver before firing.

The standard weapon is provided with a selective fire device to permit its use as a light machine-gun. The AVS suffered from excessive muzzle blast and recoil, and in an endeavour to reduce this a two-port muzzle-brake was fitted. The receiver is cut open to allow movement of the cocking handle and thus the interior of the weapon is exposed to mud and grit. Whether or not it was this defect, or simply that the unusual locking system failed to live up to its promise, the fact remains that the AVS had a very short service life. It was replaced in 1938 by the more simple Tokarev.

Length: 48.10in (1220mm)
Weight unloaded: 9lb 8oz (4.37kg)
Barrel: 24.40in (620mm), 4 grooves, right-hand twist
Magazine: 15-round detachable box
Muzzle velocity: c.2550fps (776mps)

SAMOZARIADNYIA VINTOVKA TOKAREVA OBRAZETS 1938G (SVT38)
Union of Soviet Socialist Republics
State factories
7.62mm patron o91g
The Tokarev-designed weapons relied on gas operation with a locking block cammed downwards at the rear into a recess in the receiver floor. The SVT38 had a

two-piece wooden stock with a prominent magazine; there were two steel barrel bands and the forward portion of the wooden handguard was replaced by one of sheet steel with circular cooling apertures drilled into each side. Immediately behind these, rectangular cooling slots were cut into the wooden guard. The principal distinguishing feature was the positioning of the cleaning rod, inserted along the right side of the stock rather than underneath the barrel of the weapon. The rifle was originally fitted with a six-baffle muzzle brake, replaced in late 1940 or early 1941 by a two-baffle unit. Owing to its fragile construction, manufacture of the 1938 pattern was abandoned in 1940, but not before some selected weapons had been fitted with telescopic sights.

Length: 48.10in (1222mm)
Weight unloaded: 8lb 10oz (3.95kg)
Barrel: 25.00in (635mm), 4 grooves, right-hand twist
Magazine: 10-round detachable box
Muzzle velocity: c.2725fps (830mps)

SAMOZARIADNYIA VINTOVKA TOKAREVA OBRAZETS 1940G; AVTOMATICHESKAIA VINTOVKA TOKAREVA O1940G
Union of Soviet Socialist Republics
State factories
7.62mm patron o91g
A more robust version of the 1938 Tokarev design, the SVT40 was characterised by the removal of the earlier rifle's externally mounted cleaning rod, which was instead mounted—according to convention—beneath the barrel. There

▼A carbine version of the SVT40 rifle, made from a cut-down rifle, c.1942 (RSAF).
▼A Chinese Type 56 rifle, a native-built SKS; note the bayonet (RSAF).

was only a single barrel band, beyond which a sheet metal handguard extended forward; on the SVT40 is was of wrap-around type as opposed to the 'metal-and-wood' forward guard of the SVT38. Air circulation holes were drilled into the guard, and four rectangular slots appeared through the wooden continuation. Two variations in muzzle brake design existed: the first had six slim baffles, replaced in later production by a unit having only two large baffles. These self-loading rifles were issued mainly to NCOs although, as with the SVT38 models, selected specimens were equipped with telescopic sights and issued to snipers.

A fully automatic version, called the AVT40, was outwardly identical to the self-loading SVT40 from which it was converted except for alteration to the surround of the safety catch to permit the addition of an automatic fire adjustment. Only very few rifles were thus converted.

Carbine versions, some converted and some of new manufacture, are also known to exist.

Length: 48.10in (1222mm)
Weight unloaded: 8lb 9oz (3.90kg)
Barrel: 24.60in (625mm), 4 grooves, right-hand twist
Magazine: 10-round detachable box
Muzzle velocity: c.2725fps (830mps)

SAMOZARIADNYIA KARABINA SIMONOVA OBRAZETS 1946
Union of Soviet Socialist Republics

State Factories
7.62mm patron obrazets 1943g

The SKS carbine was the first weapon developed by the Soviets to use their 'intermediate' round, which was copied from that of the Germans. Although important for that reason, the SKS was not a particularly inspired design. It was simple, easy to operate and quite strong, but a little heavy for the ammunition that it fired; this is understandable as the Soviets produced the first models under the stress of war. The system of operation and the locking of the bolt appear to have been taken from the PTRS anti-tank rifle, locking being achieved by the same type of tipping bolt. Stripping is very easy, and the pivoting bayonet and the one-piece wooden stock are also prominent features of the weapon—both of which are now thought to be rather old-fashioned ideas. Loading can be accomplished either by clips or by pushing single rounds into the magazine from the top. Unloading can be quickly effected by releasing the pivoting magazine cover, swinging it away below the receiver, and catching the rounds as they spill out downwards.

Enormous numbers of this carbine have been made, and although it is no longer in current service in the Soviet Union it has appeared in almost every Communist country in the world. The SKS has been made in slightly different versions in different factories. In Yugoslavia it is known as the M/59, and has an integral grenade launcher on the muzzle, while in China it seems to have inspired a new indigenous design altogether with a slightly longer barrel.

Length: 40.20in (1022mm)
Weight unloaded: 8lb 8oz (3.86kg)
Barrel: 20.50in (520mm), 4 grooves, right-hand twist
Magazine: 10-round box, fixed to receiver
Muzzle velocity: c.2410fps (735mps)

AVTOMAT KALASHNIKOV OBRAZETS 1947G, AVTOMAT KALASHNIKOV MODIFICATSIONNII (AKM)
Union of Soviet Socialist Republics
State factories
7.62mm patron o43g

The 'Kalashnikov' is the standard Soviet assault rifle. After observing German development of an intermediate cartridge and a rifle to match, the Russians, appreciating the logic, developed their own version which evolved into the Kalashnikov. It is probably one of the best automatic rifles in service today and certainly the most widely distributed, having been supplied to all the satellite nations, many of whom have manufactured their own variations (see APPENDICES): more than thirty-five million are reputed to have been produced. In addition, the AK will always be found where Communist-inspired Nationalist movements are pressing their causes.

The AK is gas-operated and is rather unusual in having the gas piston rod permanently attached to the bolt carrier. A cam-track on the carrier rotates the

Variations of the AK and AKM

▼A Bulgarian AK, without a cleaning rod and without a bayonet lug (SIM).
▼A Chinese rifle Type 56/1, an AK with the addition to the muzzle of a folding bayonet similar to that of the SKS (RSAF).

▼An East German MPiKM, with a plastic stock and pistol-grip but a wooden fore-end (RSAF).
▼A Romanian AKM, with a forward pistol-grip (RSAF).

bolt to lock and, during the rearward stroke, the hammer is also cocked. The barrel, like that of most Soviet weapons, is chrome-lined.

In spite of its popularity and efficiency, the AK is not without its defects. There is, surprisingly, no hold-open device on the bolt to indicate an empty magazine, or—indeed—any method of holding the bolt open.

After studying the inferior finish of the Russians' wartime weapons, it is a pleasant surprise to find that the AK reverts to more traditional methods of construction and finish, the receiver being a machined unit. This state of affairs was obviously uneconomic, and the latest Kalashnikov design, the AKM, reverts to a stamped steel construction. The bolt is parkerised instead of the polished steel of the AK, a cyclic rate reducer is fitted, and the bayonet is an ingenious model with a slot in the blade which, when engaged with a stud on the scabbard, converts the assembly into a wire-cutter—an astonishing transforma-

▼▼▼ A Polish PMK-DGN, with a grenade launcher (RSAF); a Russian AKM (authors' collection); SVD.

tion which would have been welcome in 1916 but which seems anachronistic on the modern battlefield. There are also some minor changes in the components of the AKM, but it is basically a logical development of the AK with the intention both of reducing manufacturing time and cost and improving combat efficiency.

Length: 34.25in (870mm)
Weight unloaded: 9lb 7oz (4.30kg)
Barrel: 16.34in (415mm), 4 grooves, right-hand twist
Magazine: 30-round detachable box
Cyclic rate: 800rpm
Muzzle velocity: c.2330fps (710mps)

SAMOZARIADNYIA VINTOVKA DRAGUNOVA (SVD)
Union of Soviet Socialist Republics
State factories
7.62mm patron o1891g

The Dragunov has appeared in service in the Soviet army in increasing numbers over the past few years; it is one of the small number of rifles in the world which have been specifically designed for sniping and it is one of an even smaller number which are semi-automatic. The Dragunov is replacing (or has perhaps

already replaced) the ageing bolt-action M1891/30 rifles left over from World War 2. It is an excellent weapon and much thought and effort has gone into its design and construction. The basic operating system has been borrowed from the AK and strengthened to take the greater power of the old rimmed ammunition. All parts are most carefully made and matched and a telescope sight —known as the PSO1—is issued as part of the equipment of every rifle, although iron sights are also fitted. The rifle is also easy and pleasant to handle and fire, and the trigger mechanism of the AK has been modified slightly to give a smooth pull-off with minimum shake and lock time. A civilian hunting version of the SVD exists in the Soviet Union, sold under the commercial name of *Medved* ('bear'). It has a more sporting stock, a smaller magazine, a shorter telescope and no foresight protectors, but is otherwise identical.

Length: 48.20in (1225mm)
Weight unloaded: 9lb 8oz (4.31kg)
Barrel: 24.00in (610mm), 4 grooves, right-hand twist
Magazine: 10-round detachable box
Muzzle velocity: c.2720fps (828mps)

RIFLE, AUTOMATIC, 7MM NUMBER 9 MARK 1 ('EM2')
United Kingdom
Royal Small Arms Factory, Enfield Lock, Middlesex
7mm (0.280in) SAA Ball

Although it had been realised for many years that the old series of smallarms amunition based on various cartridges from 6.5mm to 8mm was too powerful, few countries had the resources or energy to change. In postwar Britain the time seemed right for the old 0.303in bolt-action rifles were completely obsolete and, in the late 1940s, the EM2 appeared in small numbers. The rifle fired a 0.280in bullet from a short case and had been made on the premise that 1,000 yards was the maximum range at which any round would need to be effective. The rifle was a gas-operated selective-fire weapon of highly unconventional appearance and short overall length. The mechanism was very neat (though complicated) and it fired from a closed bolt at all times, which might have given rise to heat-instigated premature ignition troubles ('cook-offs') had the rifle been accepted. Locking was by front-pivoting flaps and some trouble was taken to ensure that they ran freely and would not jam if dirt and mud entered the receiver; the balance of the weapon was extremely good owing to the breech lying behind the trigger. The sight was a simple optical tube mounted in the carrying handle: it had no provision for range alteration as this was incorporated in the sight picture on the graticule. The performance of this unusual rifle was extremely good and it was proclaimed as not only highly reliable but also easy to teach and to learn. It was never taken into service, mainly because NATO was not ready for it, and political opposition was widespread largely as huge stocks of 'conventional' ammunition remained to be used up. There was also strong opposition from the USA to the idea of using a small calibre of 0.280in. The design was therefore abandoned and NATO chose the 7.62mm round a few years later. Attempts to revive the EM2 met with no success and very few now remain.

Length: 35.00in (889mm)
Weight unloaded: 7lb 9oz (3.41kg)
Barrel: 24.50in (623mm), 4 grooves, right-hand twist
Magazine: 20-round detachable box
Muzzle velocity: 2530fps (763 mps)

'US SELF-LOADING PISTOL, CALIBER .30, M1918'
United States of America
Remington Arms-Union Metallic Cartridge Company, Ilion, New York State
Cartridge, .30 M1918

In the course of studying the actions in France during 1916 and 1917 the United States Army observed that the most dangerous time for the infantryman was during his advance across 'No Man's Land', when the covering fire had stopped and the enemy was alert. With some assistance from the French, the American authorities came to the conclusion that the best solution would be to equip every man with an automatic rifle and to have him fire it from the hip as he advanced, so covering the entire area with bullets and making it most hazardous for defenders to appear over the defence parapets to see who was coming.

The prospect of producing sufficient automatic rifles for every man was out of the question and, since the normal bolt-action rifle would be required on most other occasions, the problem

▼The Pedersen device; its holster, magazine and magazine pouch (Remington).

▼▼Two views of the BAR M1918A2 (RSAF).

seemed a little difficult until it was cleverly solved by John Pedersen, who was at the time working as a designer for Remington at their Ilion plant. It was thought possible to remove the bolt from the standard M1903 rifle and replace it with a simple blowback device fitted with its own magazine and with a short barrel which outwardly resembled a standard 0.30in M1906 cartridge case. This fitted into the chamber of the rifle after the original bolt had been removed, the magazine protruded obliquely to one side, and the soldier—in fifteen seconds—had converted his rifle into a form of submachine-gun or automatic rifle. The cartridge was specially designed by Pedersen to suit the device and has never been used in any other weapon; it is rather like a much-lengthened 0.32in ACP round in appearance.

The M1903 rifle when altered to accept the device became the *Rifle, Magazine, Caliber 0.30, M1903 Mark 1* and some 65,000 of these devices (together with the special holster, two pouches of magazines sufficient to provide each man with 400 rounds, and the necessary converted rifles) were prepared by Remington in conditions of great secrecy during 1918, in order to prepare the United States Army for the 1919 spring offensive. The war then ended and a more leisurely evaluation of the Pedersen device decided that it was not entirely desirable. Soldiers who used the device invariably lost their rifle bolt or, if using the rifle, misplaced or damaged the Pedersen device. Moreover, the claimed 15-second changeover only held good in ideal conditions, and the time increased in conditions of cold, wet or darkness.

In the mid-1920s the device was sentenced for scrap, and almost the entire stock was broken up for scrap under military control.

Although the Pedersen device was originally intended for the M1903 American 'Springfield' rifle, some were made for the M1917 Enfield for trial purposes. There is also evidence that examples were made for the French Fusil M07/15 and the Russian rifle M1891, both of which were made by Remington to foreign contracts.

US AUTOMATIC RIFLE, CALIBER .30 M1918–M1922 (BROWNINGS)
United States of America
Colt's Patent Firearms Manufacturing Company, Hartford, Connecticut; Winchester Repeating Firearms Company, New Haven, Connecticut; Marlin-Rockwell Corporation, New Haven, Connecticut
.30 M1906
The Browning Automatic Rifle was designed to be fired while assaulting at the walk, derived from the French ideas which favoured this as a means of giving covering fire while crossing 'No Man's Land'. The BAR never entirely lived up to its designer's hopes; neither a rifle nor a light machine-gun, it fell between the two. As a rifle it was too heavy and could not be fired from the shoulder with any great accuracy as it vibrated from forward movement of the bolt. Set for automatic fire it was too light and moved excessively, and the small magazine capacity necessitated frequent reloading. For its day, however, it was nevertheless a brilliant design produced in record time by John Browning, and it was bought

and used by many countries throughout the world. It was the standard squad weapon for the American infantry in World War 2, and it fought in every theatre of the war. The later version was changed from that of World War 1 in that, instead of a selector switch giving semi-automatic or fully automatic fire, there was provision for two rates of automatic fire of 350 or 550rpm. The United States Marine Corps preferred semi-automatic fire and therefore modified some of their guns back to the original idea: there is, as a result, an almost bewildering variety of models of the BAR to be found around the world. After distinguished service in Korea it passed into the American National Guard Reserve, but it is still to be encountered in many of the world's smaller armies.

US Automatic Rifle, Caliber .30, M1918 (Browning). The M1918 is fitted with a smooth tapered barrel, and the stock is provided with a swivel between the pistol-grip and the stock-toe. No bipod assembly is fitted.
Length: 48.00in (1219mm)
Weight unloaded: 16lb 0oz (7.28kg)
Barrel: 24.00in (610mm), 4 grooves, right-hand twist
Magazine: 20-round detachable box
Cyclic rate: 500rpm
Muzzle velocity: c.2650fps (807mps)
US Automatic Rifle, Caliber .30, M1918-A1 (Browning). The M1918A1 shares the barrel and stock design of the M1918, with a similar butt swivel: a 'double buttplate' is fitted, the outer part of which can be hinged upwards to provide a shoulder support, and a hinged bipod is attached to the gas cylinder just forward

of the wooden forearm. The M1918A1 weighs approximately 18lb 4oz (8.30kg).

US Automatic Rifle, Caliber .30, M1918-A2 (Browning). Similar to the preceding M1918 designs, the M1918A2 has a shortened forearm with an internal metal plate intended to protect the recoil spring from barrel heat, and a bipod with 'skid feet' rather than the 'spike feet' of the M1918A1. A butt monopod of questionable utility is fitted, and the firing mechanism incorporates provision for altering the cyclic rate; unlike the two earlier patterns, the M1918A2 is incapable of firing single shots. The first M1918A2 production were originally issued with a bipod at the muzzle: later weapons returned it to a position around the gas cylinder.

US Automatic Rifle, Caliber .30, M1922 (Browning). A short-lived variation of the M1918 types, with a finned barrel to accelerate barrel cooling and a sling swivel on the left side of the stock. A bipod may be fitted and a wide groove cut around the butt is intended to accommodate the butt monopod.

PEDERSEN SELF-LOADING RIFLE, CALIBER .276, T2E1 (c.1927–30)
United States of America
Springfield Armory, Springfield, Massachusetts
0.276in Pedersen

John Pedersen was a designer who, after working commercially, joined the government designers at Springfield Armory in the years between the wars, where he developed a 0.276in cartridge and a rifle to go with it. Although the rifle (called the T2E1) was not accepted, the cartridge was regarded more favourably and indeed was almost selected in 1932 as the United States Army's service round.

The Pedersen rifle uses a toggle-joint very similar to that found on the Parabellum pistol, but designed to function as a delayed blowback arm. The thrust axis through the toggle is slightly below the pivot axis, and careful design of the toggle hinge—incorporating progressive cam surfaces rather than a simple pivot—makes the first movement of the opening so slow that the chamber pressure has time to drop before the full opening movement is developed and the empty case extracted. Unfortunately it means that when the extraction movement begins there is still sufficient pressure in the chamber to keep the cartridge case expanded against the chamber wall, and this friction leads to hard extraction, torn rims and separated cases. The only cure for this was to lubricate the cases and so Pedersen developed a system of wax-coating the cases during manufacture, and with this special ammunition the rifle worked well. But waxed or lubricated cases are anathema to most military users and—regrettably—the Pedersen was doomed.

In addition to the T2E1 rifles made for the US trials, Pedersen-system guns were made for tests in the United Kingdom by Vickers-Armstrongs Limited, c.1930–32. Similar guns were later made in Japan, c.1934–35, for trials with the Imperial army.

▼▼Two views of the Vickers-Pedersen rifle (RSAF). ▼M1 Garand (RSAF)

US RIFLE, CALIBER .30 ('Garand'), M1–M1E9, M1C, M1D, T26
United States of America
Springfield Armory, Springfield, Massachusetts; Winchester Repeating Arms Company, New Haven, Connecticut; Harrington & Richardson Arms Company, Worcester, Massachusetts; International Harvester Corporation
0.30in M1906

The Rifle M1 has the distinction of being the first self-loading rifle to be adopted as a standard weapon; this occurred in 1932 and the rifle began to enter service in 1936, and by 1941 a large part of the American regular army had it as their standard arm. Very large numbers had been made by 1945 and total production when the manufacture ceased in the 1950s was about 5,500,000. Garands were still in regular service in Vietnam in 1963, and many are no doubt still used in many parts of Asia. The weapon is itself simple and immensely strong; it is not particularly light but, by contemporary standards, the weight was reasonable enough. The system of operation is by gas action, and the bolt unlocking system was continued in the same form in the Rifle M14 of 1957. The magazine held eight rounds only and did not project below the line of the stock. This had the advantage of offering a smoother outline, but restricted the ammunition supply. Another criticism of the Garand was the method of loading, which was by a clip of eight rounds: single rounds could not be pushed in, so it was a case of a full magazine or none at all. The spent clip was automatically ejected after the last round was fired, making a distinctive sound which sometimes led to fatal results in close-quarter or concealed-firer operations. But these were small matters and the main thing was that the United States Army carried a self-loading rifle throughout World War 2.

Length: 43.50in (1103mm)
Weight unloaded: 9lb 8oz (4.37kg)
Barrel: 24.00in (610mm), 4 grooves, right-hand twist
Magazine: 8-round internal box
Muzzle velocity: c.2800fps (853mps)

US Rifle, Caliber .30, M1E1. A slight variation of the standard Rifle M1, with slight modifications made to the fit of the operating mechanism and with a more gradual cam-angle in the operating rod handle. Few were made in this pattern.

US Rifle, Caliber .30, M1E2. The first version of the Rifle M1 adapted for optical sights, an International Industries telescopic sight was fitted with suitable mounts; the M1E2 was strictly experimental issue and was quickly replaced by the Rifle M1E7.

US Rifle, Caliber .30, M1E3. Another of the experimental guns produced in an attempt to make the operation of the M1 more smooth, a roller bearing was attached to the bolt cam lug and the cam-angle of the operating rod was suitably altered.

US Rifle, Caliber .30, M1E4. An experimental arm produced in an attempt to achieve a less-violent operation by increasing the time lag between the tapping of the gas and the opening of the bolt, and also by lessening the rearward velocity of the operating rod. An expansion chamber was introduced into the gas system.

US Rifle, Caliber .30, M1E5. This was a shortened version of the Rifle M1 provided with a folding stock and the barrel was shortened to 18.00in (457mm), but although the accuracy remained virtually unimpaired muzzle blast and flash were held to be excessive.

US Rifle, Caliber .30, M1E6. An experimental project in which an offset telescopic sight was to be fitted to a sniper rifle in order that the fixed open sights could still be used if necessary.

US Rifle, Caliber .30, M1E7 (US Sniper's Rifle, Caliber .30, M1C). One of the issue snipers' rifles, the M1E7 was fitted either with a telescopic Sight M73—commercially known as the 'Lyman Alaskan' and manufactured by the Lyman Gun Sight Corporation of Middlefield—or with the Sight M73B1, commercially known as the 'Weaver 330' and made by W R Weaver Company of El Paso. A detachable leather cheekpiece was fitted to the stock, and a flash-suppressor was added in 1945. The M1E7 was renamed M1C in June 1944.

US Rifle, Caliber .30, M1E8 (US Snipers' Rifle, Caliber .30, M1D). The second issue version of the M1 intended for snipers' use, the M1E8 was fitted with the telescopic Sight M73 in a block mount in which guise it was known as the Sight M81 (crosswire graticule) or the Sight M82 (tapered-post graticule). A Sight M84 was also issued. The M1E8 was renamed M1D in June 1944.

US Rifle, Caliber .30, M1E9. An experimental variation of the M1E4, with an alteration made to the gas expansion system in which the gas piston served as a tappet for the operating rod. It was hoped by this to avoid the overheating troubles of the M1E4.

US Rifle, Caliber .30, T26. A quantity of these rifles were ordered in 1945 for the Pacific Theater, although the order was later rescinded; the rifle combined the action of the M1E5 with a shortened M1 stock.

JOHNSON SELF-LOADING RIFLE MODEL 1941
United States of America
Cranston Arms Company, Providence, Rhode Island
.30 M1906

The Johnson rifle was designed shortly before World War 2 as a light military weapon, and it was extensively tested by the American Army and Marine Corps. Neither accepted it—which is hardly surprising as the Garand had just been put into mass production—but; in the difficult days of 1941 when all rifles were in desperately short supply, the Marine Corps bought several thousand for their Special Forces and especially for their parachutists. The Dutch also bought some for their forces in Sumatra and Java. With the Japanese occupation of the Dutch East Indies, and as Garand production got under way, the Johnson fought a losing battle for official acceptance. It was only retained for the OSS and similar specialised units. The Johnson was recoil-operated, one of the few rifles so designed to be accepted into service in any army. It also had several other unusual features amongst which was the rotary magazine with its lips machined into the receiver; they were not so prone to damage as removable ones, and the magazine could be loaded or emptied with the bolt closed and the weapon safe. The barrel was largely unsupported and so rather vulnerable, but it could easily be dismounted and this aided the parachutist in carrying it. In service use the Johnson proved to be less reliable than was acceptable and throughout the war it was continually modified, although never achieving perfection before it passed out of production entirely in 1945.

Length: 45.50in (1156mm)
Weight unloaded: 9lb 8oz (4.31kg)
Barrel: 22.00in (558mm), 4 grooves, right-hand twist
Magazine: 10-round detachable rotary box (+ 1 round in magazine feedway)
Muzzle velocity: c.2650fps (807mps)

▼The Johnson V9 self-loading rifle of 1937 (RSAF), ▼and the Johnson M1941 (RSAF).

▲The Smith & Wesson Model 1940 (RSAF), and the Reising 60 (RSAF).▼

SMITH & WESSON 9MM MODEL 1940 LIGHT RIFLE
United States of America
Smith & Wesson Arms Company, Springfield, Massachusetts
9mm Parabellum

Smith & Wesson's self-loading carbine has a very clouded history. The gun was developed in 1939 as a possible police arm and, in 1940, it was offered for trials to the British. The M1940 was a blowback gun of relatively simple construction and, although of superior finish, the only truly unusual feature lay in the magazine housing; this fixed component not only accepted the box magazine but also acted as a forward handgrip, and the rear half contained a chute down which the spent cases were ejected.

The carbine was rejected by the British on the grounds of fragility and expense, especially as other models had become available which were both more reliable and cheaper. The trouble with the original Smith & Wesson guns lay in the ammunition, for the 9mm Parabellum round was more powerful than that for which the Light Rifle had originally been chambered and a series of component breakages ensued. A modified version of the gun was developed as the Mark 2 and it appears that small numbers were taken by the Royal Navy in 1941–2; there is no official record of the carbine's introduction to

the British services, although it is recorded that in 1942 the Royal Small Arms Factory at Enfield Lock designed a 'Butt, folding, Mark 2' for the 'Carbine, Self-loading, Smith & Wesson, 9mm'. Beyond this the records are silent.

It seems that a version of the Light Rifle was briefly mooted in 0.45in ACP, but it is also apparent that none was ever made; fully-automatic variations of the basic design were also considered, although none progressed past the experimental stage.

Length: 33.25in (845mm)
Weight unloaded: 8lb 10oz (3.92kg)
Barrel: 9.75in (247mm), 6 grooves, right-hand twist
Magazine: 20-round detachable box
Muzzle velocity: c.1240fps (378 mps)

REISING SELF-LOADING CARBINE MODEL 60
United States of America
Harrington & Richardson Arms Company, Worcester, Massachusetts
.45 M1911 (0.45in ACP)

The Reising Model 60 bears considerable resemblance to the Model 50 submachine-gun and is virtually the same weapon with an extended barrel, and with the mechanism altered to restrict operation to single-shot fire; like the Model 50 it operates on a retarded blowback system, the bolt being 'locked' into a recess in the receiver.

The Model 60 was developed primarily

as a police weapon although, owing to the use of a pistol cartridge, it found no application as a military self-loading rifle; it was, however, tested by a number of military agencies.

US CARBINES, CALIBER .30, M1, M1A1, M2 and M3
United States of America
General Motors Corporation, Saginaw Steering Gear Division, Grand Rapids and Saginaw, Michigan; General Motors Corporation, Inland Manufacturing Division, Dayton, Ohio; International Business Machine Corporation, Poughkeepsie, New York; National Postal Meter Company, Rochester, New York; Quality Hardware and Machine Company, Chicago, Illinois; Rochester Defense Corporation, Rochester, New York; Rock-Ola Manufacturing Corporation, Chicago, Illinois; Standard Products Company, Port Clinton, Ohio; Underwood-Elliot-Fisher Company, Hartford, Connecticut; Winchester Repeating Arms Company, New Haven, Connecticut
.30 M1 Carbine

The Carbine, Caliber .30, M1, the most prolific American weapon of World War 2, began as a 1938 request for a light rifle suitable for arming machine-gunners, mortarmen, clerks, cooks and similar grades. The request was refused but, resubmitted in 1940, it later met with a more favourable reception. In October

1940 specifications were issued to 25 manufacturing companies, although their work was delayed until Winchester had produced the ammunition. The new round was developed by them to another army specification, with a 110-grain bullet giving a muzzle velocity of 1860fps (556mps) from an 18in (457mm) barrel.

Tests began in May 1941 after some 11 different makers had submitted designs, amongst them a Springfield Armory gun designed by John Garand. Some weapons were rejected on the spot, but others showed sufficient promise for their makers to be given the chance to modify them and to remedy defects; a final trial took place in September of 1941. The result was the adoption of the Williams-designed and Winchester-manufactured prototype, which was adopted as the Carbine M1.

The M1 carbine is a semi-automatic light rifle utilising a unique operating system. A gas port in the barrel leads to a chamber containing a tappet (or short-stroke piston); when impelled by a rush of gas, this tappet is driven violently back for about 0.32in (8mm) and the end outside the gas chamber—which is in contact with the operating slide—drives back the operating slide. This operates the bolt to unlock, open and eject the spent case. A return spring then drives the slide back into contact with the tappet, repositioning it in the gas chamber; this forward movement also closes and locks the bolt, chambering the next round from the magazine in the process. The firing hammer is left cocked.

(data: M1)
Length: 35.65in (905mm)
Weight unloaded: 5lb 7oz (2.48kg)
Barrel: 18.00in (457mm), 4 grooves, right-hand twist
Magazine: 15 or 30-round detachable box
Muzzle velocity: c.1950fps (593mps)

The **US Carbine, Caliber .30, M1A1** is the same basic weapon as the M1, with the addition of a folding metal stock for the convenience of parachute and airborne troops.

US Carbine, Caliber .30, M2. The original specification for the Carbine M1 demanded provision for selective fire control, but this was dropped during the course of development and the guns appeared in due course capable only of semi-automatic fire. But after the M1 had been in service for a short time, a demand arose from the users for an automatic capability, available in emergencies, and the Carbine M2 was the result. It is simply the M1 with a selective-fire switch added to the left side of the receiver, operating on the sear mechanism.

US Carbine, Caliber .30, M3 or T3. The Carbine M3 was simply an M2 with suitable mountings prepared on the receiver to take various models of infra-red night-sighting devices. No open or conventional sights were provided. The Carbine M3, sometimes known by its development title T3, was only produced in limited numbers as a semi-prototype; only about 2,100 were manufactured compared to 5,510,000 M1 carbines, 150,000 M1A1 carbines and 570,000 M2 carbines.

◁◁◁ M1, M1A1 and M2 carbines
(RSAF).
▲The M3 or T3 carbine with an infra-
red telescope sight (RSAF).
▲▲Two views of the Armalite AR10 rifle
which later became the AR15 (Armalite).

ARMALITE RIFLE MODEL AR–10, 1955
United States of America
Armalite Division of Fairchild Engine & Airplane Company, Costa Mesa, California (see text)
7.62mm NATO

The AR10 had a short and not particularly successful career as a military rifle. Prototypes appeared in 1955, production stopped in 1961, and very few were made: Sudan is probably the only country to have bought it and then only in small numbers. Events overtook the AR10, which is a pity for it was a good rifle and might have been better than those which were chosen in its place. Most of the metallic parts were aluminium, with steel being used for the bolt, bolt carrier and barrel, and many of these few steel parts were chromium plated. The weight was considerably low and, perhaps because of this, a muzzle compensator had to be fitted to prevent—or at least reduce—muzzle climb on automatic fire. The action was the same as that now made famous by the 5.56mm AR15, a gas tube impinging on the bolt carrier and a front-locking rotating bolt. The 5.56mm rifle is in fact a smaller version of the AR10, using nearly all its characteristics. Had the AR10 started a little earlier in the race for the 7.62mm NATO rifle, it would probably have been most successful; as it was, it came too late and never made the grade with any country. The AR10 was originally envisaged as a weapons system, including a rifle, a submachine-gun and a light machine-gun, the forerunner of the Stoner and other types. Armalite granted licences to Colt's Patent Firearms Manufacturing Co Inc (1959) and Artillerie Inrichtingen (ie: NWM, 1957) for the manufacture of AR10 rifles.

Length: 40.00in (1016mm)
Weight unloaded: 7lb 8oz (3.40kg)
Barrel: 20.00in (508mm), 4 grooves, right-hand twist
Magazine: 20-round detachable box
Cyclic rate: 700rpm
Muzzle velocity: c.2500fps (761mps)

▲The Armalite AR10 rifle, fitted with a bipod (Armalite).

▲ A view of the M14 rifle, adopted in 1957 as a replacement for the old M1 Garand although in essence similar. The M14 was the victor in a series of protracted trials in which had competed the British EM2 and the FN/Harrington & Richardson T48 (RSAF).

US RIFLE, CALIBER 7.62MM NATO, M14
United States of America
Springfield Armory, Springfield, Massachusetts; Harrington & Richardson Arms Company, Worcester, Massachusetts; Winchester-Western Arms Division of Olin-Mathieson Corporation. New Haven, Connecticut; Thompson Products
7.62mm NATO
When the NATO nations decided to adopt a common cartridge in 1953, it became a matter of urgency for them all to find new weapons to fire it. The majority of the Europeans opted for versions of the FN light rifle, but in the United States this did not compete sufficiently well with a native design to be accepted. The resultant American rifle became known as the Rifle M14, in reality a modernised and improved Rifle M1 (Garand). There are many actual differences from the Garand but the parentage is there all the same. The M14 is, however, capable of both semi-automatic and fully automatic fire and in this it was the first American rifle to do so other than the BAR. The 20-round magazine is a great improvement on the 8-round one on the Garand, and there is a light bipod for use when the rifle is intended as a squad automatic. The M14 is generally used with the selector locked in the semi-automatic role. It is a little too light to be effective as a fully automatic weapon, and as the barrel is not interchangeable there is a danger of it overheating. There have been several variations on the basic design, including at least two varieties of folding stock, and a special model for snipers. The latter is most carefully selected and assembled at Fort Benning, and it is only used to fire match ammunition. Fitted with the Leatherwood Redfield telescope, it is a formidably accurate combination which has had considerable combat use in Vietnam. Mass production of the M14 finished some years ago, when roughly 1,500,000 had been made.

Length: 44.00in (1117mm)
Weight unloaded: 8lb 9oz (3.90kg)
Barrel: 22.00in (558mm), 4 grooves, right-hand twist
Magazine: 20-round detachable box
Cyclic rate: 750rpm
Muzzle velocity: c.2800fps (853mps)

▷The M16 and grenade launchers: 40mm DBCATA, 40mm CGL and 40mm XM203.

US RIFLE, CALIBER 5.56MM, M16 and M16A1 ('Armalite AR–15')
United States of America
Colt's Patent Firearms Manufacturing Company, Hartford, Connecticut (now known as Colt Industries, Firearms Division
5.56mm × 45mm (0.223in)

Eugene Stoner, a prolific and talented inventor of smallarms, produced the Armalite while he was employed by the Fairchild Engine and Airplane Company in the late 1950s. The rifle was developed in 1956 to an army specification and Stoner chose to use the existing 0.222in Remington cartridge with an improved bullet, and in many ways the rifle is a scaled-down AR10—already noted in the section on that gun. In July 1959 production of the rifle was licensed to Colt, and the AR15 made its name by being adopted by the smaller nations of South East Asia in the early 1960s, when the Communist-inspired troubles were flaring in that area. The AR15 was an ideal size for smaller men to carry in the jungle, and from this beginning it gradually came to be used and finally accepted by the United States forces operating in the same theatre. It is now the standard rifle of the United States Army and will be used in all areas of operation with the exception of NATO, where the rules of standardisation to 7.62mm will continue to apply: there is no doubt about the effectiveness of this neat and handy rifle. When the army first adopted it there were some difficulties reported from Vietnam caused by jamming which was traced to fouling in the gas passages and was quickly cured by insisting upon daily maintenance. It is a fact that direct gas-action weapons are prone to troubles from dirt and fouling, and some cleaning is essential. The AR15 was unfortunately first sold as a self-cleaning gun—something which has yet to be made. Several million AR15/M16 rifles have now been produced and are in continuous use throughout the world.

The British Army have acquired small quantities of the M16 for evaluation, especially in such jungle theatres as Malaya where the rifles' light weight was much appreciated.

Length: 39.00in (990mm)
Weight unloaded: 6lb 5oz (2.90kg)
Barrel: 20.00in (508mm), 4 grooves, right-hand twist
Magazine: 30-round detachable box
Cyclic rate: 800rpm
Muzzle velocity: c.3250fps (988mps)

STONER AUTOMATIC RIFLE
M63A1
United States of America
Cadillac Gage Company, Detroit, Michigan (see notes)
5.56mm × 45mm (0.223in)

The Stoner Rifle is part of the Stoner System of smallarms—a system unique in the world at the moment—which offers a number of possibilities for the future. The system consists of fifteen assemblies and a machine-gun tripod from which a complete smallarms series can be constructed. The assault rifle is the second in the series, coming after the carbine; it is an attractive weapon, robust and well made, but the idea of interchangeability has yet to appeal to an army. The United States Marine Corps has, however, carried out extensive testing with Stoner weapons and there have been some changes and improvements to the basic model. The rifle now has a light bipod fitted to it which folds under the handguard, and a more positive action in folding the

stock. The operating system of the Stoner patterns is not far removed from that of the Armalite series, using direct gas action from a port near the muzzle and a rotating bolt with forward locking lugs. The barrels of all the Stoner variants are easily removed and, although this is of no great importance to the rifle, it is needed in the light machine-gun role. Inevitably in a system such as this, where one set of components has to be rearranged to fulfil several tasks, there must be some compromise and it is noticeable that the carbine and rifle versions are a little heavier than some other designs specifically produced for one job. Stoner system guns are licensed to Nederlansch' Waapenen et Munitiesfabrik 'de Kruithoorn' NV.

Length: 40.25in (1023mm)
Weight unloaded: 7lb 12oz (3.56kg)
Barrel: 20.00in (508mm), 6 grooves, right-hand twist
Magazine: 30-round detachable box
Cyclic rate: 700rpm
Muzzle velocity: c.3250fps (988mps)

▲The Stoner-designed M63A1 rifle, made in Holland by Nederlansch' Waapenen et Munitiesfabrik, without magazine (NWM).
▲The M63A1 rifle with 30-round box magazine (NWM).
▲The M63A1 carbine (NWM).
▷The Stoner M63 rifle, with side-hinging butt with a bipod folded upwards under the fore-end (NWM).
▷The folding-stock version of the M63A1 carbine with the stock extended (NWM).
▷The folding-stock M63A1 carbine with the stock folded (NWM).
▷The Armalite AR18 (Armalite).

ARMALITE COMBAT RIFLE 5.56mm AR18
United States of America
Armalite Inc, Costa Mesa, California
5.56mm x 45mm (0.223in)

This rifle was developed as a result of the experience gained by the Armalite Company in the production of the other rifles in the series. There is general recognition of the fact that the 5.56mm ammunition is effective for military use and that the weapons which fire the ammunition are therefore suitable. The main Armalite weapon, the AR15, is not easy to manufacture without modern plant and machinery; it was realised that many countries who would be potential customers would also want to make the weapon under licence—but that they might not have the industrial capacity to do so. The AR18 was therefore designed to correct this. It incorporates some improvements over previous models and offers the maximum simplicity in both manufacture and maintenance.

In some respects the AR18 is similar to the AR15, although the systems are, on closer inspection, really very different. The AR18 uses steel stampings instead of the alloy forgings in the AR15, which considerably reduces the cost of manufacture. The design has been simplified, which leads in turn to greater reliability and easier cleaning and handling. The gun has been tested by the US Army, who considered that it had a military potential but did not undertake to buy.

The AR18 appears to be a robust and reliable weapon, and although its performance is very similar to that of the AR15 the manufacturers claim that it is stronger and more rugged. Production has started both in the USA and Japan (at the plant of Howa Industries in Nagoya), and civilian hunting versions and police models have been offered.

Length, stock extended: 38.00in (965mm)
Length, stock retracted: 28.75in (730mm)
Weight unloaded: 6lb 11oz (3.04kg)
Barrel: 18.25in (463mm), 4 grooves, right-hand twist
Magazine: 20-round detachable box
Cyclic rate: 750rpm
Muzzle velocity: c.3250fps (990mps)

AUTOMAT MODEL 64, AUTOMAT MODEL 64A, AUTOMAT MODEL 64B
Yugoslavia
Zavodi Crvená Zastava, Kragujevač
7.62mm Soviet M43

The Automat 64 series are assault rifles, based on the Soviet Automat Kalashnikov and developed at the Yugoslavian

▲▲Two views of the Armalite AR18 (Armalite). ▲The Yugoslavian M64.

State arms factory at Kragujevač.

The M64 is a straight copy of the AK, although the Yugoslavs have added an integral grenade-launcher sight mounted on top of the gas-tube assembly; in order to use the grenade launcher, a special muzzle attachment must be substituted for the flash-suppressor/compensator unit.

The M64A and the M64B are also similar in design to the AK, although the Yugoslavian derivatives have shorter barrels of 14.75in (375mm) instead of the original 16.50in (419mm) barrel of the AK and the M64. Grenade launchers are also fitted to both the M64A and the M64B, although the muzzle attachments still have to be altered, and the M64B also has a folding stock which swings up and over the top of the receiver.

(data: M64A)
Length: 37.68in (957mm) including flash-suppressor
Weight unloaded: 8lb 5oz (3.75kg)
Barrel: 14.75in (375mm), 4 grooves, right-hand twist
Magazine: 30-round detachable box
Cyclic rate: c.600rpm
Muzzle velocity: c.2300fps (700mps)

Machine-guns

The Billinghurst 'Battery' Gun of 1860 represented the last of the 'medieval' designs of machine-guns and for the next twenty years the hand-operated gun held complete sway, personified by the remarkably successful design of Dr Richard Jordan Gatling. This used a number of barrels on a rotating spindle with each being loaded in turn from a gravity fed hopper as it passed underneath; in its subsequent journey around the circle each barrel's breech was closed and fired, and the empty cartridge case was ejected in time for a fresh round to be fed in. The system was ingenious in that it did not make excessive demands upon the mechanism and overheating was kept at a reasonable level by the use of several barrels. In the early years the Gatling was hampered by unsuccessful cartridge cases but by the middle of the 1880s it had become an entirely reliable and useful weapon.

The principle which Gatling introduced—that of hand-operation of the mechanism—was immediately copied by a large number of inventors in various parts of the world, all of them making use of the metallic cartridge case. It is probably true to say that the greatest advance which Gatling made in the use of smallarms was in the field of ammunition, for his guns were demanding upon the cartridge case and certainly for the first years after their introduction the main research was directed to the ammunition rather than to the gun. It was not until the 1880s that the muscular power of the gunner gave way to the use of the power of the propellent in the cartridge case for the operation of the gun's mechanism. Hiram Maxim first utilized the force of the recoil which, as he explained himself, came to him as a result of firing a rifle of 0.45in calibre which he had failed to hold correctly. The bruise on his shoulder from the recoil made him realise that it was a useful force that could be harnessed to advantage in a mechanical weapon. The Maxim Gun came into its full ascendancy with the widespread adoption of smokeless powder in the 1890s and the first decade of the twentieth century, for at this time there were few contenders in the field. The use of Maxims in the Boer War (1899–1902) and the Russo-Japanese War (1904-5) gave them great publicity, upon which Maxim skilfully capitalized. The result was that by 1914 the most numerous types of machine-gun to be found in any part of the world was based upon the original Maxim design. It is, however, interesting to see (from today's standpoint) how long it took for the correct use of machine-guns to be appreciated in the armies of the world: all the early models tended to be treated more as light artillery pieces rather than as infantry close-support smallarms. There was therefore no call in the early days for the weight and bulk of the weapon to be reduced, and the results can still be seen in those few instances where there are still original Maxims in use. The most notable example of this is the Russian's Pulemet Maxim obrazets 1910, which is to be found serving some of the smaller Communist-aligned armies throughout the world, and which, with either its wheeled or sledge carriage, weighs upwards of 150lb.

By the turn of the century the system of gas operation (as well as blowback) had already been examined, the Hotchkiss medium machine-gun was in production and the first successful light machine-gun, again of Hotchkiss pattern, was being made in small quantities. The story of the light machine-gun is probably more interesting than the subsequent history of the medium gun, since it was the one which made most demands upon the designers. The

Hotchkiss 'Portative' of 1908–9 showed the way and with some reluctance other designers followed, the encouragement being given mainly by cavalry since the infantry had not yet fully realized the virtues to be gained from having a light man-portable gun within the infantry section. The early success of the light machine-gun largely stemmed from the Lewis, which was introduced to Europe by Colonel Isaac Lewis of the US Army in 1913. The Lewis Gun could be carried and operated by one man and could be produced more quickly and more cheaply than the Vickers, Maxim and similar medium guns. Because it was small and light, it was easy to conceal and it served as a first-class infantry weapon, supplementing the firepower of the infantry battalion and using the same 0.303in ammunition as the riflemen.

The success of the Lewis, not only mechanically but also tactically, brought with it a wide variety of other designs, not all of them entirely successful. The US Army was unfortunate in that it either chose or was forced to select some notably unsuccessful French designs which probably influenced their thinking for the next thirty years. As a result the American authorities turned to John Browning's very attractive automatic rifle, which seemed to offer everything that the unreliable French machine guns did not. The BAR stayed in their infantry until replaced in the early 1950s by the M60, although it was never a particularly successful light machine-gun. Since its replacement the whole idea has not been pursued in the USA.

European countries, on the other hand, continued after World War 1 with the development of light machine-guns, resulting in a wide variety of highly successful designs—most of which have now disappeared, to be replaced by the more modern concept of a general purpose machine-gun (GPMG) which is intended to fulfil both the light and the medium roles.

Despite the enormous variety of designs, and the astonishing ingenuity which is displayed in the mechanism of the machine-guns which have been made in the last eighty years, all of them are operated by the very small number of basic methods outlined in the opening chapter of this book.

By and large, the major advance in machine-guns during the twentieth century has been in the reduction of weight and in the improvement of the reliability of the mechanism; in many cases this has also led to simplification. In spite of the efforts of many ingenious inventors no totally new system has come to light, although two world wars and many lesser wars have certainly provided sufficient stimulus to do so.

SKODA-MASCHINENGEWEHRE, 1888–1913
Austria-Hungary
Waffenwerke Skoda, Pilsen, Bohemia
8mm Patrone M90 and M93

The 'Skoda' machine-guns were based on the letters patent granted in 1888 to Karl Salvator—an Austrian archduke—and Georg Ritter von Dormus, who was at that time a major in the army of Austria-Hungary.

The guns relied upon an unusual system of delayed blowback operation in which resistance to the opening of the breech was afforded by a system of pivoting blocks and a large coil spring housed in a tube at the rear of the receiver; the principal locking member was, in fact, reminiscent of the Martini dropping block which had undergone considerable vogue in the period 1870–90, and which had seen considerable military application.

A special feature of the early Skoda models was the provision of a 'rate regulator' which, in the form of a pendant lever fitted with a sliding weight, hung below the receiver where it oscillated as the weapon fired. Through the variable centre of gravity of the pendant lever, and the frictional forces inherent in the mechanism, it was possible to vary the cyclic rate to enable between 180 and 250 rounds to be fired in one minute.

Mitrailleuse (Maschinengewehr) Modell 1893. The M93 was the first machine-gun to be adopted by the authorities of Austria-Hungary when the Skoda gun was adopted for the use of the navy and of personnel engaged in manning land fortifications; in these guises the gun generally appeared on a pedestal mount. The external appearance of the M93 was more than a little strange: apart from the pendant lever assembly protruding beneath the receiver and the spring housing (to which a shoulder stock was usually fitted) extending rearwards, the mechanism was fitted with a skeletal top-mounted gravity-fed box magazine clamped to the receiver's left side. The Mitrailleuses M93—the Austro-Hungarians adopted the term from the French language, although they later reverted to the German 'maschinengewehr'—saw little action during the decade in which they served, apart from the handful of guns present in the Boxer Rebellion of 1900 where they were used in the defence of the Austro-Hungarian legation at Peking. The guns' principal advantage was in the few working parts and—for the era—they were quite reliable; but the design of the action precluded the use of all but the lowest-powered of service cartridges, and the top-mounted magazine was very prone to damage and malfunction.

Maschinengewehr Modell 1902. The water-cooled M02 was a modified version of the M93, intended for more widespread land service and generally mounted on an unusual 'cranked' tripod to which an armoured shield was often added. The shield was almost essential to compensate for the very high mounting made necessary by the pendant lever. Much redesign was made of the feed and rate mechanisms to eliminate—with no great success—the more undesirable features of the earlier gun. A much stronger 30-round magazine was provided to reduce the feed problems, but the gravity system defied the efforts and was replaced on later weapons by an equally-strange belt feed. Few M02 guns saw service, for in the same period the Schwarzlose was developed and brought to an end the aspirations of the Skoda company.

Maschinengewehr Modell 1909. To compete with the Schwarzlose-system guns, which had been adopted in 1905 as the official machine-gun of the Austro-Hungarian services, Skodawerke entirely redesigned their gun and the M09 was the result. The external pendant lever was discarded and the components of the M02 lock were redesigned, although the principle remained the same; a lubricator was added to the mechanism to oil the cartridges before they were chambered (just as in the Schwarzlose), which permitted an increase in the cyclic rate to 425rpm. The gravity feed was replaced by a system making use of a 250-round fabric belt which entered the left underside of the receiver and emerged from the left top—which must have done little to alleviate feed troubles. An improved optical sighting device was provided for the machine-gun to replace the leaf sights of the earlier models.

Maschinengewehr Modell 1913. The M13 was the last of the long-obsolescent Salvator-Dormus system guns; it saw limited service in World War 1—with unspectacular results—in the hands of the reserve and was thereafter replaced by supplies of the Maschinengewehr M07/12. The machine-gun M13 was mechanically similar to the earlier M09 with slight alterations made to the feed unit. A new heavy-duty tripod—the Dreifuss 13, smaller than those of 1902 and 1909—was introduced to lower the unit's silhouette, although in most instances the armoured shield was retained.

MASCHINENGEWEHR MODELL 05, MASCHINENGEWEHR MODELL 07, MASCHINENGEWEHR MODELL 07/12, 'FLUGZEUG MASCHINENGEWEHR MODELL 07/16' (Schwarzlose system)
Austria-Hungary
Osterreichische Waffenfabrik-Gesellschaft, Steyr
8mm Patrone Modell 93 ('8mm Austrian Service'), 7.92mm Gew Patr 98 (German), 6.5mm patroon M95 (Dutch)

The Schwarzlose machine-gun was the only unlocked-breech design (the Fiat-Revelli had a form of locking wedge) to see widespread service use. It relied entirely upon the mass of the breech-block and a toggle lever which worked at a severe mechanical disadvantage when the breechblock first started to open. The barrel was short to ensure that the breech pressure dropped as soon as possible, and this affected the muzzle velocity and maximum range. The first models of 1905 and 1907 were fitted with an oil pump to lubricate the rounds as they were fed into the breech, but by 1912 this was abandoned and more weight was added to the bolt in order to force the dry rounds into the chamber. There are disadvantages to the blowback method of operation for medium machine-guns, but the Schwarzlose was popular for its simplicity and strength. It was, however, sensitive to adverse conditions and ammunition variations. It was sold commercially throughout Europe until 1918 and was adopted by several mid-European countries. It was still in use in Italy and Hungary in 1945 as a second-line weapon. A lightened version of the basic design—sometimes called the Maschinengewehr 07/16—was also manufactured for aircraft use during World War 1: largely owing to the low cyclic rate and the short barrel, it was not a success.

Length: 42.00in (1066mm)
Weight unloaded: 44lb 0oz (19.9kg)
Barrel: 20.75in (526mm), 4 grooves, right-hand twist
Magazine: 250-round fabric belt
Cyclic rate: 400rpm
Muzzle velocity: c.2050fps (620mps)

MITRAILLEUR A GAZ (MAG)
Belgium
Fabrique Nationale d'Armes de Guerre, Herstal-lèz-Liège
7.62mm NATO

Like most Fabrique Nationale designs, the MAG machine-gun is a sound, reliable and well engineered weapon which has been adopted—especially by NATO-aligned countries—throughout the world. In common with many other manufacturers, FN had looked at the numerous designs which World War 2 had thrown into prominence and, also like many others, were impressed by the simple and effective feed systems developed for the German MG42. Fabrique Nationale had been involved with Browning designs for so many years that it is hardly surprising to find that the gas operation of the MAG is basically that of the Browning Automatic Rifle. The principal difference lies in the inversion of the bolt so that the locking movement is in a downward direction. This permits a lug to be formed on the top surface of the bolt which, engaging in a cam track in the cover plate, drives the belt feed mechanism.

There are minor variations in the appearance of various models of MAG—finned barrels, smooth barrels, stocks, spade grips and so forth—which largely reflect the national preference of the customers. They are all basically of

▶The Skoda-MG Modell 1902.
▶The Skoda-MG Modell 1909.
▼An example of the Schwarzlose machine-gun, in this case the Modell 07/12, mounted on its tripod (USMC).
▼Fabrique Nationale's Mitrailleur à Gaz (MAG), with a bipod fitted and folded to the rear (FN).

MAG type. Apart from Belgium and Sweden, where it is known as the Kulspruta m/58, the MAG has been adopted by the United Kingdom—see MACHINE-GUN L7A1.
Length: 49.20in (1250mm)
Weight unloaded: 22lb 4oz (10.15kg)
Barrel: 21.50in (546mm), 4 grooves, right-hand twist
Magazine: ∞-round metallic link belt
Cyclic rate: 850rpm
Muzzle velocity: c.2800fps (853mps)

KULOMET VZ/26
Czechoslovakia
Ceskoslovenská Zbrojovká, Brno
7.92mm Gew Patr 98 (German)
The Czech armament firm commonly known as ZB was formed after World War 1, and the ZB vz/26 was its first original design. The gun was an immediate success and, together with its later variants, it sold in large numbers throughout Europe. The vz/26 was similar in concept to many other light guns being produced at the same time, but it was far better than the majority. The gas cylinder was unusually long, running under the barrel nearly to the muzzle, but this feature led to a slower and more easily controlled rate of fire and less strain on the working parts because the action was not so fast or violent. The piston and cylinder were made in stainless steel to prevent corrosion, and the barrel could be quickly and easily changed by a rotating collar and a carrying handle. A tripod mounting was available as an extra which helped to give the gun some measure of stability in sustained-fire. The vz/26 was derived from the firm's box-fed 'Kulomet Praga vz/24', which never passed out of the prototype stage. Many Czechoslovak vz/26 guns served the German army during World War 2, in which guise they were known as the *Maschinengewehr 26(t)*.
Length: 45.75in (1161mm)
Weight unloaded: 21lb 5oz (9.60kg)
Barrel: 26.50in (672mm), 4 grooves, right-hand twist
Magazine: 30-round detachable box
Cyclic rate: 500rpm
Muzzle velocity: c.2500fps (762mps)

KULOMET VZ/30
Czechoslovakia
Ceskoslovenská Zbrojovká, Brno
7.92mm Gew Patr 98 (German), 7.65mm (Bolivia), 7mm (various South American countries)
As its title suggests, the ZB vz/30 was a direct descendant of the ZB vz/26, incorporating certain internal improvements although the two guns are difficult to tell apart. The changes were in the cam surfaces which worked the bolt and in a different method of striking the firing pin. A few changes in the machining operations of manufacture were also made, so that the gun was marginally easier to make and more reliable to use.

In fact, both the vz/30 and the vz/26 were expensive to make as they were designed to be built from expensive and time-consuming milling operations in which quite large blocks of metal were cut away until only a shell remained. This gave great accuracy of dimension and could be done with lower capital costs in equipment, but it made heavy demands on the skill of the workmen and the diligence of the inspectors. China liked the gun, whatever its manufacturing difficulties, and made it in substantial numbers in the 1930s. Britain was also interested and adopted a variant of it as the well-known Bren light machine-gun. Production continued in Czechoslovakia throughout World War 2 and the German Army used the gun as a second-line equipment under the title *Maschinengewehr 30(t)*. The vz/30 was also made in Iran, and a variant made in Spain was known as the FAO—after its manufacturer, Fabrica de Armas de Oviedo. The Spanish also developed an improved belt-fed version in 7.62mm NATO, but never produced it in quantity.
Length: 45.75in (1161mm)
Weight unloaded: 21lb 5oz (9.60kg)
Barrel: 26.50in (672mm), 4 grooves, right-hand twist
Magazine: 30-round detachable box
Cyclic rate: 500rpm
Muzzle velocity: c.2500fps (762mps)

KULOMET ZGB VZ/33
Czechoslovakia
Ceskoslovenská Zbrojovká, Brno
0.303in SAA Ball (British)
The ZGB vz/33 is extremely rare. Exactly how many were made is no longer clear, but it is unlikely to have been more than ten or twelve. It was nothing more than the ZB vz/30 incorporating the alterations desired by the British to bring it to their acceptance standards; the gun was chambered for 0.303in rimmed ammunition, the barrel was shortened, the gas port brought nearer the breech and the sights regraduated in yards. The gun was then tried by the British, and from it the Bren was drawn up and the pattern sealed. The ZGB vz/33 never saw service—it was really little more than a design sample—but it deserves mention because of the importance of the weapon which sprang from it and the evidence which it supplies of the application and attention to detail which so characterised the Brno company.
Length: 45.50in (1156mm)
Weight unloaded: 22lb 2oz (10.03kg)
Barrel: 25.00in (635mm), 6 grooves, right-hand twist
Magazine: 30-round detachable box
Cyclic rate: 550rpm
Muzzle velocity: c.2450fps (745mps)

KULOMET VZ/53 ('Kulomet vz/37')
Czechoslovakia
Ceskoslovenská Zbrojovká, Brno
7.92mm Gew Patr 98 (German)

▷The Czechoslovakian Kulomet vz/26 (also known as the Lehky Kulomet vz/26, model 1926 light machine-gun, and often so marked), shown here without its straight-sided box magazine (RSAF).
▷The ZGB light machine-gun, clearly marked 'Lehky Kulomet ZGB vz/33' on the side of the action behind the magazine, made in 1933 for trials in Britain. The curved box magazine was designed for the 0.303in rimmed British cartridge (RSAF).
▷An example of the Kulomet vz/53 on its tripod mounting (RSAF).

The ZB vz/53 was produced in 1937 and is generally known in military circles as the Kulomet vz/37, under which guise it was accepted by the Czech army. However, the factory always knew it as the vz/53 and it was exported under that title. It is an air-cooled gas-operated weapon of robust and simple design, belt-fed and having two rates of fire. It was made in large quantities for export by the firm and was built under licence (in 7.92mm calibre) in Britain as a tank gun, where it was known as the Besa. The action resembles in some respects that of the ZB light guns, although the forward motion of the piston lifts the rear of the breech block and engages it with lugs in the barrel extension—thus, unlike the light guns, barrel and block can move together. After firing, the two recoil together until the piston unlocks the block and the barrel returns to battery. The idea is unusual but good; despite the apparent complication, the gun is highly reliable and the barrel can be removed without much difficulty (and changed if the fire mission is a long one). The gun was mounted on a tripod of rather complicated design. The vz/53 was used during World War 2 by the Germans as a substitute standard gun, the *Maschinengewehr 37(t)*.

Length: 43.50in (1104mm)
Weight unloaded: 41lb 0oz (18.60kg)
Barrel: 26.70in (671mm), 4 grooves, right-hand twist
Magazine: 100-round belt
Cyclic rate: 500 or 700rpm (adjustable)
Muzzle velocity: c.2600fps (792mps)

KULOMET VZ/52, KULOMET VZ/52-57
Czechoslovakia
Ceskoslovenská Zbrojovká, Strakonice
7.62mm náboj vz/52 (vz/52), 7.62mm náboj vz/43 (Soviet M43) (vz/52-57)
Although classed as a light machine-gun and bearing obvious affinities with the ZB vz/26 design, this weapon leans more to the general purpose machine-gun concept in its ability to fire from magazine or metallic belt without requiring any adjustment or modification. Chambered for the Czechs' 7.62mm vz/52 'Intermediate' round, selection of semi-automatic or full-automatic fire is by a dual trigger system—pressure on the lower portion gives automatic fire; pressure on the top portion gives semi-automatic fire.

The operating system relies upon gas, with a piston and bolt assembly very like the ZB vz/26 but locking into the body in a slightly different way. The barrel can be easily changed, using the magazine port cover as an unlocking lever. The gun body is largely stamped out, with a machined receiver inserted in the appropriate space—an interesting essay in production engineering and cheaper to produce, but of otherwise doubtful value.

A later version of this weapon, the vz/52-57, was produced in small numbers. This was chambered for the Soviet M43 short cartridge, but in all other respects it is identical to the vz/52.

Length: 41.00in (1041mm)
Weight unloaded: 17lb 9oz (8.00kg)

▲The Lehky Kulomet vz/52.

Barrel: 27.00in (686mm), 4 grooves, right-hand twist
Magazine: 25-round detachable box or 100-round belt
Cyclic rate: 900rpm (magazine) or 1150 rpm (belt fed)
Muzzle velocity: c.2450fps (746mps)

KULOMET VZ/59, KULOMET VZ/59L KULOMET VZ/59N, KULOMET VZ/59T
Czechoslovakia
Ceskoslovenská Zbrojovká, Strakonice
7.62mm náboj vz/91 (Soviet) (vz/59, vz/59L), 7.62mm NATO (vz/59N)
The dual feed (magazine or belt) capability of the CZ vz/52 appears more useful than it really is, and after some years of experience the Czechs appear to have come to the conclusion that it introduced more trouble than it was worth. The vz/59, therefore, does away with the magazine feed and is belt-fed only. In most respects it is no more than an improved vz/52 but, while dispensing with the magazine, the general purpose concept is retained and—indeed—improved. This model is provided with two alternative barrels: a light one with bipod attached for use in the squad light machine-gun role, and a heavy barrel some four inches longer for use in the sustained fire role in which the gun is mounted on a tripod of unusual appearance and design.

An unusual ballistic reversion is evident: the model vz/52 was chambered for the Czech intermediate cartridge, but the vz/59 is chambered for the Russian 7.62mm M1891 rimmed rifle round (7.62mm × 53mm) or, at least, for the Czech equivalent. It seems that the Czechs are willing to encumber the squad light machine-gun with a non-universal cartridge (for the remainder of the squad weapons use the intermediate round) so that, in the medium machine-gun role, it can be provided with a round having a heavier bullet and longer range. A light barrel version of the vz/59 is manufactured as the CZ vz/59L, and a version is made for export—in 7.62mm NATO—as the CZ vz/59N. A tank version known as the vz/59T makes use of a firing solenoid.

Length: 48.00in (1220mm)
Weight unloaded, heavy barrel: 21lb 0oz (9.50kg)
Weight unloaded, light barrel: 19lb 0oz (9.60kg)
Barrel, heavy: 27.30in (694mm), 4 grooves, right-hand twist
Barrel, light: 23.30in (591mm), 4 grooves, right-hand twist
Magazine: 50-round belt
Cyclic rate: 750rpm
Muzzle velocity: c.2700fps (823mps)

LET MASKINGEVAER MADSEN, c.1904
Denmark
Dansk Rekylriffel Syndikat AS 'Madsen', København (later known as Dansk Industri Syndikat AS 'Madsen'—or DISA)
8mm Patron m/89 and many others

The Madsen is a remarkable gun in almost every way. It was undoubtedly the first light machine-gun ever to be produced in quantity; the same model continued to be produced with only minor variations for over fifty years and it featured in innumerable wars both large and small—yet it was never officially adopted by any major country. Special models were fitted in tanks, armoured cars and aeroplanes. Finally it possessed a mechanism which, although compact and light, exceeded most others in ingenuity and complexity.

The Madsen was really an automatic form of the Peabody-Martini hinged-block action and as such it had several peculiarities. With no bolt to move the cartridges in and out of the breech, the Madsen was provided with a separate rammer and a powerful extractor. The action worked by recoil, part long and

part short, and the movement of the hinged breechblock was controlled by a system of cams and lugs on the block and on a plate in the side of the receiver. The box magazine was another "first" and probably was used as a model by other designs which followed.

Despite the complexity, which might appear to be a drawback, the Madsen was remarkably successful and was sold in at least thirty-four countries, remaining in production until the late 1950s. Its manufacturers were quick to appreciate that the experience of World War 1 indicated that it was desirable in some circumstances to have a machine-gun which combined the characteristics of a light weapon when mounted on a bipod with those of a medium gun when mounted on a tripod. The Madsen was offered with these possibilities and the necessary associated equipment. It was accepted by most of the Latin American countries and bought by them in quantity.

In British service the Madsen gun gained a reputation for jamming frequently, which was due to the rimmed 0.303in cartridge. With rimless ammunition, however, the guns' performance was excellent. Apart from the 0.303in

▼An example of the 1950 model Madsen Maskingevaer, with the marking on the left side of the receiver (in front of the magazine) of the Thailand navy (RSAF).

▲A Madsen aircraft observer's gun, c.1933–5; the ring sights, for which the mountings can be seen, are missing from this gun. The tube protruding from the rear of the receiver contains the recoil spring, normally held within the butt (RSAF).

◁A Madsen light machine-gun, captured and modified in World War 2 by the Germans. Originally an aircraft gun, it has been altered by the addition of a German-type bipod, and a disintegrating metallic-link belt feed is used. Note the bag for collecting spent cases (RSAF).

◁The Madsen-Saetter light machine-gun, fitted to its tripod for use as a 'medium' or support gun (authors' collection).

◁An example of the Lahti aircraft observer's machine-gun, supplied for the British trials of c.1927. The ring sights are missing from this example (RSAF).

cartridge, Madsen guns were offered in a wide variety of calibres—amongst them 7.92mm, 7.65mm, 7mm, 6.5mm rimmed, and others.

(data: 0.303in model)
Length: 45.00in (1143mm)
Weight unloaded: 20lb 0oz (9.07kg)
Barrel: 23.00in (584mm), 4 grooves, right-hand twist
Magazine: 25, 30 or 40-round detachable box
Cyclic rate: 450 rpm
Muzzle velocity: 2350fps (715mps)

MASKINGEVAER MADSEN-SAETTER
Denmark
Dansk Industri Syndikat AS 'Madsen', København and Herlev
7.62mm NATO

This, the latest and last of the Madsen line of weapons, is a general purpose machine-gun which can be used either as a man-portable light gun or a tripod-mounted sustained-fire support gun. It is made in a variety of calibres, though chiefly 7.62mm NATO, and it can be quickly changed to accept other calibres (assuming the case's base diameter is similar) simply by substituting an appropriate barrel. If the case diameter is different, a new bolt is also needed. The rate of fire is adjustable to any speed between 650rpm and 1,000rpm; by using two barrels and changing them at the correct intervals, the manufacturers claim that a sustained rate of 7,000 or 8,000 rounds per hour can be maintained. Simple production techniques are predominantly used and much of the gun is made by punching, turning and precision casting. The bore is chromium-plated to prolong barrel life and is locked to the gun by a quick-action handle. The gun operates by gas action and locks by lugs being forced into the receiver wall. It fires from an open bolt, so giving the breech the best possible chance of cooling between shots. As a light machine-gun, the Madsen-Saetter was adopted and produced by Indonesia; but the gun has elsewhere failed to find favour. A prototype 0.50in calibre machine-gun employing the basic mechanism was also constructed and showed great promise.
Length: 45.90in (1165mm)
Weight unloaded: 23lb 8oz (10.80kg)
Barrel: 22.20in (565mm), 4 grooves, right-hand twist
Magazine: 49-round belt
Cyclic rate: 650rpm to 1000rpm (adjustable)
Muzzle velocity: c.2800fps (853mps)

AUTOMAATTIKIVAARI LAHTI-SALORANTA MALLI 26
Finland
Valtion Kiväärithedas (VKT), Jyväskylä
7.62mm patruuna m/91 (Soviet)
Designed in 1926 by Aimo Lahti, the m/26 machine-gun is a good example of the generation of guns produced after World War 1. It is simple and strong,

yet not too heavy. It had been hoped to offset some of the development and production costs by selling the gun in Europe, but this did not happen and the m/26 equipped only the Finnish Army. It was used extensively in the Russo-Finnish war of 1939–40 and only passed out of service in the late 1940s when Russian equipment was introduced. It was a recoil-operated gun which seems to have used some ideas from similar weapons of the time: unlike many other guns, however, it was reasonably light. The feed system used two types of magazine—a 20-round box or a 75-round drum, both of which fed from underneath and did not affect the balance of the gun. The barrel could be removed quite easily and quickly but the bolt had to come out with it—sometimes making it impractical to change a barrel in the field. Single-shot or automatic fire could be selected by a lever on the receiver and the rate of fire was rather low at 500 rounds per minute. Nevertheless, whatever its shortcomings, the Lahti design was among the best of its time.
Length: 46.50in (1180mm)
Weight unloaded: 19lb 0oz (8.60kg)
Barrel: 22.3in (566mm) approximately, 4 grooves, right-hand twist
Magazine: 20-round detachable box or 75-round drum
Cyclic rate: 500rpm
Muzzle velocity: c.2630fps (800mps)

MITRAILLEUSES HOTCHKISS, 1897–1918
France
Société de la Fabrication des Armes à Feu Portatives Hotchkiss et Companie, St. Denis
8mm Cartouche Mle 86; 7mm (Mauser), for export
The Hotchkiss machine-gun was a significant advance in the design of repeating arms at a time when most of the systems of operation were carefully covered by patents which almost totally precluded evasion. By 1893 only Maxim and Browning had produced truly workable machine-guns (although others had tried), and both had used recoil of the barrel to power the mechanism. In the same year, however, an Austrian aristocrat named Odkolek brought to Hotchkiss & Cie a prototype of his gas-operated machine-gun; seeing the potential of the weapon, although it required considerable development, the Hotchkiss organisation promptly acquired the rights in a manner none too satisfactory from the viewpoint of the luckless inventor. Hotchkiss & Cie would countenance only a straight cash payment, with exclusion of such things as royalties from the contract, with the result that Odkolek scarcely benefited from the transaction.

The chief engineer of the Hotchkiss company was an American, Laurence Bénét (whose father at one time held the office of Chief of Ordnance in the United

▲The Hotchkiss-system machine-gun, Modèle 1914, mounted on the Affut-Trepied Modèle 1916 (RSAF).

States Army) to whom fell responsibility for the redesign and perfection of the gun mechanism. The Hotchkiss Gun first appeared in 1895—a gas-operated pattern locked by a pivoting locking flap which securely locked the bolt to the barrel until impinging gas removed the components from alignment. The Mle 95 was given a smooth barrel to facilitate air cooling, as it was held to be a little difficult to adapt a system of water cooling to a gas-operated gun. The machine-gun was adopted by the French army in 1897, and a number of subsequent improvements were made to the basic design, which saw good use throughout the period of World War 1.

Mitrailleuse Hotchkiss Modèle 1897. The first of the official patterns, the Mle 97 was closely based on the experimental Mle 95; brass cooling fins were added to the barrel in an attempt to cure the overheating problems inherent in the experimental weapons, but although this improved the situation the guns were still notorious for the rapidity with which the barrel absorbed heat. The Mle

97 used a normal Hotchkiss feed—perhaps the greatest single failing of the design—of metallic (originally brass but later steel) strips, holding either 24 or 30 8mm rounds. A second failing of the Mle 97 lay in the design of the mounting, a spindly tripod known as the Affut-trepied Mle 97, which had provision for neither elevation nor traverse. The gun weighed 56lb 0oz (25.50kg) and the mount contributed a further 36lb 7oz (16.50kg).

Mitrailleuse Hotchkiss Modèle 1900. A modified pattern of the Mle 97, the principal recognition feature of the Mle 00 was the steel-finned barrel substituted in yet another attempt to reduce barrel heat-absorption. A new type of mount—the Affut-trepied Mle 00—was provided with elevation and traverse, and either of the two patterns of machine-gun could be mounted on it. The later Affut Mle 07 could also be adapted to the gun.

After the Hotchkiss had seen service for several years, the French designers attempted to improve it by adding such things as a variable-fire rate device and

returning once again to brass cooling fins. The results of their deliberations, the machine-guns Mle 05 ('Puteaux') and Mle 07 ('Saint-Etienne') are separately described: neither proved anything more than a failure, and the authorities returned to the proven Hotchkiss.

Fusil Mitrailleur Hotchkiss Modèle 1909. The Mle 09 was originally designed as an attempt to provide a light automatic arm which fitted the French theories of 'assaulting at the walk' but which ultimately proved to be too heavy and was therefore relegated to such things as tanks, aircraft and fortifications. The Mle 09 deviated from the normal Hotchkiss guns in the design of the locking mechanism—the new pattern was as a result often called the 'Hotchkiss-Mercié' or the 'Bénét-Mercié'—which replaced the well-tried locking flap by a 'fermature nut' which locked the bolt and barrel together and was rotated out of alignment by gas pressure. At the same time, the opportunity was taken of reversing the feed unit so that the cartridges were on the underside of the feed strip, greatly complicating the problems of feeding ammunition to the weapon. These strictures apart, the mechanism was relatively simple although not as efficient as some competing designs. The Mle 09 was actually adopted by the United States of America as the *Machine Rifle, Bénét-Mercié, Caliber .30 M1909*, and by the United Kingdom as the *Gun, Machine, Hotchkiss Mark 1*.

Mitrailleuse Hotchkiss Modèle 1914. The Mle 14 was no more than a slightly redesigned version of the original Mle 00, with the elimination of the safety system and the revision of certain action components. The Mle 14 was issued with a number of tripod mounts: the Affut Modèle 1914 was designed specifically for the Mitrailleuse Mle 14, although both the Affut Mle 15 Type Omnibus and the Affut Mle 16 could also be used. The Affut Mle 16—the most advanced of the mountings—was the most eagerly sought.

Although rather heavy the Hotchkiss was reliable, which meant much to those whose lives depended on it, and it survived in the hands of the French troops until World War 2. The principal drawback lay in the method of feeding the rounds into the gun, although in the Mle 14 the authorities attempted to overcome this by supplying a form of 'metallic-strip belt' in which 249 rounds could be held: the new feed took the form of short metallic strips, each holding three rounds, with a hinge at each joint.

Hotchkiss heavy machine-guns were exported in 7mm calibre to Brazil, Mexico and Spain, where the guns were extensively used by their armies. The 8mm French version was used by Greece and other Balkan states, and the American Expeditionary Force to Europe in 1917 used Hotchkiss guns on a divisional basis.

Length: 50.00in (1270mm)
Weight unloaded: 52lb 0oz (23.58kg)
Barrel: 30.50in (775mm), 4 grooves, left-hand twist
Magazine: 24 or 30-round metallic strips (see text)
Cyclic rate: 600rpm
Muzzle velocity: c.2380fps (725mps)

Mitrailleuse Hotchkiss, dit 'Modèle de Ballon', 1917. The Hotchkiss 'Balloon model' was used to combat the menace of the German observation balloons which had proved so useful to the Germans' artillery direction control, although it had originally been conceived

as a heavy infantry machine-gun. It was found that the large 11mm bullet was sufficient to carry an incendiary filling to the balloons, and to then penetrate the hydrogen-filled gas envelope. The gun itself was relatively heavy and immobile and its use did not extend into the postwar years; the only lasting contribution to weapon design made by the Balloon gun was that by its example the American authorities were inspired to develop the 0.50in Browning heavy machine-gun and its cartridge.

MITRAILLEUSE MODELE 1905 DIT 'PUTEAUX', MITRAILLEUSE DE LA FORTIFICATION MODELE 1907 DIT 'PUTEAUX'
France
Manufacture d'Armes de Puteaux, Puteaux
8mm Cartouche Mle 86

The Puteaux machine-gun was an abject failure and lasted in service for just two years before it was relegated to static and reserve use. The design began as an attempt to provide the French Army with a gun superior to the Hotchkiss patterns then in service. The Modèle 1905 was hardly an improvement on its predecessors and, when compared with the work progressing in other European countries at the time, well illustrates the ineptitude of the era's French ordnance personnel.

The Puteaux operated in similar fashion to the gas-operated Hotchkiss

to which it bore several affinities and with which it shared the same 24 or 30-round strip feed, the first feature which should have been discarded. The normal cyclic rate was 500rpm, but the French incorporated a rate regulator theoretically capable of infinitely varying the rate between 8rpm and 650rpm; the device (a poor copy of Maxim's 1884 device) was all but useless.

The external appearance of the Puteaux foreshadowed the Mitrailleuse Mle 07 ('Saint-Etienne') for which it served as a prototype, but the barrel of the Puteaux was entirely covered by brass cooling fins which, in the event, rapidly overheated. Owing to the many deficiencies in the design, the Puteaux was withdrawn and supplied to fortresses as a defensive gun—in order to camouflage the troubles discovered in the field. In this guise it was known as the 'Mitrailleuse de la Fortification Mle 07'.

MITRAILLEUSE MODELE 1907 DIT 'SAINT-ETIENNE', MITRAILLEUSE MODELE 1907 TRANSFORMEE 1916 DIT 'SAINT-ETIENNE'
France
Manufacture d'Armes de Saint-Etienne, Saint-Etienne
8mm Cartouche Mle 86

This gun represents a hopelessly unsuccessful attempt to improve upon the abortive Mle 05 Puteaux—itself an attempt to improve upon the Hotchkiss types then in French service. The Mle 07

►The 'Saint-Etienne': the Mitrailleuse Mle 07T16 (RSAF).

was designed by a small group working at the French Government arsenal at Saint-Etienne, all of whom seem to have been poorly versed in the operating principles of automatic weapons. The group began with the Puteaux and promptly reversed the piston operation so that, instead of moving backwards, it moved forwards—and so a rack-and-pinion mechanism had to be introduced to· reverse the motion. The bolt was locked by an over-centre cam lever instead of the Hotchkiss link, and the gas cylinder could be varied in volume to adjust the cyclic rate: it was hardly worth the trouble as it further complicated the mechanism and gave rise to still further stoppages. The return spring was placed below the barrel, but the temper in the spring was quickly destroyed by heat if enclosed and so it was consequently exposed to the elements. In the trenches of the Western front, the Saint-Etienne's deficiencies were quickly evident, particularly as the exposed spring rapidly clogged with mud, and the guns were promptly replaced by the Hotchkiss.

Modifications were made to the gun in an attempt to improve it, including the substitution of new patterns of gas pressure regulator, firing pin and foresight, and a form of drum sight replaced the old type of leaf rearsight—if such the peculiar assembly could be called—and the altered weapon was called the 'Modèle 1907 transformée 1916' (Mle 07T16, or simply Mle 07T). After tests, the French military decided that the Saint-Etienne was suited to arid regions—another way of ridding themselves of the gun without actually saying so—and therefore many were shipped to France's African colonies.
Length: 46.50in (1180mm)
Weight unloaded: 56lb 12oz (25.40kg)
Barrel: 28.00in (710mm), 4 grooves, right-hand twist
Magazine: 24 or 30-round metallic strips
Cyclic rate: 400-500 rpm
Muzzle velocity: c.2300fps (700mps)

FUSIL MITRAILLEUR MODELE 1915, US MACHINE RIFLE, CHAUCHAT, CALIBER .30, M1918 (FUSIL MITRAILLEUR MODELE 1918) ('CSRG' or 'Chauchat')
France and United States of America
Manufacturers unknown
8mm Cartouche Mle 86 (Mle 15), .30 M1906 (M1918)
The CSRG light machine-gun was designed by a commission of French designers towards the end of 1915 and like most commission-instigated weapons, the result was nothing to be admired; it has been described as the worst design of machine-gun ever formulated and it was universally execrated by those who used it. To start with, it is a long-recoil weapon in which the barrel and bolt are locked together for the full stroke; the bolt is then held and the barrel is returned to battery. Once the barrel has returned, the bolt is

released to chamber and fire the next round. It is not a system which readily lends itself to a light weapon in which steadiness of aim is all-important and, to compound the mischief, the CSRG was poorly manufactured of inferior material although it foreshadowed later production techniques; issue of it to the troops was an unending tale of malfunction

The peculiar semicircular magazine was forced upon the French designers by the abrupt taper of the Modèle 1886 cartridge: they do not seem to have thought of using a different round. When the United States Army arrived in France in 1917, approximately 16,000 of the CSRG Mle 15 were passed to them; in order to rationalise the ammunition supply the gun was redesigned to accept the American 0.30in round and the resulting weapon, slightly over 19,000 of which were supplied to the luckless American troops, was called the M1918. The principal difference between the two models lies in the design of the magazine, as the M1918 was fitted with a straight box magazine suited to the 0.30in round. Although the rechambering was theoretically advantageous, the more powerful 0.30in cartridge further strained the already inferior gun and components often expired through overloading.

In spite of the poor combat showing, the CSRG was briefly adopted by Greece and by Belgium (both in 8mm). The Greeks listed the weapon as the 'Gladiator' and the calibre as 7.8mm but, as this was their term for the French 8mm cartridge, the weapons were neither rechambered nor rebarrelled.
Length: 45.00in (1143mm)
Weight unloaded: 20lb 0oz (9.07kg)
Barrel: 18.50in (469mm), 4 grooves, right-hand twist
Magazine: 20-round detachable box
Cyclic rate: 250rpm
Muzzle velocity: c.2300fps (700mps)

MITRAILLEUSE DARNE MODELE 1918
France
Manufactured by Unceta y Compania, Guernica (Spain) for R et P Darne et Cie, Saint-Etienne
8mm Cartouche Mle 86, and others
The Darne company, long renowned as the manufacturers of a variety of sporting weapons, became interested in the machine-gun as a result of a World War 1 contract to produce Lewis guns for the French Government. However, unlike many traditional manufacturers, they saw no need to spend excessive amounts of time and money on producing a military weapon to commercial standards of finish and they succeeded in producing one of the cheapest and crudest machine-guns ever marketed. Although their name is attached to the weapon by virtue of their having designed it, the vast majority of the Darne guns came from Unceta's Spanish factory—where they were made under licence at an even lower price than that

▷The infamous 'Chauchat', the Fusil Mitrailleur Mle 15, with its peculiar semicircular magazine made necessary by the abrupt taper of the French service cartridge (RSAF).

▲A specimen of the Darne light machine-gun, manufactured in Spain for the French parent company. The inferior finish of the weapon is very evident, although the Darne worked quite well (RSAF).

▲A Darne aircraft gun, supplied for the British trials of the late 1920s which ultimately led to the adoption of the Browning (RSAF).

at which the original French firm could have produced them.

For all its cheapness, the gun was undeniably efficient, serving the French and other European nations as an aircraft gun throughout the 1930s. The Darne was among several weapons evaluated by the Royal Air Force just prior to World War 2 but it was turned down in favour of the Browning. Gas-operated and belt fed, it had the high rate of fire desirable in an aircraft weapon, although this was one of the features which prevented it from gaining wide following as an infantry accompanying gun.

It is also recorded that the Darne gun was manufactured in Czechoslovakia prior to the appearance of the vz/26; it is thought that these guns were made in 7.92mm calibre.

HOTCHKISS LIGHT MACHINE-GUN, 1922-6
France (Greece/Czechoslovakia)
Société de la Fabrication des Armes à Feu Portatives Hotchkiss et Cie, Saint-Denis, and others
Various calibres

The Hotchkiss light gun was offered in the immediate postwar years to those who were interested. The gun was a standard type of gas-operated weapon, locked by a tilting flap, although it incorporated a rate-reducing mechanism in a housing in front of the pistol grip/trigger assembly. Versions of the basic design were made using either a top-mounted box magazine or a side-feeding metallic strip, in standard Hotchkiss fashion; in the latter case there is also evidence that a belt, consisting of short three-round sections of strip joined together to form

◁ The Hotchkiss light machine-gun; this, a strip- or articulated-belt fed model, was supplied for trials in Britain (c.1922). It is chambered for the 0.303in rimmed cartridge (RSAF).

◁ A box-fed version of the Hotchkiss, in 0.303in calibre and supplied to Britain c.1922 (RSAF).

◁ A Greek 6.5mm Hotchkiss gun, model 1926; similar guns were used in Spain (RSAF).

◁ The 'Chatellerault' machine-gun, the Fusil Mitrailleur Mle 24/29, shown without its magazine (RSAF).

▲ The Mle 24/29 complete with its box magazine (RSAF).

an articulated string, was also developed. Other features of the light Hotchkiss were the 'rocker-feet' bipod and the muzzle compensator/flash suppressor, which was cut obliquely to provide the necessary downward thrust—but whether or not this in any way helped to stabilise the gun is not recorded.

The gun saw little commercial use: apart from some 0.303in examples tested in the period 1922-3 by the British ordnance authorities (when the gun was tried and found wanting), 1,000 were used in Czechoslovakia in 1924 for extended trials. The Czech guns, in 7.92mm calibre and manufactured by Hotchkiss of Saint-Denis, were rejected in favour of the ZB vz/26. It is known, however, that examples of the Hotchkiss —perhaps 5,000—were acquired in 6.5mm by the Greek army, and used in Greece for a number of years; 7mm examples were also used in the Dominican Republic and Brazil, which suggests that Hotchkiss found the markets sufficiently lucrative to market the guns (as the modèle 1924) for several years.

(data: Greek M/1926)
Length: 47.75in (1214mm)
Weight unloaded: 21lb 0oz (9.52kg)
Barrel: 22.75in (577mm), 4 grooves, right-hand twist
Magazine: 25-round (?) strip feed
Cyclic rate: c.450rpm
Muzzle velocity: c.2450fps (745mps)

FUSIL MITRAILLEUR MODELES 1924, 1924/29 and 1931
France
Manufacture d'Armes de Chatellerault; Manufacture d'Armes de Saint-Etienne
7.5mm Cartouche Mle 24 (Mle 24), 7.5mm Cartouche Mle 29 (Mles 24/29, 31)

The French light machine-gun at the end

of World War 1 was the infamous Chauchat, and it was patently obvious that something better was vitally necessary. Since the 8mm rimmed Mle 86 (Lebel) cartridge was of an awkward size and shape for use in automatic weapons, the French began very wisely by developing a new 7.5mm rimless round broadly based on the German 7.92mm service cartridge. With this in hand, work then began on a suitable machine-gun and in due course a limited number—known as the Mle 1924—were produced for trials. This gas-operated weapon was based on the Browning Automatic Rifle and used a similar form of breech locking.

The gun was more successful than its predecessor (although still some way from perfection) but the cartridge had some ballistic shortcomings, and it was redesigned with a shorter case. The gun was modified to suit and was tested c.1928 with the new round, the combination was found to be successful and the weapon was standardised for issue as the Mle 24/29.

In 1931 a slightly modified version was issued for use in fixed defences—notably along the Maginot Line—and this was later adopted as a tank gun. This, the Mle 31, was distinguished by its peculiar butt and handgrip and the 150-round drum magazine was mounted on the right side.

The 'Chatellerault' guns remained in the hands of the French Army until the middle 1950s; indeed, during World War 2 numbers were seized by the German Army and put to use, principally in the anti-invasion defences on the coasts of France and the Channel Islands.

Length: 42.60in (1182mm)
Weight unloaded: 20lb 4oz (9.24kg)
Barrel: 19.70in (500mm), 4 grooves

▲The French Mle 31 tank machine-gun, also noted for its employment in the fortifications of the Maginot Line—to no great purpose. The side-mounted drum magazine, which contains 150 rounds, was rated of great importance when the gun first appeared (RSAF).
▲The AAT Mle 52 on its tripod mount (authors' collection).

Magazine: 25-round detachable box
Cyclic rate: 500rpm
Muzzle velocity: c.2700fps (823mps)

ARME AUTOMATIQUE TRANS-FORMABLE MODELE 52 (AAT 52, sometimes known as the MAS 52)
France
Manufacture d'Armes de Saint-Etienne, Saint-Etienne
7.62mm NATO
The MAS 52, or Arme Automatique Transformable Modèle 52 (AAT Mle 52) is the French entry in the general purpose machine-gun field. It is a considerable improvement on earlier French designs but still manages to exhibit that flair for 'la difference' which characterises most French weapons.

Used with a light barrel and bipod as a light machine-gun, it can be fitted with a 23.50in (596mm) heavy barrel and mounted on a tripod to act as a sustained fire weapon. In the light machine-gun role it also boasts that old and useless Continental appendage, a butt monopod.

The belt feed system owes a good deal to the MG42 while the general system of operation also stems from Germany through the CETME rifle. The AAT 52 operates by delayed blowback, using a two-piece bolt unit in which the bolt-head is blown back but has first to operate an unlocking device before the main bolt body is permitted to recoil. Like all blowback guns, the extraction of the empty case is liable to be violent and—in order to prevent sticking and possible separations—the chamber is fluted to float the case on a layer of gas. In spite of this, the system is taxed to its utmost and a random handful of empty cases will inevitably exhibit a number of expansions and splits. The AAT 52 works—but only just.
Length: 39.00in (990mm)
Weight unloaded: 21lb 12oz (9.88kg), light barrel version
Barrel: 19.30in (488mm), 4 grooves, right-hand twist
Magazine: 50-round belt
Cyclic rate: 700rpm
Muzzle velocity: c.2700fps (823mps)

△MG08 and MG08/15▽

▲An example of the MG08 with the elaborate Schlitten (sledge) 08 mount. This gun is fitted with a muzzle booster to increase the cyclic rate; such conversions, executed in 1915, were often known as the MG08/15 or sMG08/15. This led to confusion with the light gun of the same year (RSAF).

▲The light Maschinengewehr Modell 08/15, based on the MG08 with the addition of a shoulder-stock and a pistol-grip. The receiver was redesigned in an attempt to lighten it (RSAF).

▲An example of the Bergmann-designed Maschinengewehr 15nA with its magazine drum (which contained a belt) fitted to the receiver. The lightweight tripod is notable (RSAF).

▲ The Bergmann 15nA with the feed cover open and the magazine drum removed (RSAF).

MASCHINENGEWEHR 08, MASCHINENGEWEHR 08/15, LUFTGEKUHLT MASCHINENGEWEHR 08/15, MASCHINENGEWEHR 08/18 (all Maxim-system)
Germany
Königlich Gewehr- und Munitionsfabrik Spandau; Deutsche Waffen- und Munitionsfabriken AG, Berlin
7.92mm Gewehr Patrone 98; various calibres, among them 7mm and 7.65mm, were available for export

The German experiments with machine-guns began in 1887 with the demonstration by Hiram Maxim of a weapon designed by him; as a result of the demonstration, extensive field trials were held in the period 1890 to 1894. Limited quantities of Maxim-system guns had, however, been purchased in 1895 by the army and in 1896 by the navy. Widespread trial issue in 1899 was followed in 1901 by the official introduction of the gun to the German Army.

The Maschinengewehr 08 was the ultimate outcome of the German trials and was promptly issued to the German Army; in August 1914 the Germans were the only army to appreciate the value of a machine-gun and each of their infantry regiments was supplied with six guns of MG08 pattern, the total number of machine-guns in the armed services being approximately 12,500. The MG08 (sometimes called the 'schweres Maschinengewehr 08'—sMG08) is of typical Maxim design, working on short-recoil principles in which the barrel and breechblock move approximately 0.70in (18mm) securely locked together. The barrel is then halted and the toggle locking the breechblock breaks to permit the block to continue towards the rear: the recoil spring then halts the movement and propels the breechblock back into battery, having

stripped a round from the belt. The toggle then locks once again. In 1915 many MG08 guns were fitted with muzzle boosters to increase the cyclic rate, giving an additional thrust to the recoiling barrel by deflecting some of the propellant gases to impinge upon it. This increased the cyclic rate by approximately 45%, and weapons so modified were called 'MG08 mit Rückstossverstärker S'. The MG08 was originally issued with a heavy sledge called the 'Schlitten 08', but this made the combination heavy—as the basic gun weighed 58lb 5oz (26.50kg) unloaded (but with 4 litres of coolant in the water jacket) and the sledge weighed 70lb 8oz (32.00kg). Together with the two extra barrels and the two extra locks which made up the 'Maschinengewehr-Gerät 08 (System Maxim)', this meant a total weight of about 137lb 0oz (62.00kg).

As a result, the German authorities issued a lighter pattern of the MG08—the MG08/15—which was fitted with a light bipod, a pistol grip and a shoulder stock; the weapon weighed some 39lb 0oz (18.00kg) with the bipod but with an empty water jacket, which was too heavy for a true light machine-gun. At the same time a lightened version, the lMG08/15 (the 'l' for *luftgekühlt*—air-cooled—and not for *leichte* or light), was supplied as an aeroplane gun; it was fitted with a skeleton jacket suited to air cooling and could also be adapted for the German interrupter gear for firing through a rotating propeller.

In 1916 a tripod, the 'Dreifuss 16', was introduced to replace the sledge mounting of the MG08: assorted Maxim-system weapons captured in Belgium and Russia were also converted for this mounting.

The last of the wartime guns, the Maschinengewehr 08/18, was introduced as a last attempt to make a light machine-

gun from the MG08 in which the water jacket of the MG08/15 was discarded and a light casing adopted instead. The MG08/18—1kg (2.2lb) lighter than the MG08/15—was not supplied with a readily removable barrel, greatly restricting the volume of fire which could be delivered because the barrel soon overheated. In an attempt to avoid this, the Germans often grouped the guns in threes and advised alternate use of them.

The MG08 continued to be issued to the German Army until the 1930s when the MG34 was perfected. Many MG08 guns remained, however, in the hands of the reserve formations and the German police forces, with whom they served until 1945.

(data: MG08)
Length: 46.25in (1175mm)
Weight unloaded: 58lb 5oz (26.50kg)
Barrel: 28.30in (719mm), 4 grooves, right-hand twist
Magazine: 250-round fabric belt
Cyclic rate: 300rpm without booster, 450rpm with booster
Muzzle velocity: c.2925fps (900mps)

MASCHINENGEWEHR 10 (BERGMANN), MASCHINENGEWEHR 15, MASCHINENGEWEHR 15 NEUER ART (MG15 nA–Bergmann)
Germany
Theodor Bergmann Waffenbau AG, Suhl
7.92mm Gewehr Patrone 98

These guns were recognised as the work of the noted designer Theodor Bergmann, although it is quite probable that they were the brainchildren of Louis Schmeisser. The first Bergmann machine-gun was patented in 1900 and the first production—on a limited scale—was undertaken as the Bergmann-Maschinengewehr Modell 02: a slight modification appeared in the following year and the first model

▲The Parabellum MG17 (or MG14/17) with a lightened barrel casing (RSAF).
▲The Parabellum-type luftgekühlt Maschinengewehr Modell 14, an air-cooled aircraft observer's gun (RSAF).

to achieve reasonable success was the MG10, excessively tested by the German Army.

The MG10, and its wartime successor, the MG15, are water-cooled guns, belt fed and utilising short-recoil principles to operate the mechanism; the recoiling components travel approximately 0.50in (12.70mm) rearwards before a locking block is cammed downwards from the underside of the breechblock, thereafter permitting the block to continue in its travel. The action of the recoil spring then returns the breechblock to battery and cams the vertically swinging locking-piece back into place. A notable feature of the water-cooled MG10 and MG15 is the provision of a quick-removable barrel, remarkable in weapons of this class.

A much-lightened version of the basic design, the MG15 nA (nA represents *neuer Art,* 'new pattern'), was issued in 1916 to troops on the Italian front. The MG15 nA discarded the water jacket of the MG10 and MG15, and instead adopted a pierced casing suited to air cooling. A bipod, a pistol grip, and a shoulder pad—hardly a stock in the conventional sense—were also added and the weapon fed from a drum magazine fixed to the right side of the receiver. The MG15 nA weighed 28lb 8oz (12.92kg) unloaded.

The Bergmann designs never gained the acceptance they perhaps deserved, particularly as they incorporated several advanced features (amongst which was the disintegrating aluminium link belt—a definite advance over the canvas belts of most contemporaries). It is perhaps fair to record that the success of the Maxim-pattern MG08 blinded the German authorities to the features of the Bergmann which was, after all, an indigenous product. In retrospect, how-ever, the authorities deserve recognition for ignoring chauvinism and not veering from the MG08 at a time when such a change was at best ill-advised.

(data: Bergmann 15 nA)
Length: 44.13in (1121mm)
Weight unloaded: 28lb 8oz (12.92kg) without mount
Barrel: 28.50in (726mm), 4 grooves, right-hand twist
Magazine: 200-round belt
Cyclic rate: c.500rpm
Muzzle velocity: c.2925fps (900mps)

PARABELLUM-MASCHINEN-GEWEHR MODELL 14, LEICHTES PARABELLUM-MASCHINEN-GEWEHR MODELL 1914, PARA-BELLUM - MASCHINENGEWEHR MODELL 1917

Germany
Deutsche Waffen- und Munitionsfabriken AG, Berlin
7.92mm Gewehr Patrone 98

The Parabellum light machine-gun was the standard aircraft flexible gun and was mounted singly or in pairs on many German aeroplanes; it was also used as a Zeppelin gun and occasionally appeared in a ground role, particularly during 1918 when the Germans were experiencing an arms shortage.

The Parabellum arose from a 1909 specification for a weapon suited to air-borne service and much lighter than the service MG08: none of the government arsenals was at that time capable of designing and manufacturing such a gun and so the authorities turned to the Berlin firm of DWM, who were then producing Mauser-system rifles. The project was assigned to Karl Heinemann who, after two years' work, produced the Para-bellum in 1911, having taken the Maxim design as his starting point. The Para-bellum was a much-lightened Maxim with the toggle inverted so that it broke up-wards—in the manner of the Parabellum pistol and the British Vickers—rather than downwards as in the original MG08. The Parabellum-MG was otherwise operated by short-recoil principles, although careful attention to the mechanism's size, weight and fit gave a cyclic rate of 700rpm without recourse to a muzzle booster.

The most common guise of the Para-bellum-MG is that of the aircraft flexible gun (lMG14), with a pistol grip and a shoulder stock: the weapon was drum-fed from the right side of the receiver. Some of these appeared with a large barrel casing and others (the so-called MG17 or MG14/17) with one of much slimmer proportions. Most of the heavier Zeppelin guns (MG14) were water-cooled to prevent the too-ready dissipation of heat to the flammable surroundings.

Optical sights sometimes appeared on the airborne weapons and ground guns were provided with simple bipods, with which they weighed about 23lb 0oz (11.00kg).

The Parabellum-MG was an efficient gun—the best, perhaps, of the flexible guns produced during World War 1 and lacking only a readily-changeable barrel. Rather than bothering to convert the MG08 to a light machine-gun (as the MG08/15 and MG08/18) it might well have paid the Germans to have concen-trated on the lighter Parabellum; the majority of such weapons were, however, required for air use.

Length: 48.13in (1223mm)
Weight unloaded, without bipod: 21lb 9oz (9.80kg)
Barrel: 27.75in (705mm), 4 grooves, right-hand twist
Magazine: 250-round belt
Cyclic rate: 650-750rpm
Muzzle velocity: c.2925fps (900mps)

DREYSE-MASCHINENGEWEHR MODELL 10, DREYSE-MASCHINENGEWEHR MODELL 15
Germany
Rheinische Metallwaaren- und
    Maschinenfabrik AG, Sömmerda
7.92mm Gewehr Patrone 98
The 'Dreyse' machine-guns were based on the 1907 patents granted to Louis Schmeisser and they were manufactured by RM&M of Sömmerda. The name ascribed to the design is confusing as Johann Niklaus von Dreyse, the inventor of the Zündnadelgewehr and whose name had been chosen to grace the machine-guns, had died some forty years before Schmeisser's patents were granted. In fact, RM&M had acquired von Dreyse's weapons business in 1901 and from then named their smallarms in honour of the famous connection.

Like the Bergmann designs the Dreyse guns, although possessing advanced features, found little success in view of the successful MG08. Both the Dreyse-MG10 and the Dreyse-MG15 were water-cooled weapons: the former was mounted on a tripod for use in a sustained-fire role and the latter was provided with a light bipod fixed to the breech end of the water jacket. The MG15 was also provided on occasion with a crude monopod which, positioned beneath the receiver in line with the cocking handle, was sometimes needed to prevent the gun from resting on the spade grips as no shoulder stock was provided. The MG15 was a reworked version of the MG10 intended to supply a somewhat rudimentary light machine-gun for use in Palestine, Turkey and Mesopotamia but the improvements were at best marginal.

Both patterns operate by short recoil with a hinging breechblock cammed upwards at the rear by tracks cut in the receiver, and consequently lowering the front or locking portion of the block. Further rearward travel of the block permits the novel three-claw feed unit to remove a cartridge from the belt; the recoil spring then returns the breechblock to battery and cams the lock upwards. The guns are hammer-fired, and an accelerator augments the recoil which is then checked by a buffer, resulting in a cyclic rate higher than many contemporary weapons of comparable class.

Although taken into service during World War 1 in reasonable numbers, most surviving Dreyse guns were converted in 1933–4 to the MG13 (qv) and ultimately sold to Spain or Portugal.

GAST-MASCHINENGEWEHR, 1917–1918
Germany
Vorwerk- und Companie, Barmen
7.92mm Gewehr Patrone 98
The Gast-MG can rightly be described as one of the oddities produced during World War 1, although it was nevertheless a remarkable development. The gun was designed in response to a 1917 request from the military authorities for a machine-gun capable of a high rate of fire and therefore suited to the flexible armament of aircraft, as the single-mounted Parabellum aircraft gun had a cyclic rate of only 700rpm—which was held to be too low. The Gast-MG was the design of Ingenieur Carl Gast and was in direct competition with such weapons as Siemens' powered machine-gun, which was never satisfactorily developed; Gast's solution was to provide two barrels on a single mounting and controlled by a single trigger unit. The units are recoil-operated and are cross-connected so that the recoil of one barrel unit provides the power for the other's feed cycle; large spring-operated drum magazines were placed on either side

The Gast-MG was secretly developed and tested in the spring of 1918 and it was not until the war had been over for some months that the Allied disarmament commissions heard of it: it was even longer before they each managed to obtain one. Each nation then tested the design, and all expressed themselves amazed at the gun's performance and reliability. For all that, however, no further development was forthcoming and the Gast-MG was forgotten. It is possible that the drum magazines would have provided a weakness to the gun as the springs aged, but none of the post-war trials showed this—possibly because few of them used more than 4,000 rounds in the course of tests.

▼The extraordinary double-barrelled Gast machine-gun of 1917. By a system of cross-connecting the barrels and actions, a high fire-rate (for its day) was achieved. A large spring-operated drum magazine was fitted to each side of the receiver (RSAF).

MASCHINENGEWEHR MODELL 13 (MG13)
Germany
Rheinische Metallwaaren- und Maschin-enfabrik, Sömmerda (originally)
7.92mm Gew Patr 98

The MG13 was a light machine-gun constructed by rebuilding the old 1918 model 'Dreyse' guns left over after World War 1. The only significant change was the adaptation to air-cooling by using a perforated barrel jacket and mounting a bipod at the front. When sufficient quantities of the much more efficient MG34 became available, the majority of the remaining MG13 guns were sold in 1938 to Portugal where the design was adopted as the Metralhadora M938, and remained there in service until the late 1940s.
Length: 57.75in (1466mm)
Weight unloaded: 23lb 15oz (10.89kg)
Barrel: 28.25in (717mm), 4 grooves, right-hand twist
Magazine: 25-round detachable box or 75-round saddle drum
Cyclic rate: 650rpm
Muzzle velocity: c.2700fps (823mps)

MASCHINENGEWEHR 15 (MG15)
Germany
Rheinmetall AG, Düsseldorf
7.92mm Gewehr Patrone 98

The MG15 was an aircraft gun which was pressed into ground service when Germany began to run short of weapons and replacements in the late stages of World War 2. The background of the MG15 is of interest because from it evolved another and more widely used gun, the MG34.

In the inter-war years Rheinmetall—then known as Rheinische Metallwaaren-und Maschinenfabrik—acquired control of the Solothurn company in Switzerland, in which they then had an outlet unrestricted by the provisions of the Versailles Treaty. The Rheinmetall designers, through Solothurn, developed a variety of machine-guns and other weapons and in 1930 produced the Modell 30 machine-gun for aircraft installation.

In 1932 Rheinmetall produced in Germany an improved version firing from an open bolt, later known as the MG15. The design had been lightened, the locking system was new, it was capable only of automatic fire, and it used a 75-round saddle-drum magazine which fed rounds from each side alternately so that the balance of the weapon did not change as the ammunition was expended.

The first experimental version was known as the T6-200 and was for fixed installation. It was soon followed by the T6-220 for flexible application, but this terminology was dropped on the military acceptance of the weapons and both versions became the MG15. An open-bolt weapon is, however, inconvenient for synchronisation with a revolving airscrew and a new model firing from a closed bolt —the MG17—superseded the MG15 in fixed installations.

When adapted to the ground role, a stock was clamped to the receiver, a bipod was pinned to the barrel and simple sights were fitted to the barrel casing. The resulting gun was long, rather heavy, and definitely clumsy; it was not issued in large numbers.
Length: 52.50in (1334mm)
Weight unloaded: 28lb 0oz (12.70kg)
Barrel: 23.50in (595mm), 4 grooves, right-hand twist
Magazine: 75-round saddle drum
Cyclic rate: 850rpm
Muzzle velocity: c.2480fps (755mps)

MASCHINENGEWEHR MODELL 34 (MG34)
Germany
Mauser-Werke AG, Berlin, and others
7.92mm Gewehr Patrone 98

The MG34 was derived from the Swiss-manufactured (but German-designed) Solothurn Maschinengewehr Modell 30. Simply by changing the type of mount, the MG34 could be used in a number of widely-differing roles; a bipod, which was adjustable for height, could be attached to the muzzle to make a light machine-gun of the basic weapon and a light tripod —called the Dreifuss 34—was issued to convert it into a light anti-aircraft machine-gun. A heavy sprung-cradle tripod, called the Maschinengewehr-Lafette 34, was used to turn the gun into a heavy machine-gun in which role only the belt-feed could be used owing to the form of the mount; an anti-aircraft adaptor could also be supplied for the MG-Lafette 34. Various patterns of mount intended for service on vehicles were also available upon request, and various sighting devices—amongst them telescope and periscope types—could be supplied amongst the accessories.

The MG34 was introduced to the services in 1936, and although officially superseded in 1943 by the MG42, supplies of the earlier weapon were never withdrawn. The gun introduced two radical ideas: the concept of a general or multi-purpose machine-gun, and the use of a belt feed in a 'light' gun. The MG34 was manufactured to a high standard of tolerance and finish—a factor which greatly contributed to its being superseded by the MG42, as the factories (originally Mauser-Werke, but later including in the process such companies as Steyr-Daimler-Puch AG and Waffenwerk Brünn) could not keep pace with demand arising from the greatly enlarged German Army and the wartime rate of attrition. Too much effort was required to produce the MG34, although this made for an excellent result.

The trigger was large and rocked about its centre; pressure on the upper portion marked 'E' (for 'Einzelfeuer'—single fire) gave semi-automatic fire, and pressure on the lower half marked 'D' ('Dauerfeuer' —continuous fire) gave automatic fire. It was recommended that the barrel should be changed after firing 250 rounds at the rapid rate and this was done by

▷The Dreyse MG13, an alteration to the old water-cooled MG10 used in small numbers in World War 1. The conversion was executed c.1933–4 to supply the Wehrmacht with a suitable light machine-gun pending the development and issue of the MG34 (RSAF).
▷An example of the MG15 aircraft gun converted for ground use by the addition of a bipod and a shoulder-stock. The conversions were made in the closing stages of World War 2 when machine-gun demands far outstripped supply (RSAF).
▷Three views of the MG34 multi-purpose machine-gun developed by Mauser-Werke in the early 1930s from the Solothurn MG30 (RSAF).

▶A cutaway drawing of the MG3, the current German army version of the MG42 (Rheinmetall).
▷▷▷ Three views of the wartime MG42, thought by many to have been the best machine-gun produced during World War 2—and certainly one which has since influenced many guns, including the American M60 (RSAF).

unlatching the receiver, swinging it through 180°—so exposing the breech—and withdrawing the barrel to the rear: not the easiest of tasks with a hot barrel.

The normal feed was by 50-round belts which could be linked together to give 250 rounds, and a special feed cover allowed the use of the 75-round 'saddle drum' of the MG15, which was normally done for anti-aircraft work as the magazine was convenient for such use and the reduced effort required to strip the rounds into the chamber served to increase the cyclic rate.

The MG34 utilised short-recoil operation, with an additional thrust imparted to the mechanism by a muzzle booster. The bolt was locked by means of an interrupted screw rotated by cam faces on the receiver walls which revolved it through 90° and into the barrel extension.

On the infantry tripod (MG-Lafette 34) the gun was steady and effective to 3800yd, but on the bipod it was by no means so efficient and was accurate only when firing single shots. The gun was strong but suffered from a tendency to jam in dust, dirt and snow, although despite this it lasted throughout the war in large numbers and was at some time present in practically every German first-line unit.
Length: 48.00in (1219mm)
Weight unloaded: 26lb 11oz (12.10kg)
Barrel: 24.75in (627mm), 4 grooves, right-hand twist
Magazine: 50-round belt or 75-round saddle drum
Cyclic rate: 800-900rpm
Muzzle velocity: c.2480fps (755mps)
Maschinengewehr 34S, Maschinengewehr 34/41. The MG34S served as a prototype, it seems, for the 1941 modification intended to provide a higher rate of fire. The MG34/41 used the shortened barrel of the MG34 and a modified lock was used in which lugs replaced the interrupted threads; the trigger mechanism was altered to eliminate the provision of single-shot fire, and the gun was only capable of using the belt feed. There were numerous internal modifications which led to non-interchangeability between

parts of the designs of 1934 and 1941. Although mooted as a replacement for the MG34, the advent of the MG42—which was, above all, a much more simple manufacturing proposition—spelled the MG34/41's rapid demise and official adoption was not forthcoming.

MASCHINENGEWEHR MODELL 42 (MG42)
Germany
Mauser-Werke AG, Berlin, and others
7.92mm Gewehr Patrone 98
Faced in 1941 with a critical shortage of infantry weapons, Germany looked for a machine-gun that could be produced more easily and more quickly than the MG34, yet still retain its more admirable characteristics. A new gun was conceived, using the MG34 as its basis but introducing certain changes and employing to some extent the manufacturing techniques of the equally successful MP40 submachine-gun: as much metal stamping as possible was used in production and the finish on the MG42 never equalled that of its predecessor. Despite this, however, it was a better gun and became most popular in the Wehrmacht. Like the MG34, the MG42 was a general-purpose weapon meant to be used from either a bipod or a tripod, and it used the same ammunition, belts and ammunition carriers as the preceding design. Some major mechanical changes were introduced: the locking system was entirely new and used locking rollers forced outwards into the receiver walls by the bolt. The locking action was much smoother and easier, and the rate of fire was increased to the remarkable figure of 1200rpm.

At such a high rate the barrel quickly heated and a second innovation was an excellent and simple barrel change. The barrel casing was as square in outline as the receiver, the right-hand side was cut away for most of its length, and the barrel was held at the breech by a yoke and at the muzzle by a simple bearing. The yoke was located by a latch and this swung forwards both to release the breech end of the barrel and to allow the

entire barrel to be pulled out to the right and to the rear, clear of the gun. A fresh barrel entered in the reverse direction and the entire change could be completed by a trained gunner in five or six seconds.

The high rate of fire made the gun difficult to control in the bipod role, but the Germans felt that any loss of accuracy was more than compensated for by the resultant fire-power.

More reliable than the MG34 and better able to resist dirt and rough treatment, the MG42 made an enviable name for itself with both the Wehrmacht and the Allies—the latter treating it with great respect. By the end of the war, over 750,000 had been made and many were sold by the Allies to countries in need of smallarms. In 1957 the design was revived in NATO 7.62mm calibre for the new Bundeswehr, in which form it has also travelled abroad.
Length: 48.00in (1219mm)
Weight unloaded: 25lb 8oz (11.50kg)
Barrel: 21.00in (533mm), 4 grooves, right-hand twist
Magazine: 50-round belt
Cyclic rate: 1200rpm
Muzzle velocity: c.2480fps (755mps)

MASCHINENGEWEHR 1—MASCHINENGEWEHR 3A1 (MG1–MG3A1), MASCHINENGEWEHR 42/59 (MG42/59)
Germany
Rheinmetall GmbH, Düsseldorf
7.62mm NATO
The West German Army's MG1 series all derive from the wartime MG42, although the calibre has been changed from the 7.92mm Gewehr Patrone 98 to 7.62mm NATO. The MG1, commercially known as the MG42/59, was re-engineered from an actual specimen of the MG42 as the original manufacturer's drawings had disappeared in the aftermath of World War 2; there are consequently a few minor departures from the basic design, and more modifications have been made in the light of service experience. The operation of the weapons, however, remains unchanged from the MG42—although in some

pivot pin of cover · belt-feed pawl · cocking slide · cover · safety nut · feed tray · transport lever · cover catch · buffer spring · oval-head screw · recuperator · bolt · recoil spring · rear cover catch · thrust bold · locking rollers · trigger · safety device · pistol grip · rear cover · butt · sear weapons the rate of fire can be altered by changing the bolts and buffers: Rheinmetall's Type N buffer and light bolt V550 (which weighs 550gm) give a fire-rate of 1150–1350rpm, while the Type R buffer and heavy bolt V950 (weight 950gm) gives a cyclic rate of 750–950rpm. The variants of the basic design are as follows:

7.62mm Maschinengewehr 1. The initial design reconstructed from the MG42, the MG1 is virtually identical to its predecessor: the bolt and feed unit have been slightly modified, but the two guns are externally virtually indistinguishable. The old pattern of muzzle booster, with fins and gas ports, is fitted.

7.62mm Maschinengewehr 1A1 and 1A2. Both of these are experimental weapons which were not taken into the inventory of the Bundeswehr; the MG1A1 had a slightly modified trigger mechanism, a chromed bore, and modified sights. The MG1A2 served as a prototype for the MG3 and had the feed unit suitably modified to accept the American M13 disintegrating link belt.

7.62mm Maschinengewehr 1A3. A developed form of the MG1, alterations have been made to the bolt, the trigger, the bipod and the feed mechanism. A new type of muzzle booster has been added which is integral with the flash-hider. The MG1A3 can be used in an anti-aircraft role by discarding the shoulder stock in favour of a rubber pad and using a special mount.

7.62mm Maschinengewehr 1A4. The fixed gun version of the basic MG1, the bipod and carrying strap have been discarded along with the anti-aircraft sight, and the rubber shoulder pad is fitted as standard. A third pattern of muzzle booster is fitted.

7.62mm Maschinengewehr 1A5. A conversion of the MG1A3 to MG1A4 standards, it is fitted with the third pattern muzzle booster.

7.62mm Maschinengewehr 2. A conversion of wartime examples of the MG42 from 7.92mm to 7.62mm NATO, with the attendant alterations to the barrel feed and the bolt. These guns can easily be recognised by the appearance on the receiver of dates prior to 1945.

7.62mm Maschinengewehr 3. An improved version of the MG1 based on the experimental MG1A2, the feed unit has been modified to accept with equal ease the German DM1 continuous belt, the DM13 disintegrating link belt or the American M13 disintegrating link belt. Provision is made for the attachment of a 100-round magazine case to the receiver, and a larger ejection port has been added. The barrel is externally tapered and has been given a chromed bore lining.

MG3 data essentially similar to MG42 (qv)

7.62mm Maschinengewehr 3A1. The fixed version of the MG3, the gun has been modified in a similar fashion to the MG1A4.

In addition to the above variants four others exist, called the MG1 ZUB, MG1A3 ZUB, MG2 ZUB, and MG3 ZUB: the suffix ZUB indicates *mit zubehör*—'with accessories'—and indicates that the guns are issued with tripods and other impedimenta.

HECKLER & KOCH MASCHINEN-GEWEHR HK13
Germany
Heckler & Koch GmbH, Oberndorf-am-Neckar
5.56mm × 45mm (0.223in)

The HK13 is a light machine-gun which is capable of both fully automatic fire and semi-automatic fire, and it is intended to provide the main firepower of an infantry squad equipped with 5.56mm weapons. The general design and system of operation has been derived from the highly successful Heckler & Koch rifles and the action closely resembles that of the 7.62mm G3 rifle. It has a semi-rigid bolt, sliding locking rollers and a fixed barrel. Operation is by delayed blowback, and feed is by a variety of magazines including a 100-round dual drum. Despite a promising start, this gun showed itself in need of several modifications, particularly in respect of the feed where failures were not unknown, and the firm continued with a programme of improvement and adaptation. The design of the gun is extremely good and manufacture is to a high standard, using a large number of precision stampings or pressings; the weapon bears a distinct external resemblance to the G3 and is also robust and practical. Like other designs in Europe, this one awaits a major change

in calibre policy by the military forces before large sales are possible.
Length: 37.13in (943mm)
Weight unloaded: 9lb 10oz (4.36kg)
Barrel: 22.00in (558mm), 6 grooves, right-hand twist
Magazine: 20-round box or 100-round drum
Cyclic rate: c.600rpm
Muzzle velocity: c.3250fps (990mps)

HECKLER & KOCH MASCHINEN-GEWEHR HK21
Germany
Heckler & Koch GmbH, Oberndorf-am-Neckar
7.62mm NATO

The HK21 is a selective-fire light machine-gun capable of single shots or automatic fire. Like the others in Heckler & Koch's weapon family, it is a delayed blowback gun with a fixed barrel. Single shots are fired from a closed bolt, which improves accuracy by permitting a short lock time and no movement of the working parts before the cartridge is fired. Automatic fire is from an open bolt in order to keep the breech cool between bursts and so eliminate premature ignition caused by heating the chambered round 'cooking-off'. The barrel is easily changed by means of a handle on its right side: lifting the handle unlocks the barrel from the body and it is then pushed forward to clear the housing, drawn to the right and pulled back clear of the gun. The action is both simple and fast to perform. The gun is meant to feed from a belt, but the feed mechanism can be easily removed and replaced by a special magazine adaptor which accepts the normal range of Heckler & Koch

▲The DM1 continuous-link belt. ▼The US M13 disintegrating-link belt.

▼The DM6 disintegrating-link belt.

▲The 5.56mm HK13 light machine-gun, shown here with a drum magazine; a box unit is also available (Heckler & Koch). ▼▼Two versions of the 7.62mm HK21 light machine-gun; the upper gun has an 80-round dual drum magazine, while the lower has provision for a belt-feed (Heckler & Koch).

magazines. The bipod can be either at the front or at the rear of the barrel casing—which allows flexibility in mounting the weapon—and the legs are adjustable for height. The HK21 shares 48% of its components with the original G3 rifle and there is full interchangeability between HK21 parts. Another useful item is a recoil booster which allows the gun to operate with blank cartridges.

Length: 40.00in (1016mm)
Weight unloaded: 14lb 9oz (6.60kg)
Barrel: 17.70in (448mm), 4 grooves, right-hand twist
Magazine: 50-round metallic belt, or various 20 or 30-round boxes
Cyclic rate: c.750rpm
Muzzle velocity: c.2625fps (799mps)

HECKLER & KOCH MASCHINEN-GEWEHR HK23
Germany
Heckler & Koch GmbH, Oberndorf-am-Neckar
5.56mm × 45mm (0.223in)
The HK23 is a direct descendant of the HK13, from which it differs only slightly. It is a light, belt-fed, air-cooled machine-gun of modern conception and manufacture incorporating several advanced features. It retains the distinctive delayed blowback system of operation with its locking rollers, and the overall outline shape closely resembles the previous model. However, the feed is changed to a belt which is pulled through the receiver by a stud working in a channel in the belt. The channel is angled and the stud moves from side to side as the bolt reciprocates. This motion is transferred to two star wheels which engage with rounds in the belt. There is adequate power to drive the feed mechanism and also to ensure that the gun works in adverse conditions. This latter capability is usually the weakness of blowback systems, particularly when firing small-calibre ammunition.

The HK23 is an excellent modern light weapon which is probably the best of its kind in Europe at the time of writing. Stripping and cleaning are straightforward, accuracy is good, and the gun appears to be able to withstand considerable rough handling. Its smooth outline and the absence of apertures give it a good resistance to dust and mud, and the plastic furniture resists wear and warping. Heckler & Koch's simple manufacturing processes are quite obviously intended to produce a weapon at a highly competitive price, yet there is nothing cheap or nasty about the resulting product. As with the HK13, the eventual success of the HK23 depends upon the universal acceptance of 5.56mm as a viable military calibre.

Length: 40.00in (1016mm)
Weight unloaded: 17lb 10oz (7.99kg)
Barrel: 22.00in (558mm), 6 grooves, right-hand twist
Magazine: 50-round belt
Cyclic rate: c.600rpm
Muzzle velocity: c.3250fps (990mps)

DROR MACHINE-GUN, c.1952
Israel
Israeli Metal Industries, Tel Aviv
7.92mm Gew Patr 98 (German); 0.303in SAA (British)
This weapon, resembling the Johnson designs (particularly the Johnson light machine-gun of 1944), was developed by the Israeli Army in the early 1950s. Although a sound weapon, only a small quantity was produced and it seems likely that the Israeli Government found it more economical to buy a foreign design of proven worth and commercial availability rather than involve themselves in the considerable expense of laying out a plant to produce the relatively small

◁The HK23 light machine-gun, in 5.56mm calibre, which utilises a belt-feed (Heckler & Koch).

◁The Israeli Dror, really no more than a modified version of the American Johnson M1944 design. Note the sharply-curved box magazine for—in this case—the 0.303in British round (RSAF).

numbers they required.

The Dror is recoil-operated, an unusual feature in a light machine-gun, and magazine-fed. The usual quick-change barrel and bipod are fitted. Difficulties with barrel stability in the original Johnson design dictated that the Dror should have a longer barrel support. The modified gun was not completely successful under harsh Middle East conditions.

MITRIAGLICE SISTEMA PERINO, 1900–1913
Italy
Manufacturer unknown
6.5mm cartucchia pallottola modello 95

The Perino machine-gun, patented in 1900 by Guiseppe Perino, was an interesting weapon with several creditable features. It was operated by a combination of recoil and gas action, in reality a recoil gun augmented by impinging the muzzle gases on a fixed muzzle section, which thus boosted the recoil of the moving portion of the barrel. The breech locking was done by a bell-crank lever system which gave a very positive action. The feed unit was originally a metal chain carried on a drum on the side of the gun (each link of the chain carried a cartridge) but this was later replaced by a feed box carrying five trays of twelve rounds, similar to the feed system used on many Italian machine-guns in later years.

A notable feature was the enclosure of the recoiling barrel within a sleeve; the barrel was carried on two piston rings which—working in the sleeve—acted as an air pump to force cool air through ports alongside the breech, which were themselves angled to direct a flow of cooling air into the chamber every time the bolt was opened. A modified version was also produced in which the whole length of the barrel was covered by a casing and water was pumped around the barrel by the same piston ring arrangement. A further refinement common in that era, provided for the alteration of the fire-rate by controlling the return of the bolt.

It has frequently been said that the highly-esteemed Perino was treated with considerable secrecy by the Italian Government and this may be, so as far as service adoption was concerned, but the gun was commercially available to everyone and, in 1911, an improved version was offered to the British Army by the English importer. This was somewhat modified from Perino's original design, water-cooled by an external pump and having the tray-feed system. The trials showed that the gun was robust and reliable, although owing to the large proportion of sliding mechanical components, it was thought likely to give trouble in dusty or sandy climates. The main drawback was one of weight, almost fifty pounds without water or tripod, and this was sufficient to lead the trials committee to the conclusion that it showed no advantage over the

Vickers-Maxim. In 1913 the agents returned with news of an improved '1913 Model' which, they claimed, was simpler in its mechanism and more reliable than any other known machine-gun—and reduced in weight to a few ounces under thirty pounds; it is not known whether trials were ever made of this version, and the details of how it differed from the earlier model are not clear.

The Italian Government were much taken with the idea of promoting indigenous inventions—and rightly so, for the Perino was quite a serviceable weapon for its day—but they wasted too much time in endless trials against Maxim, Vickers, Colt and other weapons without committing themselves to production. When they had ultimately decided, World War 1 was upon them and they were forced to take what they could get instead of having a Perino production line.

MITRIAGLICE LEGGERA SIA SISTEMA AGNELLI, c.1913–1925
Italy
SAI G Ansaldo, Armstrong & Company
6.5mm cartucchia pallottola modello 95

The SIA machine-gun—the initials stand for an abbreviated form of Societa Anonima Italiana G Ansaldo, Armstrong & Company—was a relatively simple light machine-gun of dubious value. There is no evidence to suggest that it was ever accepted into military service in any numbers, though it appears to have been employed by the Italians as a training weapon in the 1930s.

The design is a questionable form of retarded blowback based upon the patents of Giovanni Agnelli, which relate to a system of locking the rotating breech-bolt by using a positively-located firing pin with a lug riding in helical grooves within the breech-bolt. Thus, as the pin went home under the pressure of the return spring, the bolt was revolved to lock to the breech, but the pin was held clear of the cartridge cap by an auxiliary spring which was overcome only by the blow of the firing hammer.

Like every other inventor of a blowback gun, Agnelli had his share of troubles owing to sticky extraction of the bottlenecked cartridge case, and he must be credited as the first patentee of the idea of machining flutes in the chamber in order to equalise the pressure on each side of the case and thus overcome this problem.

The Ansaldo-Armstrong combine took over the Agnelli patents and produced a gun shortly before World War 1, but it was not developed into a workable proposition until the 1920s, by which time there were many other and better ideas available. Probably the worst feature of the SIA was the open-sided magazine which allowed the dust and dirt roused by firing to thoroughly coat the rounds waiting to be fed into the chamber, which may account for the rest of Agnelli's extraction troubles.

MITRIAGLICE SISTEMA REVELLI MODELLO 14 ('Fiat-Revelli')
Italy
FIAT SpA, Torino
6.5mm cartucchia pallottola M95

The modello 1914 Revelli was the first Italian-designed machine-gun to appear in any numbers. It was chambered for the underpowered 6.5mm M95 rifle round but was as heavy as any of the more powerful Maxims to which it bore a considerable resemblance. The action was novel, for it worked by a retarded blowback system in which the barrel recoiled for a short distance before the bolt moved away from the breech. This arrangement did not allow for any primary extraction and, to ensure that the cartridge cases did not rupture, each round was oiled as it was fed into the chamber, the oil being kept in a reservoir on top of the receiver. Another curiosity was a buffer rod attached to the top of the bolt and working outside the receiver on the top surface. This rod buffered against a stop immediately in front of the firing handles, in which position it was a constant source of danger while the gun was firing—and where it also picked up grit and dust and fed it into the mechanism. In any case, the oiled

cartridges attracted dirt and the gun was noted for stoppages.

The modello 14 was fitted with an extraordinary pattern of magazine which contained ten compartments, each of five rounds. As the device emptied a projection at the rear of each compartment raised a pawl to allow an arm to push the magazine to the right, in so doing presenting the next of the magazine compartments to the feed. The peculiar feed arrangements constituted an example of the needless mechanical complexity usually evident in Italian machine-gun design but, even so, it survived in first-line use throughout World War 2 (although many were modernised in 1935).

Length: 46.50in (1180mm)
Weight unloaded: 37lb 8oz (17.00kg)
Barrel: 25.75in (643mm), 4 grooves, right-hand twist
Magazine: 50-round strip-feed box
Cyclic rate: 400rpm
Muzzle velocity: c.2100fps (645mps)

MITRIAGLICE SISTEMA BREDA, 1925–1938
Italy
Societa Anonima Ernesto Breda, Brescia
6.5mm cartucchia pallottola modello 95,

▲The Revelli machine-gun, shown here in the 1935 form (at which time the water-cooled jacket of the modello 14 was discarded) (RSAF)
▲The Breda modello 28 aircraft gun (RSAF).
▲The Fucile Mitriagliatori Breda modello 30, in 6.5mm calibre (RSAF).
▷The Mitriaglice Breda modello 37, 8mm calibre, on its tripod (RSAF).
▷A specimen of the Breda tank machine-gun of 1938 (RSAF).

7.35mm cartucchia pallottola modello 38, 8mm cartucchia pallottola modello 35, 13.2mm

The Breda company produced a number of machine-guns for the Italian army which, for the sake of convenience, might be considered together. The first design produced by the Breda company was the Mitriaglice sistema Breda modello 1924, which was little different to the succeeding pattern of 1930 adopted on a large scale by the army.

Mitriaglice Breda calibro 6.5 modello 30 (in 1935 renamed **Fucile Mitriagliatori Breda modello 30**). The design of 1930 was the result of trials undertaken with the earlier machine-guns of 1924 (known commercially as the Mitriaglice Breda tipo 5C), 1928 and 1929. It was an ungainly-looking weapon which must have been difficult to clean and maintain in dusty conditions; the modello 30, like its predecessors, was blowback operated and since blowback operation invariably means difficult extraction the gun carried an oil pump to lubricate the rounds prior to chambering. The magazine on the right side of the receiver hinged forward, in which position it could be loaded from rifle chargers. This design offered a theoretical advantage in that the lips could be properly machined and were therefore less liable to damage than those of detachable magazines. But there were disadvantages, principally that the rate of fire was greatly reduced owing to the difficulties of loading and—should the magazine become in any way damaged—the gun could be easily put out of action.

The barrels of these guns could be changed quite rapidly, but it is notable that there was no form of handle or grip with which to hold the hot barrel; nor, indeed, was there any carrying handle, and so the unfortunate gunner had either to carry the gun across his shoulder or cradle it in his arms.

The modello 30 differed from the earlier 1924 design in having a bipod instead of a tripod, and in being given a pistol grip and shoulder stock in place of spade grips and a thumb trigger.
Length: 48.40in (1230mm)
Weight unloaded: 22lb 8oz (10.20kg)
Barrel: 20.50in (520mm), 4 grooves, right-hand twist
Magazine: 20-round detachable box
Cyclic rate: 475rpm
Muzzle velocity: c.2000fps (609mps)
Mitriagliera Breda RM modello 31. In 1931 the Italians introduced a 13.2mm heavy machine-gun intended primarily as a tank gun, although it could be mounted on a tripod and issued in an infantry support role. It has few unusual features apart from some exceptionally sensitive explosive bullets, although from a design aspect it seems to have been an intermediate step towards the development of the modello 37.

Mitriaglice Breda calibro 8 modello 37. The modello 37, which became the standard Italian army machine-gun in World War 2, was a fairly conventional gas-operated pattern with several unusual features which placed it in a class of its own. The design of the mechanism was such that the cartridges were not given a primary extraction movement to loosen them in the chamber prior to ejection: it was still necessary, therefore, to oil the rounds before they were fed into the mechanism. The second unusual feature was the system of feeding the rounds into the gun from a series of trays inserted from the side; the action of the gun was to remove the cartridges from the feed-tray, chamber and fire them, and then to extract and replace them in the tray. The full tray fed into one side of the gun and appeared at the other loaded with empty cartridge cases. Precisely what this mechanical complication was meant to ensure is open to question: not only was a lot of energy devoted to the useless task of placing the empty cases back into the 'magazine', but the poor gunner was also forced to pull the empties from the tray before he could attempt to reload it. In spite of this, however, the modello 37 managed to serve in front-line service throughout World War 2 and emerged from it with a reputation for reliability.

M37
Length: 50.00in (1270mm)
Weight unloaded: 43lb 0oz (19.58kg)
Barrel: 26.75in (679mm), 4 grooves, right-hand twist
Magazine: 20-round strip
Cyclic rate: 450rpm
Muzzle velocity: c.2600fps (791mps)
Mitriaglice Breda calibro 8 modello 38 per carri armati. This was the basic small-calibre tank and armoured vehicle gun and was a far more sensible design than some of its predecessors, using a top-mounted spring-fed box magazine and supplied with a heavy barrel which was capable of a measure of sustained fire. **Fucile Mitriagliatori Breda calibro 7.35 modello 38.** In 1938 the Italians introduced a larger 7.35mm cartridge in an attempt to improve the efficiency of their rifles; at the same time they took the opportunity of rechambering some of the

Fucile Mitriagliatori modello 30 for the larger round, and the modello 38 was the result. The 6.5mm and 7.35mm cartridge cases were virtually identical except for the size of the case-mouth, so few changes apart from the barrel were necessary to execute the conversion.

Aircraft versions of the Breda-system guns were also manufactured.

MITRIAGLICE LEGGERA SISTEMA SCOTTI MODELLO 28
Italy
Isotta-Fraschini SpA, Torino
7.7mm (0.303in British)
The Scotti light machine-gun was one of a range of weapons designed by Alfredo Scotti of Brescia. He was a free-lance designer who was for the most part associated with the Italian aircraft firms and most of his weapons were intended for use in air warfare, although he also produced some submachine-guns and a few light guns for infantry use. The pattern of 1928 was the best of his light infantry guns. It utilised the Scotti patent principle of operation, which is a form of locked blowback. Gas is tapped from the barrel and used to unlock the bolt, which is then carried to the rear by residual pressure in the breech. Both belt and drum feed were offered, but the design was not taken up by anyone

and few were made. The gun is included here because it shows a different approach to the problem of operating the mechanism. In larger form, as a 20mm cannon, the Scotti system was used by the Italian Air Force in World War 2.
Length: 42.00in (1068mm)
Weight unloaded: 27lb 0oz (12.25kg)
Barrel: 25.00in (636mm), 4 grooves, right-hand twist
Magazine: 250-round belt
Cyclic rate: 500rpm
Muzzle velocity: c.2400fps (731mps)

MITRIAGLICE FIAT CALIBRO 8 MODELLO 35 ('Mitriaglice Sistema Revelli Modello 35)
Italy
Fiat SpA, Torino
8mm cartucchia pallottola modello 35
The modello 35 is actually the 1914 gun brought up to date. The water-cooled barrel gave way to an air-cooled one, the feed was changed to a belt, the oiler was discarded and a fluted chamber substituted, and the calibre was changed to 8mm. This should have insured some success, but sadly it did not. There were too many of the old Revelli features still left to allow the gun to work at all well. Despite the fluted chamber the cartridge cases still stuck and, in the end, either the oiler had to be reinstated or

◁The Scotti-designed modello 28 light machine-gun, shown here as an aircraft flexible gun made by Isotta-Fraschini SpA of Torino (RSAF).
◁The FIAT modello 35 machine-gun, an air-cooled gun converted from stocks of the old modello 14 (RSAF).

the rounds had to be greased before going into the belt. The gun fired from a closed bolt, which is always undesirable in a sustained-fire weapon, and it led to premature ignitions ('cook offs') when the breech got hot. In fact, the modello 35 was actually a worse gun than the one upon which it supposedly improved. It lasted the war but went out of service immediately afterwards.

Length: 50.00in (1270mm)
Weight unloaded: 40lb 0oz (18.10kg)
Barrel: 25.75in (653mm), 4 grooves, right-hand twist
Magazine: 50-round belt
Cyclic rate: 500rpm
Muzzle velocity: c.2600fps (792mps)

TAISHO 3 NEN KIKANJU
('Machine-gun Taisho 3') 1914
Japan
State manufacture
6.5mm Meiji 30 ('Arisaka')
The Taisho 3 is really a Japanese version of the Hotchkiss Modèle 1900. In the Russo-Japanese war of 1904–5, the first in which machine-guns were employed in significant numbers, the Japanese Army used the French Hotchkiss to great effect. Kijiro Nambu used the 1914 pattern Hotchkiss to design a gun suitable for Japanese manufacture and the resulting close copy of the original is chambered for the 6.5mm Japanese Meiji 30 rifle cartridge. The only obvious external differences lie in the barrel finning and the fittings on the tripod. It was adopted in 1914 and some of the original weapons continued in service throughout World War 2. The Taisho 3 inherited from its French ancestor the merits of reliability and strength,

although the necessity to oil the cartridges was always a possible source of trouble in dusty conditions. Like the models which followed it, the Taisho 3 had sockets in the tripod feet through which the crew passed poles so that they could carry the gun and tripod in one lift—something which was unique to the Japanese machine-guns.

Length: 45.50in (1370mm)
Weight unloaded: 62lb 0oz (28.10kg)
Barrel: 29.50in (749mm), 4 grooves, left-hand twist
Magazine: 30-round metal strip
Cyclic rate: 400rpm
Muzzle velocity: c.2400fps (731mps)

TAISHO 11 NEN KIKANJU, 1922
Japan
State manufacture
6.5mm Meiji 30 reduced load
The Taisho 11 was brought into service in 1922 as the first light machine-gun the Japanese had designed on their own. It was unusual in several ways and was probably never entirely satisfactory, but it survived until 1945 and gave a good account of itself. Apart from its ungainly outline and angular shape, it possessed some features seldom found in other machine-guns. The chief one was the feed system in which a hopper on the left of the gun accepted clips for the Meiji 38 (Ariska) rifle, stripped the rounds out and fed them into the breech. Thus any rifleman could provide ammunition for the gun without having to load a magazine or a belt. However, the system was complicated and led to stoppages. Another feature of the feed was that the rounds were oiled as they passed into the breech, for the Taisho 11

▼The Taisho 3rd year (1914) heavy machine-gun on its tripod. Note the style of the spade grips, which readily differentiates the Taisho 3 from the later Type 92 (RSAF).

had no primary extraction and without some sort of lubrication the empty case could not easily be withdrawn from the chamber. A special cartridge loading, somewhat less powerful than the standard infantry rifle round, was generally used to prevent case ruptures. The Taisho 11 was only capable of automatic fire.

Length: 43.50in (1104mm)
Weight unloaded: 22lb 8oz (10.19kg)
Barrel: 19.00in (482mm), 4 grooves, right-hand twist
Magazine: 30-round hopper
Cyclic rate: 500rpm
Muzzle velocity: 2300fps (701mps)

91 SHIKI KIKANJU, 1931 (Type 91 Machine-gun)
Japan
State manufacture
6.5mm Meiji 30
The Type 91 was the tank version of the Taisho 11. It differed very little from the Taisho 11, except for the feed: it was found necessary to give the tank gunner more than 30 rounds at one filling of the hopper and so this was enlarged to almost twice the original size. This cannot have been such a great advantage as the gunner still had to refill it with clips in the confined space of the turret. It does not seem that the Type 91 was in service for long, although some were converted to infantry use by fitting a bipod and also, in many cases, a long telescopic sight. They can hardly have

been popular in the infantry role since they were heavier than any other Japanese 'light' machine-gun and no more effective. It is not recorded if the larger hopper conferred any advantage.
Length: 42.00in (1066mm)
Weight unloaded: 24lb 7oz (11.00kg)
Barrel: 19.20in (488mm), 4 grooves, right-hand twist
Magazine: 50-round hopper
Cyclic rate: 500rpm
Muzzle velocity: c.2300fps (700mps)

92 SHIKI KIKANJU, 1932
Japan
State manufacture
7.7mm 'semi-rimless' Shiki 92 and 7.7mm rimless Shiki 99
The Type 92 is no more than an improved Taisho 3 and in all aspects except the ammunition, barrel and breech it is the same gun. It was recognised in the late 1920s that the 6.5mm Meiji 30 round was inadequate for machine-gun use and the more powerful 7.7mm was introduced in 1932—hence Type 92, from the equivalent numbering of the Japanese calendar. Strangely, the 7.7mm round still needed to be oiled and the opportunity was lost to abandon this undesirable feature. The Type 92 round was semi-rimless and its successor, the Type 99, was rimless. The Type 92 gun was fortunate in being able to fire both kinds and it became one of the most widely used guns in the Japanese Army during World War 2. The rate of

▼The Type 92 heavy machine-gun; like the preceding Taisho 3 of 1914, it is really a modification of the Hotchkiss. Note the style of the spade grips and the sockets at the end of the tripod legs, into which fitted carrying poles (RSAF).
▷The Taisho 11th year (1922) light machine-gun, again based on the French Hotchkiss, clearly showing the unusual hopper feed mechanism on the left side of the receiver. Although not evident in the photograph, the butt and the sights are offset to the right (RSAF).
▷An example of the Type 96, without magazine; many of these guns were fitted with flash-hiders (and were therefore of similar appearance to the later Type 99) and long telescope sights on the right side of the action (RSAF).

fire was low, and because of a curious stuttering effect in the firing the gun was nicknamed the 'woodpecker'—although the sound hardly resembles that bird. Examples of the Type 92 are still in use with some armies in the Far East. A modified version was introduced in 1941 and was rather confusingly known as the Type 1. It was a little lighter than the Type 92, the barrel could be removed more easily and it only fired the Type 99 ammunition.

Length: 45.50in (1156mm)
Weight unloaded: 122lb 0oz (55.30kg), with tripod
Barrel: 27.50in (698mm), 4 grooves, right-hand twist
Magazine: 30-round strip
Cyclic rate: 450rpm
Muzzle velocity: c.2400fps (732mps)

96 SHIKI KIKANJU, 1936
Japan
State manufacture
6.5mm Meiji 30 (see notes)
The Type 96 was introduced in 1936 as an improvement on the Taisho 11. The cartridge hopper was replaced by a box magazine holding 30 rounds of the same 6.5mm ammunition and the cartridge oiler was abolished. The rounds were still oiled, with all the objections that accrue from doing it, but in the Type 96 the oil was introduced in the magazine loader and so the pump was divorced from the gun; the barrel was thus easier to change, which was a distinct advantage, but apart from these small advances the Type 96 was little better than the Taisho 11 which it was meant to replace. In fact, the Type 96 never did replace the Taisho

11 because Japanese arms manufacture could not possibly satisfy the demands made upon it. The two versions therefore existed alongside each other for the whole war.

One feature of the Type 96 rarely found on other machine-guns is the sight, for in many cases a low-power telescopic sight was fitted. The exact reason for this is no longer clear, since the inherent lack of consistent accuracy in the gun makes the use of a telescope largely unnecessary. The standard ammunition for the Type 96 was a reduced-charge version of the standard Meiji 30 infantry cartridge: the lower charge was essential in preventing case ruptures and head separations.

Length: 41.50in (1054mm)
Weight unloaded: 20lb 0oz (9.07kg)

Barrel: 21.70in (552mm), 4 grooves,
  right-hand twist
Magazine: 30-round detachable box
Cyclic rate: 550rpm
Muzzle velocity: c.2400fps (732mps)

97 SHIKI SENSHA KIKANJU, 1937 (Type 97 tank machine-gun)
Japan
State manufacture
7.7mm semi-rimless Shiki 92

The Type 97 is the successor to the Type 91, and not to the Type 96 as one might be led to imagine from the numbering. A tank machine-gun, it was used throughout World War 2 alongside the Type 91, although it never replaced it as it was obviously meant to do. It is a straightforward copy of the Czech ZB vz/26 firing the Japanese 7.7mm round, and it retains almost all the characteristics of the Czech weapon. It can hardly have been a success in a tank since the feed is by a box magazine, although this is undeniably better than the old hopper. The barrel is too light for the sort of shooting required of a tank gun and this either means that the gunner is restricted in the rate at which he could fire his magazine or that the barrel would rapidly overheat and be shot out—the latter fault being the most likely. In fact an improved Browning-system gun (the *4 Shiki Sensha Kikanju*) was designed; no more than the prototypes and a few preproduction guns were completed by Japan's fall.
Length: 34.00in (864mm)
Weight unloaded: 24lb 0oz (10.80kg)
Barrel: 28.00in (711mm), 4 grooves,
  right-hand twist
Magazine: 30-round detachable box
Cyclic rate: 500rpm
Muzzle velocity: c.2400fps (732mps)

99 SHIKI KIKANJU, 1939
Japan
State manufacture
7.7mm Shiki 99

When the decision was taken in 1939 to introduce the 7.7mm Type 99 rimless round, the Japanese Army had no light machine-gun to accommodate it; the Type 99 machine-gun was therefore designed for it. Since time was short, the design team worked from modifications to existing service guns and the accepted Type 99 was a development of the Type 96, itself a new weapon at that period. The Type 99 was a great improvement on its predecessors and more nearly resembled the light machine-guns which were in use in Europe. The new rimless round did not require oiling, there was adequate primary extraction to reduce stoppages, tolerances were held to fine limits, and a new pattern of barrel change was used. It was a good gun, but it came too late to be effective and never saw service in large numbers. Japanese industry was overloaded when it appeared, and the factories never caught up with the demand. There was more

than a hint of the ZB vz/26 in its outline, although the Type 96 ancestry was also clear. A small monopod was fitted to the toe of the butt to allow the gun to be used for firing on fixed lines somewhat after the manner of a tripod-mounted gun; this has been used on some other guns, but it is not stable or accurate enough to be of great value. The virtues of the Type 99 lay in its powerful ammunition and its magazine feed. In common with the majority of the Japanese machine-guns, it was only capable of automatic fire.
Length: 46.50in (1185mm)
Weight unloaded: 23lb 0oz (10.40kg)
Barrel: 21.50in (545mm), 4 grooves,
  right-hand twist
Magazine: 30-round detachable box
Cyclic rate: 850rpm
Muzzle velocity: c.2350fps (715mps)

62 SHIKI KIKANJU (Type 62 machine-gun), 1962
Japan
Nittoku Kogyo Kyokai, Tokyo
7.62mm NATO

The Type 62 is a general purpose machine-gun similar in outline and performance to the many that exist in NATO and those that have emanated from Europe. The specification which led to the Type 62 was laid down in the same period as elsewhere—the mid-1950s—and the gun was adopted in 1962. In appearance it is similar to the MAG of Fabrique Nationale, though the mechanisms are not the same. The Type 62 is a simple gas-operated gun of good design and of high quality finish, which can fire both the full charge round and a reduced charge version using the United States' disintegrating metal link belt. The Type 62 is also fitted on to the American M2 buffered tripod when used as a support gun. There is no selector lever as such, as the gun is only capable of automatic fire and it has a quick change barrel. There are indications that Japan may now change to 5.56mm ammunition, in which case the Type 62 will presumably be superseded.
Length: 47.50in (1205mm)
Weight unloaded: 23lb 9oz (10.70kg)
Barrel: 23.60in (599mm), 6 grooves,
  right-hand twist
Magazine: ∞-round disintegrating link
  belt
Cyclic rate: 650rpm
Muzzle velocity: c.2800fps (853mps)

FUSIL AMETRALLADOR MENDOZA MODELO B–1933
Mexico
Fabrica de Armas Nacionales, Mexico City
7mm cartucho modelo 1895 (7mm Mauser)

Mexico has been fortunate in having the talented arms designer Rafael Mendoza as the driving force behind smallarms production in the country, which has enabled Mexico to develop a range of

cheap weapons for her own specialised uses. The modelo B–1933 machine-gun is an original design, but it owes something of its inspiration to both the Hotchkiss light machine-gun and the Lewis. The bolt-locking action is of improved Lewis type, with some of the locking friction in the system diminished by using two cam slots. The gas cylinder is broadly of Hotchkiss form, though with improvements. The overall layout, the feed system and the quick-change barrel are purely of Mendoza's conception. The operating stroke of the piston is short and the gas is quickly released to the atmosphere. The bolt then continues under its own momentum.

The gun was much lighter than its contemporaries, provision was made for selective fire and the magazine was small and easily handled. At the time it was produced it represented an advance on most other similar guns in the world. It was taken into service in the Mexican Army, and remained in first line use until after 1945.
Length: 46.00 (1168mm)
Weight unloaded: 18lb 8oz (8.30kg)
Barrel: 25.00in (635mm), 4 grooves,
  right-hand twist
Magazine: 20-round detachable box
Cyclic rate: 450rpm
Muzzle velocity: c.2700fps (822mps)

AMETRALLADOR MENDOZA MODELO 45
Mexico
Fabrica de Armas Nacionales, Mexico City
.30 M1906

By 1945 it was apparent that the 7mm cartridge was becoming outdated, and at the same time great quantities of United States 0.30in ammunition existed. Mexico has always enjoyed a close relationship with the United States and it became expeditious, as well as good sense, to develop weapons which could take advantage of common calibres. Mendoza took the opportunity to improve his 1933 design whilst still retaining the main features. The modelo 45 has a slightly shorter barrel, a perforated muzzle brake and a simplified receiver. There is also a slight cleaning-up of the outline, but it is otherwise the same gun as the 1934 type.
Length: Approximately 45.00in (1142
  mm)
Weight unloaded: Approximately 18lb 0oz
  (8.15kg)
Barrel: 24.50in (622mm), 4 grooves,
  right-hand twist
Magazine: 20-round detachable box
Cyclic rate: 500rpm
Muzzle velocity: c.2750fps (837mps)

FUSIL AMETRALLADOR MENDOZA MODELO RM2
Mexico
Productos Mendoza SA, Mexico City
.30 M1906

The RM2 is the latest of the Mendoza

▲The 7.7mm Type 97 tank machine-gun, a slightly modified version of the Czechoslovakian vz/26 (RSAF).

▲The 7.7mm Type 99 light gun, without its box magazine (RSAF).
▼The Mexican Mendoza RM2 (RSAF).

machine-gun designs and its main features are low cost and simplicity of manufacture. It is also remarkably light—so light that it can almost be considered as an automatic rifle roughly in the same class as the BAR. The RM2 does not have a readily-detachable barrel and, for a light machine-gun, this is a distinct drawback since it denies the gunner the ability to fire more than a small number of magazines before having to stop to let the barrel cool down. One feature of the gun which is an advance on others is its method of stripping, the rear of the receiver being hinged so that it folds downwards and allows the working parts to be easily and quickly withdrawn. This method is reminiscent of the Fabrique Nationale's series of rifles and the inspiration for it may have been drawn from there. So far as is known, the RM2 has not appeared in large numbers.
Length: 43.00in (1092mm)
Weight unloaded: 14lb 0oz (6.30kg)
Barrel: 24.00in (609mm), 4 grooves, right-hand twist
Magazine: 20-round detachable box
Cyclic rate: 600rpm
Muzzle velocity: c.2750fps (837mps)

AMETRALLADOR ALFA MODELO 44, AMETRALLADOR ALFA MODELO 55
Spain
Fabrica de Armas de Oviedo, Oviedo
7.92mm Gewehr Patrone 98 (German) (ALFA 44), 7.62mm NATO (ALFA 55)
The ALFA Modelo 44 is a medium machine-gun, usually found mounted on a tripod. It is gas-operated and belt fed, feeding from a fixed cartridge box on the left-hand side. The operation is quite conventional in that a gas piston in a cylinder beneath the barrel is employed to unlock the bolt and drive it back while operating the belt feed mechanism and cocking the weapon. A return spring then sends the bolt back into battery, locking it and preparing it to fire the next round. A selector mechanism permits the firing of single shots.

A 1955 model also exists which is no more than the 1944 type chambered for the 7.62mm NATO round.
Length: 57.00in (1447mm)
Weight unloaded: 28lb 8oz (12.92kg)
Barrel: 29.50in (750mm), 6 grooves, right-hand twist
Magazine: 100-round metal link belt
Cyclic rate: 800rpm
Muzzle velocity: c.2500fps (761mps)

KULSPRUTA KJELLMAN, c.1907
Sweden
Manufacturer unknown (Husqvarna Vapenfabrik?)
6.5mm patron m/96
The Kjellman machine-gun was never adopted for service, but it deserves a place in history for it pioneered a locking system that has since become widely used and well known. The original idea

was conceived by a Swedish officer named Friberg, but it was not developed for over twenty years until it was incorporated into a gun designed in 1907 by Rudolf Kjellman. The locking system utilised two pivoting locking lugs which were forced into recesses in the receiver as the firing pin moved forward. The moving masses were thus kept light and could move quickly. At the same time, the gun could not fire until the breech was locked since the pin could not reach the base of the cartridge until the lugs had been pushed out of the way. The system was used in the Russian Degtyarev light machine-guns and also in the German MG42, which had an impressively high rate of fire. The Kjellman gun was produced both as a light machine-gun on a bipod mount with a box magazine and as a tripod-mounted gun with belt feed.

KULSPRUTA LH33; MASCHINEN-GEWEHR KNORR-BREMSE MODELL 35
Sweden/Germany
Knorr-Bremse AG, Berlin-Lichtenburg (German models)
6.5mm patron m/96 (Sweden); 7.92mm Gew Patr 98 (Germany)
This weapon first appeared in the early 1930s as a Swedish design called the 'LH33' in 6.5mm calibre. It was intended as a simple and cheap light machine-gun, and after the Swedish Army bought a few for evaluation the inventor made a few small improvements and looked around for an export market. He tried the Norwegians but they declined the weapon, and he then sold his patents to the German Knorr-Bremse company who—as their name implies—were in the automobile brake business. They appear to have rushed blindly into the arms trade in the hopes of a German Army contract, and in 1935 they began manufacture of a slightly simplified version of the LH33 under their own name. The modified pattern was capable only of automatic fire and therefore discarded the double trigger of the original LH33.

Feeding from a box magazine on the left side, the Knorr-Bremse had one or two odd features. The barrel was retained by a quick-release nut and for no apparent reason the rifling ended three inches from the muzzle. The safety catch was a trap for the unwary since, if wrongly applied, it would hold the bolt three-quarters cocked without engaging the sear; releasing the safety thus released the bolt and fired the gun. The butt was secured by a metal clip plate which vibrated loose so that the butt dropped off during firing—which is, to say the least, disconcerting.

Although the gun worked, the general standard of design and manufacture was poor even allowing for the intention to keep it cheap. The Waffen-SS purchased a few which were used for training and then unloaded on to the various 'legions' of foreigners formed in the war, amongst

▷The German MG35 manufactured by Knorr-Bremse to a Swedish design. Few guns of this type were ever made (RSAF).
▷The Swiss Fürrer-system IMG25 together with some of its components, including the receiver housing (above the unfinished forging from which it was made) and the toggle mechanism: although ingenious and beautifully made, the Fürrer's complexity doomed it to limited use (SIG).

them the Latvian Legion. Apart from this the only major sales were in 1940 to the hard-pressed Finns—who were glad of anything—and a few more to Sweden, where it was adopted as the m/40. Production thereafter ceased.

Length: 51.48in (1308mm)
Weight unloaded: 22lb 0oz (10.00kg)
Barrel: 27.25in (691mm), 4 grooves, right-hand twist
Magazine: 20-round detachable box
Cyclic rate: 490rpm
Muzzle velocity: c.2600fps (792mps) (7.92mm)

LEICHTES MASCHINENGEWEHR MODELL 25 (lMG25 or 'Fürrer')
Switzerland
Waffenfabrik Bern, Bern
7.5mm Patrone M11

This Swiss design, taken into service as the lMG25, is typical of its origin: exceptionally well conceived, beautifully made, and far too expensive to be considered as a mass-production weapon.

It is a recoil-operated gun which, not to put too fine a point on it, is virtually the Parabellum pistol turned on its side insofar as the locking system used is the Parabellum's toggle joint. However, Fürrer took a leaf from the submachine-gun world and used the differential recoil theory to produce a weapon with a very light recoil. Basically, the system is to fire the weapon while substantial portions of the recoiling mass are still moving forward, so that the recoil force of the exploding cartridge is largely absorbed in bringing the mass to rest and then reversing its direction of motion. Most applications of this system are in the blowback weapons in which

firing takes place while the heavy bolt is still moving. In the Fürrer, however, the breech toggle is closed and locked while the entire barrel and action unit are still moving forward into battery. The sear is released during this movement, so that the entire mass of the barrel and bolt must be stopped before recoil can begin.

Although a very efficient system, it demands careful manufacture—which is why the Fürrer never achieved success outside Switzerland.

A twin-barrel weapon for aircraft use was also designed

Length: 45.80in (1163mm)
Weight unloaded: 23lb 6oz (10.66kg)
Barrel: 23.00in (583mm), 4 grooves, right-hand twist
Magazine: 30-round detachable box
Cyclic rate: 450rpm
Muzzle velocity: c.2450fps (746mps)

MASCHINENGEWEHR MODELL 30 ('Solothurn MG30')
Switzerland
Waffenfabrik Solothurn AG, Solothurn
7.92mm Gewehr Patrone 98

The Solothurn firm was originally a watch manufacturing concern, but it was bought and converted to arms manufacture in the 1920s. In 1929 Rheinische Metallwaaren- und Maschinenfabrik AG gained control of Waffenfabrik Solothurn and it seems that they used the Solothurn factory as an assembly shop for their own designs. The first of these was the Modell 29, which was quickly changed to the Modell 30 and sold in Austria and Hungary. The Modell 30 had a quick-change barrel which was removed by rotating the stock and pulling it off. The main spring and guide stayed with the stock. Barrel and bolt could then be shaken out of the receiver and another inserted. Another feature was a rocking trigger: pressure on the top half gave single shots, and pressure on the lower half gave automatic fire. On firing, the barrel recoiled a short way and the bolt rotated to unlock. The barrel then returned to battery and the bolt continued rearwards until returned by the main spring. It was a simple and rapid action with low inertia forces involved and a high rate of fire. The MG34 inherited it all. The Solothurn fed from a box magazine mounted horizontally on the left of the receiver, an unusual idea which is rarely seen because of the centre-of-gravity changes as the magazine is emptied. However, whatever the disadvantages of the gun, over 5,000 were made between 1930 and 1935; and of these, a large proportion must have seen service in World War 2. The real contribution of the Modell 30 is that it acted as the starting point from which the MG15 and MG34 were developed.

Length: 46.25in (1174mm)
Weight unloaded: 17lb 0oz (7.70kg)
Barrel: 23.50in (596mm), 4 grooves, right-hand twist
Magazine: 25-round detachable box
Cyclic rate: 800rpm
Muzzle velocity: 2500fps (761mps)

SIG MASCHINENGEWEHR MODELL KE7, c.1936
Switzerland
Schweizerische Industrie-Gesellschaft, Neuhausen-am-Rheinfalls
7mm cartucho modelo 93 (Spain), 7.65mm Cartouche Mle 89 (Belgium), 7.92mm Gew Patr 98 (Germany), 0.303in SAA Ball (Britain)

Developed before World War 2 in the late 1930s, the KE7 was a purely commercial venture of SIG and the designers Kiraly and Ende, unsupported by the Swiss army. It was an attempt to produce a practical light machine-gun at a realistic price. However, it had only limited success in overseas sales although China took several large consignments, and it was not manufactured after the war. The KE7 was an interesting recoil-operated design, and although few light machine-guns have used this system it has some advantages over gas, particularly in barrel changing, fouling of the working parts and simplicity. Recoil operation is less successful in that the power of the mechanism cannot be easily altered to compensate for ammunition of varying characteristics. The KE7 was very light for a full-power light machine-gun— even lighter than the Browning Automatic Rifle—and it was probably difficult to hold on continuous fire, but, as the magazine only held 20 rounds there would not be many bursts before it would be necessary to change it. A good point was that the gun fired from an open breech at all times, and it had remarkably few parts in its construction. A light bipod was attached to the fore-end and there was an optional large tripod not unlike that provided for the MG34 or the Bren. This tripod gave the weapon a measure of stability for fixed fire tasks, but the construction of the gun would not really allow it to be employed in support fire roles since the barrel was too light. Another inconvenience would have been the constant replacement of the small magazines.

Length: 46.87in (1190mm)
Weight unloaded: 17lb 4oz (7.80kg)
Barrel: 23.63in (600mm), 4 grooves, right-hand twist
Magazine: 20-round detachable box
Cyclic rate: 550rpm
Muzzle velocity: c.2450fps (746mps)

SIG MASCHINENGEWEHR MG51
Switzerland
Schweizerische Industrie-Gesellschaft, Neuhausen-am-Rheinfalls
7.5mm Patrone M11 (Swiss), .30 M1906 (American)

The MG51 was developed from the German MG42 in the immediate postwar years. It was only used in Switzerland in small numbers and the only sale of any significance was to Denmark, who equipped her army with it. The MG51 was a heavy gun, as it was milled from solid metal rather than stamped from sheet like the MG42. Another minor change was the introduction of locking flaps on the bolt rather than the rollers of the MG42. These changes did not affect its performance and the gun was both reliable and fast-firing; it was usually mounted on a robust tripod which was provided with carrying straps and back pads. It has now been replaced by the German MG42/59 firing NATO 7.62mm ammunition.

Length: 50.00in (1270mm)
Weight unloaded: 35lb 6oz (16.00kg)
Barrel: 22.20in (564mm), 4 grooves, right-hand twist
Magazine: 250-round belt
Cyclic rate: 1000rpm
Muzzle velocity: c.2600fps (793mps)

SIG MASCHINENGEWEHR MG710-1, SIG MASCHINENGEWEHR MG710-2
Switzerland
Schweizerische Industrie-Gesellschaft, Neuhausen-am-Rheinfalls
6.5mm, 7.62mm NATO, 7.92mm Gew Patr 98 (German)

The SIG710 series of machine-guns were developed in the postwar years not only for service in the Swiss army but also for sale abroad. They bear certain likenesses to the last models of the MG42 and are direct derivations from the STG57 assault rifle. The rifle's delayed blowback locking system is once again employed

▲The Solothurn-made MG30, built under German control in Switzerland and later developed into the MG34.

▲The SIG-manufactured KE7 light machine-gun, designed by the Swiss Ende and the Hungarian Kiralý (SIG). ▼The SIG Maschinengewehr Modell 50 (MG50), based on the German MG42.

▼The SIG MG710-2, or MG552, belt-fed and mounted on its tripod. This weapon was submitted for the British trials which ultimately led to the adoption in Britain of the MAG.

◁ The SIG Maschinengewehr 710-1, once known as the MG55-1. The cut-out in the right side of the barrel casing permits the barrel to be replaced (SIG).
◁ The MG710-3, a modified version of the preceding model intended for low-cost production from as many stampings as practicable. The belt is contained in a removable box placed below the receiver (SIG).
◁ An example of the MG710-3 mounted on a tripod (SIG).

and, despite apparent complication, it is successful. The models 1 and 2 differ in respect of the barrel change; the 710-1 has a perforated barrel casing with flash-hider and it looks very similar to the MG42, and the barrel is changed by swinging it to the right and withdrawing to the rear, clear of the gun. The 710-2 barrel has a vertical carrying handle which is also used to carry the gun, and this handle is turned and pushed forward to remove the barrel. The guns are offered with a wide range of extras including a tripod, a drum magazine, and a carrying attachment. They are remarkably well made weapons and finished to very fine limits. The 710-1 and 710-2 have not been adopted by the Swiss army, which is already well-equipped, and their sales abroad have probably been affected by the later model 710-3.

(data: MG710-1)
Length: 45.75in (1160mm)
Weight unloaded: 25lb 0oz (11.30kg)
Barrel: 19.75in (500mm), 4 grooves, right-hand twist
Magazine: ∞-round belt
Cyclic rate: 750-1400rpm
Muzzle velocity: c.2600fps (792mps)

(data: MG 710-2)
Length: 46.75in (1190mm)
Weight unloaded: 24lb 0oz (10.90kg)
Barrel: 21.75in (550mm), 4 grooves, right-hand twist
Magazine: ∞-round belt
Cyclic rate: 750-1400rpm
Muzzle velocity: c.2600fps (792mps)

SIG MASCHINENGEWEHR MG710-3
Switzerland
Schweizerische Industrie-Gesellschaft, Neuhausen-am-Rheinfalls
7.62mm NATO

The 710-3 is the latest in the 710 series, still using the same method of operation as the preceding two types but with a less expensive form of manufacture. It is also slightly lighter. In this gun steel stampings are used as much as possible and this has resulted in a small change of outline. The barrel change is once again altered, returning to one similar to the 710-1 in which the barrel is held in a casing extending more than half way along its length and providing a front bearing for the barrel. The barrel has a large plastic handle on the right-hand side and this permits a hot barrel to be taken off the gun by pulling to the right and to the rear, as on the 710-1; the barrel is itself held by a simple latch. The basic gun is again offered with many extras and, like the others in the series, it is meant to be used as a general purpose gun. It is remarkably well made but is doubtless expensive though sales have been made, particularly in South America.
Length: 45.00in (1146mm)
Weight unloaded: 21lb 4oz (9.65kg)
Barrel: 22.00in (560mm), 4 grooves, right-hand twist
Magazine: ∞-round belt

Cyclic rate: 900rpm
Muzzle velocity: c.2600fps (792mps)

PULEMET MAXIMA OBRAZETS 1910 GODA, and variants
Union of Soviet Socialist Republics and Tsarist Russia
State factories
7.62mm patron o91g

The first machine-guns in service with the Tsarist were supplied by the Vickers' Sons & Maxim Machine Gun Company from England, but by the end of the Russo-Japanese War in 1905 the indigenous arms industry was capable of producing its own weapons and production was started at the Tula Arsenal. The first machine-gun was a Maxim with minor variations called the PM (or *Pulemet Maxim*) 1905; it had a bronze water jacket for the barrel. The next model was the PM1910 and on this the water jacket reverted to the sheet-steel material used by all other countries and the opportunity was also taken to make a slight alteration to the feed. A later variant of this model had a fluted water jacket, and the last version had a distinctive big water-filling port on top of the jacket to facilitate rapid refilling or topping-up.

This last version of the PM 1910 was produced in vast numbers and remained in front line service with the Soviet Army until replaced by the SG43. It is still to be seen in the hands of troops in various Asian armies, and is in second-line service with several armies in the Eastern Bloc. It is probably the longest-lived of the Maxim variants.

In the late 1920s the Red Army attempted to lighten and improve the design in the hope of producing a light machine-gun, for infantry use, which could be made with the machinery used for the medium gun. There were two trial types, one designed by Tokarev and called the MT and another designed by Koleshnikov, whose product was called the MK. Neither was a success and the idea was abandoned as impracticable. In the end Degtyarev produced a design which became the DP light gun of 1928.

Most Soviet Maxims are seen with the 'Sokolov' mounting, a pair of wheels supporting a large turntable (to allow traversing) and a U-shaped trail. Early models had two extra legs which folded underneath when the gun was being moved but could be put out in front for extra stability or to raise the gun well clear of the ground to shoot over high cover. Sometimes a steel shield was fitted, but this was unpopular because of its weight and the marginal protection that it offered. For winter warfare there was a sled fitting and all models could be fitted with drag ropes.
Length: 43.60in (1107mm)
Weight unloaded: 52lb 8oz (23.80kg)
Barrel: 28.40in (721mm), 4 grooves, right-hand twist
Magazine: 250-round fabric belt
Cyclic rate: 520-580rpm
Muzzle velocity: c.2830fps (863mps)

▲ The Maxim-Tokarev of c.1926
▼ The Maxim-Koleshnikov of c.1926

These two light machine-guns were designed to compete in the trials which led to the adoption in 1928 of the Degtyarev-designed DP. The Maxim-Tokarev was the work of Fedor Tokarev (responsible for the TT pistol and the SVT rifles), and it had a conventional pistol-grip butt quite unlike the strange dropping butt of the competing Koleshnikov type. Neither gun was successful, and although a few were made most ended up in Spain or China.

(Museu Militar, Lisbon)

◁A specimen of the Russian Maxim gun on the 'Sokolov' wheeled mount. This particular Maxim, model 1910, is a late version (made in 1943) with the addition of a large filling port to the top of the barrel's water-jacket (RSAF).

▼The DT tank machine-gun of 1929 (RSAF).
▼The Degtyarev machine-gun of 1928, showing the flat pan magazine to advantage. The DP was an outstandingly successful gun, marred only by the design of the bipod and the positioning of the recoil spring (SIM).

PULEMET DEGTYAREVA PEKHOTNII (DP), 1928
Union of Socialist Soviet Republics
State manufacture
7.62mm patron o91g

The DP was adopted by the Soviet Army in 1928 after two years of trials, and it was the first truly original development in Russia. It is extremely simple, yet remarkably reliable and robust. It remained the standard light gun until the 1950s and huge numbers were made, many of which survive today in the Eastern bloc countries and in Asia. The secret of the DP was the simple locking system, a modification of one of the earliest known types—the Friberg-Kjellman—which makes use of locking flaps on the bolt pushed out by the firing pin. The DP proved to be resistant to dust and dirt and free from any serious vices. Its weak point was the ammunition, as the long Russian 7.62mm rimmed rifle cartridge was difficult to load into an automatic gun without jamming. The distinctive flat pan magazine almost overcame this fault, but was in itself liable both to damage and to distortion. The operating spring was housed beneath the barrel in the piston tube, but it tended to lose its tempering when the barrel became hot. The gun was capable only of automatic fire and the bolt remained open between bursts to allow the chamber to cool. The success of this weapon brought about a series of similar guns which were derived from it, all of which proved to be equally good.
Length: 50.80in (1290mm)

Weight unloaded: 20lb 8oz (9.12kg)
Barrel: 23.80in (605mm), 4 grooves, right-hand twist
Magazine: 47-round drum
Cyclic rate: 500-600rpm
Muzzle velocity: 2760fps (840mps)

PULEMET DEGTYAREVA TANKOVII (DT), 1929
Union of Soviet Socialist Republics
State manufacture
7.62mm patron o91g

The DT is one of the variants of the original DP and was designed for the armament of tanks and armoured cars. The stock is made of metal and can be telescoped to reduce the inboard length, and there is an added pistol grip for greater control when the stock is not used. The barrel is a little heavier than on the DP and it cannot be quickly replaced. The drum magazine remained, which is an undesirable feature in an armoured vehicle, but it was of a smaller diameter and greater depth. This accommodated sixty rounds in two tiers.

This gun was intended to serve as a ground gun in an emergency and so it had a detachable bipod, carried in the vehicle, and a removable foresight. As with the DP the return spring gave trouble through overheating.
Length: 47.00in (1193mm)
Weight unloaded: 28lb 0oz (12.70kg)
Barrel: 23.80in (605mm), 4 grooves, right-hand twist
Magazine: 60-round drum
Cyclic rate: 650rpm
Muzzle velocity: c.2750fps (840mps)

◁ Shpitalny and Komaritsky's KM35 aircraft machine-gun, in this case an observer's flexible gun although various patterns were manufactured for fixed installations (RSAF).

◁ The DShK heavy gun of 1938; note the design of the feed cover (on top of the receiver in front of the sight) which protects Shpagin's rotating-block feed (RSAF).

◁ The DShKM of 1946. The rotating-block feed was discarded in favour of a more simple pawl mechanism (RSAF).

◁ The SGMB vehicle gun, shown with a support for the ammunition box and a bag for collecting the spent cases. Note also the retractable shoulder-stock (RSAF).

▲ The SGM, set on its tripod for anti-aircraft fire and with a large ring sight (USMC).

ShKAS AIRCRAFT GUNS, 1932-1941
Union of Soviet Socialist Republics
State manufacture
7.62mm ShKAS patron o33g

There were four models in the ShKAS series—KM33, KM35, KM36 and KM41 —starting in 1933 and ending in 1941. The gun was designed by two men, Shpitalny and Komaritsky, from whose names the first letters of the title are derived. The 'AS' was added to show that the gun was for aircraft use and capable of a high rate of fire. It was a complicated and expensive gun, but had the necessary high rate of fire and a good reputation for reliability. It may be that the early guns were all hand-made and it is distinctly possible that mass production in the normally accepted sense was never achieved with the ShKAS designs. The gun is gas-operated and belt fed, but the belt is picked up by a rotating mechanism sometimes called a 'squirrel cage' and the rounds are taken out and fed to the breech. The same mechanism takes the empty cases and ejects them in two stages *forward* out of the gun. The intention was to keep the cockpit clear of spent brass, and the gun is highly unusual in going to such trouble to achieve this. The concept of the gun incorporates several systems from other guns, but these are skilfully combined to produce a harmonious (if involved) whole.

KRASNOI PULEMET DEGTYAREVA-SHPAGINA OBRAZETS 1938G, KRASNOI PULEMET DEGTYAREVA-SHPAGINA OBRAZETS 1938/46G (DShK and DShKM)
Union of Soviet Socialist Republics
State manufacture
12.7mm patron o34g

The DShK is still in service in the Soviet Army; it started in 1938 as a joint design by Degtyarev and Shpagin, using Degtyarev's gas operation and locking system and a feed mechanism by Shpagin. The feed had a rotating cylinder which extracted the rounds from the belt and fed them into the chamber, although the latest model (the DShK1938/46 or DShKM) has abandoned this idea and turned instead to the simpler system used on the RP46 whereby a lever mechanism extracts each round and presents it in front of the bolt. The DShK was the standard Soviet heavy machine-gun throughout World War 2 and the Korean War, and it was used in both conflicts as an anti-aircraft gun. The DShK was provided with a wheeled mount which converted into an anti-aircraft tripod. Its perfomance is very similar to that of the 0.50in Browning. The latest models are carried on most of the Soviet armoured vehicles as secondary armament, particularly as hand-controlled anti-aircraft guns, and in some cases they are turret-mounted as co-axial guns. Both the DShK and the DShKM are

widely distributed throughout the Eastern bloc and Asia.
Length: 62.50in (1586mm)
Weight unloaded: 78lb 8oz (35.50kg)
Barrel: 42.00in (1066mm), 4 grooves, right-hand twist
Magazine: 50-round belt
Cyclic rate: 550rpm
Muzzle velocity: c.2825fps (860mps)

STANKOVII PULEMET GORYUNOVA OBRAZETS 1943G (SG43)
Union of Soviet Socialist Republics
State manufacture
7.62mm patron o91g

The Goryunov was developed during World War 2 as a replacement for the PM1910 (Maxim). An earlier replacement gun, the DS of 1939 designed by Degtyarev, had failed to meet its specifications, and by 1942 a modern medium machine-gun which was easy to manufacture and simple to use was urgently needed in the USSR. Goryunov used some of the features of the unsuccessful Degtyarev gun in order to save time, but the design of the locking system was radically changed. A tilting breechblock is used, similar to that of the Bren but moving sideways instead of vertically and locking into the side of the receiver. The feed is not straightforward, as the gun fires the 7.62mm rimmed rifle round and this has to be withdrawn rearwards from the belt before ramming into the breech. The reciprocating motion is achieved by using two claws to pull the round from the belt, and then an arm pushes the round into the cartridge guide ready for the bolt to carry it to the breech: despite this complication the Goryunov is remarkably reliable and feed jams are apparently few.

The barrel is air-cooled and massive in construction thereby contributing to the fairly high overall weight. The bore is chromium-plated and is able to withstand continuous fire for long periods, although the barrel can be easily changed by releasing a simple barrel lock and the carrying handle allows a hot barrel to be lifted clear without difficulty. The wartime version of the gun had a smooth outline to the barrel and the cocking handle was under the receiver: this gun was produced in limited quantities before 1945, but it never entirely replaced the Maxim.

Pulemet 'Stankovii Goryunova obrazets 1943 goda' ('machine-gun, Heavy Goryunov, model of the year 1943'). Commonly known as the SG or the SG43, this was the original version of the design with a smooth barrel, a plain barrel lock, no dust covers to the feed and ejection ports and an operating handle betwen the spade grips.

Pulemet 'Stankovii Goryunova modificatsionnii'. Known either as the SGM or as the SG43M, this model represents the first improvements to the original gun; dust covers were added to the feed and ejection ports, and a new pattern of barrel lock was fitted. A splined barrel was fitted to improve cooling and an operating handle appeared on the right-hand side of the receiver. There is a little confusion over the designation of this gun, as the term SG43M is sometimes used to denote a variation of the SG fitted with the new micrometer barrel lock and dust covers to the ports. As it is also possible to find early variations of the SGM without the dust covers, it is not thought that there are two separately recognised patterns. **SGMT and SGMB.** These are respectively the tank and vehicle versions of the basic SG43 design; the tank version has a firing solenoid mounted on the backplate, the vehicle gun appears in a special cradle mounting.

It must also be noted that several of the satellite countries, amongst them Hungary and the People's Republic of China, have manufactured their own guns to the basic SG design. Although the Chinese pattern is virtually that of their Russian counterparts, the Hungarian gun has a pistol grip, an RPD butt and a bipod: the result is a weapon that at first glance resembles the Kalashnikov-designed PK.

The Goryunov is one of the oldest designs of machine-gun remaining in first-line service in the hands of a major power, although there are now signs that its era is being drawn to a close in favour of the PK. It is not easy to see why the process has taken so long to come about, for the Goryunov was virtually obsolescent at the time of its inception and it has become more markedly so as the war years recede. Perhaps reliability saved the SG.

PULEMET DEGTYAREVA PEKHO-
TNII MODIFICATSIONII, 1944
Union of Soviet Socialist Republics
State factories
7.62mm patron o91g
The Degtyarev DP1928 was not without certain faults; the return spring weakened with the heat from the hot barrel and the bipod legs bent and broke from rough handling. Heavy use in the German invasion of Russia made these drawbacks particularly noticeable, and a modified gun was built. This was the DPM, M representing 'modified'. The return spring was moved to the rear of the bolt and protruded over the small of the butt in a cylindrical housing, where it prevented the gunner from grasping the gun in the usual way and so induced the fitting of a pistol grip.

The bipod, which had been the cause of continuous complaint, was replaced by a stronger version attached to the barrel casing. This raised the roll centre of the gun and made it easier to hold upright. The grip safety was replaced by a conventional safety lever, but apart from these changes no others were made. The resulting gun was apparently popular with the troops and was said to be more accurate and easier to hold and

shoot than the original of 1928.
Length: 49.80in (1265mm)
Weight unloaded: 26lb 13oz (12.20kg)
Barrel: 23.80in (605mm), 4 grooves, right-hand twist
Magazine: 47-round detachable pan
Cyclic rate: 520-580rpm
Muzzle velocity: c.2770fps (844mps)

PULEMET DEGTYAREVA TANK-
OVII MODIFICATSIONII, 1944
Union of Soviet Socialist Republics
State factories
7.62mm patron o91g
The DTM of 1944 is simply the tank version of the DPM and the same remarks apply to it. Apart from the position of the return spring it is almost exactly the same gun as the original DT of 1929 and it was fitted with the same 60-round pan magazine.
Length: 46.50in (1181mm) (stock extended)
Weight unloaded: 28lb 6oz (12.90kg)
Barrel: 23.50in (597mm), 4 grooves, right-hand twist
Magazine: 60-round detachable pan
Cyclic rate: 600rpm
Muzzle velocity: c.2755fps (839mps)

RUCHNOI PULEMET OBRAZETS
1946G (RP46)
Union of Soviet Socialist Republics
State manufacture
7.62mm patron o91g
The RP46 is a variation on the basic DP intended for use as a company level sustained-fire support gun. It is capable of delivering a high volume of fire, but it is not as portable as the original DP and DPM light guns. It has a heavier barrel and a belt feed system. There is a carrying handle (something conspicuously absent on the DP) and an improved barrel change. Despite the belt feed, it is still possible to fit the 47-round pan if required. This gun has now been replaced in first-line service, but it undoubtedly remains in second-line service in many parts of the Eastern bloc.
Length: 50.00in (1270mm)
Weight unloaded: 28lb 12oz (13.00kg)
Barrel: 23.80in (605mm), 4 grooves, right-hand twist
Magazine: 50-round belt or 47-round drum
Cyclic rate: 650rpm
Muzzle velocity: c.2750fps (840mps)

RUCHNOI PULEMET
DEGTYAREVA (RPD), c.1953
Union of Soviet Socialist Republics
State manufacture
7.62mm patron o43g
The Ruchnoi Pulemet Degtyarev (Degtyarev light machine-gun, or RPD) has for some years been the standard light machine-gun of the Soviet Army, having been introduced in the 1950s as the complimentary squad weapon to the AK rifle. It was the logical development of the earlier DP (1928) and DPM (1944), and it has been pro-

▷The DPM light machine-gun of 1944. The design of the bipod and the position of the recoil spring (in a housing at the rear of the receiver) distinguish the DPM from the earlier DP. A pistol grip was also added to the stock of the later gun (RSAF).
▷The DTM tank machine-gun of 1944; this was a DPM-type modification of the old DT of 1929 (RSAF).
▷The RP46, basically a belt-fed version of the DPM; the pan magazine of the earlier Degtyarev weapons will fit the RP46 provided that the feed mechanism is removed (USMC).
▷The RPD, in this instance a Chinese-made Type 56. Note the design of the gas piston housing (under the barrel) and the reciprocating handle on the right side of the receiver (SIM).

◁A Russian RPDM; note the non-reciprocating cocking handle on the side and the enlarged gas-piston housing (SIM).
◁The KPV heavy machine-gun, used in some instances as a tank gun in place of the DShK or DShKM (RSAF).
◁The RPK, a light machine-gun derivative of the standard AK assault rifle.
◁An example of the PK, the new Russian medium machine-gun, showing the unusual configuration of the butt (USMC).

gressively improved during its life. The original model used a cup-type piston head, had a straight cocking handle which oscillated back and forth as the gun fired, and was without a dust cover. The piston was then modified to the more usual plunger pattern and the dust cover added, and then came a change in the cocking handle to a folding type which remained still as the gun was fired.

The fourth modification, sometimes known as the RPDM, has a longer gas cylinder and a recoil buffer incorporated in the butt—measures intended to improve stability, which has always been a problem with this somewhat light weapon, and also to try and improve the reserve of power available to lift the feed belt.

The final version was very slightly changed, having a combined magazine bracket/dust cover and a sectional cleaning rod housed inside the butt.

The RPD fires the 7.62mm M43 'Intermediate' round and (unlike the DP, DPM and RP46) is belt-fed from a drum clipped beneath the gun at the centre of gravity. The mechanism has therefore to lift the belt up to the breech, and there is evidence that the power available to do this is barely sufficient even after the changes incorporated in the RPDM, giving rise to malfunctions under adverse conditions.

The replaceable barrel of the DP was abandoned in this fresh design, and it became a matter of drill and training for the gunner to avoid firing more than 100 rounds in one minute to prevent overheating the barrel. The remainder of the mechanism is similar to the DP, suitably scaled down for the smaller ammunition; and, like its predecessor the DP, the RPD is capable of automatic fire only.
Length: 41.00in (1041mm)
Weight unloaded: 15lb 7oz (7.00kg)
Barrel: 20.50in (520mm), 4 grooves, right-hand twist
Magazine: 100-round belt
Cyclic rate: 700rpm
Muzzle velocity: c.2410fps (734mps)

KRASNOI PULEMET VLADIMIROVA (KPV), c. 1955
Union of Soviet Socialist Republics
State manufacture
14.5mm patron o41g
The KPV is an anti-aircraft machine-gun of a sophisticated and advanced design. It came into service in the 1950s, when there was a general overhaul of Soviet equipment and it has since appeared on a number of wheeled mountings in single (ZPU1), twin (ZPU2) and quadruple (ZPU4) form. It is now being mounted on Soviet armoured personnel carriers and some other vehicles. It is widely used in the Eastern bloc countries and some of the anti-aircraft mounts have been installed in North Korea. The gun is unusual in Soviet designs in that it operates by recoil and the bolt is locked by turning to engage two projections on the outer surface of the breech. The

chromium-lined barrel can be easily and quickly changed, and the number of parts in the mechanism is small. The ammunition was originally used in the Soviet PTRS and PTRD anti-tank rifles of World War 2 and has been developed to include a variety of different types.
Length: 78.80in (2002mm)
Weight unloaded: 108lb 0oz (48.90kg)
Barrel: 53.10in (1349mm), 8 grooves, right-hand twist
Magazine: ∞-round belt
Cyclic rate: 600rpm
Muzzle velocity: c.3250fps (988mps)

RUCHNOI PULEMET KALASHNIKOVA (RPK), c.1960
Union of Soviet Socialist Republics
State manufacture
7.62mm patron o43g
The RPK is replacing the RPD, and may have already replaced it, as the standard light gun of the Soviet infantry. It can really be regarded as an enlarged AK assault rifle since it uses most of the same parts and spares in its manufacture. The system of operation is the same as the AK and the gun accepts the magazines from the AK as well as those designed especially for it. Like the RPD the barrel is fixed so that the tactical use of the gun is to some extent restricted, but as Soviet squad members all carry AKs the limitation is perhaps not so critical since the combined volume of fire is high. The finish on the RPK is good and, like the AK, the bolt and bore are chromium-plated to reduce wear.
Length: 41.00in (1041mm)
Weight unloaded: 10lb 8oz (4.70kg)
Barrel: 23.20in (589mm), 4 grooves, right-hand twist
Magazine: 30 or 40-round detachable box, or 75-round drum
Cyclic rate: 600rpm
Muzzle velocity: c.2400fps (734mps)

PULEMET KALASHNIKOVA (PK), STANKOVII PULEMET KALASHNIKOVA (SPK or PKS), c. 1965
Union of Soviet Socialist Republics
State manufacture
7.62mm patron o91g.
The PK is a true general purpose machine-gun—the first to be seen in Soviet service. It is a replacement for the now elderly RP46 and it uses the same 7.62mm long rimmed cartridge; in this respect it is remarkably old-fashioned, because this round dates back to 1891 (although a similar stricture can be applied to others) and the rim gives rise to feed complications. As in the RP46 each cartridge has to be taken from the belt before it can be rammed into the breech; there are, presumably, sufficiently large stocks of the 7.62mm rifle round to make it uneconomical to change to another. The PK is intended as a company support gun and so requires a more powerful round than the M43 'Intermediate' round of the assault rifles and light machine-guns. The mechanism is a clever combination of that of the

AK together with an original feed system, the barrel is replaceable, the gas regulator can be adjusted without tools, the finish is very good and the weight low; it is an impressive gun. There are versions of it for use in armoured vehicles and a tripod is supplied for the sustained-fire role with which the gun is known as the PKS. When mounted on the tripod, the box holding the belt is attached to the left-hand side of the receiver; in the bipod role this box clips underneath the receiver, as in the RPD, and centralises the centre of gravity. A tank machine-gun—the PKT—is also manufactured; it, of course, lacks the shoulder stock and pistol grip assemblies.
Length: 47.00in (1193mm)
Weight unloaded: 19lb 12oz (8.90kg)
Barrel: 26.00in (660mm), 4 grooves, right-hand twist
Magazine: 100, 200 or 250-round belt
Cyclic rate: 650rpm
Muzzle velocity: c.2700fps (822mps)

MAXIM MACHINE-GUNS, 1884—c.1925
United Kingdom
Albert Vickers Limited, Crayford, Kent (later known as Vickers' Sons & Maxim Limited and then simply as Vickers Limited)
0.303in SAA Ball and others
Hiram Maxim was one of the geniuses produced by the nineteenth century: his inventions, an astonishing list, covered many fields. The one for which he is remembered in the armaments world is his machine-gun pattern, first demonstrated in 1884 and later adopted by many nations. Amongst the countries to

test the Maxim Gun were the United Kingdom (first trial 1887), Austria-Hungary (1887–8), Italy (1887), Germany (1887), Russia (1887) and Switzerland (1887), and the United States of America (1888). Most of the trials were successful although few of those countries who tried the Maxim adopted it much before 1900—largely owing to the prevalent conservatism existing in the minds of the contemporary military authorities. In 1891, however, the Maxim Gun had been issued to British troops and had proved its effectiveness in combat; adoption of the weapon by Switzerland followed in 1894, and the United States Navy took a limited number in 1896.

Most of the earlier guns were manufactured in the United Kingdom by Vickers, who held most of the patents. The parent company later developed a modified design—usually known as the 'Vickers' or the 'Vickers-Maxim'—which ultimately supplanted the Maxim in many armies.

Some nations produced Maxim-system machine-guns in their own plants, especially Germany and the USSR. The following list gives some idea of the more important models of the Maxim Gun used throughout the world.

Many of these guns are covered separately in these pages: see also GERMANY for the MG08, its derivatives and the Parabellum; UNITED KINGDOM for the Vickers guns; UNION OF SOVIET SOCIALIST REPUBLICS for the PM05, PM10 and their derivatives. Apart from the infantry machine-guns, assorted Maxim-system arms were made in calibres as large as 37mm.

Length: 46.50in (1180mm)
Weight unloaded: 40lb 0oz (18.00kg)
Barrel: 28.25in (717mm), 4 grooves, right-hand twist
Magazine: 250-round cloth belt
Cyclic rate: 600rpm
Muzzle velocity: c.2750fps (838mps)

LAIRD - MENTAYNE MACHINE - GUN, 1908–1914
United Kingdom
Coventry Ordnance Works, Coventry, Warwickshire
0.303in SAA Ball and others
The Laird-Mentayne machine-gun was produced in England by the Coventry Ordnance Works to the designs of Mentayne and Degaille, whose patents were taken out in 1908. Laird was a later co-patentee with Mentayne in respect of one or two very minor modifications to the original designs, and one is inclined to feel that Laird's name is attached to the gun out of courtesy simply in return for his assistance in producing the weapon.

The gun itself was a long-recoil type, using the firing pin to lock the bolt: when fired, the barrel and bolt recoiled for the full stroke, the firing pin was held and the barrel and bolt began to move forward again. This withdrew the firing pin and unlocked the bolt, which was then held while the barrel returned. Feed was from a bottom-mounted box magazine and the gun could be fitted to a tripod, although versions were also submitted with a light folding bipod under the barrel. The barrel was designed to be quickly interchanged when overheated and, reading the trial reports of the

Maxim-type machine-guns

year/**model**/country/calibre/system

1900	**Maschinengewehr Modell 00**/Switzerland/7.5mm Patrone M89/Maxim
1900	**Mitrailleuse Modèle 00**/Belgium/7.65 mm Patrone Mle 89/Maxim
1901	**Maschinengewehr Modell 01** (MG01)/Germany/7.92mm Gew Patr 98/Maxim
1904	**US Machine-gun, caliber .30, M1904**/United States of America/.30 M1906/Maxim
1905	**Pulemet Maxim o1905g**/Russia/7.62mm patron o1891g/Maxim
1908	**Maschinengewehr Modell 1908** (MG08)/Germany/7.92mm Gew Patr 98/Maxim
1908	**Model 1908**/Bulgaria/8mm Patrone Modell 93 (Austro-Hungarian)/Maxim
1909	**Maschinengewehr Modell 09** (DWM commercial)/Germany/7.92mm Gew Patr 98/Maxim
1910	**Pulemet Maxim o1910g**/Russia/7.62mm patron o1891g/Maxim
1910	**Mitrailleuse Modèle 10**/Belgium/7.65mm Patrone Mle 89/Maxim
1911	**Maschinengewehr Modell 11**/Switzerland/7.5mm Patrone M11/Maxim
1911	**Parabellum-Maschinengewehr Modell 11** (experimental)/Germany/7.92mm Gew Patr 98/Parabellum
1914	**Parabellum-Maschinengewehr Modell 14**/Germany/7.92mm Gew Patr 98/Parabellum
1915	**Maschinengewehr Modell 08/15** (MG08/15)/Germany/7.92mm Gew Patr 98/Maxim
1915	**luftgekühlt Maschinengewehr Modell 08/15**/Germany/7.92mm Gew Patr 98/Maxim
1915	**Gun, Machine, Vickers 0.303in Mark 1**/United Kingdom/0.303in SAA/Vickers-Maxim
1915	**US Machine-gun, caliber .30, M1915**/United States of America/.30 M1906/Vickers-Maxim
1916	**Maschinengewehr Modell 16** (experimental)/Germany/7.92mm Gew Patr 98/Maxim
1917	**leichtes Parabellum-Maschinengewehr Modell 14/17**/Germany/7.92mm Gew Patr 98/Parabellum
1918	**leichtes Maschinengewehr Modell 08/18**/Germany/7.92mm Gew Patr 98/Maxim
1922	**PV1 aircraft gun**/USSR/7.62mm patron o1891g/Maxim

▲A Maxim machine-gun of 1904 compared to a Vickers of 1915 (USIM)

▲Maxim's first working machine-gun of 1884, the base from which all subsequent Maxim guns rose. The device on the right of the action is capable of varying the rate of fire (USMC).

period, one has the impression that here was a fairly sound and serviceable light machine-gun—certainly better-designed than some which followed. The military of the time were regrettably unaware of the light machine-gun concept: machine-guns, as everyone well knew, were large pieces which were water-cooled and fired from tripods.

Tested in 1912 by the British Army, the 0.303in version weighed 17lb (7.71kg) and fired from an interchangeable 25-round magazine. It survived its trials reasonably well, with slight feed troubles, but the eventual conclusion was: 'The Committee do not consider this gun would meet any want except possibly for mounting in aeroplanes, for which purpose it would require considerable modification, as at present it is not adapted to a central pivot.' Had there been the necessary recognition, the tactics of World War 1 could well have been considerably revised.

GUN, MACHINE, HOTCHKISS, 0.303in MARKS 1 and 1*
United Kingdom
Royal Small Arms Factory, Enfield Lock, Middlesex (?)
0.303in SAA Ball
During World War 1 the supply of machine-guns for the British Army was augmented by purchasing the rights to the Hotchkiss gun and manufacturing it in Britain in 0.303in calibre. The result was basically the French Army's 'Fusil Mitrailleur Mle 09' (see FRANCE) and it was known to the British as the Mark 1, introduced in March 1916. Fitted with a butt and bipod it became a useful light machine-gun.

The basic design was then altered to ensure that the gun could be loaded either from the standard metallic strips or from a form of 'belt-feed' which consisted of no more than a series of short three-round strips hinged at their joints. This was primarily accomplished in order to use the guns for tank weapons, and was based on similar French developments. The revised gun, known as the Mark 1*, was introduced in June 1917.

Although superseded by the Lewis Gun and later by the Bren Gun, the Hotchkiss was retained in service throughout World War 2 as a reserve and Home Defence gun and was not declared obsolete until June 1946. In c.1926, however, the guns had become the *Guns, Machine, Hotchkiss, 0.303in Number 2, Marks 1 and 1**.
Length: 46.75in (1187mm)
Weight unloaded: 27lb 0oz (12.25kg)
Barrel: 23.50in (596mm), 4 grooves, right-hand twist
Magazine: 30-round metallic strip
Cyclic rate: c.500rpm
Muzzle velocity: c.2425fps (739mps)

LEWIS MACHINE-GUN
United Kingdom
Birmingham Small Arms Company Limited, Birmingham
0.303in SAA ball
The 'Lewis' light machine-gun was the first light automatic to be used on a large scale in time of war. It was adopted by the Belgian army in 1913 and soon afterwards the British Army expressed an interest and BSA obtained manufacturing rights; the first combat use of the gun occurred in the 1914 retreats of the Belgian army, though small numbers were already in the hands of the contemporary British Army. It was made in large numbers throughout the war, one reason for its success being that six Lewis Guns could be made for the time and expense involved in making one of Vickers type. The other reason was that it could be carried by one man who would nonetheless be able to move fast enough to keep up with an infantry battle. It was, of course, extensively adopted as an aircraft gun.

The original design was evolved from the designs of one Samuel Maclean by Colonel Isaac Lewis (of the United States of America) and, as originally patented, was intended for production as a heavy or medium gun cooled either by air or water and mounted on a tripod; it had the distinctive Lewis action and drum feed, but it was without the peculiar cooling system later added when the gun

▷A Mark 1 Lewis light machine-gun fitted with a 'fire simulator'. This, on the side of the barrel jacket at the breech, was no more than a ratchet device which produced a clattering noise—in no way comparable to machine-gun fire! The device dates from World War 1 (RSAF).
▷A Mark 1 Lewis, with a repositioned bipod of a different design and a bag for collecting spent cartridge cases (RSAF).

▼An example of the Hotchkiss Mark 1 machine-gun on its diminitive tripod (RSAF).

was transformed into a light weapon.

The action is based on a turning bolt with rear locking lugs and is very similar to the Swiss Schmidt-Rubin rifle action, from which Maclean perhaps drew inspiration. A post on the gas piston extension engages in a helical slot in the bolt and also carries the striker, riding within the bolt. With the gun cocked, and the piston to the rear, pressure on the trigger releases the piston which is driven forward by the helical return spring—another distinctive Lewis feature. As the piston moves so the post carries the bolt forward, chambering a round, rotating the bolt by the helical slot until the lugs engage in the receiver body, and finally carrying the striker on to the cartridge cap.

Gas pressure on the piston after firing drives it to the rear, withdrawing the striker, unlocking the bolt and opening it, ejecting the spent case and rewinding the helical return spring. Cooling of the barrel is accomplished by forced draught, as the barrel is in contact throughout its length with a finned aluminium radiator enclosed in a cylindrical steel casing which is open at the rear but which projects some distance in front of the muzzle. The expansion of propellant gases at the muzzle induces a flow of air into the rear opening and along the aluminium radiator. When the gun was adapted to aircraft installation this device, held to be unnecessary, was abandoned and during World War 2 (when many of these aircraft guns were put to ground use) they seemed to work as well as the forced-cooling type—though prolonged firing might well have shown the difference.

Although Colonel Lewis had energetically promoted his invention to various American authorities, and tests had been made, it was not until the gun had been produced by the thousand in Europe and proved in war that it was finally adopted in the land of its inception. In spite of subsequent combat experience, the United States Army only retained a small number after the war for training purposes, though the Army Air Service adopted the gun as a standard weapon.

The Lewis Gun continued in service with many European and Asian countries until World War 2. By that time the British Army had replaced it in first line service with the Bren gun, but after Dunkirk the many weapons in store were issued to units as a temporary measure until sufficient Brens were available; they continued to be used for the remainder of the war by the Home Guard and the Merchant Marine.

The Lewis Gun's principal virtue was that it was the first in the field: its drawbacks lay in the excessive weight and the astounding variety of malfunctions and stoppages which could result from its complicated mechanism.

Length: 50.50in (1283mm)
Weight unloaded: 26lb 0oz (11.80kg)
Barrel: 26.25in (666mm), 4 grooves, left-hand twist
Magazine: 47-round or 97-round pan
Cyclic rate: 550rpm
Muzzle velocity: c.2450fps (745mps)

The following list gives the nomenclature and distinctive features of the various models of Lewis Gun:

Gun, Machine, Lewis 0.303in Mark 1 (introduced on 15th October 1915). This is the original model, sighted to 2000 yards and supplied with a 47-round magazine. It was officially declared obsolete on 16th August 1946, though none had been seen in use for years.

Gun, Machine, Lewis 0.303in Mark 2 (introduced on 10th November 1915). The Mark 2 differed from Mark 1 in having the cooling arrangements removed for aircraft use. A spade grip was fitted in place of the butt. The 97-round magazine was introduced for this gun in November of 1916.

Gun, Machine, Lewis 0.303in Mark 2* (introduced on 13th May, 1918). This differed from Mark 2 in having a larger gas port and certain other parts modified to produce a faster rate of fire. Mark 2* guns were modified from existing weapons.

Gun, Machine, Lewis 0.303in Mark 3 (introduced on 13th May 1918). The

◁◁ Two views of the Mark 2 Lewis, an aircraft gun fitted with an enlarged 97-round pan magazine and a spade grip (RSAF).

◁ An automatic rifle derivative of the Lewis Mark 1, produced c.1940 for the use of the Home Guard. The style of the muzzle compensator, the addition of a gas-piston guard, and the provision of a wooden fore-end characterised these guns. The conversion was of similar appearance to the later naval Mark SS (RSAF).

◁ The Savage-Lewis 0.30in weapon, originally the American M1918 aircraft gun but modified for the use of the British Home Guard, c.1940 (RSAF).

Mark 3 was exactly the same as Mark 2* but of new manufacture and not a modification of existing weapons.

Gun, Machine, Lewis 0.303in SS (introduced on 27th August 1942). For Naval use 'to guide modification of existing guns to Shoulder Shooting'—so said the official announcement. The modification consisted of removing the radiator assembly and fitting a new short butt and a muzzle compensator, and adding a cylinder guard and foregrip. It could be applied to any mark, whereupon the mark had a 'star' added to the nomenclature; these guns, however, were also referred to rather indiscriminately as the 'Mark XI SS', which tended to confuse matters.

Gun, Machine, Lewis 0.303in Mark 1* (introduced on 16th August 1946). A conversion of Mark 1 guns to Mark 4 standard. It is doubtful if any were ever converted, for they were declared obsolete on the day of approval.

Gun, Machine, Lewis 0.303in Mark 4 (introduced on 16th August 1946). A conversion of Mark 3 guns to simplify manufacture. It is again doubtful if any were ever made, as the gun was declared obsolete on the day it was approved.

Gun, Machine, Savage-Lewis 0.30in. This was the American 0.30in Lewis aircraft gun made by the Savage Arms Corporation, purchased some time in 1940 for Naval use (although it was later taken into use by the Home Guard). As supplied, they had no adjustable sights and were instead later fitted with simple battle sights zeroed to 400 yards; the spade grip originally provided was extended into a skeleton butt by welding strip metal on and adding wooden shoulders and cheek pieces. Some of the first guns supplied were provided with spare standard wooden butts from store, but the welded model was developed when this supply ran out.

The name 'Savage-Lewis' was adopted by the Naval authorities to distinguish the guns from the British 0.303in versions. In addition, a two-inch wide red band was painted around the body in front of the magazine post and the rear half of the magazine centre disc was painted red, to remind users of the 0.30in calibre.

GUN, MACHINE, VICKERS, 0.303in MARKS 1—7, 1915—1967
United Kingdom
Manufactured in the Royal Ordnance Factories, and by Vickers' Sons and Maxim (later Vickers - Armstrongs Limited)
0.303in SAA Ball

The Vickers machine-gun was an improvement on the original Maxim. The main difference lies in the fact that the toggle locking action was inverted but the weight was also considerably reduced by careful stress calculations and the use of good grade steel and aluminium. The gun was adopted by the British Army in November 1912 and remained as the standard support-fire machine-gun until

the middle 1960s, when it was replaced by the L7A1 GPMG. In its time, the Vickers pattern went through twelve or more modifications—mostly minor—and was substantially the same gun after fifty years of service. It was heavy, fairly slow-firing, prone to a number of stoppages from the ammunition but reliable in itself and well loved by all. It would work in the most adverse conditions, and its water-cooled barrel ensured a long life for the bore by helping to maintain a low temperature. It was used in aircraft (for which it was air-cooled), in ships, in tanks, as a ground AA gun, on armoured trains, on armoured cars, and in a host of other roles. It is still in use in some countries as a first-line gun, and it retains a strong following who maintain that it still has much to offer in modern armies. While firing the standard types of 0.303in ammunition, a special round was developed for the Vickers—the boat-tailed Mark 8z—and this round added an extra 1000yd (914m) to the maximum range.

(data: Vickers Mark 1)
Length: 45.50in (1155mm)
Weight unloaded: 40lb 0oz (18.10kg)
Barrel: 28.50in (723mm), 4 grooves, right-hand twist
Magazine: 250-round fabric belt
Cyclic rate: 450rpm
Muzzle velocity: c.2450fps (745mps)

Gun, Machine, Vickers, 0.303in Mark 1 (introduced in 1912). This, the standard water-cooled weapon described above, remained in service until 1965. It was finally declared obsolete in 1968.

Gun, Machine, Vickers, 0.303in Mark 1* (1916). An air-cooled aircraft gun, introduced in 1916 as the armament of the Sopwith 1½ Strutter. The barrel jacket was louvred to permit the circulation of air around the barrel and the entire machine-gun, excluding the Constantinesco interrupter gear, weighed 28lb (12.70kg).

Gun, Machine, Vickers, 0.303in Mark 2 (1917). A minor variant of the Mark 1* and also intended for air service; a smaller casing pierced with holes was fitted, and the unit weighed 22lb (10kg).

Gun, Machine, Vickers, 0.303in Mark 2* (1927). Identical to the Mark 2, but with slightly different feed arrangements; the Mark 2* 'A' was provided with a left-side feed and the Mark 2* 'B' with a right-side feed.

Gun, Machine, Vickers, 0.303in Mark 3 (c.1928). Another of the aircraft guns, the Mark 3 was virtually the Mark 2* with an elongated flash-hider designed to protect the aircraft's engine cowling.

Gun, Machine, Vickers, 0.303in Mark 4 (c.1929–30). An experimental armoured vehicle machine-gun derived from the Mark 1; it was never adopted and remained in the prototype stage.

Gun, Machine, Vickers, 0.303in Mark 4B. An armoured vehicle gun manufactured with a suitably modified barrel casing and provided with an integral block carrying the mounting trunnions.

Gun, Machine, Vickers, 0.303in Mark 5

(c.1932). An aircraft gun similar in design to the Mark 3, but with a modified method of opening the body.

Gun, Machine, Vickers, 0.303in Mark 6 (1934). A gun similar to the Mark 4B and similarly intended for use in armoured vehicles. It was given a better mount and had a corrugated barrel casing; versions existed with left or right-side feed.

Gun, Machine, Vickers, 0.303in Mark 6* (1938). Similar to the Mark 6, but with inlet and outlet pipes attached to the barrel casing to allow attachment to a header tank—or some similar reservoir—in the vehicle.

Gun, Machine, Vickers, 0.303in Mark 7. Another of the vehicle guns, and again similar to the Mark 6; the mounting, which seems to have given constant trouble, was once again strengthened. A thicker barrel casing was used and the surface left plain; the machine-gun weighed 48lb (21.75kg).

Marks 4 to 7 were declared obsolete in 1944 and none of the aircraft guns saw service in World War 2.

Vickers-system medium machine-guns were also used by the US Army under the title **US Machine-gun, Caliber .30, Model of 1915.** They were made by Colt's Patent Firearms Manufacturing Company, of Hartford in Connecticut, to a licence granted by Vickers; chambered for the Cartridge .30 M1906, some were

commercially marketed after World War 1 in a variety of calibres, and some in 0.30in calibre were purchased c.1922 by the Mexican army—where they were known as the **Ametrallador modelo 1915.**

Vickers themselves are also known to have marketed commercial machine-guns in various calibres, amongst them 7.65mm (Mauser). Guns in this calibre are known to have been supplied to Bolivia and Paraguay, and possibly to Argentina.

GUN, MACHINE, BEARDMORE-FARQUHAR, 0.303in EXPERIMENTAL, c. 1917–1924
United Kingdom
Beardmore Engineering Company
0.303in SAA Ball

The Beardmore-Farquhar machine-gun —designed by the Farquhar of the Farquhar-Hill rifle and manufactured by Beardmore—was developed during World War 1 but was not developed to a suitable standard for testing until the war was over. Thus, with the immediate urgency removed, the gun was somewhat more stringently examined than might have been the case had it been ready more quickly. It was an early contender in the light machine-gun field, for it must be borne in mind that until World War 1 was into its third year the light machine-gun had little or no place on the battlefield, and it was not until the Lewis had

▲The Gun, Machine, Vickers 0.303in Mark 1 on the Mount, Tripod, Mark 4B (RSAF).

▷The Beardmore-Farquhar light machine-gun, an outstanding design that deserved better success than it achieved. The specimen here, in 0.303in calibre, was made in 1921 (SIM).

▷The Vickers-Berthier, an Anglo-French design, which competed with some success in the trials to find a light gun for the British Army. It was beaten by the Czech vz/26, which became the Bren. This particular VB dates from 1928-9 (RSAF).

been demonstrated as a useful adjunct to the rifle section that the philosophy took firm hold.

In addition to its possible use as an infantry weapon, this model was also proposed as an aircraft observer's gun and it was in this role that it was first tested. The report on the tests was favourable; indeed, had finance been available at the time and had the climate of events been otherwise, there is every reason to suppose that the Beardmore would have been accepted as a service weapon. As it was, circumstances militated against it and no further development of the Beardmore-Farquhar took place.

The principle of operation in this gun is quite unusual. Most gas-operated guns rely on the push of a gas piston to directly operate the bolt, but here the piston actually compresses a powerful spring and the pressure generated by this spring upon the bolt is very carefully balanced against the pressure placed on the bolt by the exploding cartridge. Until the chamber pressure—and thus the pressure on the bolt—has dropped to a safe level, the spring pressure is not sufficient to unlock the bolt. Once the pressure has dropped, the spring performs the unlocking and bolt retraction with a very smooth movement unlike the usual 'slam-bang' action of a gas piston.

The result is a smooth action with less liability to stoppages and difficult extraction, and a slower rate of fire than any of its contemporaries. Moreover, owing to the gentle action and low recoil forces developed by this system, the whole weapon is considerably lighter—without sacrificing the robustness demanded in military service—than had previously been thought possible.

VICKERS-BERTHIER MACHINE-GUNS, 1925–1945
United Kingdom, India
Vickers-Armstrong Limited, Crayford, Kent
0.303in SAA

The Vickers-Berthier was designed by the Frenchman Adolphe Berthier and patented in the early 1920s; manufacturing rights were acquired by Vickers in 1925. Limited numbers were made in the United Kingdom and a few sales were made to minor powers, amongst them Bolivia, in the first years of the 1930s. In 1933 the Indian government adopted the Vickers-Berthier as their army's standard light machine-gun, in whose hands it replaced the Lewis and the Hotchkiss. It is also possible, but for the appearance in 1932/3 of the original models of the Bren gun, that the Vickers design would have been adopted by the British. The VB was gas-operated gun with few moving parts, a smooth action and the ability to be dismantled and assembled without special tools. The action locked by the tilting of the bolt into a recess in the top of the receiver; it was said to be reliable and trouble-free in adverse conditions.

Amongst the variants of the VB were the following:

Mark 1. Introduced in 1928, this was the first model and could be recognised by a slab-sided forearm under the receiver. The barrel was finned.

Mark 2. (c.1929/30). Essentially similar to the Mark 1, the forearm was rounded and extended forward of the receiver. A bipod and a butt monopod were fitted, similar patterns to those of the Mark 1.

Light Mark 2. Produced in 1931 as an experiment for the Indian Government. The gun had a smooth barrel, a light forearm, no monopod and a cutaway butt.

Mark 3 and Mark 3B. The Mark 3 was adopted in 1933 by the Indian authorities, and was basically a heavier-looking version of the Light Mark 2. The gun, made by the rifle factory at Ishapore, was officially known as the *Gun, Machine, 0.303in Vickers-Berthier, Indian Mark 3*; the Mark 3B was a minor variant in which alterations were made to the gas system to improve reliability.

Length: 46.50in (1180mm)
Weight unloaded: 22lb 0oz (10kg)
Barrel: 23.50in (552mm), 5 grooves, right-hand twist
Magazine: 30-round box
Cyclic rate: 600rpm
Muzzle velocity: c.2450fps (745mps)

VGO. The VGO (or 'Vickers Gas Operated' machine-gun) was originally designed as an aircraft observers' weapon. A flat pan magazine, like that of the Lewis but non-rotating, fed 96 rounds into the breech at nearly 1000 rpm. It was later used by SAS and other jeep-borne light reconnaissance troops, and as the rear gun in a few two-seat aircraft.

GUN, MACHINE BREN, 0.303in, MARKS 1–4; GUN, MACHINE, 7.62mm BREN, L4A1–L4A6; c.1935–1971
United Kingdom
Royal Small Arms Factory, Enfield Lock, Middlesex
0.303in SAA Ball (Marks 1–4), 7.62mm NATO (L4A1–L4A6)

In the early 1930s the British Army was searching for a light machine-gun which would show some improvement on the Lewis. The Vickers-Berthier was the strongest contender but before a decision had been taken a British military attaché brought the Czechoslovakian ZB vz/26 machine-gun to the army's attention. Specimens of the gun were obtained and it performed so creditably under test that

butt was fitted with a strap to go over the firer's shoulder and a pistol grip beneath it for his non-firing hand; this particular style of grip did not commend itself to the British soldier, and when modification and simplification were called for the butt fittings were the first to go.
Length: 45.25in (1155mm)
Weight unloaded: 22lb 5oz (10.15kg)
Barrel: 25.00in (635mm), 6 grooves, right-hand twist
Magazine: 30-round detachable box
Cyclic rate: 500rpm
Muzzle velocity: c.2400fps (731mps)

Gun, Machine, Bren, 0.303in Mark 2. In June 1941 the Mark 2 was introduced. This changed the rearsight to a more conventional leaf type; the telescopic bipod was replaced by one of fixed

◁The Vickers-Berthier Indian Mark 3B, adopted in the 1930s by the Indian Army because of insufficient supplies of the Bren, and successfully used throughout World War 2 (SIM).
▲A 7.92mm version of the Bren Mark 1; note the straight-sided magazine, which distinguishes this gun from the normal 0.303in type (RSAF).
◁The 0.303in Bren Mark 1 on its short-lived tripod mount (RSAF).

it was adopted forthwith for service. The only difficulty was that the ZB vz/26 had been designed for the 7.92mm rimless German cartridge, and so it had to be redesigned to accommodate the British 0.303in rimmed round which accounts for the characteristic curved magazine of the Bren. Once the necessary modification had been made, the gun went into production at the Royal Small Arms Factory at Enfield Lock in 1937. In subsequent years large numbers were made in Canada, including a quantity redesigned to the original 7.92mm chambering for supply to Nationalist China.

Without doubt, the Bren is one of the finest light machine-guns ever made. Gas-operated, its mechanical components are simple and easily understood; it can be stripped and assembled by a trained soldier in a very short time indeed. There are only a few possible stoppages, and the Bren built up an enviable reputation for accuracy and reliability during World War 2.

Gun, Machine, Bren, 0.303in Mark 1 (officially introduced in August 1938). This was a direct copy of the original design and was equipped with a rather luxurious drum-pattern rearsight. The

length; the butt was simplified; the cocking handle did not fold and certain lightening grooves in the original body design were omitted in the interests of faster production in wartime.

Gun, Machine, Bren, 0.303in Marks 3 and 4. The Mark 3 gun was introduced in July 1944 and so too was the Mark 4. The Mark 3 was similar to the Mark 1 but was generally lighter and had a shorter barrel. The Mark 4 was a similar conversion of the Mark 2.

Gun, Machine, Bren, 0.303in Mark 2/1. In 1948 the Mark 2/1 was introduced; the gun was the same as the Mark 2 but with a new cocking handle and slide assembly.

7.62mm Machine-guns, L4A1–L4A6. When the 7.62mm NATO cartridge was adopted by the British Army, the Bren L4 series was introduced. By and large this consists of conversions of later marks of Bren to the new cartridge, but there are a number of distinct models: the L4A1 was a conversion of Mark 3 by the fitting of a new barrel, flash eliminator, ejector assembly, a Canadian 7.92mm Bren extractor and a Canadian 7.92mm breechblock suitably modified; the body and magazine cover were altered to suit the new magazines of 29 or 30 rounds.

◁The Bren Mark 1, right side; this gun dates from 1939 (SIM).

◁The Bren Mark 3, a shortened and lightened version of the Mark 2. Note the leaf rearsight, which replaced the drum pattern of the Mark 1 on Marks 2 and 3 (SIM).

◁The Bren Mark 4, a conversion of the long Mark 2 to approximate to the Mark 3 (RSAF).

▲An example of the 7.62mm Bren L4A1, this gun being a converted 0.303in Mark 2 produced in 1959. The straight-sided box magazine is missing from this weapon (SIM).

▲The Mark 1 Besa tank machine-gun, based on the Czechoslovakian vz/53 (RSAF).

The L4A2 was the L4A1 with some minor design improvements. The L4A3 was a conversion of Mark 2 models by modification of the body and the fitting of a new barrel, butt slide and gas deflector. Obsolete for army use, it is still in service with the Royal Navy. The L4A4 was similar to the L4A2 except that the interior of the barrel was chromium-plated, a step which so extended the life of the barrel that the provision of a spare barrel was unnecessary. The L4A5 was never produced, the number being allotted to a development model, and the L4A6 was a conversion of the L4A1 by replacing the barrel with a chromium-lined one which obviated the need for a spare barrel.

GUN, MACHINE, BESA, 7.92mm, MARKS 1–3/3, c.1939–1965
United Kingdom
Birmingham Small Arms Company Limited, Redditch, Worcestershire
7.92mm SAA Ball

After purchasing the vz/26 design from Czechoslovakia, the British authorities were offered a tank machine-gun, the ZB vz/53, from the same source. This weapon was accepted in 7.92mm chambering and in view of the trouble which had arisen in converting the vz/26 design from the 7.92mm rimless round to a 0.303in rimmed round (after which it became the Bren Gun), it was felt preferable to retain the original calibre of the gun and place a quantity of ammunition under manufacture in England. This course was acceptable since the gun was intended for use in armoured vehicles and the logistic problem was not therefore of the proportions which would have arisen had the gun been in general service.

When modified to suit production techniques and placed in production by the Birmingham Small Arms Company, the gun became known at the Besa. It is gas-operated but it is unusual in having a recoiling barrel as well, the movement of which provides a system of recoil control known as the differential system. (This system, first used in 1906 on field artillery, is currently undergoing a revival under the new title 'soft recoil'.) The point of it is that the cartridge is inserted into the chamber while the weapon is recoiled and is fired while the barrel is still moving forward into battery; the resultant recoil force has first to arrest the forward motion of the barrel before causing it to recoil. This enforced change of direction absorbs a good deal of the recoil energy and reduces the stresses on the rest of the gun. Whether or not this system was responsible for it, the Besa was renowned in the British Army for the accuracy of its shooting.

Gun, Machine, Besa, 7.92mm, Mark 1. This was officially introduced in June 1940, although numbers were in use well before that date. It was declared obsoles-

cent on the day of its introduction.
Length: 43.50in (1105mm)
Weight unloaded: 47lb 0oz (21.46kg)
Barrel: 29.00in (736mm), 4 grooves, right-hand twist
Magazine: 225-round belt
Cyclic rate, low: 450-500rpm
Cyclic rate, high: 750-850rpm
Muzzle velocity: c.2700fps (823mps)

Gun, Machine, Besa, 7.92mm, Mark 2.
This variant was introduced on the same day as Mark 1. Both these guns had a selection device allowing two different rates of fire. With the accelerator set at 'H' (for high) the guns fired from 750 to 850 rounds per minute. Set at 'L' (for low) the rate was 450 to 550 rounds per minute. The idea was to have a low rate for routine covering fire, with a high rate in hand for repelling attacks. The differences between the Marks 1 and 2 are relatively minor. In the Mark 2, the accelerator is cranked to the rear instead of forward; the barrel sleeve is shorter; the flash guard has no vent holes, and there are minor changes in the body and cover to facilitate production. At 48lb (21.84kg), the Mark 2 weighs 1lb (0.46kg) more than the Mark 1.

Gun, Machine, 7.92mm, Besa, Marks 2*, 3 and 3*. In August 1941 the Marks 2*, 3 and 3* guns were introduced. The Mark 2* is a transitional model between the Mark 2 and the Mark 3. Some components are of simplified pattern, but all are interchangeable with Mark 2 guns; the Mark 3 is a simplified design, components of which are not interchangeable with earlier marks. The greatest change in the Mark 3 is that the rate-of-fire selector is omitted: only the high rate of fire—750rpm to 850rpm—is consequently available.

The Mark 3*, on the other hand, had the rate of fire fixed at the low level of 450rpm to 550rpm. Except for this, there is no difference between the two guns.

Gun, Machine, 7.92mm, Besa, Marks 3/2 and 3/3. The Besa design remained stationary until 1952 when the Mark 3/2 was introduced, which was simply a conversion of the Mark 3* gun to accept a new bracket and cover. Then in 1954 came the Mark 3/3, which differed from the Mark 3/2 in having a new pattern of barrel and sleeve and a new gas cylinder with larger gas vents. It was introduced in order to ensure that guns using belts of mixed ammunition would function satisfactorily. A number of existing Mark 3/2 guns were modified to Mark 3/3 pattern but, so far as is known, no new manufacture to this mark ever took place.

GUN, MACHINE, BESAL, 0.303in MARK 1; GUN, MACHINE, BESAL, 0.303in MARK 2, c.1940
United Kingdom
Birmingham Small Arms Company Limited, Birmingham
0.303in SAA Ball
During World War 2, the Bren gun was exclusively produced in the United Kingdom by the Royal Small Arms

Factory at Enfield Lock. In the early days of the war, it became patently obvious that one large air-raid on the plant would completely disrupt production for some time. BSA were consequently asked to prepare an alternative design capable of rapid and uncomplicated production by almost any engineering shop.

The resultant design was known as the Besal, although later rechristened the Faulkener in recognition of the gun's designer. The Besal was in many ways a simplified Bren designed with production limitations in mind; the body and gas cylinder are simple pressings, the trigger mechanism is basic in the extreme, and the piston and breechblock—devoid of any frills—are of square section. The block locks by two lugs which are forced by a ramp into recesses cut in the receiver, and the return spring is contained in the piston and retained by a removable pin pushed up from underneath. Cocking the Mark 2 was achieved by pulling the pistol grip to the rear. The gas plug was a finned cylinder offering four sizes of port, which could be changed by rotating the unit with a bullet nose. A handle projects from the left side of the barrel and is used as a handgrip when changing the barrel unit: it is of little value as a carrying handle as it does not rotate. The rearsight has two positions only, and the legs of the bipod are not adjustable for height, but the Besal is nevertheless an impressive gun, and on trial it shot well with few stoppages. Only a few pilot models were made, as Bren production at Enfield was never seriously impaired.

Length: 46.63in (1185mm)
Weight unloaded: 21lb 8oz (9.74kg)
Barrel: 22.00in (558mm), 4 grooves, right-hand twist
Magazine: 30-round detachable box (Bren)
Cyclic rate: 600rpm
Muzzle velocity: c.2450fps (745mps)

GUN, MACHINE, BESA, 15mm MARK 1, 1940
United Kingdom
Birmingham Small Arms Company Limited, Redditch, Worcestershire
15mm SAA Ball.
The Besa 15mm Mark 1, introduced in June 1940, was also of Czech design—a modification of the ZB vz/60. Basically, it was an enlargement of the 7.92mm weapon and, like it, was destined solely for use in armoured vehicles. It had however one additional feature in that it was possible to fire single shots from it. Only one mark was ever introduced, and the 15mm Besa never appears to have been very popular; in 1942 there was an abortive attempt to redesign the 15mm Besa to 20mm calibre to use Hispano-Suiza ammunition. It was declared obsolescent in 1944 and obsolete in 1949. The design's principal drawback was said to be its weight and size, but it is of interest to see that similar heavy machine-guns now form the armament of armoured personnel carriers of other

▷ The Besal prototype, an emergency design characterised by extreme simplicity. It was expected that this gun could be produced by machine-shops with the minimum amount of equipment.
▷ The finalised version of the Besal, an interesting gun of more conventional appearance than its prototype and looking a little like the Bren. It was a little ironic that the Besal—an emergency design—was the only BSA weapon to be accepted by the British Army for volume production, and that none were thereafter produced (SIM).
▷ The experimental Rolls-Royce heavy aircraft machine-gun, showing its clean lines to good advantage (RSAF).

countries and it has also been said that the 15mm Besa would have been well suited to such employment had it remained in service, although in British service this particular role has been taken over by the 30mm Rarden cannon.

Length: 80.70in (2050mm)
Weight unloaded: 125lb 8oz (57.70kg)
Barrel: 57.60in (1462mm), 8 grooves, right-hand twist
Magazine: 25-round belt
Cyclic rate: 450rpm
Muzzle velocity: c.2700fps (823mps)

GUN, MACHINE, ROLLS-ROYCE EXPERIMENTAL, 1941
United Kingdom
Rolls Royce Limited, Derby
0.50in Browning and 0.55in Boys
Although their design was never finally developed as a service weapon, the fact

that Rolls Royce once made the venture into the machine-gun field is felt to be of sufficient interest to warrant a mention here.

In 1941 Rolls Royce began to develop a gas-operated machine-gun for use in aircraft turrets; it was intended to fire the standard American 0.50in Browning cartridge. In order to reduce weight and size to a level suited to aircraft use, the barrel was some 5in (126mm) shorter than that of the Browning and the body and cover of the gun were to be made from RR50 aluminium alloy. As finally developed, the gun was recoil-operated and used a breech-locking system based on the Friberg - Kjellman - Degtyarev system with refinements by Rolls-Royce. As the barrel and breechblock recoiled, a pair of accelerator levers carried back a wedge-like 'balance piece' and retracted the striker. The withdrawal of this balance piece allowed the bolt-lock arms to fold in and unlock the breech, after which the accelerators threw the block back at high speed to strike an oil buffer at the rear of the body. At the same time, a feed claw withdrew the next round from the belt and this was guided down and back to rest on guide lips ready to be rammed into the chamber.

The barrel returned into battery under the power of its own return spring while the bolt was returned not by a spring but by the pressure of the oil in the buffer, collecting the fresh round en route and loading it. As the mechanism went forward, the balance piece opened out the breech locks and then carried the firing pin on to the cap to fire the round.

In March 1941 the gun was delivered for trial and taken to the Proof and Experimental Establishment, Pendine, to be fired. Owing to the short barrel, a long flash-hider had to be used—which rather detracted from the original intentions— and the trial was bedevilled by minor stoppages, culminating in the breaking of the extractors. A month later, Rolls Royce decided to redesign the gun around the high-velocity belted 0.55in round from the Boys anti-tank rifle, the result of which would have produced a very formidable weapon. The Ordnance Board agreed that the idea showed promise and furnished 2000 rounds for use in preliminary trials, but it would seem that shortly after this Rolls Royce decided that they had enough to occupy their minds in the matter of making aeroplane engines, and in 1942 came notification that the development had been dropped.

Length:
Weight unloaded: 49lb 0oz (22.34kg)
Barrel: 40.00in (E016mm), 4 grooves, right-hand twist
Magazine: 250-round belt
Cyclic rate: 1000rpm
Muzzle velocity: c.2340fps (712mps)

GUN, MACHINE, HEFAH V 0.303in MARK 1 (1942)
United Kingdom
Ductile Steel Company, Short Heath, Staffordshire (originally); Hefah and Company, Wednesfield, Staffordshire (finally)
0.303in SAA Ball
The Hefah machine-gun was developed as a private venture by the Ductile Steel Company in 1940 and was first submitted for trial in June of the same year. It was basically a modified Lewis action, simplified to facilitate rapid manufacture. The breechblock used only one locking lug, a slightly altered Bren magazine was fitted beneath the gun, and the return spring was contained within a tube projecting from the rear of the receiver. On trial it was noted that this return spring housing tended to bruise the cheek of the firer, and with the gun resting on bipod and butt there was but a bare half-inch clearance beneath the magazine.

Although these small faults weighed

against it when considered for use as an infantry squad weapon, the Director of Naval Ordnance—who was desperate for anti-aircraft machine-guns for small coastal vessels—felt that the simple design was of value in view of the production capacity available at that time, and he recommended its adoption. The Director General of Munitions Production, however, suspended all work on the gun for some months because there was no factory available to make and rifle the barrels.

Capacity was eventually found and the Hefah, by this time the product of the Hefah Company of Wednesfield, went into production for the Royal Navy, formally approved for service as the 'Gun, Machine, Hefah V, 0.303in Mark 1' in May 1942.

The gun's subsequent employment is not entirely clear, although it seems that only a limited number were made; it was declared obsolete in November 1944.

GENERAL PURPOSE MACHINE-GUN, 7.62mm, L7 SERIES
United Kingdom
Royal Small Arms Factory, Enfield Lock
7.62mm NATO
The L7 series of machine-guns is basically Fabrique Nationale's MAG pattern (see BELGIUM) with many minor modifications made at the hands of the Royal Small Arms Factory to suit production to British methods; the operation, however, remains unchanged—a gas-operated tipping-bolt design. Amongst the British variants are the following:
General Purpose Machine-gun, 7.62mm, L7A1 (GPMG L7A1). This is the basic model, with a pistol grip, a butt and a stamped-steel bipod; the action is fed from the right side by means of a disintegrating-link metallic belt, usually containing 250 rounds of ammunition.
General Purpose Machine-gun, 7.62mm, L7A2. The L7A2 differs from its predecessor only in the provision of mounting points for a box containing a 50-round belt, and the provision of double feed pawls in the mechanism.
Tank Machine-gun, 7.62mm, L8A1. Intended for use in the Chieftain tank, this weapon is fitted with a bore evacuator to keep the tank's interior free of fumes. It is also fitted with a variable-aperture gas regulator and provision for a firing solenoid is also made.
General Purpose Machine-gun, 7.62mm, L19A1. The L19 is a version of the L7 fitted with a heavier barrel to reduce the number of changes of barrel necessary when the gun is used for prolonged firing. It is not an issue weapon.
General Purpose Machine-gun, 7.62mm, L20A1. The L20 is intended for pod-mounting on the army's helicopters and aircraft; fitted with an L8 gas regulator and an L7 barrel (which lacks the bore evacuator) the gun is capable of either left or right side feed.
Tank Machine-gun, 7.62mm, L37A1. This weapon is a version of the basic

▷A specimen of the Hefah V Mark 1. Despite the position of the magazine, and the apparent position of the pistol grip, the weapon is not upside-down. They were generally mounted in pairs on a naval anti-aircraft mount, in which a separate trigger unit was used; this conveyed the movement to the guns' triggers by a linkage (RSAF).
▷The Enfield-designed X11E2 machine-gun, an unsuccessful competitor to the Belgian MAG which in due course became the L7A1.
▷The BSA-designed X16E4 machine-gun, another competitor to the MAG. It was based on the well-tried Bren and was belt-fed (RSAF).
▷The L7A1, a modified version of the MAG manufactured by Fabrique Nationale (SIM).

design intended for use in tanks other than the Chieftain and sundry other armoured vehicles. It is basically an L8 gun with an L7 barrel, and can be sometimes found with a folding pistol grip unit which—together with the bipod, butt and trigger assembly carried in the vehicles—enables the L37 to be dismounted in an emergency to do duty as a standard ground gun.
Data—see Belgian MAG

US COLT-BROWNING MACHINE-GUNS, 1895–1917
United States of America
Colt's Patent Firearms Manufacturing Company, Hartford, Connecticut
Caliber 0.30 US Service, and others
The original Colt machine-gun of 1895 was developed by John Browning from an action based on a rifle he had produced while experimenting to determine whether or not the muzzle blast of a weapon could be put to some practical use. The unique feature of this gun was a swinging arm beneath the barrel. Gas was tapped off at a point just before the muzzle to drive the end of this arm down and back through an arc of about 170°. The arm was connected to a linkage which opened the breech, extracted the spent case and loaded the new one into the chamber. The action of the arm led to the gun being called the 'potato digger' and, of course, prevented it from being used too close to the ground without first digging a pit. However odd this action may appear there is no doubt that, owing to the mechanical linkage, it produced a very progressive and gentle movement of the bolt which gave particularly effective and clean extraction and kept the rate of fire down to a practical value.

Numbers of these guns were purchased by the United States Navy in the 1890s, in 6mm (0.236in) calibre, and even larger numbers were sold by Colt to various other countries in various national calibres. The gun first saw action with the United States Marine Corps at Guantanamo Bay, Cuba, in 1898. It was later used by the United States Army in both .30–40 and .30 M1906, but was largely relegated to use as a training weapon. Very few were used in action during World War 1. It had, of course, been obsolete for many years, but it was taken as the starting point for improvements which later led to the Marlin machine-gun. The gun was extensively used in Spain (7mm calibre) and Italy (6.5mm modello 95).

US TANK MACHINE-GUN, CALIBER .30 M1918 ('MARLIN')
United States of America
Marlin-Rockwell Corporation, New Haven, Connecticut
.30 M1906
The Marlin gun was a variation of the original Colt gas-operated light gun of 1895 (the well known 'potato digger'). The Marlin-Rockwell Company were given a contract in World War 1 to make the Colt design, and they produced the modification for aircraft use. The pendant lever below the barrel was replaced by a piston, and several other alterations were also incorporated. The Marlin version was much lighter than the Colt and it was undoubtedly a better gun. As an aircraft gun (M1916 and M1917) it remained in use with the United States Air Corps throughout World War 1 and for several years afterwards. Altogether 38,000 aircraft guns and 1,470 tank machine-guns were made, the latter differing slightly from the aircraft gun. There was also a projected version for infantry use as a light machine-gun but this was not pursued. In 1941, when Britain was desperately short of all types of weapons, several thousand Marlins were supplied by the United States, all of them dating from World War 1 and all heavily protected in preservative grease. These guns were activated in a very short time and use for anti-aircraft defence on small merchant ships. In this role, the Marlin was valuable though inconspicuous. It was not used to any extent elsewhere.
Length: 40.00in (1016mm)
Weight unloaded: 22lb 8oz (10.10kg)
Barrel: 28.00in (711mm), 4 grooves, right-hand twist
Magazine: 250-round cloth belt
Cyclic rate: 600rpm
Muzzle velocity: c.2800fps (853mps)

BROWNING MACHINE-GUNS, 1917–1971
United States of America
Various manufacturers
.30 M1906; .50
After experimenting with gas-operation, John Browning came to the conclusion that recoil offered the greater possibilities and as early as 1900, therefore, he began to take out patents which covered the operating system later developed in his machine-guns.

The Browning guns utilised the recoil force of the expanding powder gases to push the barrel and the bolt to the rear; after a short recoil, the bolt is unlocked and the barrel is halted. An accelerator then throws the bolt to the rear and the movement of the bolt, by cam surfaces, operates the belt-feed mechanism. The bolt is then returned by the recoil spring until it once again joins the barrel, when the parts are once again locked together and return to battery.

Although the design was fully developed by c.1910, it was not until America's 1917 entry into World War 1 that Browning was able to interest the authorities in his design. The machine-gun was, however, very promptly accepted as the Model 1917.
US Machine-gun, Caliber .30, M1917.
In appearance, the M1917 is similar to the Maxim and Vickers patterns with a water jacket of conventional form, although the pistol grip at the rear of the breech readily distinguishes the Browning design. Slightly more than 68,000 of the

▷ The components of the light and heavy barrel versions of the FN MAG tested by the British.
▷ The Browning machine-gun of 1917, shown mounted on its tripod and with an ammunition box (RSAF).

HEAVY

LIGHT

◁◁ Two views of the British Browning aircraft gun (this is the Mark 2*), some examples of which are still used as the L3 series (RSAF).
◁ The American M1919A6 light machine-gun (RSAF).
◁ Fabrique Nationale's version of the water-cooled 0.30in Browning (FN).

M1917 were manufactured before the close of World War 1 by the Remington Arms-Union Metallic Cartridge Company, Colt's Patent Firearms Manufacturing Company, and the New England Westinghouse Company. As a result of the limited combat experience made possible, the M1917 underwent several small modifications in the early 1920s and, in 1936, the opportunity was taken of revising the basic design with the consequent appearance of the M1917A1.

US Machine-gun, Caliber .30, M1917A1, introduced in 1936. The M1917A1 is virtually identical to the M1917 from which it was modified; alterations were made to the feed unit, the sights were regraduated, and the tripod was altered. Service weapons were reworked by Rock Island Arsenal in 1936–7 and further small modifications were made to them in the period 1942–4 as a result of combat experience.

Length: 38.50in (978mm)
Weight unloaded: 32lb 10oz (14.98kg) (without water)
Barrel: 24.00in (610mm), 4 grooves, right-hand twist
Magazine: 250-round fabric belt
Cyclic rate: 500rpm
Muzzle velocity: c.2800fps (853mps)

US Machine-guns, Caliber .30, M1918 and M1918M1. The M1917 was a water-cooled gun, and consequently it was ill-suited to airborne use. Modified patterns were therefore designed by discarding the water jacket in favour of light pierced casings, and by lightening components where at all possible. The M1918 designs led to the introduction of the M1919.

US Machine-gun, Caliber .30, M1919. Intended to be the definitive Browning-type tank gun of World War 1 (but appearing too late), it was fitted with a heavier barrel than that of the M1917 ground pattern. The water jacket was discarded and a slim casing cut with long slots was adopted instead.

US Machine-gun, Caliber .30, M1919A1. A variant of the M1919 intended to be mounted in the Mark VIII tank, suitable modifications were made to the mounting

US Machine-gun, Caliber .30, M1919A2. A version of the M1919 intended for the use of mounted cavalry, the M1919A2 was fitted with an especially-small tripod and could be packed on to a special saddle for transportation.

US Machine-gun, Caliber .30, M1919A3. A general-purpose derivative of the basic M1919, it served as a prototype for the M1919A4.

US Machine-gun, Caliber .30, M1919A4. This gun was issued in fixed and flexible forms; the fixed gun was intended to be used in tank and multiple anti-aircraft gun installations, and the flexible pattern was intended for use in other combat vehicles or—mounted on a tripod—for infantry use.

Length: 41.00in (1041mm)
Weight unloaded: 31lb 0oz (14.26kg)
Barrel: 24.00in (610mm), 4 grooves, right-hand twist

Magazine: 250-round fabric belt
Cyclic rate: 500rpm
Muzzle velocity: c.2800fps (853mps)

US Machine-gun, Caliber .30, M1919A4E1. A post-World War 2 version of the M1919A4, it has the slide retracting mechanism of the M1919A5.

US Machine-gun, Caliber .30, M1919A5. This was a special weapon intended to be mounted in the Light Tank M3: a special bolt-retracting slide was fitted.

US Machine-gun, Caliber .30, M1919A6. Adopted in April 1943, the M1919A6 is essentially similar to the M1919A4 with the addition of a shoulder-stock, a bipod, a carrying handle, a lighter barrel and a flash suppressor.

Length: 53.00in (1346mm)
Weight unloaded: 32lb 8oz (14.94kg)
Barrel: 24.00in (610mm), 4 grooves, right-hand twist
Magazine: 250-round fabric belt
Cyclic rate: 500rpm
Muzzle velocity: c.2800fps (853mps)

US Machine-gun, Caliber .30, M37. A tank version of the basic M1919 series, the feed mechanism was changed to permit either left or right-hand feed. An ejection chute was also added for the metallic-link belt.

US Machine-gun, Caliber .30, M2. This variety was designed specifically as an aircraft weapon; the principal differences between the M2 and the earlier M1918 lie in the provision of a special retracting mechanism. A solenoid sear-release mechanism was supplied for fixed aircraft guns, and spade grips could be fitted to the flexible guns.

Length: 39.90in (1014mm)
Weight unloaded: 23lb 0oz (10.48kg)
Barrel: 23.90in (608mm), 4 grooves, right-hand twist
Magazine: 250-round metallic link belt
Cyclic rate: 1200rpm
Muzzle velocity: c.2800 fps (853mps)

US Machine-gun, Caliber 7.62mm NATO, Mark 21 Model 0. This strangely-named gun is a conversion of the M1919A4 intended for the United States Navy. Apart from the rechambering of the gun with the attendant barrel and feed modifications, it is a standard M1919A4.

US Machine-guns, Caliber .50, M1921, M1921A1, M2, M2HB. All the foregoing weapons were of 0.30in or 7.62mm calibre but, during the latter days of World War 1, a request was made for a weapon comparable in power to the French 11mm Hotchkiss machine-gun and capable of attacking observation balloons and aircraft. After some experimentation, a Browning-system machine-gun was developed in 0.50in and eventually introduced to the service as the 'US Machine-gun, Caliber .50, M1921', a modified form of which later appeared as the M1921A1. During the 1930s, the M2 version appeared in which provision was made to enable the water to constantly circulate through the water jacket, which greatly helped dissipate the heat produced during long periods of sustained fire.

After this gun had been developed, an air-cooled version—which was still called the M2—also appeared, having been developed for aircraft use. Like the 0.30in M2, this also came in fixed and flexible guise. The cooling of the 0.50in M2 barrel was soon overtaxed by the power of the cartridge, and no more than a 75-round burst could be fired without stopping to allow the barrel to cool. Such a restriction was unacceptable for ground use and so the M2HB ('Heavy Barrel') was developed; this was supplied with a much thicker barrel which permitted faster dissipation of heat (and, of course, was capable of absorbing proportionately more heat) and therefore allowed firing over a long period without the danger of overheating the barrel. This was again made available in fixed, flexible and anti-aircraft form: the fixed gun was mounted in the bows of the Heavy Tank M6 and in multiple-gun anti-aircraft units, while the flexible gun was used on combat vehicles' turret tops or as a heavy ground-support gun.

(data: M2HB)
Length: 65.10in (1643mm)
Weight unloaded: 84lb 0oz (38.22kg)
Barrel: 45.00in (1143mm), 8 grooves, right-hand twist
Magazine: 110-round metallic link belt
Cyclic rate: 500rpm
Muzzle velocity: c.2950fps (898mps)

(data: M2 air-cooled)
Length: 57.00in (1447mm)
Weight unloaded: 65lb 2oz (29.92kg)
Barrel: 36.00in (914mm), 8 grooves, right-hand twist
Magazine: 110-round metallic link belt
Cyclic rate: 800rpm
Muzzle velocity: c.2900fps (884mps)

(data: M2 water-cooled)
Length: 66.00in (1666mm)
Weight unloaded: 100lb 0oz (45.60kg) (without water)
Barrel: 45.00in (1143mm), 8 grooves, right-hand twist
Magazine: 110-round metallic link belt
Cyclic rate: 600rpm
Muzzle velocity: c.2900fps (884mps)

During and after World War 2, several attempts were made to improve upon the basic Browning designs: none was particularly successful, and the Browning-designed machine-guns continue to serve all over the world.

JOHNSON LIGHT MACHINE-GUNS MODEL 1941 and 1944
United States of America
Cranston Arms Company, Providence, Rhode Island
Cartridge, .30 M1906

The Johnson light machine-gun was developed between 1936 and 1938 from the rifle of the same designer. The United States Marine Corps tried it without adoption, and the only sizeable order the company ever received came from the Dutch armies in the Netherlands East Indies. Before this could be entirely fulfilled, the Japanese invaded and the orders ceased, although use by the United States Army Rangers and Special Services ensured that a small continuous output emanated from the factory

The Johnson was one of the few light machine-guns to operate on recoil principles and, although an elegant design manufactured to a high standard, it was too flimsy and too prone to jamming for prolonged field use. An interesting milestone in the history of arms designs, it perhaps deserved a better fate, but the gun appeared at a time when the army had made up its mind regarding light machine-gun policy and had settled upon the Browning Automatic Rifle and the machine-gun M1919A4. The Johnson possessed a number of unusual features, including firing from an open bolt in an automatic mode and from a closed bolt as a single shot. The box magazine was on the left side of the gun, but it was also possible to reload the magazine through the right side without replacing the box; standard five-round chargers or single rounds could be utilised, which was Melvin Johnson's method of overcoming the authorities' demands for a belt-fed gun. The cyclic rate could be

◁The Belgian Browning aircraft gun, manufactured at Herstal by Fabrique Nationale (FN).
◁Fabrique Nationale's version of the water-cooled 0.50in Browning heavy gun, shown here on its tripod (FN).
◁◁◁Three views of the US M2 0.50in calibre aircraft machine-gun. The gun at the bottom is fitted with a cable retraction device fitted to the cocking mechanism (authors' collection).
▼The Johnson light machine-gun of 1941 (RSAF).

altered by changing the tension in the buffer spring and was theoretically variable between 300 and 900 rounds per minute.

Two basic models were manufactured by the Cranston Arms Company, the M1941 and the M1944. The earlier pattern was provided with a bipod and a wooden butt, whereas the 1944 pattern was marketed with a light tubular monopod and a 'butt' made from two parallel pieces of tubing finished by a butt-plate.

Length: 42.00in (1066mm)
Weight unloaded: 14lb 5oz (6.57kg)
Barrel: 22.00in (558mm), 4 grooves, right-hand twist
Magazine: 20-round detachable box, with a further 5 in the action
Cyclic rate: 300-900rpm
Muzzle velocity: c.2800fps (853mps)

US MACHINE-GUN, CALIBER 7.62mm NATO, M60 AND M60E1
United States of America
Bridge Tool & Die Manufacturing Company, Philadelphia, and Inland Manufacturing Division of General Motors, Dayton, Ohio
7.62mm NATO

The M60, with its modified successor the M60E1, is the standard squad general purpose machine-gun in the United States Army. It was designed during the last years of the 1950s and has been in service since the early 1960s. The M60 is interesting in that it uses the feed system of the German MG42 and the bolt and locking systems the FG42, an impressive example of imitation being the sincerest form of flattery. Much expense and effort went into producing the gun

▲▲Two views of the experimental T161E3 machine-gun, later adopted by the US Army as the M60 (authors' collection).

which in its original form barely justified the work. Despite its illustrious forebears the original M60 had some serious drawbacks, the most noticeable of which was in the barrel change. Each barrel had its own gas cylinder and bipod attachment to it—but no handle. It was therefore not only an expensive item but also unnecessarily heavy and dangerous to handle when hot. An asbestos glove formed part of the gun's equipment.

The more recent M60E1 has a simple barrel with the gas cylinder and bipod fixed to the gun, and it also has a handle for barrel changing. There are other less important changes which bring the M60E1 more into line with current practice and improved reliability. A feature of both models has been the very good stellite lining to the barrels which prolongs their lives beyond that normally experienced with unprotected steel, and both models have a constant-energy gas system to work the piston.

Length: 43.75in (1100mm)
Weight unloaded: 23lb 0oz (10.40kg)
Barrel: 25.50in (647mm), 4 grooves, right-hand twist
Magazine: ∞-round metallic link belt
Cyclic rate: 600rpm
Muzzle velocity: c.2800fps (853mps)

▼A partially-dismantled view of the T161E3. This clearly shows the bipod attached to the barrel, one of the gun's objectionable features.

STONER LIGHT MACHINE-GUN M63A1
United States of America
Cadillac Gage Company, Detroit, Michigan
5.56mm × 45mm (0.223in)

The M63A1 light machine-gun is one of the latest weapons in the Stoner small-arms system. When assembled into the machine-gun form, the weapon fires from an open bolt and is only capable of automatic fire. The method of operation is by a conventional gas system, with the piston and gas port on the underside of the barrel. The gun can be fed either from a box magazine or from a belt. If the magazine is used, it feeds vertically downwards in the same way as the Bren or ZB vz/26. For belt feeding, a different receiver cover has to be fitted in order to incorporate the feed pawls and stops. It will be noticed that the box is clipped under the centre of the receiver, with the feed coming up under a cover. There are several extras offered with this gun, including different varieties of ammunition box and methods of attachment. The Stoner is a most attractive system with much to recommend it, but it has yet to sell in large numbers although it has been undergoing evaluation by the United States Marine Corps in Vietnam.

Length: 40.24in (1029mm)
Weight unloaded: 12lb 8oz (5.65kg)
Barrel: 21.69in (551mm); 4 grooves, right-hand twist
Magazine: 30-round box, or belt
Cyclic rate: 700rpm
Muzzle velocity: c.3250fps (990mps)

US MACHINE-GUN M73
United States of America
manufacturer unknown
7.62mm NATO

The M73 machine-gun was designed as a tank weapon, with the specific aim of producing a gun with short inboard length and one in which all the necessary immediate actions and maintenance, including barrel changes could be done from inside the vehicle. Another important design consideration was the necessity to avoid powder fumes inside the turret. The design is attributed to Russell Robinson, an Australian who had worked with the British in the post-war years, and uses a horizontal sliding breechblock instead of the more usual axially-moving block; it is this feature which gives the desired shortness of body. Other advantages in tank use accrue from the fact that the top cover is side-hinged and thus demands less headroom when opened, and the entire body section can be swung to one side to allow the barrel to be withdrawn from its jacket from inside the tank.

Length: 34.75in (883mm)
Weight unloaded: 28lb 0oz (12.70kg)
Barrel: 22.00in (558mm)
Magazine: ∞-round disintegrating belt
Cyclic rate: 500rpm
Muzzle velocity: c.2800fps (853mps)

PUSKO MITRAJEZ MODEL 65A,
PUSKO MITRAJEZ 65B
Yugoslavia
Crvena Zastava, Kragujevač
7.62mm M43 Soviet Service

The M65A and M65B are the Yugoslavs' standard light machine-gun designs, the equivalents of the Soviet RPD and RPK patterns. Both are designed to use as many of the parts as practical of the Yugoslav M64 assault rifles, which ensures uncomplicated production.

Both the M65A and the M65B are fitted with light bipods, and heavier barrels than the assault rifles, although the utility of this is questionable as the barrels are apparently non-interchangeable. This, of course, means that sustained fire from these weapons is impossible; and the 30-round box magazine imposes another shortcoming. The Yugoslavs are obviously prepared to discount these drawbacks in order to share as many parts as possible with their rifle types.

Length: 43.11in (1095mm) including
*　flash-suppressor*
Weight unloaded: 12lb 2oz (5.50kg)
Barrel: 18.50in (470mm), 4 grooves,
*　right-hand twist*
Magazine: 30-round box
Cyclic rate: c.600rpm
Muzzle velocity: c.2445fps (745mps)

◁An example of the Stoner M63A1 light machine-gun with its plastic ammunition box attached under the receiver (NWM).
◁The Stoner M63A1 with the feed cover hinged forward and the ammunition belt exposed (NWM).
◁◁Two interesting threequarter views of the Stoner M63A1 (both NWM).
▼The Yugoslavian M65A (authors' collection).

Anti-tank rifles

The career of the anti-tank rifle lasted a mere three decades from the first tanks of World War 1 to the close of World War 2.

The advent of the tank on the Western Front caused the German army to seek a weapon powerful enough to harm the vehicle, yet light enough to be man-portable; a field-gun would, of course, destroy any of the early tanks by a direct hit but they were nevertheless immune to the impact of small-calibre rifle and machine-gun bullets. The answer was the T-Gewehr of 1918, an enlarged bolt-action rifle firing a projectile of hardened steel at a velocity in the region of 3,000fps.

The interwar years saw little development of the big Mauser-designed rifle, although some nations made attempts at adding box magazines to the basic pattern. Efforts were aimed more at improving the ammunition and one notable advance was the development of tungsten-cored bullets, which greatly improved penetrative performances. Another idea that showed promise was the coned or 'squeeze' bore theory, developed in Germany by Gerlich and in Czechoslovakia by Janaček. The former advocated achieving the desired velocities by tapering the bore in its entirety—a difficult and expensive piece of machining—while the Czech designer's work was aimed at providing a short tapered-bore adaptor which could be fixed to the muzzle of an otherwise normal barrel.

Results were spectacular in the extreme and velocities in excess of 5,000fps were obtained, but the principal drawback, of course, was the limited life of the barrel or adaptor.

The thickness of tank armour rapidly outstripped the efforts of the designers to produce a tank-killer light enough to be operated by one man yet still fire conventional fixed-case ammunition, and so the military turned to handheld rocket projectors, recoilless guns and similar devices: the anti-tank rifles, cumbersome and ineffective, were discarded.

'TANK' – GEWEHR MODELL 1918 ('T–Gew')
Germany
Waffenfabrik Mauser AG, Oberndorf-am-Neckar
13mm anti-tank rifle

The first anti-tank rifle ever developed was produced in 1918 by Mauser; it was little more than an enlarged Mauser rifle action fitted to a long barrel with a heavy butt and furniture. Supported on a light bipod, it was a one-man weapon firing a 13mm jacketed bullet with an armour-piercing steel core. While the Allied tanks of the time were immune to rifle bullets, they were not proof against such a heavy missile, delivered—thanks to a powerful cartridge and long barrel—at an extremely high velocity. The Mauser of 1918 set the pattern for a number of similar weapons.

Length: 66.13in (1680mm)
Weight unloaded: 39lb 0oz (17.69kg)
Barrel: 38.69in (983mm), 4 grooves, right-hand twist
Magazine: None, single-shot
Muzzle velocity: c.3000fps (913mps)
Armour penetration: 25mm/200m/0°

PANZERBUCHSE MODELL 38 (PzB38)
Germany
Rheinmetall-Borsig AG, Düsseldorf (?)
7.92mm/13mm anti-tank rifle

The PzB38 was a much improved weapon compared with the Mauser of 1918, gaining greater velocity and penetrative effect by combining a 7.92mm bullet of new construction with a necked-down cartridge case based on the 1918 Mauser design. The bullet contained a core of armour-piercing steel, together with a capsule of lachrymatory gas which (or so it was hoped) would contaminate the air inside the tank and either disrupt the crew's effectiveness or actually drive them from the vehicle. It was entirely useless in this respect; the bullet had a satisfactory penetrative capability but none of the victims ever complained of sneezing, and the lachrymatory capsule was not discovered until captured ammunition was examined.

The PzB38 was a single-shot rifle making use of a vertical sliding-wedge breechblock — almost a scaled-down artillery piece in its operation. On firing, the barrel recoiled in the stock and on return operated a cam system to open the breechblock and eject the spent case, the block then remaining open for reloading. Inserting a fresh round caused the block to close.

During the Polish campaign of 1939 the Germans captured numbers of the Polish wz/35 anti-tank rifle and stocks of its ammunition. This was also of 7.92mm calibre and the bullet carried a tungsten carbide core of much better penetrative power than the original German model; the Polish design was quickly copied.

Length: 51.00in (1295mm)
Weight unloaded: 35lb 0oz (15.88kg)
Barrel: 43.00in (1092mm), 4 grooves,
*   right-hand twist*
Magazine: None, single-shot
Muzzle velocity: c.3975fps (1210mps)
Armour penetration: 30mm/100m/60°

▲The Mauser T-Gewehr of 1918 (RSAF).
▲The Panzerbüchse 38 (RSAF).
▲▲The Panzerbüchse 39 (RSAF).

▲The Granatbüchse 39 (RSAF).
▲The Polish wz/35 'Marosczek' rifle
(RSAF).

PANZERBUCHSE MODELL 39 (PzB39), GRANATBUCHSE MODELL 39 (GrB39)

Germany
Rheinmetall-Borsig AG, Düsseldorf, and —amongst others—Steyr-Daimler-Puch AG
7.92mm/13mm anti-tank

While the PzB38 was a satisfactory weapon, it was felt to be a little too expensive to manufacture and a slightly simplified version replaced it. While of the same general appearance, the mechanism was changed by discarding the recoiling barrel and semi-automatic breech and instead operating the vertical breechblock by the pistol grip, which slid along the receiver. Some small modifications were also made in the interest of simplifying manufacture.

Length: 62.25in (1581mm)
Weight unloaded: 27lb 4oz (12.43kg)
Barrel: 42.75in (1086mm), 4 grooves, right-hand twist
Magazine: None, single-shot
Muzzle velocity: c.4150fps (1265mps)
Armour penetration: 30mm/100m/60°

As the tank gained the ascendancy, and armour improved, so these weapons were withdrawn. Numbers of them were converted into grenade launchers by cutting down the barrel and adding a discharger cup (Schiessbecker). The modified guns were known as the *Granatbüchse Modell 39*, or GrB39.

KARABIN PRZECIWPANCERNY WZ/35 ('MAROSCZEK')

Poland
State manufacture
7.92mm special chambering

Towards the end of 1935 the Polish Army was issued with an anti-tank rifle of conventional bolt-action pattern, generally based on the 1918 Mauser pattern but stripped of every unnecessary ounce to provide the lightest weapon of the class ever made. The tungsten-cored bullet was fired from an over-sized case, and it has been claimed that it was this which led the Germans and Russians to develop similar cored bullets; it was certainly responsible for a British development in which a 0.303in cored bullet was married to a necked-down 0.55in Boys cartridge case for a modified Boys anti-tank rifle.

Loaded from five-round clips, and with a muzzle brake to cut down the recoil force, it was ahead of its contemporaries for ease of handling and, owing to the cored bullet, had a slight supremacy of penetrating power. Unfortunately such virtue had to be paid for somehow—and the price in this case was a barrel life of but 200 rounds, after which the muzzle velocity had dropped to 3775fps (1150 mps) and penetration began to fall off rapidly.

Length: 70.00in (1780mm)
Weight unloaded: 19lb 8oz (8.85kg)
Barrel: 47.25in (1200mm), 4 grooves, right-hand twist
Magazine: 10-round detachable box
Muzzle velocity: c.4198fps (1280mps)
Penetration: 20mm/300m/0°

In 1939 work began on a coned bore weapon on the Gerlich principle, using a tungsten core surrounded by a soft lead jacket and cupro-nickel envelope, formed with a raised band around the centre. The breech calibre was 11.00mm and the emergent calibre at the muzzle 7.92mm, so that the squeeze action of the bore deformed the raised portion of the bullet and reduced the diameter. This gave a velocity of nearly 5000fps (1524mps) and almost doubled the penetrative performance. When Poland was overrun, the rifle and drawings were smuggled to France where development was continued. At the time of the French collapse in 1940, the weapon was undergoing its final tests at Versailles and was scheduled to have gone into production and issue later in 1940. In the confusion following the German advance, the rifle was lost;

▲ The Boys Mark 1 (RSAF).
▲ The PTRD of 1941 (RSAF).

neither it nor the drawings have since been seen, and no specimen is now known to exist.

RIFLES, ANTI-TANK, 0.55 INCH BOYS MARK 1 and MARK 2
United Kingdom
Royal Small Arms Factory, Enfield Lock
0.55in SAA Boys

This weapon was developed in the mid-1930s by the British Small Arms Committee and one of the principal designers was Captain Boys. The gun was originally code-named 'Stanchion' but Boys died after development had been completed while the weapon was being prepared for manufacture; as a mark of respect the Small Arms Committee decided that the weapon should be named after him.

The Boys Rifle was an enlarged bolt-action weapon feeding from a top-mounted magazine and equipped with a muzzle brake and a monopod firing support. The barrel was permitted to recoil in the stock and the butt was heavily padded—both measures to reduce the extraordinary recoil forces.

The bullet was steel-cored and was placed in a belted cartridge case, one of the few instances where this case-type has seen military use. The design was originally intended for high-powered sporting rifles, and the belt gave the base immense strength to resist high internal pressure. In 1940 a tungsten-cored bullet in a plastic/aluminium body was approved and

issued, but shortly afterwards the Boys was withdrawn from service and replaced by the PIAT.

In 1942 the gun had a brief return to popularity when a short-barrel Mark 2 version was developed for use by airborne troops, but the requirement was dropped and the weapon was never adopted. Another attempt to revive it was the 1942 development of a taper-bore version; this was successful in trials as far as its penetrative performance went, but it was a singularly unpleasant weapon to fire (so, too, was the airborne model) and it was not accepted for service.

Length: 63.50in (1614mm)
Weight unloaded: 36lb 0oz (16.56kg)
Barrel: 36.00in (915mm), 7 grooves, right-hand twist
Magazine: 5-round detachable box
Muzzle velocity: c.3250fps (990mps)
Armour penetration: 21mm/300m/0°

PROTIVOTANKOVYI RUZHE DEGTYAREVA OBRAZETS
1941G ('Degtyarev anti-tank gun model 1941') (PTRD41)
Union of Soviet Socialist Republics
State manufacture
14.5mm

This rifle, which appeared in 1941, fired a 14.5mm bullet (slightly larger than the British 0.55in) from a massive cartridge case, probably the heaviest 'smallarms' round in regular service, which when redundant in its anti-tank role became a

▲The action of the PTRS, a gas-operated autoloader using a five-round clip — which could only be loaded into the gun one way (RSAF).
▲The PTRS of 1941 (RSAF).

heavy machine-gun round.

The rifle itself—while it appeared to be simple—was in fact quite an ingenious design and probably owed something to the German PzB38. The barrel was allowed to recoil in the stock and during this movement the bolt rode on a cam which rotated and unlocked it. At the end of the recoil stroke, the bolt was held and the barrel moved back into battery, moving away from the bolt to open the breech and eject the spent case. A fresh round was then inserted and the bolt was manually closed: in some respects this could be described as a 'long recoil' system.

The bullet was originally a steel-cored streamlined armour-piercing type but this was later superseded by a non-streamlined tungsten-cored armour-piercing-incendiary pattern.
Length: 79.00in (1966mm)
Weight unloaded: 38lb 0oz (17.44kg)
Barrel: 48.30in (1227mm), 8 grooves, right-hand twist
Magazine: None, single-shot
Muzzle velocity: c.3320fps (1010mps)
Armour penetration: 25mm/500m/0°

PROTIVOTANKOVYI RUZHE SIMONOVA OBRAZETS 1941G (PTRS41)
Union of Soviet Socialist Republics
State manufacture
14.5mm
This design was a contemporary of the

PTRD, and it fired the same ammunition although of a more complex self-loading design. A gas piston acted on a bolt carrier to open the bolt, eject, and reload in the usual fashion, and the gas regulator could be adjusted to give sufficient force to overcome dirt or freezing conditions. A clip-loaded magazine was fitted.

In spite of its theoretical superiority the PTRS was less robust, much heavier and considerably longer than the PTRD and fewer of the more advanced model were issued. Both rifles remained in Soviet service until the end of World War 2 (long after they had been superseded in other nations) probably because no suitable replacement was forthcoming.
Length: 84.00in (2006mm)
Weight unloaded: 46lb 0oz (20.96kg)
Barrel: 48.00in (1216mm), 8 grooves, right-hand twist
Magazine: 5-round clip-loaded box
Muzzle velocity: c.3320fps (1010mps)
Armour penetration: 25mm/500m/0°

The indices are organised on a code system. The entry following the letter **E** refers to the pages on which a major reference to the designer or the manufacturer can be found. A bracketed reference after the **E** indicates a minor entry. The letter **I** signifies the pages on which pertinent illustrations can be found.